Historical Fiction for Teens

Recent Titles in
Genreflecting Advisory Series

Diana Tixier Herald, Series Editor

Historical Fiction for Teens

A Genre Guide

Melissa Rabey

Genreflecting Advisory Series

Diana Tixier Herald, Series Editor

LIBRARIES UNLIMITED

AN IMPRINT OF ABC-CLIO, LLC
Santa Barbara, California • Denver, Colorado • Oxford, England

Library of Congress Cataloging-in-Publication Data

Rabey, Melissa.
  Historical fiction for teens : a genre guide / Melissa Rabey.
    p. cm. -- (Genreflecting advisory series)
  Includes bibliographical references and index.
  ISBN 978-1-59158-813-9 (acid-free paper) 1. Historical fiction,
American--Bibliography. 2. Young adult fiction, American--Bibliography.
3. Historical fiction, American--Stories, plots, etc. 4. Young adult
fiction, American--Stories, plots, etc. 5. Young adults'
libraries--Book lists. 6. Readers' advisory services--United States. 7.
Teenagers--Books and reading--United States. I. Title.
  Z1231.H57R33 2011
  [PS374.H5]
  016.813'081099283--dc22   2010041101

ISBN: 978-1-59158-813-9

15 14 13 12 11   1 2 3 4 5

This book is also available on the World Wide Web as an eBook.
Visit www.abc-clio.com for details.

Libraries Unlimited
An Imprint of ABC-CLIO, LLC

ABC-CLIO, LLC
130 Cremona Drive, P.O. Box 1911
Santa Barbara, California 93116-1911

This book is printed on acid-free paper ∞
Manufactured in the United States of America

For James and Marie Rabey: not just the best parents a girl could have, but the most enthusiastic cheerleaders, typists, and researchers that any writer could have.

Contents

Acknowledgments

There are so many thanks to be given to the people who assisted me in the creation of this guide. Without their help and support, it would have taken me twice as long to complete this project.

My family and friends have been willing to listen to me discuss this book and have cheered me on whenever I was discouraged.

My professional colleagues and friends Sophie Brookover, Elizabeth Burns, and Carlisle Webber have been with me since the beginning, reviewing my initial proposal and listening to my thoughts during the writing process. A special thanks to Carlisle Webber, who encouraged me to submit my proposal in the first place.

The staff at the Frederick County Public Libraries have been incredibly supportive of this book. With their questions and encouragement, I was inspired to keep working. I am particularly grateful to Mary Cramer, my supervisor and Assistant Branch Manager at the C. Burr Artz Public Library, and Dolores Maminski, FCPL's Associate Director.

Thank you to Libraries Unlimited for this wonderful, challenging opportunity, and to Barbara Ittner, a fantastic editor who has vastly improved my original manuscript.

If I have omitted anyone who's worthy of thanks, I can only blame a mind that's been filled entirely with historical fiction for the past two years. When I come back to the present day, I will be sure to express my appreciation.

Introduction

Young adult publishers are producing more books every year. The vast amount of historical fiction available for teens has led to a need for a guide like this book, which attempts to illustrate both traditional and innovative approaches to YA historical fiction. There are other guides to historical fiction for teens, but they focus on award-winning titles and those useful for the curriculum. This guide features books popular with today's teen readers, and it organizes titles according to broad reading interest, including subgenres as well as the traditional categories of eras and locations.

Purpose and Scope

This guide covers historical fiction written for teenagers, published between 1975 and 2010. Some of the titles may fall within the children's or adult collections at some libraries or bookstores due to local standards. For the most part, books were selected if they would appeal to a reader who was in the fifth grade and up. Of course, identifying appeal for readers is an art, not a science, and some titles may skew younger than your readers.

There are some exceptions for important works published before 1975 or originally published for adults. It would be difficult to create a readers' advisory guide to YA historical fiction and leave out classics such as *Johnny Tremain*, *The Witch of Blackbird Pond*, or *To Kill a Mockingbird*. These exceptions are kept to a minimum, including only those titles that are significant and lasting contributions.

At least the first fifty pages of each book included in this guide have been read to gain a feel for the novel. Reviews were consulted to get further information on titles and gauge the standing of the book. Furthermore, book lists and recommendations found on blogs and listservs were reviewed to discover lesser-known titles.

Every attempt has been made to include only titles that accurately capture the historical facts of the period. Novels that fall prey to known historical inaccuracies are not included. This is not to say that novels that touch lightly on the historical period are excluded. Like any genre, historical fiction is made up of a myriad of elements, and they are highlighted differently in each novel. In some stories, the historical setting is sketched out with only a few strokes, whereas in others the historical setting is richly re-created for the reader. But in each case, the history had to be accurate and relatively authentic.

Organization of This Book

Freestanding titles are listed in alphabetical order below the author's name. Series are also listed under the author's name, and titles within the series are listed in series order. If an author has both freestanding books and series, the freestanding titles are listed first.

For each title in this guide, bibliographic information and a subject annotation are included. Both hardcover and softcover editions are listed if available, regardless of in-print status. In some cases, there may be additional editions that have not been included, such as mass market paperback, audiobook, library edition, or electronic version.

Some titles are enhanced with a suggested read-alike, usually a nonfiction title that helps explore the historical facts. For those titles honored with a significant or noteworthy award, the awards are listed at the end of the annotation. Finally, keywords are listed for each title to provide a quick guide to important aspects of the novel. You can find other novels that share a keyword by consulting the keyword index.

The following symbols are used throughout this guide:

Award-winning title. A selected list of awards is included in appendix A.

☐ Recommended for book discussions.

A title's grade level is indicated by the following icons:

M Middle school, grades 6–8

J Junior high, grades 7–9

S Senior high, grades 10–12

Chapter 1 explains and defines historical fiction for young adults, using published books and articles on the subject. Chapters 2 and 3 explore traditional historical fiction, with chapter 2 focusing on world historical fiction and chapter 3 on novels set in the Americas. Chapters 4 through 7 explore historical fiction titles that feature genreblending: historical mysteries, action-adventure titles, historical fantasy, and time-travel stories. Finally, Chapter 8 and the appendixes offer print resources, award-winning historical fiction titles, and booklists.

Although every attempt was made to be as thorough and sensitive to reader interests as possible, omissions and oversights are possible. Yet this guide should provide enough titles to meet the needs of today's teen readers and those who serve them.

Suggestions for Use

Depending on your needs, this guide can be a quick, as-needed resource or an in-depth research tool. Following are some suggestions for using this guide.

1. Using the keyword index, create displays, bookmarks, or other exhibits about popular topics.

2. Use the ready-made booklists in appendix B or be inspired to create your own.

3. When working with teen readers who are reluctant to read historical fiction, find out their preferred genre and look for a crossover title. For example, consult chapter 6 for a work of historical fantasy to recommend to a fantasy reader who must read a historical fiction title.

4. Increase the circulation or use of lesser-known titles from your collection by pairing them with a contemporary blockbuster. Why not match up Ally Carter's <u>Gallagher Girl</u> series with Celia Rees's *Sovay*?

5. Work with teachers from your school to offer historical fiction that ties in with language arts or social studies curriculum. Or consider more unusual links: drama, art, and science classes could read a work of historical fiction that involves these subjects.

Of course, this guide can also be used for traditional readers' advisory and collection development tasks. Need more books on the American Revolution? Can't keep your teens supplied with books about supernatural creatures? Hopefully, this guide will help you meet those needs and more.

Chapter 1

Living in the Past: Historical Fiction for Young Adults

The phrase "like nailing Jell-O to a wall" takes on a particular significance when we try to define historical fiction. On the surface, it seems easy: any novel set in the past. But like any simple definition, upon further consideration, it's not so clear-cut. How long ago is "the past?" In a novel identified as historical fiction, how much should be based on fact and how much may be imagined by the author? Does the genre have other identifying factors? And just how does the definition change when the novel is written for young adults? Do some concerns become more important when a novel is written for a nonadult reader?

This chapter is designed to define what historical fiction is. After reviewing a variety of definitions, the definition that shaped the creation of this reference guide is explained. Information is also provided that clarifies the process of selecting novels for this guide. The chapter discusses historical fiction concerns and how YA historical fiction differs from adult novels. Finally, I explore the big question: Do teens really like historical fiction?

What Is Historical Fiction?

Some of the earliest works of literature could be defined as historical fiction. The *Iliad*, the *Odyssey*, and the *Aeneid* combined historical events with storytelling. Although these works were considered histories at the time of their creation, a modern definition would classify these ancient works as historical fiction. More recently created works are even more recognizable as historical fiction. Two authors seen as the founders of modern historical fiction are Sir Walter Scott and James Fenimore Cooper. For these authors, the historical setting is the backdrop for the actions and lives of the characters. In *The Distant Mirror: Reflections on Young Adult Historical Fiction*, Joanne Brown and Nancy St. Clair state that, "the crucial interaction between character and the historical events of the era set a pattern in the genre . . . that has endured (to its advantage) down to the present" (2006, 6).

For a writer to create a historical novel, it's not enough to take a generic character and put him or her on the *Titanic* or in ancient Egypt. The character has to act like someone who lived in the period and place, with the values and attitudes of people in that time. Otherwise, the character will be an anachronism, not in the correct place in time. Such flaws and inauthenticities can undermine the author's attempt to transport readers into the past. As Sarah Johnson notes, "The best historical novelists make the history an integral part of the story but weave it in gradually so that readers aren't overwhelmed" (2005, 5).

Just what is meant by "historical?" Many books set in the past are not considered historical fiction. This is often because they are set in the contemporary present, the time when they were written. Thus, novels like *Jane Eyre* or *Seventeenth Summer*, both of which are set in the past, cannot be considered historical fiction. Each reflects the time period its was written in—the 1820s–1830s and the 1940s, respectively.

There are various opinions about how far in the past a novel should be set to be considered historical fiction, ranging from a generation to beyond living memory. For example, Sarah Johnson includes as a criterion for historical fiction that the novels be "set before the middle of the last century [1950s] and ones in which the author is writing from research rather than personal experience. This usually means that the novels will take place before the author's life and times" (2005, 1). Although it is important to ensure an author has done proper research, rather than creating a novel that is a memoir in disguise, this rigidity does more harm than good. By eliminating any historical fiction set after the 1950s, we do not expose teens to a wealth of information about the recent past. In many teens' history and social studies classes, it is this very period that is often overlooked. For some teens, historical fiction might be the only way they are exposed to subjects like the civil rights struggle or the Vietnam War. Because it covers historical fiction written for teenagers, a cut-off of 1980 was set for any work included in this guide. Any novel of historical fiction set after 1980 was not included. Although works on the Vietnam War and what seems like the recent past to many of us are included, keep in mind that these events happened before today's teens were born.

What other factors or guidelines should be included in a definition of historical fiction? Joyce Saricks (1999) identified four important aspects of historical fiction:

- historical detail regarding characters, event, and setting;

- authentic characterizations without anachronisms;

- storylines that represent the lives in context with time and setting; and

- a pace that allows the plot to unfold and span a broad scope.

This commonsense definition offers flexibility, applying to novels that cross genres or cover a broad range of audiences. An additional factor, of particular value when discussing YA historical fiction, is some kind of conflict in the storyline.

Therefore, for this guide, historical fiction is defined as a novel with authentic details and a certain prominence of its historical setting, with characters that act in accordance with those historical details. The plot grows out of the setting, generally presenting an internal or external struggle that reflects people's concerns and problems in that time period. Finally, the novel allows its story to unfold at a rate that is appropriate for both the setting and the plot.

YA Historical Fiction and Its Tensions

Although this definition is fairly straightforward, it doesn't address all concerns. When it comes to historical fiction for teens, questions remain about accuracy, appropriateness, and ownership, which can lead to disagreements about how to judge historical fiction and how to recommend the best novels to teen readers.

Within any form of historical fiction, there are certain tensions. Practically any librarian or teacher, when suggesting historical fiction to readers, is asked "Is it real?" This question and variations on it highlight the greatest balancing act in the genre: the need to use fact to tell a story, without diminishing either history or fiction. If the story gets little attention, readers will be left unmoved by an ineffective plot or stock characters. If the author can't control factual exposition, the story is bogged down with too much detail. Sarah Johnson notes that

> [r]eaders seek out authors who evoke or re-create the past by providing detail on all aspects of life in earlier times: customs, food, clothing, religious beliefs, architecture, and much more. This historical frame must be presented as authentically as possible so as not to shatter the illusion, but accuracy in historical facts isn't nearly enough to satisfy readers. (2005, 5)

Even worse is the historical novel that does not separate modern ideals from actions in the past. "Too much historical fiction for children is stepping around large slabs of known reality to tell pleasant but historically doubtful stories" is a criticism made by Anne Scott MacLeod (1998, 26). Novels such as *Sarah, Plain and Tall*, *The True Confessions of Charlotte Doyle*, *Lyddie*, and *The Midwife's Apprentice*—all award-winning, critically acclaimed works—could be criticized on the grounds of injecting modern ideas about women and education inappropriately into historical settings. To be more specific, a medieval noblewoman or a nineteenth-century factory girl is unlikely to obtain literacy, and therefore books like *Lyddie* or *Catherine, Called Birdy* are inauthentic—even though there are historical examples of women who accomplished just this feat. For much of the nineteenth and twentieth centuries, the ability to read in English was seen as a critical aspect of gaining the American Dream and rising to a higher station.

Good Writing, Bad History:
Examples from Anne Scott MacLeod

Sarah, Plain and Tall
1985 Newbery Medalist
Errors: Ignores nineteenth-century mores regarding unmarried women and men living in the same house; does not reflect the never-ending toil of life on a farm.

The True Confessions of Charlotte Doyle
1991 Newbery Honor Book
Error: A teenage girl, alone on a sailing ship full of men, is not sexually abused or otherwise molested.

Catherine, Called Birdy
1995 Newbery Honor Book
Error: Resistance to parents' wishes would have drawn harsh beatings and punishment, as children were possessions in the medieval period.

MacLeod comments that these novels and many others "evade the common realities of the societies they write about." Such evasion may result in a good book, but not a historically accurate one. It remains for librarians and teachers to determine which factor is more important: the accuracy or the literary quality. Some of the conceits of literature, like the novel in letters or the diary format, require the reader to accept that the format is just the way the story is being told. Questioning whether the protagonist would actually be able to write or read may be overthinking, analyzing the novel too closely. Attempting to make blanket statements, such as that all medieval women were treated cruelly or that all poor children were illiterate, seems more inaccurate exploring the idea of one teenager gaining freedom or literacy.

These concerns about accuracy reflect some of the questions about appropriateness in young people's literature. Anne Scott MacLeod stated that, "didacticism dies hard in children's literature. Today's publishers, authors and reviewers often approach historical fiction for children as the early nineteenth century did—as an opportunity to deliver messages to the young" (1998, 31). Authors must walk a delicate line when writing for teens; attempts to be historically accurate can lead to charges of exposing impressionable readers to crude, unsavory subjects. For example, Kathryn Lasky wrote about the shunning of a rape victim in one of her novels. When a reviewer criticized this, Lasky responded that such treatment was reflective of the historical period (Brown and St. Clair 2006, 44).

It does appear that such attitudes are beginning to change. Authors are less often held to a different standard when writing for young adults. Michael Cart writes that though nostalgic works show us the best of the past, it is equally important for historical fiction to show us the worst of the human condition. Such exposure, in Cart's opinion, makes these kinds of books "required reading for all teens who wish to become fully realized—and, for me, that means civilized—adults" (2007, 37). Instead of the burden being placed on authors and publishers to protect young adults, it seems the focus has become providing teen readers with a wider range of choices, including books that twenty years ago would have been accused of being coarse and exploitative.

Questions about exploitation also arise about historical fiction dealing with ethnic or racial groups. Some authors, such as William Armstrong or Ann Rinaldi, have been criticized for their portrayals of ethnic groups of which they are not members. Rinaldi, in her diary-style story of one girl's experience at the Carlisle Indian School, used the names of real students for characters, an action seen as lacking respect for those now-dead individuals and their families. Such books have led to acrimonious attacks on their authors for telling stories that are not their own. Yet as Kathryn Lasky has argued, "this new insistence on certain rules for authorship and provenance of a story (who writes what or where) is indeed threatening the very fabric of literature and literary criticism" (Brown and St. Clair 2006, 52).

To answer such concerns, perhaps the best approach is that offered by Debbie Reese, a leading authority on Native American books for children and teens. She recommends that authors perform in-depth research and have a true connection to the culture; otherwise, "an author may unwittingly tread on territory the members of that culture would prefer [the author] walk around, rather than tramp through" (1999). In this vein, Katherine Paterson's experience of living in China as a child and studying and living for years in Japan would make her suited to write novels set in Asia.

Young Adult Historical Fiction in the Classroom

Perhaps the most common way for teens to be exposed to young adult fiction in their classroom is when studying history. Although young adult fiction is generally sidelined in favor of the classics in the English classroom, social studies teachers have been assigning YA historical fiction for years. With the number of awards that recent historical fiction titles have won, it has become easier for teachers to find high-quality works of historical fiction written for teens.

The benefits to using young adult historical fiction in the classroom are numerous. Historical novels supplement textbooks, providing struggling readers with an engaging story that still communicates needed information. A student can read a 200-page novel and gain a better feel for a historical period than by reading ten pages in a textbook. What's more, historical fiction can provide a wealth of viewpoints and attitudes within one book, handling such transitions more smoothly than a textbook.

Perhaps the strongest benefit of historical fiction in the classroom is that it allows students to more readily cross the divide between the present and the past. "Good historical fiction creates an emotional connection between children of today and their historical counterparts" (Rycik and Rosler 2009, 163). This connection allows teens to better understand historical events by providing a context and a rationalization for decisions. Textbooks can provide a multitude of facts on why the American colonies chose to revolt against Great Britain, but novels like Esther Forbes's *Johnny Tremain*, *Chains* by Laurie Halse Anderson, or *Just Jane* by William Lavender can illuminate the struggle of individuals while also presenting the colonial viewpoint as a whole.

More information on resources that can assist teachers in using historical fiction in their classrooms is included in chapter 8.

But Do Teens Like It?

For decades, librarians and teachers have been saying that teens don't like historical fiction because it is too much like school—especially when a teacher assigns historical fiction. Judith Ridge noted that the prevailing opinion was that "Australian children . . . aren't interested in history. They don't read historical fiction, and they're especially not interested in Australian history" (2002, 795). No less a figure than Patty Campbell declared YA historical fiction dead in a 1980 article. Yet by the mid-1990s, Campbell had to change her position. Thanks in part to Pleasant Company's <u>American Girls</u> series, children and teens were coming into libraries asking for historical fiction. And publishers wanted to cash in on this new interest.

Moving beyond formulaic series, historical fiction for young adults has remained popular since Campbell's reassessment. In 2007 Michael Cart ascribed interest in historical fiction to a reaction to the events of September 11, 2001. "Suddenly, the traditional setting of YA literature-the contemporary, the here and now had become downright scary and, accordingly, the past, previously considered a yawn by teens, became more enticing" (37). Anita Silvey, writing more generally, said that "instead of craving realistic stories about people like themselves, today's teens are crazy about characters (and scenarios) that have little in common with their own everyday lives" (2006). Genres like historical fiction and fantasy have benefited from teens seeking escape from modern-day problems.

Just like any other genre, historical fiction has its fans among young adult readers. Though some teens may equate historical fiction with schoolwork, there are more and more titles being published that defy this categorization. This lack of pigeonholing as "school books" has led to more teens seeing historical fiction as leisure reading, a trend that will only continue as authors and publishers create genrebending works that engage teen readers.

Conclusion

It's an exciting time to be a fan of historical fiction. There are more works set in the past being published every year, and authors have given free range to their creativity and inventiveness. This variety and breadth lead to confusion, though: Just what is historical fiction? How can we organize and categorize all these novels? How do we find the good titles? By exploring these questions, this guide seeks to provide one set of answers. Whether you consider yourself an expert or a newcomer, asking questions about historical fiction allows you to better understand the genre and serve teen readers more effectively. With the ideas and suggestions set forth in this guide, you now have the foundation to answer readers' advisory questions, even if you read very little historical fiction.

Enjoy your time in the past!

References

Brown, Joanne, and Nancy St. Clair. 2006. *The Distant Mirror: Reflections on Young Adult Historical Fiction*. Lanham, MD: Scarecrow Press.

Cart, Michael. 2007. "Of Innocence—and Experience." *Booklist* (April 15): 37. Available at www.gale.cengage.com/PeriodicalSolutions/generalOnefile.htm.

Johnson, Sarah L. 2005. *Historical Fiction: A Guide to the Genre*. Westport, CT: Libraries Unlimited.

MacLeod, Anne Scott. 1998. "Writing Backwards: Modern Marvels in Historical Fiction." *The Horn Book Magazine* 74, no. 1 (January and February): 26–33. Available at www.gale.cengage.com/PeriodicalSolutions/generalOnefile.htm.

Reese, Debbie. 1999. "Authenticity and Sensitivity: Goals for Writing and Reviewing Books with Native American Themes." *School Library Journal*, December 1. Available at www.schoollibraryjournal.com/article/CA153126.html.

Ridge, Judith. 2002. "Our Story: Rediscovering Australian History." *The Horn Book Magazine* 78, no. 6 (November/December): 795–802. Available at www.gale.cengage.com/PeriodicalSolutions/generalOnefile.htm.

Rycik, Mary Taylor, and Brenda Rosler. 2009. "The Return of Historical Fiction." *The Reading Teacher* 63, no. 2 (October): 163–66. Available at www.gale.cengage.com/PeriodicalSolutions/generalOnefile.htm.

Saricks, Joyce. 1999. "Historical Fiction—Rules of the Genre." *Booklist* (April 1): 1392. Available at http://www.gale.cengage.com/PeriodicalSolutions/generalOnefile.htm.

Silvey, Anita. 2006. "The Unreal Deal." *School Library Journal*, October 1. Available at www.schoollibraryjournal.com/article/CA6376083.html.

Chapter 2

Traditional Historical Fiction: World History

Calling a work a traditional historical fiction can be a double-edged sword. The word "tradition" calls to mind dry, plodding stories of great white men, glorying in their accomplishments. However, the novels in this chapter and chapter 3 are rarely like that kind of historical novel. These novels are traditional in that the historical background is central to their appeal and they do not cross over into another genre. This chapter features a range of works spanning the breadth of human history.

Traditional historical fiction is also a thriving field, thanks in part to the richness and vastness of history. Even in well-mined areas like American and British history, there are little-known events that have yielded works of historical fiction. We are only now seeing novels exploring the history of some countries, giving us a look at the history of African nations that are little known to most readers. In addition, we are also getting a richer portrait of countries that are often known for only one era. Japan has been explored beyond the samurai era, for example.

The works in this chapter cover historical fiction set outside the Western Hemisphere, ranging from the ancient past to the twentieth century in the geographical regions of Asia, Africa, the Middle East, and Europe.

Ancient Lands: Before the Common Era

Many teens, especially when younger, have an interest in ancient Greece or Egypt. The novels in this section play on that interest, telling stories of long-ago times that will be of interest to teens. Whether set in Egypt, Rome, or Greece, these stories balance the setting with some of the concerns that teens have today.

Stories that feature aspects of mythology are covered in chapter 6.

Albin, Henry T.

Rise of the Golden Cobra. **Annick Press, 2007. 978-1-55451-060-3 (hardcover); 978-1-554510-59-7 (softcover). 200pp.** **M** **J**

> Treachery and loyalty are concepts as old as humankind. In the land now known as Egypt, a young servant boy sees his master killed. With his dying breath, his master bids Nebi to travel to King Piankhy of Kirsh. The king must know of the treachery of Lord Nimlot, who has broken his vow of allegiance to Piankhy and joined forces with another warlord. These actions could spell doom for the people of South Egypt. Nebi must travel through the desert, trying to escape Nimlot and deliver this news to King Piankhy. As Nebi joins the king on his campaign, he must decide whether to forgive his enemy or seek revenge. The ancient world in the eighth century BCE comes to life, with some of the same questions we face today.
>
> **Keywords:** Egypt; Eighth Century BCE

Carter, Dorothy Sharp.

His Majesty, Queen Hatshepsut. **HarperCollins, 1987. 978-0-397-32178-0 (hardcover). 256pp.** **M**

> Even a princess or a queen can feel trapped. Hatshepsut has been told her whole life that she should be grateful for how fortunate she is. But Hatshepsut only sees that she has to marry her sickly half-brother Thutmose II and have duty and responsibility with no choices. Yet slowly, she chooses to do what she wants. And with the death of the pharaoh, she gets her chance. Hatshepsut is appointed regent to her husband's son and heir, but soon she has pushed aside the heir and has taken the throne for herself, ruling as sole monarch. And as pharaoh, Hatshepsut will do much to make Egypt strong and secure.
>
> **Keywords:** Egypt; Fifteenth Century BCE; Royalty; Women's Roles

Cowley, Marjorie.

The Golden Bull. **Charlesbridge Publishing, 2008. 978-1-58089-181-3 (hardcover). 216pp.** **M** **J**

> In a time of drought, farmers are hit hard. When there is no longer enough food for the whole family, Jomar's father arranges an apprenticeship for Jomar. He will work for Sidah the goldsmith, in the nearby city of Ur. Jomar is nervous about leaving the farm, especially when he learns his younger sister Jefa will go with him. Jefa is just twelve, and her only skill is her musical talent. Within the great city of Ur, the fourteen-year-old Jomar sees fabulous sights and is quickly welcomed. But Jefa is seen as an extra mouth to feed and is even accused of stealing. With the help of a high priestess, Jomar rescues his sister and protects her from harm. The world of ancient Mesopotamia is vividly re-created in a story about a brother and a sister.
>
> **Keywords:** Brothers and Sisters; Mesopotamia; Music

Dickinson, Peter.

A Bone from a Dry Sea. **Delacorte Books for Young Readers, 1993. 978-0-385-30821-2 (hardcover); 978-0-440-21928-6 (softcover). 199pp. J S**

Two girls, millions of years apart, show how humans have evolved yet still display many of the same characteristics. Vinny is joining her paleontologist father on a dig in Africa in contemporary times. The dig site might yield proof of early human evolution. There's tensions and jockeying for positions, observed by Vinny. At the same time, two million years earlier a group of primitive humans live on the shore of a great inland sea. They have few tools and little brainpower. But one girl seems to have a special ability to go beyond the boundaries. She can create tools out of available objects. What's more, she knows how to gain power without upsetting the male leaders. And this girl will leave behind proof of her evolution—something that lasts until it's discovered at the dig site Vinny is visiting.

Read alike: Find out more about the first humans in *Lucy Long Ago: Uncovering the Mystery of Where We Came From* by Catherine Thimmesh.

Keywords: Africa; Parallel Narratives; Women's Roles

Friesner, Esther.

Nefertiti. J

A young woman in ancient times finds a way to gain power without hurting others. By developing her skills and talents, Nefertiti is different from other women, like her aunt Tiye.

Keywords: Egypt; Family; Friendship; Slavery; Women's Roles

Sphinx's Princess. Random House, 2009. 978-0-375-85654-9 (hardcover); 978-0-375-85655-6 (softcover). 384pp.

Nefertiti is a beautiful and kind girl, caring for her half-sister and loving to dance and sing. She doesn't think much about the things she takes for granted, like the household's slaves. But then an old family friend starts to offer her lessons in reading and writing. As she learns, Nefertiti starts to question the way things are. Her lessons must kept secret, and not just because females are not supposed to have an education. Nefertiti's aunt, Queen Tiye, has great power, thanks to the use of scribes—female scribes. Her father has tried to protect Nefertiti, but when her dancing talent attracts royal attention, she will have to protect herself when she moves to the Pharaoh's city of Thebes. She learns how to drive a chariot and use weapons, but will that be enough when her opponent is a queen? If Nefertiti wants to do what she thinks is right, she has to discover just how strong she really is.

Sphinx's Queen. Random House, 2010. 978-0-375-85657-0 (hardcover). 368pp.

> Nefertiti may have escaped from Thebes, but she is still in plenty of danger. After being accused of a crime she didn't commit, her betrothal to the future pharaoh Thutmose was ended. Although she escapes with Thutmose's brother Amenophis and the young slave girl Nava, Nefertiti knows that Thutmose will not let her go. She knows her only chance is to travel to Dendera in search of the Pharaoh. If Nefertiti can travel along the banks of the Nile, reach the city, and tell the Pharaoh the truth, her name can be cleared and the true criminals will be punished. But such a journey for a beautiful young woman is full of terrors, from both man and beast. It will take all of Nefertiti's courage to succeed.

Gormley, Beatrice.

Poisoned Honey. **Knopf Books for Young Readers, 2010. 978-0-375-85207-7 (hardcover); 978-0-375-84404-1 (softcover). 320pp. 🚹 🅂**

> In the ancient past, the times covered in Bible stories, women and girls had no power. They were expected to do as their fathers or husbands ordered. That's how it is for Mariamne, nicknamed Mari. Although she hears voices that tell her she has a great destiny, she can do nothing to create this future. Instead, she does as she's told. At first she thinks she's lucky to be betrothed to a handsome, kind, young man. Perhaps this is Mari's destiny. But then a fever spreads through her hometown of Magdala. Many are sickened, and among the dead are Mari's father and betrothed. Now Mari has to follow her brother's orders, including marrying a man she does not love. Mari's only comfort is the new skill she has been taught by Ramla, an Egyptian wise woman. Mari travels into the spirit world, where unbelievable wonders are hers to create and control. Will Mari stay in her new refuge or find that it is just an illusion?

> **Keywords:** Biblical Retelling; Brothers and Sisters; Women's Roles

📖 *Salome.* **Knopf Books for Young Readers, 2007. 978-0-375-83908-5 (hardcover); 978-0-440-23979-6 (softcover). 288pp. 🚹**

> Many have heard the name of Salome. But who was this girl who asked for the head of John the Baptist? In this novel Salome is the daughter of an old, emotionally distant king and a young, immature mother. Salome has a talent for dancing, which can only be exercised in service to the goddess Diana. Although Salome and her parents are Jewish, they have little faith in any god. Salome is very close to her mother, calling her by her first name. But when her mother divorces her father and marries another man, Salome is hurt and confused. Her mother has less and less time for her, and Salome becomes willing to do anything to keep her mother's love. After she performs the enthralling Dance of the Seven Veils, Salome finds out what her mother wants. Is she willing to send an innocent man to his death, just to be loved?

> **Keywords:** Biblical Retelling; Mother and Child; Women's Roles

Lasky, Kathryn.

The Last Girls of Pompeii. **Viking Juvenile, 2007. 978-0-670-06196-9 (hardcover). 160pp.** Ⓜ

> In the city of Pompeii, all the blessings and curses of life are thanks to the gods. Twelve-year-old Julia may be the daughter of a wealthy citizen, but her withered arm indicates the Curse of Venus upon her. Because of this, she will never marry or have children. At least Julia has the comfort of her best friend, Sura. She may be a slave, but Sura is beautiful and a good friend to Julia. Sura stands by Julia as Julia's future is being planned—a terrible future. But before this happens, an even worse event occurs: Mount Vesuvius erupts. Julia and Sura are separated and on their own. Will they escape to safety and freedom or fall victim to the volcano?
>
> **Keywords:** Disasters; First Century; Italy; Physical Disability; Slavery

Lawrence, L. S.

Escape by Sea. **Holiday House, 2009. 978-0-8234-2217-3 (hardcover). 195pp.** Ⓙ Ⓢ

> Life in Carthage as a senator's daughter has granted Sara riches and privilege, but she is also restless and lonely. She runs her father's household and worries about her beloved older brother, a soldier in the Carthaginian Army. She pays little attention to the Roman ships that sail in the harbor . . . until one horrible day. The news that her brother is dead and the Romans will soon invade the city sends Sara into action. Shepherding her father, who has momentarily lost his wits, Sara manages to get them onto a ship and escape the Roman advance. Sailing into the Mediterranean seeking safety, they instead confront storms and pirates, not to mention the Roman Navy itself. Soon Sara finds herself alone, needing to survive. With her instincts and abilities, Sara has confidence in herself.
>
> **Keywords:** Africa; Women's Roles

Lester, Julius.

Pharaoh's Daughter: A Novel of Ancient Egypt. **Harcourt Children's Books, 2000. 978-0-15-201826-9 (hardcover); 978-0-06-440969-8 (softcover). 192pp.** Ⓙ

> Many know the story of Moses through the Old Testament or popular culture. Yet the movie versions of the story have distorted historical facts, and the biblical accounts are one-sided. In this novel we meet Almah, the eldest sister of Moses and the adopted sister of the Pharaoh's daughter Meryetamyn. When the princess adopts Moses, claiming this Hebrew baby was given to her by the goddess Taweret, Almah comes to the palace of Rameses the Great. There Almah will watch over her little brother, seeing him grow up into a strong, intelligent Egyptian. Yet Almah and Moses both

know that he is really a Hebrew . . . and there will come a day when he will have to accept his true identity.

Keywords: Biblical Retelling; Brothers and Sisters; Egypt; Religious Conflicts

Marston, Elsa.

The Ugly Goddess. **Cricket Books, 2002. 978-0-8126-2667-4 (hardcover). 224pp.** ⬛

The lives of three very different people become intertwined in sixth-century BCE Egypt. Princess Meret is preparing to take on her ceremonial role as the divine wife of the god Amun. But once she meets the dashing yet intelligent Hector, a Greek soldier, she starts feeling even more disgruntled about becoming the Divine Wife. With Egypt's security and safety threatened by other countries, the Pharaoh needs to eliminate any internal tensions by having his daughter become the Divine Wife, and Meret will have the protection of the goddess Taweret by carrying a statue of the goddess into her new life in the temple. But then the statue disappears, only to be found by Bata, a servant in the sculptor's shop. He will have to find a way to get the sculpture to the princess—an adventure that will bring Bata into contact with Meret and Hector. And only with the help of Taweret can these three young people get through this quest.

Keywords: Egypt; Sixth Century BCE

Miklowitz, Gloria D.

Masada: The Last Fortress. **Eerdmans Books for Young Readers, 1998. 978-0-8028-5165-9 (hardcover); 978-0-8028-5168-0 (softcover). 184pp.** ⬛ ⬛

After years of rebellion, Rome has nearly brought all of Jewish Judea under its control. The only remaining holdout is Masada, a mountain fortress that was designed to withstand attack. Simon is the son of the Jewish leader. He begins recording his thoughts on the eve of the Roman siege. In his journal he describes what it's like in Masada as the Romans surround the city and try to starve them out. Since he helps the only doctor in Masada, Simon sees firsthand the injuries suffered by Masada's defenders. At the same time, Simon records his feelings for Deborah, a beautiful girl who is involved with his best friend. Simon struggles to keep living his life in the middle of a horrible battle.

Keywords: Coming-of-age; Middle East; Religious Conflicts

Mitchell, Jack.

The Ancient Ocean Blues. **Tundra Books, 2008. 978-0-88776-832-3 (softcover). 200pp.** ⬛ ⬛

How do you cope when you have a talent for something you don't want to do? That's the dilemma facing Marcus Oppius, a teenager in Rome. His cousin Gaius is a skilled political operative, the best bribe-maker in the whole city. He gets Marcus to help him with the biggest challenge yet: electing to the position of

High Priest an ambitious unknown, Julius Caesar. When Caesar is elected, Gaius insists that Marcus help him more. But the task that Marcus is assigned might just be impossible. He is to sail to Athens, trying to prevent Admiral Pompey from meeting with Cicero. These two men are Caesar's greatest rivals, and they could overthrow him if they can coordinate an attack against him. But how is Marcus to stop these two powerful men? With the help of Homer, a Greek publisher, and Paulla, his romantic but unwanted betrothed, Marcus just might pull this off.

Keywords: Italy; Politics

The Roman Conspiracy. **Tundra Books, 2005. 978-0-88776-713-5 (softcover). 164pp. M J**

When a band of discharged soldiers begins attacking the farmers on his family's lands, Aulus Lucinus Spurinna must grow up quickly. He is left the only male in his family when his uncle is killed—and his uncle's death and the attacking soldiers seem to be connected. The family's only hope is to get the help of their Protector, Cicero. The problem is that Cicero is in Rome, five days' travel from the Spurinna farm. Now the head of the family, Aulus sets off for the city he has always wanted to see, accompanied by the Greek slave Homer. In Rome Aulus gets some help from Tullia, Cicero's daughter. But in the midst of a political crisis, there is little that Cicero can do to help. So it is left to Aulus, helped by Tullia and Homer, to find his uncle's killer and save his family's land.

Keywords: Italy; Politics

Provoost, Anne.

In the Shadow of the Ark. **Arthur A. Levine Books, 2004. 978-0-439-44234-3 (hardcover); 978-0-425-20277-7 (softcover). 384pp. S**

When the coastline marshes overflow and start to flood, Re Jana and her parents pack their belongings and head inland. Her father is a confident, impatient man, while her mother used to be a talented fisherwoman but is now paralyzed. Re Jana is a young woman looking for love, for respect. She works as a masseuse, attracting men with her scented oils and a natural appeal. In the desert a woman who can find fresh water is highly prized, and Re Jana has an uncanny ability to find the sweetest water. This draws the attention of Ham, the son of the local mad man named Noah. Known as the Builder, Noah tells everyone that he has been ordered to build a giant ark, one that will withstand a coming season of great rains. Of course no one believes him—they live in the middle of the desert! But then the rains start. Ham and Re Jana work desperately to convince Noah to allow Re Jana and her family on the ark. But will Noah's God allow that? Re Jana doesn't understand why a god would destroy the world . . . and she just wants to survive.

Keywords: Biblical Retelling; Middle East; Women's Roles

Williams, Susan.

Wind Rider. **Laura Geringer Books, 2006. 978-0-06-087236-6 (hardcover); 978-0-06-087238-0 (softcover). 320pp. ⚙ Ⓢ**

> For Fern, being a girl means staying indoors and sewing and caring for children. Meanwhile, her twin brother Flint is free to roam across the steppes, learning to hunt. Fern would rather spend time with animals, using her special talent to connect to beasts of all kinds. When she finds a young horse buried in the bog, Fern is excited. She hides it, names the horse Thunder, and takes care of it. Soon she has taught Thunder to accept her as a rider and follow her commands. But when Fern reveals her prize, her people are fearful. They think she's a witch, casting spells on animals. Can Fern find a way to convince her tribe of this advantage? Ancient Asia's nomads are described through the story of a girl's love for a horse.
>
> **Keywords:** Animals; Asia; Women's Roles

Asia: Medieval to Modern Times

A vast region spanning thousands of miles, Asia includes countries like China, Japan, and India. These countries are rich in history, yet they are only beginning to be explored in YA historical fiction. The novels set in these places feature stirring conflicts and intriguing characters, reflecting the personality of each country.

Compestine, Ying Chang.

📖 *Revolution Is Not a Dinner Party*. **Henry Holt, 2007. 978-0-8050-8207-4 (hardcover); 978-0-312-58149-7 (softcover). 256pp. Ⓜ ⚙**

> In China there was a period known as the Cultural Revolution. Chairman Mao, the leader of the country, wanted to make China strong, communist, and loyal. So doctors and lawyers were sent to the country to work with peasants. Workers did poor work for half the day, then gave speeches praising Mao. It is a very confusing time, especially for a girl like Ling. She's smart and spirited, liking flowered fabric and learning English from her father. But the Cultural Revolution takes all this away from her. As she slowly adapts to this new harsh life, Ling clings to her hopes: that her father will come home, that they will all have enough to eat, that someday she will see the Golden Gate Bridge. The Cultural Revolution can't last forever, can it?
>
> **Keywords:** 1970s; China; Family; Political Rebellions

Finn, Mary.

Anila's Journey. **Candlewick, 2008. 978-0-7636-3916-7 (hardcover). 320pp. ⚙ Ⓢ**

> Anila is not ready to consider herself an orphan. True, her mother is dead, but her father is just missing. Staying in Calcutta is the next-best thing to looking for

him. But without any friends or family, a half-Indian, half-Irish girl like Anila will have difficulties living on her own, especially in late eighteenth-century India. ThenAnila gets a wonderful opportunity to serve as a draughtsman for a scientist who is studying birds along the Ganges. Anila is known as the Bird Girl of Calcutta and has surpassed her father's talent for drawing. Getting this position will allow her to travel, seeking news of her father, as well as doing something that she loves. The only sticking point? Convincing the scientist to give a job meant for an Englishman to a half-breed girl. But Anila has to try . . . .

Keywords: Art; Eighteenth Century; Family; India; Women's Roles

Flood, Nancy Bo.

Warriors in the Crossfire. **Front Street, 2010. 978-1-59078-661-1 (hardcover). 142pp. 🗊**

At age thirteen, Joseph is expected to act more like a man than a child. But often his anger takes over, at the treatment of him and the other island natives by their conquerors. Japan has ruled over Saipan for many years, and Joseph has grown up an inferior. But Joseph feels equal to his half-Japanese friend and cousin, Kento. As American troops come closer to the island in their struggle with Japan, Kento looks to Joseph to train him in survival. And Joseph, who longs to be more than a warrior, learns to read and write from Kento. Soon both boys will have to defend and protect their families, as Saipan becomes a battleground. As the Americans approach, the Japanese civilians will be taken to a spot known as Banzai Cliff. After that day's events, it will be renamed Suicide Cliff.

Keywords: 1940s; Coming-of-age; Family; Japan; World War II

Gavin, Jamila.

The Blood Stone. **Farrar, Straus & Giroux, 2005. 978-0-374-30846-9 (hardcover); 978-1-4052-1284-7 (softcover). 352pp. 🗊 🅂**

Filippo is twelve years old and has never met his father. That's because his father, Geronimo, left for Hindustan—what is now Afghanistan—before he even knew his wife was pregnant. Years later the family is facing hard times thanks to their guardian Bernardo Pagliarin, who is married to Filippo's oldest sister. Bernardo is pressing the family for money when news arrives that Geronimo is alive and being held for ransom. The ransom demanded is a vast, priceless diamond—one that Bernardo covets as well. It will be up to Filippo to journey to far-off Hindustan, carrying the diamond inside his skull. But will that be enough to keep the diamond safe? A life-changing journey takes a young boy from Venice to Kabul in the seventeenth century.

Keywords: Asia; Family; Italy; Seventeenth Century

Gratz, Alan.

Samurai Shortstop. **Dial, 2006. 978-0-8037-3075-5 (hardcover); 978-0-14-241099-8 (softcover). 288pp.** 🄹 🅂

Toyo is entering Ichiko, the most elite school in Tokyo. He hopes to do well in his classes and find a place on the school's baseball team. Japan in 1890 is changing, old traditions being replaced with new ways. This transition has been on Toyo's mind ever since he was a witness at his Uncle Koji's *seppuku*, or ritual suicide. According to Toyo's father, the samurai code of *bushido* demanded Koji's death. Sixteen-year-old Toyo doesn't understand *bushido* at all, though. His questions inspire his old-fashioned, emotionally distant father to teach Toyo *bushido*. As Toyo slowly learns the code, he is able to apply it to his new, modern life. *Bushido* helps Toyo lead his classmates against the upperclassmen's bullying and even assists Toyo in getting on the baseball team. But hanging over these victories is Toyo's worries about his father. Will Toyo fulfill *bushido* by serving his father at his *seppuku*?

Keywords: Father and Child; Japan; Nineteenth Century; Sports

Ho, Minfong.

📖 *The Clay Marble.* **Farrar, Straus & Giroux, 1991. 978-0-374-31340-1 (hardcover); 978-0-374-41229-6 (softcover). 163pp.** 🄼 🄹

Years of war have damaged both Cambodia and Dara's family. The brutal Khmer Rouge regime is retreating, and twelve-year-old Dara journeys with her mother and her older brother Sarun from their destroyed village. They arrive at a refugee camp on the Thai–Cambodian border, where food, seed, and tools are plentiful and freely distributed. They start to form a new family with a group of fellow refugees. Dara spends time with Jantu, playing and growing strong. Jantu's ability to create toys out of clay seems magical to Dara. But soon the border camp is caught between guerrilla groups, and Dara and Jantu are separated from the rest of their family. Dara will draw her strength from a clay marble made by Jantu. With that marble, she knows she can find her family.

Keywords: 1970s; Cambodia; Family

Kadohata, Cynthia.

A Million Shades of Gray. **Atheneum, 2010. 978-1-4169-1883-7 (hardcover). 216pp.** 🄼 🄹

For as long as he can remember, all Y'Tin has wanted is to be an elephant handler. He thinks up new ideas for training and using elephants and plans to open a school for elephant handlers someday. The bond between Y'Tin and Lady, his elephant, is strong. But can it withstand the turmoil that is tearing apart Vietnam? It is 1975, and the North Vietnamese Army has been invading the Central Highlands of South Vietnam. Y'Tin's village is hidden deep in the jungle; everyone thinks the dense foliage will protect them. But then the North Vietnamese arrive, taking over the village and destroying the life that Y'Tin once had. Now Y'Tin faces a choice: to stay in the village and obey the Vietcong or take his elephant and escape into the jungle.

Keywords: 1970s; Animals; Vietnam

Matthews, Andrew.

The Way of the Warrior. **Dutton Juvenile, 2008. 978-0-525-42063-7 (hardcover). 192pp.** Ⓜ Ⓙ

Revenge is difficult to exact when you become familiar with your potential victim. At the age of ten, Jimmu's parents are dishonored due to the treachery of Lord Ankan. Rather than live with their shame, they kill themselves and leave Jimmu in the charge of a bodyguard. Jimmu knows he will get revenge for his parents, so he spends the next seven years being trained for this task. He learns combat methods and steels his heart against unnecessary emotion. Then he makes his way to Lord Ankan's castle, taking a position as guard. Jimmu observes and plans, trying to find the right time to strike. But Lord Ankan's respect for Jimmu—and his arrogant yet beautiful daughter—makes him start to question his goal.

Keywords: Coming-of-age; Japan; Medieval

McCaughrean, Geraldine.

The Kite Rider. **HarperTeen, 2002. 978-0-06-623874-6 (hardcover); 978-0-06-441091-5 (softcover). 320pp.** Ⓜ Ⓙ

With the death of his father, Haoyou's family is put in jeopardy. The man who indirectly caused his father's death presses Haouyou's mother, now a widow, to marry him. With the help of a relative, a fake medium named Mipeng, Haoyou is able to prevent the wedding and find a job as a kite rider. Strapped to a giant kite, he rides air currents for the entertainment of the visitors to the Jade Circus. With his talents, Haoyou gains fame and fortune for himself and for Miao, the owner of the circus. He sends money home to his mother, but is money all she needs? Perhaps things look different once Haoyou comes back to the ground and sees life up close . . . .

Awards: Carnegie Medal Finalist

Keywords: China; Coming-of-age; Family; Medieval

Napoli, Donna Jo.

Bound. **Atheneum, 2004. 978-0-689-86175-8 (hardcover); 978-0-689-86178-9 (softcover). 192pp.** Ⓜ Ⓙ

Xing Xing knows that her future is bleak. With no mother and father of her own, there's no one to plan a marriage for her. Her stepmother focuses on her own daughter and makes Xing Xing do housework, even changing the bandages on her half-sister's bound feet. Worst of all, Xing Xing is educated, something that is not valued in medieval China. But Xing Xing is a good daughter and sister, until her stepmother commits an unspeakable act. Then Xing Xing decides to look to the examples of her mother and her father and find her own path. Although her stepmother forbids her to go, Xing Xing attends the local cave festival, dressed in the rich clothes and shoes left by her mother. Not even losing one of her shoes dims her happiness at attending the event. But when a prince comes to town, looking for the girl who wore the tiny golden shoes at the festival, Xing Xing will discover her reward.

Keywords: China; Family; Medieval; Women's Roles

Park, Linda Sue.

A Single Shard. **Clarion Books, 2001. 978-0-395-97827-6 (hardcover); 978-0-440-41851-1 (softcover). 160pp. Ⓜ Ⓙ**

Tree-Ear is an orphan, living under a bridge with his friend and father-figure Crane-Man. Tree-Ear is strong and thoughtful, grateful for the little he has. That's how Crane-Man raised him, and this humility and intelligence will serve him well. The village they live in, Ch'ulp'o, is famous for its celadon pottery. Twelve-year-old Tree-Ear becomes more and more interested in the work of the potters, and one potter in particular. He watches Master Min work, eager to learn his secrets. After an accident, Tree-Ear repays Min with days of hard work, slowly earning the master's trust. Tree-Ear becomes an apprentice, learning how to craft pottery. But he is eager to do even more for his master—even travel to the royal court to display Min's finest work. When disaster strikes, Tree-Ear will carry on with his mission.

Awards: Newbery Medal

Keywords: Art; Korea; Orphans; Twelfth Century

📖 *When My Name Was Keoko.* **Clarion Books, 2002. 978-0-618-13335-2 (hardcover); 978-0-440-41944-0 (softcover). 208pp. Ⓜ Ⓙ**

For thirty years Korea has been part of Japan. It is illegal to speak Korean or to display the Korean flag. Students like ten-year-old Sun-hee and her older brother Tae-yul spend most of their time in school learning Japanese. But starting in 1940, with the onset of World War II, Japan does even more to tighten its control over Korea. All Koreans must have Japanese names. Rose of Sharon bushes, the national tree of Korea, are destroyed and replaced with Japan's symbolic cherry tree. Any protests against the Japanese—such as the one by Sun-hee's uncle—are brutally repressed. For Sun-hee, now known as Keoko, it is a terrible time. And it becomes even worse when Tae-yul, who loathes being "Japanese," leaves home to try to rescue their uncle. Will Sun-hee ever see her brother again or get to use her true name?

Keywords: 1940s; Brothers and Sisters; Identity; Korea; Multiple Voices; World War II

Paterson, Katherine.

Of Nightingales That Weep. HarperCollins, 1974. 978-0-690-00485-4 (hardcover); 978-0-06-440282-8 (softcover). 170pp. **M** **J**

> The daughter of a samurai has many expectations to live up to. Takiko has a difficult time adjusting when those expectations change. The death of her father means her mother will remarry, and to a mere potter. Living in the country, Takiko slowly learns to care for her new father as she becomes a young lady and improves her musical skills. Those skills bring her back to the city. There may be war and famine in the far-off-north, but in the city Takiko's beauty and voice gain her many admirers. Eventually she falls in love with Hideo, a brave warrior. But when it's revealed that Hideo is an enemy spy, Takiko flees the city, trying to make a choice between her love and her loyalty. Takiko will have to learn which is more important for a samurai's daughter.
>
> **Keywords:** Coming-of-age; Japan; Medieval; Music; Women's Roles

Perkins, Mitali.

Secret Keeper. Delacorte, 2009. 978-0-385-73340-3 (hardcover); 978-0-440-23955-0 (softcover). 240pp. **J**

> The 1970s was a time of change all over the world. But change comes more slowly in some places. Asha feels confined in Delhi, living in her uncle's house. With her mother and her beautiful older sister Reet, Asha is waiting for word from their father. He has gone to America for work, leaving his family to live with his brother and the rest of the family. Asha tries to keep her spirits up by writing in her diary, reading, and telling stories. But in a world where all the talk is about Reet's beauty and the need to arrange marriages, Asha feels trapped. A secret friendship with the boy next door—a friendship that might be more—does much to help Asha. But when her father finally sends the letter they've been waiting for, Asha has to choose. She will have to decide if a new life of independence in America is worth all she will leave behind.
>
> **Keywords:** 1970s; India; Women's Roles

Ruby, Lois.

Shanghai Shadows. Holiday House, 2006. 978-0-8234-1960-9 (hardcover). 282pp. **J** **S**

> In 1939 few countries would accept Jews escaping Europe. At first Ilse and her family think they are lucky, being able to resettle in Shanghai. China is very different from beautiful Vienna, but they're able to get by at first. Eleven-year-old Ilse learns English from her mother, tries to go to any American movie she can, and plays with Tanya, who lives in the same house. When the Japanese bomb Pearl Harbor in 1941, though,

conditions quickly deteriorate. Ilse's older brother joins the resistance against the Japanese and is arrested. Her mother, who never told them that she has American citizenship after studying in California, is taken away. Ilse, now a teenager, will have to take care of her father and find a way to survive.

Keywords: 1930s; 1940s; China; Family; Holocaust; World War II

Sheth, Kashmira.

Keeping Corner. **Hyperion, 2007. 978-0-7868-3859-2 (hardcover); 978-0-7868-3860-8 (softcover). 288pp. 🄹 🅂**

Imagine knowing that you've been engaged since you were two years old—and that you'll start living with your husband at thirteen. That's how it is for Leela, a pretty, spoiled girl in early twentieth-century India. She's never paid much attention in school and doesn't know anything about the current political state of India. What Leela worries about is bangles and ribbons. When Leela's husband dies, she's left a widow at the age of twelve. According to tradition, she will now have to spend the next year in her house, not to mention shave her head and give away all her pretty things. Leela might just go crazy from the boredom, until her old schoolteacher offers to give her lessons at home. Education gives Leela a way to cope with her isolation and allows her to blossom. Her hopes then turn toward college, but there are many barriers that Leela must surpass to realize her dreams.

Keywords: 1920s; Coming-of-age; India; Women's Roles

Smith, Roland.

Elephant Run. **Hyperion, 2007. 978-1-4231-0402-5 (hardcover); 978-1-4231-0401-8 (softcover). 336pp. 🄼 🄹**

It's a case of going from the frying pan into the fire for Nick Freestone. After the apartment he shares with his mother and stepfather is bombed during the London Blitz, his mother decides to send him to his father's plantation in Burma. She thinks Nick will be safer there, and Nick is excited to return to the country he left at the age of five. After all, his father's plantation has elephants that he can ride! When he arrives, everyone is talking about the threat posed by the Japanese. Soon it's more than a threat: The Japanese invade Burma, fighting their way to the Freestone plantation. The Japanese soldiers take Nick's father as a prisoner, leaving Nick in the local village to act as a servant to the Japanese. Nick is very worried about his father, and he's not going to wait idly for help or rescue. With the help of Mya, the daughter of one of his father's mahouts, Nick plans to escape and save their families. It will be a dangerous trip, but with their elephants, Nick and Mya will take the risk to save their families.

Keywords: 1940s; Animals; Burma; World War II

Venkatraman, Padma.

Climbing the Stairs. **Putnam Juvenile, 2008. 978-0-399-24746-0 (hardcover); 978-0-14-241490-3 (softcover). 256pp. 🇯 🇸**

Vidya is an intelligent girl, brought up by her parents to speak her mind. That's very unusual in 1941 India, and it will be a challenge for Vidya when her life changes. Her father is injured by British police during a nonviolent protest march, with the result that Vidya and her family have to move into the extended family home. Headed by her grandfather, it's a traditional household, with little freedom for a girl like Vidya. Only her grandfather's library helps Vidya accept all these changes. Meanwhile, her older brother studies to become a doctor, but then announces he will be joining the British Army to fight in World War II. That's something the family will not accept, and he is disinherited. Vidya is worried for her brother and herself. Will she get to go to college, as she has dreamed? Or will her family's traditional values win out over her wishes?

Keywords: 1940s; Family; India; World War II

Wilson, Diane Lee.

I Rode a Horse of Milk White Jade. **Scholastic, 1998. 978-0-531-30024-4 (hardcover); 978-0-06-440773-1 (softcover). 232pp. 🇲 🇯**

Ever since the day when her foot was crushed by a horse, Oyuna has been considered unlucky. She's kept confined within her family's yurt, not allowed to go near the horses she loves. Yet she can't stay away, so she sneaks out to ride. But her freedom leads to disaster and upheaval. The only way Oyuna can bring luck back to her family is by winning one of the great horse races. But how can a girl with a crippled foot and an old mare win such a race? Oyuna attempts a journey across the Mongolian steppes of the fourteenth century that will change her life.

Keywords: Animals; Medieval; Mongolia; Physical Disability; Women's Roles

Yep, Laurence.

Hiroshima: A Novella. **Scholastic, 1995. 978-0-590-20832-1 (hardcover); 978-0-590-20833-8 (softcover). 56pp. 🇲 🇯**

On a day in August, a day like any other day, a tragedy occurred. An atomic bomb was dropped on the city of Hiroshima in Japan. It killed thousands of people and injured even more. One of the injured was Sachi, who received burns on her face and a damaged arm. She was lucky enough to go to the United States and receive free surgeries, which repaired her arm and fixed some of her burn scars. But that didn't change the fact that many people were still dying from the bomb, from the radiation it spewed forth. Slowly the world learns that nuclear weapons are too dangerous, giving hope to people all over the world, even those like Sachi.

Keywords: 1940s; Japan; World War II

Australia: 20th Century

Australia, an island that is a continent, has called to many people since its discovery. By the twentieth century it had become a diverse nation, with many different languages and ethnic groups living in close quarters. Although this can create tension, it also makes Australia an unusual country, full of intriguing stories.

Disher, Gary.

The Divine Wind: A Love Story. **Arthur A. Levine Books, 2002. 978-0-439-36915-2 (hardcover); 978-0-439-36916-9 (softcover). 157pp. 🔲 🅂**

Love can cut across many lines. In 1940s Australia, Hart lives in a multiethnic town on the northwest coast. He works with his father on his fleet of pearling boats. He is also in love with his sister's best friend, Mitsy. They've been friends for years, but friendship turned into love as they grew older. But Mitsy is Japanese, and as World War II begins, all Japanese citizens are under suspicion. Hart watches his friends enlist while he stays home, unable to serve due to an injury. When Hart's sister Alice, an army nurse, is reported missing, his divided loyalties get their greatest test. Can he love a woman who should be his enemy?

Keywords: 1940s; Australia; Romance; World War II

Herrick, Steven.

Cold Skin. **Front Street, 2009. 978-1-59078-572-0 (hardcover). 279 pp. 🔲 🅂**

This novel in verse examines what happens in a small town when a terrible crime is committed. Eddie longs to quit school and go to work in his Australian town. But Eddie's father, bitter over his service driving trucks during World War II, refuses to let Eddie or his brother Larry become miners. So Eddie keeps dreaming, and he also has Sally, the girl who was his friend and is now his girlfriend. Larry just wants to finish school and leave town for the big city. But then a beautiful girl is murdered—a girl Larry had a crush on. As suspicion widens to include most of the men in town, Eddie sees how secrets and revenge are part of his home.

Keywords: 1940s; Australia; Murder; Novel in Verse

Newton, Robert.

Runner. **Knopf Books for Young Readers, 2007. 978-0-375-83744-9 (hardcover). 224pp. 🔲**

Responsibility for his family has been on Charlie's shoulders ever since his dad died of the flu. His mother wants him to stay in school, but fifteen-year-old Charlie can't find the concentration to learn. He wants to take care of his mother and younger brother. So he starts working for Squizzy Taylor, the mobster. Charlie's a runner, going all over Richmond and Melbourne delivering messages or parcels. It's an exciting and good-paying job. But slowly Charlie starts to see the downsides of this job. Carrying illegal liquor into the bad part of town, roughing up the people who owe Squizzy money . . . it's not what Charlie wants. Can he find a way to get out without getting on the wrong side of Squizzy?

Keywords: 1920s; Australia; Coming-of-age; Family; Sports

Middle East: Ancient to Modern Times

Often called the cradle of civilization, some of the world's first settlements were in the Middle East, in the countries now known as Iraq, Iran, and Saudi Arabia. This region is little understood by most Americans, and there are few works of historical fiction set here. Yet reading even one of these works can open teens' eyes to life in this remarkable area and go beyond the images in the nightly news.

Fletcher, Susan.

Alphabet of Dreams. **Ginee Seo Books, 2006. 978-0-689-85042-4 (hardcover); 978-0-689-85152-0 (softcover). 304pp.** 🄹 🅂

In first-century Persia, to oppose the King was to risk your life and the lives of your family. Mitra and her younger brother Babak hide in the City of the Dead, concealing their royal blood and hiding from the King's spies. Mitra has disguised herself as a boy, because thirteen-year-old girls can't go around on their own. All Mitra wants is a way to get to far-off Palmyra, to find family members who could protect Babak and herself. They need money for such a journey, and the only way to get it is with Babak's unusual power. If he sleeps with a piece of someone's clothing, he will dream about that person's future. Such a gift is both profitable and dangerous. Will Mitra be able to protect her brother and reach Palmyra? Or will the King finish his revenge on Mitra's father and his family?

Keywords: Brothers and Sisters; Disguised as Boy; First Century; Persia; Political Rebellions

Garcia, Laura Gallego.

The Legend of the Wandering King. **Arthur A. Levine Books, 2005. 978-0-439-58556-9 (hardcover); 978-0-439-58557-6 (softcover). 224pp.** 🄹

In Arabia, in the time before Islam, a young royal learns how to be a man. Prince Walid is widely regarded as the best poet in the kingdom of Kinda. But when his father the King insists he prove his reputation as a poet, Walid holds a poetry competition. Instead of winning, Walid loses to a poor carpet weaver named Hammad. Two more annual contests confirm that Hammad is the true poet. His losses twist Walid, turning the formerly good prince into a young man filled with hate. He seeks revenge upon Hammad, but his revenge will hurt Walid more. Desperate to redeem himself, Walid sets out on a journey that will take him across the Middle Eastern deserts. As he meets merchants and peasants, bandits and a beautiful woman, Walid will become that which he most desired: a great poet.

Keywords: Arabia; Coming-of-age; Fifth Century; Writing

Lottridge, Celia Barker.

Home Is Beyond the Mountains. **Groundwood Books, 2010. 978-0-88899-932-0 (hardcover). 192pp.** Ⓜ

When Samira sees three men in her family's garden, stealing melons in the middle of the night, she doesn't know that her life is about to change. It is 1918, and in the Persian villages near the border with Turkey, soldiers from the Turkish army are starting to create fear. Samira's father leads her whole family out of their village, heading for the safety of the British army. By the time they arrive, only nine-year-old Samira and her older brother Benyamin are left alive. Now orphans, they spend years living in a refugee camp, making friends, learning to read, but yearning for home. After years of waiting, Samira and Benyamin learn they can return to Persia—but the journey is more than 300 miles through the mountains. And it will be only children making this trip.

Keywords: 1910s; Brothers and Sisters; Orphans; Persia; World War I

Sayres, Meghan Nuttal.

Anahita's Woven Riddle. **Amulet, 2006. 978-0-8109-5481-6 (hardcover); 978-0-8109-9548-2 (softcover). 288pp.** Ⓙ Ⓢ

In late nineteenth-century Iran things are beginning to change. The old nomadic ways of tribes and the unique dyes used in tribal carpets are becoming lost. Anahita is a gifted weaver, beautiful and kind, and a lover of riddles. She has caught the eye of the local Khan, who desires her hand in marriage. Anahita is full of despair when her father tells her this, for even if she wanted to marry, she wouldn't want to marry the Khan. So she comes up with an unusual, daring idea: She will only marry the man who can solve the riddle she will weave into her wedding rug. News of this contest, and the prize for its winner, begins to spread, bringing several suitors to Anahita's village. Anahita meets these men, who run the gamut from a shepherd and a schoolmaster to a diplomat and a prince. Anahita begins to wonder who will solve her riddle, and if that clever man will also be able to capture her heart.

Keywords: Iran; Nineteenth Century; Romance; Women's Roles

Whelan, Gloria.

Parade of Shadows. HarperCollins, 2007. 978-0-06-089028-5 (hardcover). 304pp. **J** **S**

> Life in London is dreary and lonely for Julia. Her mother died ten years ago, and her father is often away from home, thanks to his work with the British Foreign Office. When he is home, he intimidates and patronizes Julia. She hopes for adventure and excitement but can't find it in England. So when she learns her father will be visiting the Levant—the exotic countries of the Middle East and Africa—Julia convinces her father to let her accompany him. As they travel into the Ottoman Empire, Julia sees firsthand the wonders and the heartache in these ancient lands. She will meet a French treasure-hunter, a British student revolutionary, and more. It's the trip of a lifetime for sixteen-year-old Julia, and it just might be what makes her into the woman she's supposed to be.
>
> **Keywords:** 1910s; Coming-of-age; Ottoman Empire; Women's Roles

Crusades: 1095–1291

Centuries of conflict wracked most of the known world during the period from 1095 to 1291. Many of the holiest sites for both Christians and Muslims, such as Jerusalem and Bethlehem, are located in the Middle East. In the Middle Ages Christian nations rallied to oust the Muslims who had occupied the Holy Land for centuries, sparking warfare that waxed and waned for many years.

Bradford, Karleen.

There Will Be Wolves. Dutton Juvenile, 1996. 978-0-525-67539-6 (hardcover); 978-0-00-647938-3 (softcover); 208pp. **M** **J**

> Daughter of an apothecary, Ursula knows that she has a skill for healing. Using the book of healing arts she owns, she tries to help others who are sick or injured. But her headstrong ways and outspoken tongue anger the local women, and Ursula is declared a witch. Convicted by the Church, Ursula expects to be burned at the stake. Thanks to her father, she is pardoned, but only if she goes on Crusade to free Jerusalem. Ursula is unwilling, but she accepts the cross and begins the journey to the East, with her father and her friend Bruno. Will these three find salvation in their holy mission—or be guilty of the evil ways of other Crusaders?
>
> **Keywords:** Eleventh Century; Europe; Father and Child

Cadnum, Michael.
The Crusade Series. **M** **J**

> The medieval world is brought to life through the story of Edmund and Hubert, two squires who manage to rise to a higher position even within nonmeritocratic times.

Keywords: Coming-of-age; Eleventh Century; England; Middle East

The Book of the Lion. **Viking Juvenile, 2000. 978-0-670-88386-8 (hardcover); 978-0-14-230034-3 (softcover). 208pp.**

Edmund has served his master well since he became an apprentice. Yet he knows that his master, a coin maker, is using a percentage of copper in his coins, debasing the coinage. For his crime, his master's right hand is cut off, and Edmund should meet the same fate. A bit of luck saves his hand: He is recruited to serve a knight on his journey to the Holy Land. For Edmund, this seems like a dream come true: Who wouldn't want to kill Saracens and have all one's sins forgiven? But training to be a squire is a difficult undertaking, and only the help of Hubert, another squire, will get Edmund through the training. An exciting time awaits these two squires, to participate in one of the greatest battles of the Crusades.

Awards: National Book Award Finalist.

The Leopard Sword. Viking Juvenile, 2002. 978-0-670-89908-1 (hardcover). 224pp.

For the squires Hubert and Edmund, surviving their time in the East is just the beginning. After a battle and a massacre, the Christians take ship and begin their journey back to England. But it is a journey that will be fraught with danger. Infidel ships follow theirs, a duel is fought on a Greek island, and a thieving servant chooses death over maiming. Even more fearful, both their lives and their souls will be at risk, as their ship founders and they escape the rocks to discover that Rome is split between warring families. Charged with a secret mission, the knights and squires must continue to England at any cost. Through it all, Hubert and Edmund strive to serve their masters, hoping to prove themselves worthy of becoming knights.

The Dragon Throne. Viking Juvenile, 2005. 978-0-670-03631-8 (hardcover). 224pp.

The return to England brings good fortune to Hubert and Edmund. Prince John, brother to King Richard, dubs them knights, granting them the position they have been dreaming of. Yet this gift comes with a string, for Prince John is trying to find men to carry his banner. While Hubert and Edmund, along with their former masters Ranulf and Nigel, would prefer to stay loyal to the King, they seem to have little choice but to serve John once they have been captured by his men. Then the four knights are given a holy mission by Queen Eleanor, Richard and John's mother: to escort a young maiden to Rome to allow her to pray in the Holy City. With a woman along, a difficult journey will be even harder. But the four men are knights who are up to this challenge.

Crossley-Holland, Kevin.

Crossing to Paradise. Arthur A. Levine Books, 2008. 978-0-545-05866-7 (hardcover); 352pp. **J**

Gatty appears to be nothing more than a common peasant girl. But when she opens her mouth and begins to sing, she has the voice of an angel. She is alone in the world with no family, and it's up to the lord of the manor to find a vocation for Gatty—or a husband. Then an unexpected opportunity presents itself. Gatty is sent to serve a noblewoman during her pilgrimage to Jerusalem. For Gatty, who has never been outside Wales, the journey will be long, dangerous, and life-altering. And it won't be just the people and places that change her; it will also be by entering a Christian's paradise on Earth, the holy city of Jerusalem.

Awards: Carnegie Medal Finalist

Keywords: Middle East; Music; Thirteenth Century; Wales

Goodman, Joan Elizabeth.

Peregrine. Houghton Mifflin, 2000. 978-0-395-97729-3 (hardcover). 228pp. **M** **J**

In medieval society, only a widow had a measure of control over her own life and property. After the death of her husband and her baby, Lady Edith decides to go on pilgrimage, journeying to the Holy Land. She tells her brother, her companion, and the mysterious Welsh girl she took in that she's running away from the marriage that the king could force her to make. But in truth, there's something else that Edith's running from, and it's not until she discovers the real reason for her flight that she will be able to return to England.

Keywords: England; Middle East; Twelfth Century; Women's Roles

Jinks, Catherine.
The Pagan Chronicles. **M** **J**

The Middle Ages were definitely a time that required a sense of humor. War and religious intolerance, limited food and deadly diseases—not to mention fleas and absolutely no indoor plumbing. Through the ups and downs of the Crusades, Pagan Kidrouk, a Christian Arab who was born nine months after his mother's rape, brings his sarcastic wisecracks and observations to his personal history. Pagan .

Keywords: France; Humor; Medieval; Middle East

Pagan's Crusade. Candlewick, 2003. 978-0-7636-2019-6 (hardcover); 978-0-7636-2584-9 (softcover). 256pp.

It can be tough when you're gifted with a quick mind and a sarcastic tongue. Pagan, left with no other options, joins the Order of the

Knights Templar to get the money to repay a debt. Assigned to a knight who seems more like Saint George than a man, Pagan has a lot to do in his new position of squire. At first Pagan's not happy to serve Lord Roland. But slowly, as Roland shows his kindness and belief in Pagan, a tentative trust forms between them. The Infidels, under the command of Saladin, are coming ever closer to Jerusalem, threatening the Christian pilgrims gathered there . . . as well as Lord Roland and Pagan.

Pagan in Exile. Candlewick, 2004. 978-0-7636-2020-2 (hardcover); 978-0-7636-2691-4 (softcover). 336pp.

The fall of Jerusalem to the Infidels makes the city unsafe for Christians. Pagan has accompanied Lord Roland to Europe, hoping to gather more soldiers for the Christian cause. Entering Lord Roland's home village, Pagan expected a warm welcome. Instead, he and Lord Roland are met with whispers and ugly words. Roland's brothers and father are coarse and loud, very unlike Roland. And his family is unhappy that he has returned, especially now that he is a Templar. Religious divisions also affect France, and Roland's family is on the wrong side of the Templars. Will Roland and Pagan be able to determine who is friend and who is foe before it's too late?

Pagan's Vows. Candlewick, 2004. 978-0-7636-2021-9 (hardcover); 978-0-7636-2754-6 (softcover). 336pp.

The last place you'd expect to find Pagan is in a monastery. But since Lord Roland has given up his sword to become a monk, in penance for the death of his love, Pagan has also entered the monastery. It's a rough transition for both of them. Pagan's mouth keeps getting him in trouble, and Roland feels insecure due to his lack of learning. It doesn't get any easier for Pagan to practice obedience and humility when he discovers there's corruption in the monastery. Only Pagan the outsider will be able to uncover the deceit and find the wrong-doer. And maybe, just maybe, he'll find his true place.

Pagan's Scribe. Candlewick, 2005. 978-0-7636-2022-6 (hardcover); 978-0-7636-2973-1 (softcover). 368pp.

More than twenty years have passed, and Pagan is now an archdeacon, a high position in the Church. He has been tasked to confront the growing spread of heresy through southern France by the people called Cathars. Yet he will do it in his own way, which includes mentoring a young man named Isidore. Taking him on as a scribe, Pagan helps Isidore deal with his strange fits and narrow thinking. This story is Isidore's, as he struggles to adapt to expanding his world beyond books and a small village. With appearances by Lord Roland and other past characters, Pagan's world slowly becomes Isidore's over the course of the novel.

Africa: Fourteenth Century to Today

There are few works of traditional historical fiction set in Africa. Yet this continent is one of the locations that the first humans roamed, evolving to meet threats and gain new skills. It is hoped that modern-day humans will gain new appreciation for Africa if more works of historical fiction are set in this area.

Glass, Linzi.

The Year the Gypsies Came. **Henry Holt, 2006. 978-0-8050-7999-9 (hardcover). 272pp. J S**

Emily's family lives in a big, beautiful house in Johannesburg. Her parents have an unhappy marriage, full of fights. To help cut the tension, they often invite people to stay as house guests. In the summer of 1966, when Emily is twelve, a very unusual family comes to stay. The two boys in the family are frequently beaten by their father, and neither of the boys—Otis, who is the same age as Emily's sister Sarah, and Streak, Emily's new friend—has ever been to school or lived in a house. Emily spends time with Streak, showing him her secret place and introducing him to Buza, the old Zulu watchman who tells Emily folktales. But when Otis attacks Sarah, Emily and her family will have to find a way to come together in spite of their problems.

Keywords: 1960s; Family; Sisters; South Africa

Nanji, Shenaaz.

Child of Dandelions. **Boyds Mills Press, 2008. 978-1-932425-93-2 (hardcover). 214pp. J S**

Sabine's life in Uganda has been happy and peaceful. But President Idi Amin has just decreed that all foreigners of Indian descent must leave Uganda. While Sabine's mother worries and Sabine's father offers reassurance, fifteen-year-old Sabine doesn't know how they could be forced to leave. After all, her family are all Ugandan citizens. As the ninety-day countdown ticks closer to zero, Sabine begins to realize how serious the situation is. Making things even worse is that her best friend Zena won't even talk to her. The disappearance of her uncle convinces Sabine and the rest of her family that they must leave. But is starting over in a new land better than staying in their home?

Keywords: 1970s; Family; Political Rebellions; Uganda

Temple, Frances.

The Beduins' Gazelle. Scholastic, 1996. 978-0-531-09519-5 (hardcover); 978-0-06-440669-7 (softcover). 160pp. ⬛

> While Europe in the fourteenth century was cold and dark, the desert of northern Africa was bright and hot. Amid the sands, cousins Atiyah and Halima live with their tribe, the Beni Khalid. Betrothed since birth, they love each other and look forward to their marriage. But then they are separated in two ways. Atiyah is forced by his uncle to travel to far-off Fes to study. Halima is lost during a sandstorm and taken in by another tribe—a tribe whose sheikh wants Halima for his new wife. When Atiyah hears that Halima is thought dead, he refuses to believe it. Setting off with his new friend Etienne, a French student, Atiyah will cross the desert to find Halima. But will Halima be able to withstand the orders of the sheikh and remain true to Atiyah? This companion to *The Ramsey Scallop* explores the Muslim world and its contrasts to Christian Europe.
>
> **Keywords:** Africa; Fourteenth Century; Romance

Whelan, Gloria.

Listening for Lions. HarperCollins, 2005. 978-0-06-058174-9 (hardcover); 978-0-06-058176-3 (softcover). 208pp. ⬛ ⬛

> British East Africa is the only home Rachel has ever known. She was born there, the year after her parents came from England. Among her father's patients and her mother's students, Rachel learns Swahili and about the customs of the Kikuyu and the Masai. But although Africa is remote from the rest of the world, it cannot escape the influenza epidemic of 1918–1919. The death of her parents leaves Rachel an orphan, and she falls into the care of her cruel neighbors, the Pritchards. They want Rachel to take the place of their dead daughter and impersonate her during a visit to Mr. Pritchard's father. It's all to get money, and Rachel doesn't like the idea of lying. Yet sailing to England, pretending to be Valerie Pritchard, will get her away from the Pritchards. So Rachel accepts this burden, but she makes a promise: Someday she will return to Africa and continue her parents' work.
>
> **Keywords:** 1910s; England; Family; Illness; Kenya

Europe

One of the most popular geographical settings for historical fiction, Europe features many different cultures and ethnic makeups. These cultures have often triggered conflicts, ranging from local to international. Yet there is still a sense of connection between Europeans, reflecting their close proximity to each other.

Historical fiction set in Britain—the countries of England, Scotland, Ireland, and Wales—is covered in the next section.

Medieval Darkness: Before 1000 CE

The centuries before 1000 CE cover several periods of European civilization. After the Roman Empire fell in the fifth century, Europe was beset by periods of strife and warfare, led by groups such as the Goths and the Vikings. There were highlights such as Charlemagne in this period, showing that Europe was not quite as dark as some historians once thought. But true stability and light would have to wait until the Middle Ages and the Renaissance.

Branford, Henrietta.

The Fated Sky. **Candlewick, 1999. 978-0-7636-0775-3 (hardcover). 160pp.** 🄜 🄙

Ran lives a hard life. Long winters often mean little food, raiders often sweep across the country pillaging farms, and the gods are capricious. When her father and brothers die, Ran's relationship with her mother breaks apart—especially when her mother brings a new man into their home. Things haven't improved when the three of them must set off on a three-day journey to take part in the midwinter sacrifice. Amid tragedy, Ran attempts to rebuild her life—and when it's destroyed a second time, she starts all over again.

Keywords: Medieval; Mother and Child; Scandinavia

Cadnum, Michael.

Daughter of the Wind. **Orchard, 2003. 978-0-439-35224-6 (hardcover). 272pp.** 🄜 🄙

The lives of three young people become connected in medieval Scandinavia. Gauk is a good hunter who longs to be one of the wild warriors known as beserkers. Hallgard is the daughter of the local jarl or chieftain, a great beauty who is as skilled as she is proud. And then there is Hego, a man slow in mind and body who desires to improve. When Danes attack their village, Hallgard is taken as a captive to a Danish city. When Gauk returns to their village after a hunting trip, he learns about the Danish attack. He takes up arms while the village waits for reinforcements, and together with Hego he sets off to rescue Hallgard.

Keywords: Medieval; Scandinavia

Raven of the Waves. **Orchard, 2001. 978-0-531-30334-4 (hardcover); 978-0-439-62661-3 (softcover). 224pp.** 🄜 🄙

Lidsmod and Wiglaf live very different lives. Lidsmod lives in a village in medieval Norway that is overrun with men. The only way for the men to keep occupied is to sail away on raids against the nearby Danes or to distant lands. Wiglaf lives in one of these lands. With a withered arm, he was given to the Church. He hopes to become a healer like Father Aethelwulf. But that hope is dashed when Lidsmod and his fellow villagers attack Wiglaf's home. Wiglaf is now a captive, and the Norsemen are rampaging through his village, stealing from their church and killing all the men. Wiglaf tries to make himself useful by tending to the wounds of his captors. He doesn't know it, but his actions might just get him his freedom from Lidsmod, his captor.

Keywords: Medieval; Scandinavia

Napoli, Donna Jo.

Hush. **Atheneum, 2007. 978-0-689-86176-5 (hardcover); 978-0-689-86179-6 (softcover). 320pp. Ⓜ Ⓙ**

In the year 900 CE, Ireland is often raided and attacked by Vikings, the fierce warriors of Scandinavia. They sweep in across the cold north seas, killing men and kidnapping women and children. One of these women is the Irish princess Melkorka. Taken from her home and all she knows, Melkorka is miserable during the long voyage from Ireland to Russia, suffering hunger, thirst, and abuse. Urged by a wise fellow slave, she takes a vow of silence. Being mute gives her a strange power over the men who kidnapped her and the man who buys her as a slave. Even though she suffers in silence, Melkorka is determined to return to her home, find her family, and once again use her voice.

Keywords: Ireland; Russia; Scandinavia; Slavery; Tenth Century; Women's Roles

Wilson, Diane Lee.

Raven Speak. **Margaret K. McElderry, 2010. 978-1-4169-8653-9 (hardcover); 978-1-4169-8654-6 (softcover). 252pp. Ⓜ Ⓙ**

Cold and famine have taken a great toll on the people in the clan longhouse. The winter has been long and hard, following a small harvest. Fourteen-year-old Asa Coppermane, the daughter of the clan chieftain, wants to protect her sick mother and her beloved horse Rune while her father is searching for food. But Jorgen, the clan's skald or wise man, wants to take control of the clan. Against the chieftain's wishes, Jorgen urges the remaining clan members to sacrifice a horse. When he attempts to attack Rune, Asa takes her horse and flees for safety. She cannot give up her horse . . . but then Asa meets a woman who talks to ravens. The birds say that Asa must lose something she loves in order to save her clan. Asa is faced with a horrible choice: to sacrifice her horse or risk her clan.

Keywords: Animals; Ninth Century; Scandinavia

Wright, Randall.

Hunchback. **Henry Holt, 2004. 978-0-8050-7232-7 (hardcover). 256pp. Ⓜ Ⓙ**

A visit from royalty is bound to make a medieval castle come to life. Hodge dreams of such a visit and having the chance to become a servant to a prince. Because of his hunched back, Hodge is given the dirtiest jobs around the castle. But when a prince does arrive at Castle Marlby, Hodge quickly finds that reality is quite different. This royal visit seems more like an invasion, with the prince's men guarding the castle and curtailing Hodge's freedom to move around. There seems to be much unspoken; will Hodge be able to read between the lines and discover what is going on?

Keywords: Coming-of-age; Medieval; Physical Disability

Middle Ages: 1000–1400

The Middle Ages, those centuries between the "Dark" Ages and the Renaissance, represent a transitional period. Although there was still plenty of turmoil, this period was marked by increasing power held by countries that are still known to us. Although a wide gap still separated peasants from the nobility, there was some certainty to life.

Barrett, Tracy.

Anna of Byzantium. **Delacorte Books for Young Readers, 1999. 978-0-385-32626-1 (hardcover); 978-0-440-41536-7 (softcover). 224pp.** Ⓜ Ⓙ

She is Anna Comnenus, daughter of Alexius Comnenus, Imperial Emperor of the Byzantine Empire. She is his heir, his first-born, and not even the birth of a son changes that. As the years pass, Anna prepares to become empress by learning to read and write, spending time with Simon the librarian, and preparing for her wedding. But her grandmother, Anna Dalassena, has different plans: to put Anna's younger brother John on the throne and rule through him. When her father dies, Anna is faced with a decision: work with her mother to usurp John and Anna, risking everything, or let her birthright and position be destroyed.

Keywords: Byzantine Empire; Eleventh Century; Family; Political Rebellions; Royalty; Women's Roles

Chandler, Pauline.

Warrior Girl: A Novel of Joan of Arc. **Greenwillow Books, 2006. 978-0-06-084102-7 (hardcover); 978-0-19-275410-3 (softcover). 368pp.** Ⓙ

The land known as France is in turmoil. The heir to the throne, the dauphin Charles, is unable to reach the city of Reims to be crowned King. English soldiers block his path—soldiers who would take over France and make it part of England. It is a bleak time, but then an unlikely leader appears, an uneducated peasant girl, untrained in combat but with a mission from God. The girl, named Jehanne and called the Maid of Lorraine, has been ordered by God's messengers to see Charles crowned and help defeat the English. But how will she achieve this monumental task? The help of her relatives, like her mute cousin Mariane, and the belief of a few noblemen will allow Jehanne d'Arc—Joan of Arc—to save France.

Keywords: Fifteenth Century; France; Women Soldiers; Women's Roles

Garden, Nancy.

Dove and Sword: A Novel of Joan of Arc. **Farrar, Straus & Giroux, 1995. 978-0-374-34476-4 (hardcover); 978-0-590-92949-3 (softcover). 237pp. Ⓜ Ⓙ**

> In Gabrielle's village, the war among France, England. and Burgundy is sometimes close, sometimes far away. There doesn't seem to be an end in sight, though. Unbeknown to anyone, the hope of France lies in Gabrielle's village. Jeanette d'Arc, the sister of Gabrielle's childhood playmate, has declared that three saints have instructed her to save France. No one, from the villagers to the local officials, believes Jeanette, a peasant and a girl, can lead the French armies to victory and the Dauphin Charles to his throne. But Jeanette slowly and surely proves that she has been chosen for this mission. Accompanied by her brother Pierre and by Gabrielle, Jeanette will attempt her holy mission, no matter the cost to herself!
>
> **Keywords:** Fifteenth Century; France; Women Soldiers; Women's Roles

Grant, K. M.
Perfect Fire Trilogy. Ⓙ Ⓢ

> As the Crusades sent waves of Christians into the Holy Land, there were efforts in Europe to force out Christian sects that followed practices outlawed by the pope. One such group was known as the Cathars, located in what is now southern France. This series uses this conflict as the backdrop for a love story.
>
> **Keywords:** Cathars; France; Religious Conflicts; Romance; Thirteenth Century

Blue Flame. Walker Books for Young Readers, 2008. 978-0-8027-9694-3 (hardcover). 256pp.

> In the southern part of France there is a region known as the Occitan. In the early part of the thirteenth century, the land was split between two religious factions, the Catholics and the Cathars. Each was convinced God was on its side, and both wanted to control the Occitan. In the midst of this struggle, the son of a Cathar weaver and the daughter of a Catholic count fall in love. But they cannot give into their love, for soldiers from the north and Church inquisitors are approaching their castle, all after the same thing: the Blue Flame. The mysterious flame, which sprang to life at the moment of Christ's death, is for the whole Occitan and promises enormous power. It will be up to the young lovers, Raimon and Yolanda, and the elderly knight Parsifal, to save the Blue Flame from those who would use it against the Occitan.

White Heat. Walker Books for Young Readers, 2009. 978-0-8027-9695-0 (hardcover). 272pp.

> Lovers Raimon and Yolanda are separated by situation and distance. Sentenced to death, Raimon is able to escape and carry the Blue Flame of the Occitan into hiding. As news about the flame spreads, people come to Raimon's camp, but they only want to know which side in the current religious war the Flame supports. Raimon is frustrated with this misunderstanding of the Flame's purpose. But soon Raimon will have the

French King's armies to worry about. Meanwhile, Yolanda is in Paris as the future wife of Sir Hugh. She believes Raimon to be dead; in spite of Sir Hugh's kindness to her, she is resistant to marrying him. Learning that Raimon is alive will propel Yolanda out of her stupor and send her on a journey to the Occitan. Yolanda and Raimon will struggle to save their country and their love.

Jinks, Catherine.

Babylonne. **Candlewick, 2008. 978-0-7636-3650-0 (hardcover). 400pp.** 🔲

Even though Babylonne never knew her father, some things are passed on in the blood. The daughter of Pagan Kidrouk is disobedient, sarcastic, and quick-witted. She loves living in Toulouse among all the people and bustle of a large town. What she does not like is living with a group of female relatives, women who disapprove of Babylonne because of her illegitimacy. She is often abused and mistreated, but she can't help questioning what she is told. Babylonne imagines a glittering future for herself, fighting for her Cathar faith against the forces of Catholic France. Or should she listen to the words of the Catholic priest who says he knew her father? This companion to the <u>Pagan Chronicles</u> expands upon the story told in the last novel in the series.

Keywords: Cathars; France; Religious Conflicts; Thirteenth Century; Women's Roles

Konigsberg, E. L.

A Proud Taste for Scarlet and Miniver. **Atheneum, 1973. 978-0-689-30111-7 (hardcover); 978-0-689-84624-3 (softcover). 208pp.** 🔲 🔲

In Heaven, Eleanor of Aquitaine is waiting. When she was alive, she didn't have to wait for anything. She was a brilliant, beautiful, enchanting woman, a queen to two kings. The heir to the duchy of Aquitaine, she was an heiress of great wealth, first married to King Louis VII of France. The marriage ended and she became queen of England, bringing light and beauty to the court of Henry II. Now she's waiting to see if Henry will be permitted into Heaven. To pass the time, she sits with three old friends and talks about the life she led while she was on Earth. Abbot Suger, her mother-in-law Empress Matilda, and William Marshal have been with her for most of her life, at different points along the way, and they tell her story as much as she does.

Keywords: England; France; Multiple Voices; Royalty; Twelfth Century; Women's Roles

Leeds, Constance.

The Silver Cup. **Viking Juvenile, 2007. 978-0-670-06157-0 (hardcover). 240pp.** 🔲

Anna's German village is small, full of people she has known her entire life. Some are kind and caring; some are mean and cruel. She wants to see more, but seeing more reveals things that make her uncomfortable. When she goes with her father to the large city of Worms, she first meets Jewish people. She's been brought up to believe that Jews are evil, the murderers of Christ. But when a group of men, part of the First Crusade, slaughter the Jews of Worms, Anna slowly begins to learn tolerance and brings an orphaned Jewish girl to her village.

Keywords: Eleventh Century; Germany; Religious Conflicts

McDonnell, Kathleen.

1212: Year of the Journey. **Second Story Press, 2007. 978-1-897187-11-1 (softcover). 240pp. ❶ ❺**

It didn't take long for the spirit behind the Crusades to be twisted. It became more about war than faith. In southern France, out of the conflicts and tensions of Catholics, Jews, and Cathars living in close quarters, came the Children's Crusade. A young shepherd, Etienne, has a vision of Saint Nicholas, and that vision inspires him to preach a crusade to children from all classes. Their message will be peace and harmony. Joined by Blanche, a Cathar, and the Jewish Abel, Etienne and the followers will suffer adult hardships on their journey. Yet their message of children spreading peace endures today.

Keywords: France; Religious Conflicts; Thirteenth Century

Napoli, Donna Jo.

Breath. **Atheneum, 2003. 978-0-689-86174-1 (hardcover); 978-0-689-86177-2 (softcover). 260pp. ❿ ❶**

Salz lives in a small village called Hameln. He suffers from a strange condition that makes it difficult for him to breathe. To cope with his illness, he is kept on a strict diet and forbidden to drink beer like everyone else. Meanwhile, the residents of his village start suffering from their own strange sickness, which makes people have nausea or act strangely. Even the animals are acting odd—cows are swallowing bees without even noticing. No one knows what's causing this: Is it all the rain? The sudden infestation of rats? Only Salz is unaffected . . . and he might be the only one who can find an answer. But does the answer lie with the mysterious piper who has just come to the village?

Keywords: Family; Germany; Illness; Thirteenth Century

O'Dell, Scott.

The Road to Damietta. **Houghton Mifflin, 1985. 978-0-395-38923-2 (hardcover); 978-0-618-49493-4 (softcover). 307pp. ❿ ❶**

Ricca may be barely thirteen, but her parents are already looking for a husband for her. But Ricca is already in love, with the charming Francis Bernadone. In the city of Assisi, everyone knows Francis and his wild ways, and Ricca has loved him from afar. But then Francis has a transformation, giving himself over to God. He wears a rough robe and goes begging for his food. Ricca doesn't understand the change that has come over Francis, but it hasn't affected her love for him. She will follow him to the city of Damietta, the site where Francis's faith will be tested—as will Ricca's love. The life of Francis of Assisi is presented against the backdrop of thirteenth-century Italy.

Keywords: Italy; Romance; Thirteenth Century

Sauerwein, Leigh.

Song for Eloise. **Front Street, 2004. 978-1-886910-90-4 (hardcover). 133pp. ◨ ⑤**

Like the song of a troubadour, the intertwined lives of a group of people is told to the reader. Front and center is Eloise, who is married at fifteen to a man twice her age, a rough soldier baron named Robert. Robert deeply loves his young wife and just wants to make her happy. So he hires a troubadour and a juggler to come and entertain everyone in his castle. But Robert doesn't know that Thomas the troubadour has known Eloise since childhood . . . and there's a connection between the two young people. This story and more are woven together in this complex novel of medieval Europe.

Keywords: France; Multiple Voices; Music; Twelfth Century

Skurzynski, Gloria.

Spider's Voice. **Atheneum, 1999. 978-0-689-82149-3 (hardcover); 978-0-689-84208-5 (softcover). 144pp. ◨**

Aran was born tongue-tied, unable to speak. Yet his mind is sharp, intelligent—and he longs to learn more. He escapes from his abusive, small-minded father and in Paris becomes a servant to a wise man. Not just any wise man: Aran works for Peter Abelard, the most talented and innovative teacher in all of Europe. As Aran, called Spider, learns to read, he also learns about the love between a man and a woman. For Abelard loves Heloise, the most beautiful and learned woman in Europe. Their love is timeless, living on through tragedy and separation. Spider's fortunes wax and wane, yet through it all he maintains loyalty to the star-crossed lovers as he attempts to find his own place in the world. An eyewitness account of a medieval love story gives the reader insight into the pressures faced by those in search of knowledge and truth.

Keywords: France; Physical Disability; Romance; Twelfth Century

Temple, Frances.

📖 *The Ramsay Scallop*. Orchard, 1994. 978-0-531-06836-6 (hardcover); 978-0-06-440601-7 (softcover). 310pp. **J** **S**

The return of her betrothed has engulfed Elenor in a whirlwind. It's been eight years since Thomas of Thornham left for the Crusades. Now he's a silent, strong man, scary and intimidating to young, fourteen-year-old Elenor. Father Gregory, the parish priest, sees the turmoil within both Elenor and Thomas, a turmoil that also exists within the whole village where they live. So he tasks Elenor and Thomas to set off on a pilgrimage to the shrine of Compostela in Spain, to ask forgiveness for the village's sins. As they travel, experiencing the world, Elenor and Thomas slowly develop their friendship, meeting other travelers along the way, all seeking salvation. Amid the pilgrims and along the way, their friendship becomes love.

Keywords: Crusades; England; France; Romance; Spain; Thirteenth Century

Weil, Sylvie.

My Guardian Angel. Arthur A. Levine Books, 2004. 978-0-439-57681-9 (hardcover); 978-0-439-57682-6 (softcover). 208pp. **M** **J**

This translated novel reveals the full nature of Jewish life in a French town in the eleventh century. Elvina's life is one of simple pleasures and small pains. She hates that as a girl, she must help set eggs, keeping them warm during winter. But she has the happiness of her writing. It is unusual for any girl to know how to read and write, but Elvina's grandfather is a great rabbi who had no sons. So the women of the family are educated, and Elvina especially loves writing, smoothing ink across parchment. She often writes to her mazal, her guardian angel. Elvina will need to call upon her mazal to help her with the decision she has to make. For Elvina, a Jewish girl, allows an injured Crusader to come into her family's home. Her decision might destroy the Jewish community, but her charity might reap great rewards.

Keywords: Eleventh Century; France; Religious Conflicts; Writing

Renaissance and Reformation: 1400–1700

"Renaissance" means rebirth in French. This name is given to the period when Europe began to recover the knowledge that had been lost after the fall of Rome, knowledge known to the Greeks and Romans. This sense of discovery led to much questioning by Europeans, eventually leading to the Protestant Reformation and the development of other Christian religions. These centuries are marked by dynamic events and probing questions, as well as occasional great cruelties.

Barnhouse, Rebecca.

The Book of the Maidservant. Random House Books for Young Readers, 2009. 978-0-375-85856-7 (hardcover); 978-0-375-85857-4 (softcover). 240pp. **M** **J**

In early fifteenth-century England, Dame Margery Kemp was considered the most pious woman in existence. She only thought of the sufferings of Jesus, often bursting into sobs. Such behavior didn't just gain her respect for her holiness; there were plenty who thought she was mad or afflicted with an evil spirit. For Johanna, Dame Margery's maid, her mistress was just aggravating. Even the prospect of joining Dame Margery on a pilgrimage to Rome doesn't change Johanna's opinion. Johanna finds herself serving the needs of all the pilgrims, not just her lady's—much to Dame Margery's dislike. After her mistress quarrels with the other travelers and leaves the caravan, Johanna is abandoned. She must call upon her own strength and faith if she is to reach Rome.

Keywords: England; Fifteenth Century; Germany; Italy; Women's Roles

Beaufrand, Mary Jane.

Primavera. Little, Brown, 2008. 978-0-316-01644-5 (hardcover); 978-0-316-01645-2 (softcover). 272pp. **J** **S**

Fourteen-year-old Flora is the youngest daughter in the Pazzi family of Florence. With eleven brothers and sisters, Flora is of little use to her parents, especially since she is so plain. While her older, beautiful, but empty-headed sister gets her portrait painted by Botticelli, Flora works in her garden and spends time with her grandmother. But the Pazzi family's greatest enemy, the Medici family, is growing more powerful at the expense of the Pazzis. Flora, the most overlooked in her whole family, might be the one to save her family. Renaissance Italy's political struggles are presented in the story of a stubborn, determined girl.

Keywords: Art; Disguised as Boy; Fifteenth Century; Italy; Women's Roles

Cullen, Lynn.

I Am Rembrandt's Daughter. Bloomsbury, 2007. 978-1-59990-046-9 (hardcover); 978-1-59990-294-4 (softcover). 320pp. **J** **S**

Cornelia's life is full of difficulties and hardship. Once her father was the most respected, sought-after painter in Amsterdam. But those days are long gone, and now Rembrandt van Rijn is nearly mad. He paints only what he is inspired to paint, his brush strokes thick and obvious rather than invisible. It's left to Cornelia to care for her father, especially after her brother gets married. Her father is demanding and imperious—but he possesses great artistic genius. Cornelia cannot deny his abilities, even as she wishes he could sell his work and pull them back from the brink of poverty. Yet perhaps Cornelia will be saved by another man. Will it be Carel, the rich man's son with an artistic eye? Or will it be Neel, her father's last remaining student? At a time of great sadness, Cornelia will finally make her choice.

Keywords: Art; Father and Child; Netherlands; Romance; Seventeenth Century

Dines, Carol.

The Queen's Soprano. **Harcourt Children's Books, 2006. 978-0-15-205477-9 (hardcover); 978-0-15-206102-9 (softcover). 336pp. J S**

Imagine you have a gift. You sing like an angel, an ability that you've had since birth. But in the time and place you live in, you're not allowed to fully use this talent. That's Angelica's problem. In Rome in 1670, women who perform in public are accused of prostitution. So Angelica sings inside her house, attracting listeners from all over Rome. Her mother is determined to use Angelica's gift to secure a rich or noble husband for her. But Angelica, against her mother's wishes, has fallen in love with a French artist. It seems the only way Angelica can be happy is by escaping to the quarter of Rome that's under the control of Christina, the former queen of Sweden. There women may sing in public, and Angelica might marry her love. Can Angelica be safe under Queen Christina's protection? She takes the greatest risk of her life to break out of her sheltered cage.

Keywords: Italy; Music; Seventeenth Century; Women's Roles

Grey, Christopher.

Leonardo's Shadow: Or, My Astonishing Life as Leonardo da Vinci's Servant. **Atheneum, 2006. 978-1-4169-0543-1 (hardcover); 978-1-4169-0544-8 (softcover). 400pp. J S**

The day that he falls from the roof of the cathedral changes Giacomo's life. Saved from death by landing on some scaffolding, Giacomo is taken in by Leonardo da Vinci, the great artist. Without any memories of his former life, he is renamed Giacomo and becomes da Vinci's servant. In the world of Renaissance Milan, there are saints' day celebrations, mass fights between servants and apprentices, and frequent wars with other nearby cities. But there's also the beauty of architecture and art—and no one is a greater artist than Giacomo's master. But Leonardo, for reasons of his own, is delaying the completion of a painting of the Last Supper. Since the painting is a commission from the Duke of Milan, this delay is dangerous. With money running short, Giacomo can't help worrying about his future. But he also has questions about his past, especially when signs point to a relationship between himself and da Vinci. Giacomo slowly grows up and matures as he grapples with these questions and worries.

Keywords: Art; Fifteenth Century; Identity; Italy

McCaughrean, Geraldine.

Cyrano. Harcourt Children's Books, 2006. 978-0-15-205805-0 (hardcover). 114pp. **M** **J**

The Gascon soldier and wit known as Cyrano de Bergerac is as famous for his accomplishments as he is for his peculiar physical feature. Cyrano is not an attractive man, thanks to his massive nose. Insults and jests about it roll off his back, yet he knows that no woman could love him. Knowing this doesn't make not falling in love any easier. Cyrano cares deeply about his beautiful cousin Roxanne, but she loves the beautiful but empty-headed Christian. When Christian, unaware of Cyrano's love, asks for his help in composing poetry to Roxanne, Cyrano agrees. It is painful for Cyrano, but he's determined to charm Roxanne with his wit and panache.

Keywords: France; Romance; Seventeenth Century

Meyer, Carolyn.

Duchessina: A Novel of Catherine de' Medici. Harcourt Children's Books, 2007. 978-0-15-205588-2 (hardcover); 978-0-15-206620-8 (softcover). 272pp. **J**

As the last member of a noble line stretching back to Lorenzo the Magnificent, Caterina de Medici is heiress to a powerful dukedom and great riches. But due to political shifts in power, she is often alone, kept isolated from those who love her. She does get to spend some time with her beloved Aunt Clarissa, her nursemaid Betta, and her kind cousin Ippolito. Then Catarina becomes a pawn in the political game as well as a victim of the public's disdain for the Medici family. She is imprisoned in a convent with a group of cruel nuns. She is only rescued when the French ambassador intervenes. Discovering that a marriage has been arranged for her with the heir to the French throne, Caterina is dismayed that she will be separated from her love, her cousin Ippolito. The only advantage is that as queen of France, she will have power for the first time in her life.

Keywords: France; Italy; Royalty; Sixteenth Century

Napoli, Donna Jo.

Daughter of Venice. Wendy Lamb Books, 2002. 978-0-385-32780-0 (hardcover); 978-0-440-22928-5 (softcover). 275pp. **M** **J**

To some, Donata leads a charmed life. She's the daughter of a noble family, a rich and respected one in Venice. But now that her older sister is sixteen, it's time for her to marry. Donata and her twin sister Laura, at fourteen, hope they might marry as well. But in sixteenth-century Venice, usually only one daughter in the family marries; the other girls go to convents or live with their families. Donata doesn't like that thought, but what choice does she have, as a noble girl without any trade or craft? She's kept sheltered by her family, and doesn't even know the name of the street she lives on. But Donata is a daughter of Venice, and she will find a way to explore and discover her city—and perhaps more than that.

Keywords: Italy; Sixteenth Century; Women's Roles

The Smile. **Dutton Juvenile, 2008. 978-0-525-47999-4 (hardcover); 978-0-14-241492-7 (softcover). 272pp. Ⓜ Ⓙ**

Probably the most famous painting in the world is the *Mona Lisa* by Leonardo da Vinci. But we know almost nothing about the woman in the painting. What if we knew about her life? Elisabetta, nicknamed Lisa, is the daughter of a silk merchant, approaching the time when she will be betrothed. She's not looking forward to having to marry an old or ugly man, but she knows it is expected of her—and it'll help her family. Until then, she wants to enjoy going into the woods and spending time with her friends and family. The death of Lorenzo de Medici, the ruler of Florence, brings Lisa's family to the city, where there are many people to meet. Some are old friends, like Leonardo de Vinci. Some are new friends, like Guilianio de Medici, the youngest son of the powerful noble family. And some, like Piero de Medici, could be enemies. Will Lisa be able to find happiness, or must she continue to hide her smile?

Keywords: Art; Italy; Sixteenth Century; Women's Roles

Richardson, V. A.
Windjammer. Ⓙ

Adventure and economics go hand-in-hand in these stories of a Dutch trading family. Many companies financed exploration of the New World to reap financial rewards—but if disaster struck the expedition, it also struck the company, as happens to the House of Windjammer.

Keywords: Netherlands; Romance; Seventeenth Century

The House of Windjammer. **Bloomsbury, 2003. 978-0-7475-5563-6 (hardcover); 978-0-7475-6475-1 (softcover). 352pp.**

Dutch companies took huge risks by sailing to unknown lands, exploring the world. Often they succeeded. But the House of Windjammer has just lost its entire fleet, save a ship still under construction. The companies and moneylenders, led by Hugo van Helsen, refuse to help the Windjammers, bringing the company to the brink of bankruptcy and leading to the death of the head of the family. Now Adam Windjammer, a teenager, is in charge of the company. Between his grasping uncle Augustus and the banker van Helsen, that's a tall order, made even more difficult because all of Amsterdam is glorying in the fall of Windjammer. Will Adam be able to start a new era for his family and their company or be destroyed just like the lost fleet?

The Moneylender's Daughter. Bloomsbury, 2006. 978-1-58234-885-8 (hardcover); 978-0-7475-7589-4 (softcover). 300pp.

> The House of Windjammer has fallen apart, thanks to the efforts of Hugo van Helsen. Adam Windjammer has sailed to the Americas, determined to find any survivors of the company's lost fleet. Yet his heart is still in Amsterdam, with Jade van Helsen. Even though she is the daughter of his enemy, Adam is in love with her—and Jade loves him back. But Jade is just a pawn to her father, and he has arranged a marriage for her based on money, not love. As Jade attempts to escape and prove her real worth to her father, Adam returns to Amsterdam, determined to rebuild his company. Adam and Jade struggle to gain their freedom and happiness.

Trevino, Elizabeth Borton de.

I, Juan de Pareja. **Farrar, Straus & Giroux, 1965. 978-0-374-33531-1 (hardcover); 978-0-312-38005-2 (softcover). 192pp. Ⓜ Ⓙ**

The great artist Velázquez was only able to create his remarkable paintings with the help of a slave, Juan de Pareja. Juan grew up in Seville, serving a noble family. His mistress sometimes hit him, sometimes cuddled him, but he cared for her, especially when she taught him how to read and write. Her death means that Juan will go to Madrid and become the property of her nephew, the respected painter Velázquez. In Madrid, his new master sees the intelligence in Juan. Although the law forbids it, Velázquez teaches Juan about art, training him to be an artist. In return for this gift, Juan will be a devoted servant to Velázquez until his death. The world of seventeenth-century Spain is brought to life, like a painting being created before our eyes.

Awards: Newbery Medal

Keywords: Art; Seventeenth Century; Slavery; Spain

Yolen, Jane, and Robert J. Harris.

Queen's Own Fool. **Philomel, 2000. 978-0-399-23380-7 (hardcover); 978-0-698-11918-5 (softcover). 390pp. Ⓜ Ⓙ**

Nicola is the victim of her uncle's kicks and slaps. As part of his performing troupe, she never seems to satisfy him. He dislikes her witty answers to questions and her talkativeness. But those skills will help Nicola in a way she never imagined. After the troupe performs for the new king and queen of France, Nicola leaves the troupe and becomes a jester for Mary, queen of Scots, entertaining her and keeping her spirits up when times are bad. There will be many of them ahead: the death of King Francis, Mary's return to Scotland, and political turmoil. Through it all Nicola, known as La Jardiniere, will be with Mary. But when the Scottish people stop respecting their queen, what will happen to Mary—and to Nicola?

Keywords: France; Performing; Royalty; Sixteenth Century

Revolution and Napoleon: 1700–1900

These two centuries were marked by different kinds of turmoil than the previous two. Rather than focusing on the next world, people were caught up in thoughts about their lives here on Earth. Peasants questioned their lot in life when they saw the luxurious lives of nobles and aristocrats, leading to a string of revolts and rebellions. After these upheavals, Napoleon created and ruled over an empire that stretched across most of Europe.

Ain, Beth Levine.

The Revolution of Sabine. Candlewick, 2008. 978-0-7636-3396-7 (hardcover). 224pp. **M** **J**

Paris in 1776 is in a whirlwind over its latest visitor, Mr. Benjamin Franklin, from the colonies that are rebelling against Great Britain. Every hostess wants Franklin to attend her events. Madame Durand is no different; in fact, she's desperate to improve her family's social position by landing Franklin. Her daughter Sabine is often embarrassed and resentful of her mother's actions. She feels constrained by all her mother's rules, but what other option does she have? It's only thanks to her childhood friend Michel that she begins to have her eyes opened. Meeting Franklin makes her all the more determined to make a revolutionary life for herself. Otherwise, she'll meet her fate as an aristocrat and marry a man she doesn't love. Sabine will do anything to escape her mother's control, but how can she achieve that? Sabine finds inspiration in unusual places as she stages a personal revolution.

Keywords: Eighteenth Century; France; Mother and Child; Political Rebellions

Bradley, Kimberly Brubaker.

The Lacemaker and the Princess. Margaret K. McElderry, 2007. 978-1-4169-1920-9 (hardcover); 978-1-4169-8583-9 (softcover). 208pp. **M** **J**

Within the vast, elaborate court at Versailles, one could spend years working in the palace without ever catching more than a glimpse of the King and Queen of France. But Isabelle is different. She is rescued by Marie Antoinette and selected as a companion to Therese, princess of France. As the daughter of a poor lacemaker, Isabella doesn't understand life at court and is always asking questions. Life in court is luxurious, with every whim met. As news about the troubles in France begins to reach Versailles, Isabella must decide whether her friendships are worth the sadness of others.

Keywords: Eighteenth Century; France; Royalty

Elliott, Patricia.

The Pale Assassin. Holiday House, 2009. 978-0-8234-2250-0 (hardcover); 978-0-8234-2312-5 (softcover). 336pp. **J S**

> The French Revolution turned the world upside down. Eugenie must change if she is to survive. When the hostilities between peasant and noble first explode, she is a sheltered, naïve girl. She thinks more about sweets and dresses than the ideas her radical governess is trying to introduce to her. But when her brother tells her she is betrothed, Eugenie is horrified. It's bad enough to be getting married, but her future husband is the revolutionary spy known as le Fantôme, the Phantom. If Eugenie is going to escape Paris and this arranged marriage, she must discover just what kind of brains she has.
>
> Keywords: Coming-of-age; Eighteenth Century; France; Women's Roles

Gardner, Sally.
French Revolution Colors. **J S**

> A lush, passionate look at lives caught up in the French Revolution, Gardner's series features compelling characters and a thrilling pace.
>
> Keywords: Eighteenth Century; France; Political Rebellions; Romance

The Red Necklace. Dial, 2008. 978-0-8037-3100-4 (hardcover); 978-0-14-241488-0 (softcover). 384pp.

> The winter of 1789 is one of the coldest ever in Paris. While the poor freeze, the nobles live in their luxurious chateaus. For Yann Margoza, a gypsy who works for the magician Topolain, life is a string of performances, not to mention marveling at the skills of Tetu, Topolain's assistant. When Topolain is summoned to perform at a noble's house party, he thinks it will be the start of better things for the three of them. But the party at the Marquis de Villeduval's is anything but: Topolain is killed while performing, and the sinister Count Kalliovski tries to capture Yann and Tetu. With the help of Sido, the marquis's daughter, they are able to escape, but only briefly; Count Kalliovski is now chasing them—and he already has trapped Sido. How will Yann keep his freedom while worrying about Sido? And there's also the small problem of the revolution sweeping through France.

The Silver Blade. Dial, 2009. 978-0-8037-3377-0 (hardcover); 978-0-14-241731-7 (softcover). 368pp.

> For Yann and Sido, the future looks bright even though they are separated. Yann is helping spirit aristocrats out of France to the safety of England. That's where Sido is, safe not just from the guillotine. The death of the evil Count Kalliovski means that there is no barrier to Yann and Sido's love, except Yann's secret Gypsy heritage. When it's

revealed, Sido's guardian refuses to allow her to marry Yann. Even worse, Count Kalliovski is still alive and still wants Sido. He arranges for Sido to be kidnapped and held as his prisoner. Yann will need to balance his love for Sido with his job of rescuing aristocrats. Yann is determined to save Sido and France—but can he succeed?

Gerstein, Mordicai.

Victor: A Novel Based on the Life of the Savage of Aveyron. Farrar, Straus & Giroux, 1998. 978-0-374-38142-4 (hardcover). 272pp. **J S**

In a France recovering from the French Revolution, a strange child was discovered in the district of Aveyron. The boy is a savage, covered in layers of grime and unable to communicate. It's not clear why the child is like this, but his lack of communication leads officials to send him to a home for deaf-mutes. The doctors write him off, convinced that he's hopeless. But one doctor, Jean-Marc Itard, sees something in this boy. Naming the boy Victor, Dr. Itard creates new techniques to reach the boy. Dr. Itard believes Victor can learn to speak, eat properly, and be like any French child. But is that possible with a boy who used to be a savage?

Keywords: Eighteenth Century; France

Holub, Josef.

An Innocent Soldier. Arthur A. Levine Books, 2005. 978-0-439-62771-9 (hardcover); 978-0-439-62772-6 (softcover). 240pp. **J S**

As Napoleon leads his armies across Europe, conquering every nation in his path, he continually requires new soldiers. One such new soldier is Adam. Forced to take the place of his master's son, Adam becomes George and endures the boredom and power plays of life in the army. Still, it's not quite so bad as being a farmhand. And things look up when an arrogant noble lieutenant plucks out Adam to be his new servant. Attending to his master's needs is an easy job, and Adam can even ride, one of his greatest pleasures. Then at last the day comes for the army to leave the barracks and march into battle. The lieutenant, like most of the officers, is excited to finally be on the march. Yet neither the lieutenant nor Adam realizes what this campaign means. For it is the spring of 1812, and they are marching for Russia.

Keywords: Coming-of-age; Napoleonic Wars; Nineteenth Century

Ibbotson, Eva.

The Star of Kazan. Dutton Juvenile, 2004. 978-0-0525-4734-3 (hardcover); 978-0-14-240582-6 (softcover). 416pp. **J**

Annika lives in a big house on a square in Vienna. But she doesn't live with her parents; she was abandoned in a small mountain church as a baby. She was found by Ellie and Sigrid, servants to three eccentric professors, and they took her in. Annika helps around the house, plays in the square with her friends, and spends time with the old lady in another house. But she can't help wondering whom and where her mother is. And then one day a mysterious, glamorous woman appears. She claims that she is Annika's mother, and she wants her daughter back. Annika is excited until they arrive at her new home: an old, crumbling castle. And the falling down estate in just the first clue that Annika's new family is more than it appears. As she fights homesickness, Annika discovers just what family is.

Awards: Carnegie Medal Finalist

Keywords: Austria; Family; Nineteenth Century

Meyer, Carolyn.

The Bad Queen: Rules and Instructions for Marie-Antoinette. **Harcourt Children's Books, 2010. 978-0-15-206376-4 (hardcover); 978-0-547-48249-1 (softcover). 432pp.** 🔲

Maria Antonia, the daughter of Empress Maria Theresa of Austria, has bad teeth, unmanageable hair, and poor handwriting. But once she is betrothed to the dauphin, the heir to the throne of France, only perfection is permitted. She is tutored to write better and to speak French fluently. Her hair is tamed and her teeth shifted through painful procedures. With all this, she has become perfect—and she is now Marie Antoinette. Sent to France at age fourteen, she is eager to make people like her and to be all that is asked of her. But the demands on Marie Antoinette in this strange land are too much for any one person. So she rebels by spending too much money and engaging in scandalous activities. But soon Marie Antoinette will find herself in such trouble that even being perfect won't save her.

Keywords: Eighteenth Century; France; Royalty; Women's Roles

In Mozart's Shadow. **Harcourt Children's Books, 2008. 978-0-15-205594-3 (hardcover). 368pp.** 🔲 🔲

Competing with a sibling for attention and admiration is difficult. It's even worse when your sibling is a true genius. That's the problem faced by Nannerl, older sister to Wolfgang Mozart. Nannerl loves to play the harpsichord, to sing, and to perform for the nobility. But she has to work and practice hard, while music flows in Wolfgang like the water in a river. Their father takes them to all the cities of Europe, playing for kings and queens. But Nannerl is slowly pushed aside by her brother's talent, reduced to living in their hometown of Salzburg while Wolfgang travels the world. Alone, with little outlet for her talents, Nannerl grows frustrated and disappointed. Can she be truly happy playing only for herself, especially when her brother is known by all for his talent? How can Nannerl find an answer to that question?

Keywords: Austria; Brothers and Sisters; Eighteenth Century; Music; Women's Roles

Marie, Dancing. **Harcourt Children's Books, 2005. 978-0-15-205116-7 (hardcover); 978-0-15-205879-1 (softcover). 272pp. 🅜 🅙**

> Life as a ballet dancer at the Paris Opera is very difficult. The chances of being a star are slim, leading most dancers to a life of selling themselves. This fact didn't matter to Marie's mother, though. Marie and both her sisters—one older, one younger—are all members of the ballet, but the money they make isn't much. Their mother works as a laundress, but she often drinks her wages. So Marie follows her older sister Antoinette in posing for Edgar Degas, the artist. Monsieur Degas plans to create a statue of Marie, something new and unique. But if the money from Monsieur Degas isn't enough, Marie may have to follow Antoinette's lead in other ways.
>
> **Keywords:** Art; France; Nineteenth Century; Sisters; Women's Roles

Newth, Mette.

The Dark Light. **Farrar, Straus & Giroux, 1998. 978-0-374-31701-0 (hardcover); 978-0-374-41688-1 (softcover). 256pp. 🅙 🅢**

> Even with her self-righteous grandmother, Tora finds happiness in her life in the mountains. There's her charming but flighty mother, her friend Ende, and the mountains themselves. But all this ends when she is diagnosed with leprosy. Lepers have to be isolated, so Tora is taken to Bergen to stay in the leper hospital for the rest of her life. It's a difficult adjustment; she's young and doesn't have any signs of the disease yet. But all the other patients and Tora both know that someday, her body will be ravaged. So she decides to improve her mind and lift her spirits toward God. She can help her fellow patients—and she can learn to read, in order to read the Bible herself. But to do that, she'll have to ask the disagreeable Mistress Dybendal for reading lessons. In nineteenth-century Norway, a young girl will find a way to beat the disease that will kill her.
>
> **Keywords:** Illness; Nineteenth Century; Scandinavia

Rabin, Staton.

📖 *Betsy and the Emperor*. **Margaret K. McElderry, 2004. 978-0-689-85880-2 (hardcover); 978-1-4169-1336-8 (softcover). 304pp. 🅙 🅢**

> Living on the island of St. Helena, a rocky, mountainous land, is very boring. For fourteen-year-old Betsy, newly home from boarding school, St. Helena is about finding or making mischief to pass the time. But then an event way beyond mischief occurs: Napoleon Bonaparte, the former emperor of France, is now imprisoned on St. Helena—in Betsy's own house! Betsy, who speaks good French and isn't intimidated by anyone, stands toe-to-toe with "Boney" and captures his interest. Slowly a friendship forms between the English girl and the former French emperor. It's such a strong friendship that Betsy will even dream up a plan that could free Napoleon from his exile.
>
> **Keywords:** Humor; Napoleonic Wars; Nineteenth Century

Wiseman, Eva.

Puppet. Tundra Books, 2009. 978-0-88776-828-6 (hardcover). 252pp. 🔳 🔳

Prejudice against Jewish people has existed for centuries. Some Christians even believed that Jews needed the blood of a Christian child to make their matzo. In a small Hungarian village in 1882, a maid named Esther vanishes. Even though everyone knows she was sad—what we would call depressed today—and could have drowned herself in the river, people in the village quickly suspect the Jews of murdering Esther. But Julie, Esther's friend, isn't so sure. So many Jews have been kind to her and her family. They've given her mother medicine and hired her father when no one else would. Why would anyone, much less a Jew, hurt Esther? The villagers turn on the Jewish residents, taking advantage of bubbling anti-Semitism. The authorities compel Morris Scharf, a Jewish boy Julie knows, to testify against other Jews, even his own father. As the trial goes on, drawing attention from around the world, Julie watches what happens and wonders how to tell good from evil.

Keywords: Hungary; Nineteenth Century; Religious Conflicts

Modern Times: 1900–1980

By the 1900s life had changed dramatically, thanks to inventions like electricity and cars. Yet age-old grudges and grievances would ignite to create two terrible wars that would change the very map of Europe and lead to new countries and political systems.

Bagdasarian, Adam.

Forgotten Fire. DK Children, 2000. 978-0-7894-2627-7 (hardcover); 978-0-440-22917-9 (softcover). 288pp. 🔳 🔳

Vahan is a spoiled boy, the youngest child in his family. Brought up in luxury, he's never known hardship or discomfort. But it is 1915, and in the section of Turkey known as Armenia, a massacre is being planned. As the world powers are dealing with World War I, the Muslim Turkish majority are eliminating the Christian Armenians. Vahan's father is taken away, his two oldest brothers are shot in front of the family, and then everyone is taken from their homes. Vahan manages to escape the death march and seeks safety somehow, somewhere. As he struggles to survive, Vahan discovers the courage, self-discipline, and character that he never knew he had.

Awards: National Book Award Finalist

Keywords: 1910s; Armenia; Coming-of-age; Family; Religious Conflicts

Cooper, Michelle.

A Brief History of Montmaray. **Knopf Books for Young Readers, 2009. 978-0-375-85864-2 (hardcover); 978-0-375-85154-4 (softcover). 304pp.** 🗓 🆂

Not many girls get to live in a castle as Sophie does. True, it's a crumbling, drafty building, located on a small island near Spain, but it is a castle. Sophie is a princess of the tiny Kingdom of Montmaray, living on the island among a few surviving villagers and her family. There's her mad uncle, King John, her brilliant cousin Veronica, and her tomboy sister Henry. And then there's Sophie herself, who has decided to keep a journal detailing what life is like in Montmaray. Sophie doesn't realize the changes that are coming for her; it is 1936 and war is developing in Europe. It takes the shipwreck of two men from Nazi Germany to start the chain reaction that will end the Kingdom of Montmaray. An imaginary kingdom is gripped by real politics in the 1930s.

Keywords: 1930s; Atlantic Ocean; Family; Royalty

Dunlap, Susanne.

Anastasia's Secret. **Bloomsbury, 2010. 978-1-59990-420-7 (hardcover); 978-1-59990-588-4. 352pp.** 🗓

Anastasia Romanov, like her three older sisters, is a sheltered young woman. She's a grand duchess, a member of the Russian royal family, but she knows little of the outside world, like what things cost or how normal people live. Thanks to Sasha, a young soldier, her eyes are opened. Through Sasha, Anastasia discovers the hardships that plague the Russian people and the anger that some of them feel. But Anastasia's time with Sasha isn't all sadness; there's small talk and listening to Sasha play his balalaika. Slowly Anastasia's friendship with Sasha deepens. Then at the beginning of World War I, Sasha is sent to the front. And the revolt of the Russian people will result in continued suffering for Anastasia and her family. Sadly, there is no happy ending to this story.

Keywords: 1910s; Romance; Royalty; Russia

Durbin, William.

The Winter War. **Wendy Lamb Books, 2008. 978-0-385-74652-6 (hardcover). 240pp.** 🗓

It's been just twenty years since Finland gained independence from the Soviet Union, but the Soviets have been looking for an excuse to attack Finland. In 1939 Soviet troops approach the Finnish border, bombing towns and creating fear. Marko, a young teen, is determined to do his part to defeat them. When his best friend is killed by a bomb, Marko will let nothing stop him from protecting Finland. Since his leg was weakened by polio, Marko serves as a messenger, covering the distance on skis. The odds are are not good: The Soviet Union has many more men, planes, and tanks. But in the harsh winter conditions of their homeland, the Finns have the advantage of firsthand knowledge. Can Marko and his people defeat the invaders and remain independent?

Keywords: 1930s; Finland; Political Rebellions

Fine, Anne.

The Road of Bones. Farrar, Straus & Giroux, 2008. 978-0-374-36316-1 (hardcover). 224pp. ⬛

In a country much like the Soviet Union, the people live in fear and sadness. There's never enough food, and anyone can be arrested at any moment. Twelve-year-old Yuri has grown up hearing his parents and grandmother whisper about the political upheaval. He used to believe the propaganda that his country was a shining star, led by wise, compassionate men. But as he grows older, he begins to question these assumptions. He realizes just how wrong they are when he and his schoolmates' education is halted and they're put to work in factories and cement yards. Exhausted from doing a man's work, Yuri says a few words that are seen as treason. He's soon charged with being an enemy of the state, in line for exile or even death. Yuri won't accept punishment when he committed no crime. So he strikes out, trying to escape those who would silence him.

Keywords: 1930s; Political Rebellions; Soviet Union

Lasky, Kathryn.

Ashes. Viking, 2010. 978-0-670-01157-5 (hardcover); 978-0-14-241112-4 (softcover). 320pp. ⬛

Thirteen-year-old Gabriella likes reading, Joan Crawford movies, and physics. She's happy spending time with her best friend Rosa and talking to her neighbor Albert Einstein or her parents and their friends. But all of Gabriella's pleasures are eclipsed by the growing power of the Nazi Party. Germany has suffered much since the end of World War I, and some people believe Adolf Hitler and the Nazis can restore the good times and protect Germany. But Gaby's parents don't support Hitler or his policies. And Gaby can't, either. How could she believe in a man who speaks out against books, against knowledge? As Gaby sees the impact of Hitler's rise to power, she begins to lose many of the people and things she loves.

Keywords: 1930s; Germany; Politics

MacKall, Dandi Daley.

Eva Underground. Harcourt Children's Books, 2006. 978-0-15-205462-5 (hardcover). 256pp. ⬛ ⬛

When her father tells her he's moving them to Communist Poland, it's the last thing Eva wants. She wishes there was a way she could stay in Chicago, eating pizza, listening to records, and finishing high school with her best friend and boyfriend. But her father insists it's only for a year, so Eva goes along with him. It's a rough adjustment; Eva had no idea just how bad the conditions are. Little food, cold houses, unpaved streets . . . . Poland is a miserable place, which Eva is desperate to leave at first. But as she learns more about the underground cause her father is participating in, she realizes that Poland is starting to feel like home. There's also Tomek, a university student who's moody and grumpy—but also kind and poetic. Eva and Tomek get to tell their own stories as they live in Poland in 1978.

Keywords: 1970s; Cold War; Poland; Romance

Schur, Maxine Rose.

Sacred Shadows. **Dial, 1997. 978-0-8037-2295-8 (hardcover). 224pp.** 🔟

An episodic story of life between the world wars reveals one girl's life. Lena is only five when her father dies during World War I fighting in the German Army. He is posthumously awarded the Iron Cross. As a result of Germany's defeat, Lena's hometown becomes part of the reformed country of Poland. Lena and her family— her mother and her older brother Gunther—are German Jews, a minority in Poland. Lena's mother refuses to leave, believing that they will be protected and safe. Yet Poles dislike Germans and Jews, and racial prejudice grows over the years. Many Jews become convinced their only hope lies in striking back or emigrating to Palestine. As she becomes a woman, Lena will have to decide what path to take.

Keywords: 1930s; Coming-of-age; Poland; Religious Conflicts

Whelan, Gloria.

📖 *After the Train.* **HarperCollins, 2009. 978-0-06-029596-7 (hardcover). 160pp.** Ⓜ

Thirteen-year-old Peter doesn't understand why his lessons feature so many of Germany's misdeeds. After all, it's been ten years since the war ended and Germany was divided. Peter and his classmates were all little children during the war—they're not responsible for what happened. But while working on a summer assignment, Peter comes across a letter and a photograph. The letter discusses something his mother did, and the photograph is of a woman Peter has seen in his nightmares. Putting together the pieces, Peter realizes he has different parents than the people who have brought him up. Peter is actually Jewish, the son of a woman sent to a concentration camp. With this knowledge, Peter will have to discover if this changes who he really is.

Keywords: 1950s; Family; Germany

Russian Family. 🔟

Life in Russia in the early twentieth century was a time of upheaval and change— but that doesn't mean people didn't still fall in love, get married, and have children.

Keywords: 1910s; 1930s; Family; Political Rebellions; Russia; Soviet Union

Angel on the Square. HarperCollins, 2001. 978-0-06-029030-6 (hardcover); 978-0-439-43789-9 (softcover). 304pp.

> Katya is very lucky, thanks to an accident of birth. She was born the daughter of a noble Russian family, one with money and status. In the winter of 1913 her mother is selected as a lady-in-waiting to the Empress Alexandra, and Katya is to be a friend to the Grand Duchess Anastasia. Katya has lived in comfortable luxury but is dazzled by life in the Imperial palaces. They are ornate, lavish homes, full of servants—yet food is simple and the imperial children take cold baths. Still, it's a more comfortable and safer life than that lived by most Russians, as Katya learns. Misha, who has been brought up with Katya, opens her eyes to the poor lives of ordinary Russians, for he is a student who is agitating for change. Soon that change will sweep through Russia, destroying the life that Katya knew. Will she have the strength to survive in the midst of revolution?

The Impossible Journey. HarperCollins, 2003. 978-0-06-623811-1 (hardcover); 978-0-06-441083-0 (softcover). 256pp.

> The children of Katya and Misha will have to reunite their family when political turmoil separates them. After a prominent opponent of Stalin is assassinated, Marya's parents are arrested and soon sent to Siberia. Marya isn't prepared to be without her parents and be responsible for her little brother Georgi. But somehow she must keep the two of them safe. When she gets a letter that tells her where her parents are, Marya takes a chance. She will take her brother, sneak out of Leningrad, and find the town to which her parents have been exiled. It's a long, dangerous trip, with little chance of success. But Marya would do anything to reunite her family.

World War I and World War II: 1914–1945

Originally known as the Great War, the First World War was a conflict like nothing seen before in human history. It saw massive casualties and new weapons, and the ending of the war was supposed to usher in happier, better times. But these good times could not last long, not with the still-simmering tensions beneath the surface. These tensions would spark the Second World War.

The books in this section concern the military action of the wars or life on the home front. For novels on the Holocaust and the Jewish experience during World War II, see the next section.

Bartoletti, Susan Campbell.

The Boy Who Dared. **Scholastic, 2008. 978-0-439-68013-4 (hardcover). 192pp.** ◑

The rise of the Nazi party in Germany is an exciting but troubling time. Helmuth hopes that Hitler, the new chancellor, will bring better times and get the Germans more food and money. But the Nazi stand against Jews confuses Helmuth. Swept along by patriotic fervor, Helmuth joins the Hitler Youth. He hopes that life in Germany will improve from poverty and unemployment. But as he sees more about what the Nazis want to create, Helmuth's Mormon beliefs make him start questioning more. Soon he's unable to stay silent amid the injustices he sees. Daring to speak out, Helmuth suffers the ultimate punishment.

Read-alike: *Hitler Youth: Growing Up in Hitler's Shadow*, also by Susan Campbell Bartoletti, tells more about the youth group that Helmuth joins.

Keywords: 1940s; Coming-of-age; Germany

Chambers, Aidan.

Postcards from No Man's Land. **Dutton Juvenile, 2002. 978-0-525-46863-9 (hardcover); 978-0-14-240145-3 (softcover). 320pp.** ⑤

Dual narratives show how the past informs the present. Teenager Jacob has come to Amsterdam on behalf of his grandmother. It's the fiftieth anniversary of the battle of Arnhem, and his grandmother had wanted to attend the memorial services, but after breaking her hip, she sends Jacob. Jacob was named after his grandfather, who served in the British Army during World War II and died during the battle. As one Jacob explores present-day Amsterdam, the first Jacob is cared for by a local Dutch teenager and her family. The girl, Geertrui, has seen four years of war but has been protected from the worst of its horrors. But now as war comes to her village, she will see both destruction and creation. The two storylines slowly come together as past meets present.

Awards: Printz Award; Carnegie Medal

Keywords: Family; Netherlands; Parallel Narratives

Graber, Janet.

Resistance. **Marshall Cavendish, 2005. 978-0-7614-5214-0 (hardcover). 138pp.** Ⓜ ◑

In the middle of World War II, Marianne's life has become full of danger and unhappiness. Ever since the death of her father two years before, Marianne's mother has sought revenge against the Germans by participating in the Resistance. Marianne completely disapproves of this—especially since her mother has brought Michel, Marianne's deaf brother, into the work of helping English airmen. Marianne wants to protect Michel, but she also needs to protect herself. The local German commandant has noticed Marianne, leering at and fondling her when he gets a chance. He even quarters a German soldier in Marianne's home. With an Englishman in the cellar, a German in her former bedroom, and her French mother still working for the Resistance, Marianne must find a way to protect her brother and survive the war with her family intact.

Keywords: 1940s; Family; France; Spies

Hughes, Dean.

Soldier Boys. **Atheneum, 2001. 978-0-689-81748-9 (hardcover); 978-0-689-86021-8 (softcover). 159pp. Ⓜ Ⓙ**

Two boys from different sides of World War II will come together during the Battle of the Bulge. Ever since he was ten years old, Dieter has been dedicated to the Hitler Youth. Now fifteen, he is a leader, has met the Fuhrer, and hopes for even greater glory. Meanwhile Spencer joins the army at age seventeen, determined to be a man and do his part. Training as a paratrooper pushes Spencer to his limits, but he succeeds. While Spencer is sent overseas, Dieter is transferred into the main German army, despite being only fifteen. But both boys will have their eyes opened to the nature of war.

Keywords: 1940s; Army; Coming-of-age; France; Parallel Narratives

Lawrence, Iain.

B for Buster. **Delacorte Books for Young Readers, 2004. 978-0-385-73086-0 (hardcover); 978-0-440-23810-2 (softcover). 336pp. Ⓙ Ⓢ**

To get away from his hometown, the Canadian town of Kakabeka, as well as his abusive father, Kak lies about his age and enlists. Now a member of the Canadian Air Force, sixteen-year-old Kak is in England, trained as a wireless operator and ready to start flying. It's 1943 and the Canadian Air Force, along with the Royal Air Force, is participating in bombing raids on Germany. Assigned to an old bomber called B for Buster, Kak is excited to go on his first op but scared of having his secret revealed. Kak finds that bombing runs aren't just exciting—they're terrifying. The only one who seems to understand is Bert, the caretaker of the pigeons that ride on every bomber. Kak must find a way to manage his fear or risk being branded a coward.

Keywords: 1940s; Air Force; Animals; England

Napoli, Donna Jo.

An Italian Boy. Ⓙ Ⓢ

Although Italy was an ally of Germany during World War II, Italian civilians were taken by German soldiers as forced laborers. Napoli tells the story of one boy who suffers incredible hardships.

Keywords: 1940s; Coming-of-age; Germany; Italy

Stones in Water. Dutton Juvenile, 1997. 978-0-525-45842-5 (hardcover); 978-0-14-130600-1 (softcover). 224pp.

> Due to a movie, Roberto's life goes horribly wrong. With two friends and his older brother, Roberto goes to the theater to see a rare American movie. But then Nazi soldiers take over, herding the audience of boys and young men to the local train station. Roberto manages to stick with his friend Samuele, who is Jewish, as the train moves the boys into Germany. Any resistance or sickness earns you a bullet in the head, unless you're unlucky and you're just beaten. Roberto vows to stick with Samuele no matter what. It's only when Samuele is killed that Roberto is finally willing to attempt escape. Otherwise his life consists of little food and grinding, back-breaking work until he is too weak to carry on.

Fire in the Hills. Dutton Juvenile, 2006. 978-0-525-47751-8 (hardcover); 978-0-14-241200-8 (softcover). 256pp.

> Roberto is only fourteen, but what he's seen has made him into a man. After escaping from Germany, Roberto has made his way from Sicily to the Italian mainland. Dazed and in the middle of a war zone, Roberto finds himself serving as a translator for German soldiers. Italy has surrendered to the Allies, and the Nazis are being pushed out of Italy. Roberto only wants to return to Venice, but there's so much suffering and sadness. Making a connection with a woman called Red Fox will bring Roberto into the resistance. Smuggling weapons and information to rebels makes Roberto feel like he's helping Italy. But will he ever see his family or his home again?

Pausewang, Gudrun.

Traitor. Carolrhoda Books, 2006. 978-0-8225-6195-8 (hardcover); 978-0-7613-6571-6 (softcover). 220pp. ◼

> Anna thinks for herself. She considers everything she hears and looks for the truth. But she keeps her mouth shut, because in World War II Germany, your thoughts are just your own. It's her independent nature that makes this fifteen-year-old make a risky decision. On a wintry evening she finds a sick Russian soldier inside her family's barn. He has escaped from the nearby prisoner of war camp. Something in Anna makes her help the soldier, giving him warm clothes and food. She even hides him in a better location, one of the defense bunkers near her house. The bunker is only ten miles from the Czechoslovakian border, giving the soldier plenty of distance from his pursuers. For escaping, he will be shot if he's captured. But for harboring him, Anna could be branded a traitor. She will have to decide what is the right thing to do.

Keywords: 1940s; Germany

Whelan, Gloria.

Burying the Sun. HarperCollins, 2004. 978-0-06-054112-5 (hardcover); 978-0-06-054114-9 (softcover). 224pp. ▣

> It is 1941, and the mood in the Soviet Union is slightly optimistic. People have enough food, there are jobs available, and Soviet culture is becoming vibrant again. The only problem is the Germans; even though a treaty of friendship exists between the Soviet Union and Germany, many Soviets distrust the Nazis. When the German army attacks, Soviet fears begin to come true. Georgi is too young, at fourteen, to join the army and defend his country. But he can do much to help protect Leningrad. He works with his sister Marya, taking the priceless paintings from the Hermitage and hiding them. He helps dig up the beautiful Summer Gardens to create air-raid shelters. But will Georgi have a chance to do more?
>
> **Keywords:** 1940s; Coming-of-age; Soviet Union

Wolf, Joan M.

Someone Named Eva. Clarion Books, 2007. 978-0-618-53579-8 (hardcover); 978-0-547-23766-4 (softcover). 208pp. ▣

> Even though times are hard in 1942 in Czechoslovakia, there are still happy moments. Milada's eleventh birthday is one of those. Her family and her best friend Terezie gather to celebrate as they always have. But a few short months later, Milada's whole life is changed forever. Nazis march into her hometown of Lidice, arresting everyone. Over the three days that are spent in a local gym, something strange happens to Milada. Doctors examine her, doing normal medical tests but also examining her blonde hair and blue eyes, even measuring her nose. Milada and a classmate are taken away to Poland, where it is revealed that thanks to their "Aryan" features, they are going to be trained to be proper German citizens. Renamed Eva, Milada is supposed to forget that she was ever Czech. But Milada fights to remain true to herself on the inside.
>
> **Keywords:** 1940s; Czechoslovakia; Germany; Identity

Wulffson, Don.

Soldier X. Viking Juvenile, 2001. 978-0-670-88863-4 (hardcover); 978-0-14-250073-6 (softcover). 240pp. ▣

> As World War II drags on, the German army is so low on men that boys as young as sixteen are drafted. Erik was trained as a translator, thanks to his secret Russian heritage. But on his sixteenth birthday he is on a train to the Eastern Front, joining an infantry unit. In the army the food is bad, the other men are cruel, and the threat of death hangs over all of them. Erik uses some of his language skills, but as he keeps fighting small bands of

fighters, he begins to question: Is the only way to survive the war by killing others?

Keywords: 1940s; Army; Coming-of-age; Germany

Holocaust: 1938–1945

A major aspect of World War II was the Holocaust, a term that encompasses the Nazi attempt to eradicate non-Aryan people. Although this was primarily directed at the Jews of Europe, there were also efforts to eliminate other "undesirable" groups, such as Gypsies, Roman Catholics, homosexuals, and the mentally and physically handicapped. The Holocaust remains one of the most chilling episodes in world history, and a rich subject for YA historical fiction.

Baer, Edith.
A Third Reich Childhood. 🇯 🇸

Based on the author's own experiences, these two novels vividly portray, through the eyes of a child, the coming of the Third Reich in Germany.

Keywords: 1930s; Family; Germany

A Frost in the Night: A Childhood on the Eve of the Third Reich. Knopf Books, 1980. 978-0-394-84364-3 (hardcover); 978-0-374-42482-4 (softcover). 224pp.

Eva's life in southern Germany is idyllic. She lives in a big house split into apartments, in the middle of the city. Her grandfather lives with Eva and her parents, and her aunt and uncle, as well as her favorite cousins, live in the same building. Every year passes with its string of holidays and festivals, some that are only celebrated by Jews like Eva and her family. She spends time outside, taking long walks and swimming in the river. But underneath all this quiet happiness, there is tension. The grownups talk about politics, and there are worries about the direction that Germany may be going in. As political changes lead to the end of the German Republic and the rise of Hitler, Eva's family cannot shield her from their anxiety.

Walk the Dark Streets. Farrar, Straus & Giroux, 1998. 978-0-374-38229-2 (hardcover). 272pp.

As Eva suffers in bed with sickness, it seems that Germany is also falling ill. Hitler has outlawed democracy and taken control of the country. With his rise, anti-Semitism has become common, as well as prejudice against Catholics and Communists. Eva watches in horror as her whole world starts disappearing. Her father shuts down his bookstore, several of her teachers are dismissed for being non-Aryan, and one of her uncles is beaten for being Jewish. As it becomes more dangerous to be Jewish, all of Eva's family tries to find a way to leave Germany. But when her father is taken away, Eva and her mother will do anything, even stay in Germany, to save her father from the concentration camp.

Cheng, Andrea.

Marika. **Front Street, 1998. 978-1-886910-78-2 (hardcover); 978-0-439-55696-5 (softcover). 163pp.** 🅜 🅙

> Marika should feel lucky. She lives in a nice apartment, is given lots of books, and usually gets her way. But she is embarrassed by her family's money and the way her mother draws attention to herself. To Marika the worst thing is that her father has built a wall through their apartment, creating a small private apartment just for himself. Marika doesn't realize that far worse things are coming. Marika and her family are Jewish, and even though they don't celebrate Jewish holidays or attend synagogue, their name is still Jewish. In Hungary in the 1930s, a Jewish name becomes more and more dangerous. When Hungary is invaded by Nazi Germany, Marika will learn what really matters.
>
> **Keywords:** 1930s; Family; Hungary

Chotjewitz, David.

Daniel Half-Human and the Good Nazi. **Atheneum, 2004. 978-0-689-85747-8 (hardcover); 978-0-689-85748-5 (softcover). 304pp.** 🅢

> In the early 1930s Germany is in turmoil. Government leaders come into power quickly and then fall just as fast. Communists face off against Nazis, name calling and mocking each other with graffiti. Daniel and his best friend Armin both support Hitler, although no one really thinks he'll become chancellor. But as Hitler rises quickly, Daniel discovers to his horror that his mother is Jewish. Being half-Jewish makes Daniel a half-human in the eyes of the Nazis. So he keeps his ancestry a secret, even as Armin talks about joining the Hitler Youth. Armin's abusive drunk of a father is against it, but Armin joins anyway. And that choice will change things for the thirteen-year-old blood brothers.
>
> **Keywords:** 1930s; Friendship; Germany; Politics

Friedman, D. Dina.

Escaping into the Night. **Simon & Schuster Children's Publishing, 2006. 978-1-4169-0258-4 (hardcover); 978-1-4169-8648-5 (softcover). 208pp.** 🅙

> Every day things get a little worse for Halina and her mother in the ghetto. When her mother is taken from the factory she works in, Halina is on her own. But she has a chance to escape, thanks to a tunnel that connects the local synagogue with the outskirts of town. Halina and several other Jews join a large, hidden camp deep in the forest. Hundreds of Jews are hidden there, eking out a life amid battles fought by partisans against the Germans. Will they be able to maintain the forest hideaway? Will they be able to find

enough food and supplies? And will Halina be able to create a life without her mother? These questions and more haunt Halina as she tries to survive.

Keywords: 1940s; Mother and Child; Poland

Kosistsky, Lynne.

The Thought of High Windows. **Kids Can Press, 2004. 978-1-55337-621-7 (hardcover); 978-1-55337-622-4 (softcover). 176pp.** 🅜 🅙

It's early in World War II, early enough that Jews still hold some hope of escaping danger. Esther is a plain girl from an Old Jewish family. Along with a group of Jewish children—most from more secular backgrounds—Esther has traveled from Germany to Belgium and now to southern France. France has just surrendered to Germany, but since the children are in Vichy France, they should be safe. For Esther, her personal problems outweigh the political uncertainty. The other girls don't like her, the barn they live in is full of lice, and the food is revolting. Worst of all, her friend and crush Walter barely notices her. As the Holocaust begins to reach into France, Esther finds the political will outweigh the personal.

Keywords: Coming-of-age; France

LeZotte, Ann Clare.

T4: A Novel. **Houghton Mifflin Books, 2008. 978-0-547-04684-6 (hardcover). 112pp.** 🅙

A novel in verse tells the story of a non-Jewish victim of the Holocaust. Paula has been deaf most of her life, but she has managed to communicate. She taught herself to lip-read and created her own signs for words. But in 1939 the Nazi threat is beginning to sweep through the Jewish communities of Germany. Just as bad as Jews are other "unfit" people: homosexuals, Gypsies, the mentally ill, and the disabled. Rumors say that the disabled are painfully killed, as part of a program named after its location in Berlin, Tiergartenstrasse 4. To protect her, Paula's parents hide her, getting help from the Catholic Church. Paula knows she must stay hidden, but it's difficult to cope with losing any of your freedom when you're deaf. Paula will have to struggle to survive—can she stay safe, in hiding or not?

Keywords: 1930s; Germany; Novel in Verse; Physical Disability

Matas, Carol.

Greater Than Angels. **Simon & Schuster, 1998. 978-0-689-81353-5 (hardcover); 978-0-590-51540-5 (softcover). 144pp.** 🅜 🅙

In the eyes of Germany, Jews are not citizens. Anna and her family are part of a large group who are deported, taken to France and left there as enemy aliens. Anna joins the thousand of Jews in a refugee camp called Gurs, where little food and primitive conditions start wiping out the population. But Gurs is nowhere near as bad as the camps like Dachau. After a year in the camp, Anna gets the chance to leave, to live in a small French village away from the terror of Gurs. It's difficult for Anna to be separated from her mother and her aunt, but with her imagination and her supply of jokes, she will try to survive. And maybe, just maybe, she will.

Keywords: Family; France

In My Enemy's House. **Simon & Schuster Children's Publishing, 1999. 978-0-689-81354-2 (hardcover); 978-0-689-82400-5 (softcover). 176pp. Ⓜ Ⓘ**

Fifteen-year-old Miriam, nicknamed Marisa, has always been sensitive and delicate. She's prone to fainting whenever she's upset. The Soviets have controlled Poland for two years, leaving Jews alone for the most part. But now that the Germans have taken over, Marisa and all the Jews are in great danger. Marisa slowly gains strength as Jews are shot and rounded up for the ghetto—or worse. With her blonde hair and blue eyes, she doesn't look Jewish, and that might save her. Polish girls have been ordered to report to Germany to serve as workers in German homes. Marisa takes a dead girl's papers and soon finds herself in Weimar. The family she works for likes Marisa and treats her well, but she cannot let herself forget that she works in her enemy's house.

Keywords: Poland; Germany; Coming-of-age

Danish Resistance. Ⓜ

These two novels present younger audiences with an inspiring story of resistance to the actions of Nazi Germany. Although written for younger teens, they still describe the full range of wartime horrors.

Keywords: 1940s; Coming-of-age; Denmark

Lisa's War. Atheneum, 1989. 978-0-684-19010-5 (hardcover); 978-1-4169-6163-5 (softcover). 128pp.

The invasion of Denmark by German forces marks the end of Lisa's old life. Age twelve and Jewish, she's worried about what will happen, while her older brother, Stefan, is angry at Denmark's immediate surrender and refusal to fight. Soon Stefan is part of the Danish Resistance, working against the Nazis who are treating Danes with such cruelty. Lisa joins him in his work, distributing anti-German leaflets, but when her best friend Susanne loses her parents in a bombing, the two girls decide to go beyond leaflets.

Code Name Kris. Atheneum, 1990. 978-0-684-19208-6 (hardcover); 978-1-4169-6162-8 (softcover). 152pp.

When the Nazis attempt to transport the Jews of Denmark to concentration camps, the Danish resistance manages to sneak most Jewish residents out to Sweden. Among those rescued are Stefan and Lisa. Left behind is Stefan's best friend, and Lisa's boyfriend, Jesper.

Non-Jewish, Jesper stays in Denmark to continue the work of the resistance. Known as Kris, he works on various projects. His work ranges from sabotage to writing and publishing an underground newspaper. After being betrayed by a Nazi infiltrator, Jesper goes underground to protect himself and his family. Although he's safe for a while, eventually he is captured. Tortured, Jesper won't give in and is scheduled for execution. Will he survive to see the defeat of the Nazis?

Polak, Monique.

What World Is Left. Orca Books, 2008. 978-1-55143-847-4 (softcover). 208pp. **J** **S**

Anneke and her family are among the lucky ones. They are Dutch Jews who have been deported to Theresienstadt. Although it is plagued by lice and bedbugs and they are barely fed it is a model city, not a death camp. It has streets and barracks originally built for soldiers, but now Jews are crammed into the barracks, struggling to survive. Anneke and her mother are separated from her father and brother. Sickness and absence from work could lead to deportation east, to other camps—and certainly to worse conditions. Through it all, Anneke will find reasons to survive: the secret kindness of her fellow Jews, the love of her mother; a new friend named Hannalore. And there might even be love with a boy her age . . . .

Keywords: 1940s; Germany; Romance

Spinelli, Jerry.

📖 *Milkweed.* Knopf Books for Young Readers, 2003. 978-0-375-81374-0 (hardcover); 978-0-439-67695-3 (softcover). 224pp. **M** **J**

He's small but quick. He can steal bread in the blink of an eye. He can't remember his name or his parents. An older boy named Uri takes in the nameless boy and teaches him how to survive in the streets of Warsaw. Given the name Misha, the boy becomes friends with a Jewish girl named Janina. Even though he's not Jewish, Misha joins Janina and her family when the Jackboots move the Jews into the ghetto. Since he's so small, Misha can sneak out of the ghetto and get food. Slowly he begins to learn just what kind of world he lives in, and this knowledge might save his life.

Keywords: 1930s; Identity; Poland

Thor, Annika.

A Faraway Island. Delacorte Books for Young Readers, 2009. 978-0-385-73617-6 (hardcover). 256pp. **M**

As the Jews of Europe realized the danger coming toward them, they tried to flee. Twelve-year-old Stephie and her younger sister Nellie are among a lucky few who have been brought to Sweden while their parents try to get visas to enter the United States. But as time drags on, Stephie and Nellie have to adjust to their new lives. Nellie has an easy time learning Swedish and making friends. For Stephie, it's harder to adapt. Her guardian is stern and severe, and the popular girls don't like her. Worst of all, some of the townspeople are cruel to Stephie because she's Jewish. Can she find the strength to live in this strange, lonely place?

Keywords: 1930s; Sisters; Sweden

Whitney, Kim Ablon.

The Other Half of Life: A Novel Based on the True Story of the MS **St. Louis. Knopf Books for Young Readers, 2009. 978-0-375-85219-0 (hardcover); 978-0-375-84422-5 (softcover). 256pp.** 🄹 🅂

In the late 1930s some German Jews knew that as their freedoms were restricted, even worse fates were coming. So they tried to find ways to escape Germany. In 1939 a luxury liner sails out of Hamburg, full of Jews. They are heading for Cuba, many of the passengers expecting to travel on to the United States. Among the passengers is Thomas, whose Jewish father is in Dachau while his Christian mother stays behind. On board, Thomas finds himself spending time with Priska, a beautiful girl with a sunny outlook. Thomas doesn't understand her faith in humanity's goodness; he's become bitter about the way the strong hurt the weak. Thomas's fears are justified when the ship arrives in Havana but the passengers are not allowed to disembark. Could a Nazi crew member have betrayed the passengers? Perhaps a Nazi secret agent was ordered to keep the Jews on board. Whatever the reason, the question still remains: What will happen to the nearly 1,000 Jews on the ship?

Keywords: 1930s; Atlantic Ocean; Coming-of-age

Williams, Laura E.

Behind the Bedroom Wall. **Milkweed Editions, 1996. 978-1-57131-607-3 (hardcover); 978-1-57131-658-5 (softcover). 169pp.** 🄼 🄹

Korinna is a good German. She's active in her local Jungmadel group, speaking out against those who don't put Germany first. She listens to all of Hitler's speeches and thinks he's a great man. Soon, she knows, Germany will win the war and be the strongest nation in the world, without Jews and traitors. But then Korinna learns something that turns her world upside-down. Her parents have been hiding Jews behind her bedroom wall! At first the thirteen-year-old Korinna is disgusted. Out of love for her parents, she says nothing. Slowly she starts to have sympathy for the Jews. However, when the Gestapo are alerted about the hidden Jews, Korrina must decide whether to be a good German or a good human.

Keywords: Coming-of-age; Family; Germany

Zusak, Markus.

The Book Thief. **Knopf Books for Young Readers, 2006. 978-0-375-83100-3 (hardcover); 978-0-375-84220-7 (softcover). 560pp.** ◑ ⑤

Death has a story to tell. In 1930s Germany, Death meets Liesel Memminger and sees that there is something different about this girl. Liesel doesn't know she has attracted such attention. She was abandoned by her mother and is eventually taken in by a working-class family. In her new town, Liesel gains a domino-playing friend, a kind foster father and a stern foster mother, and a new skill. She learns how to steal books, choosing to steal from the secret library that the mayor's wife has. But as World War II accelerates, German civilians are also victims of war. The residents of Liesel's town seek refuge in shelters and basements, including Max, a Jew who is hiding his true identity. And through it all, Death keeps watching Liesel. Will she become aware of Death's interest in her?

Awards: Printz Honor Book

Keywords: 1930s; Coming-of-age; Germany

Britain

Although it is a small island nation, Britain has had a major impact on world history. Whether it's the Norman invasion of 1066, the internal conflicts between England and Scotland, or British resistance during World War II, the four countries that make up Britain—England, Scotland, Ireland, and Wales—have histories that have spawned many works of YA historical fiction.

Medieval Darkness: Before 1100

Prior to the Norman Conquest, many raids were made on Britain by groups such as the Danes and the Vikings. Mingling with the native English population, these ethnic groups helped create a new culture. The Anglo-Saxons were a diverse and vital people, with characteristics that persist today.

Alder, Elizabeth.

The King's Shadow. **Farrar, Straus & Giroux, 1995. 978-0-374-34182-4 (hardcover); 978-0-440-22011-4 (softcover). 192pp.** ◑

All Evyn wants is to be a storiawr, a traveling storyteller roaming the land, who is the servant of no lord. Even as a serf, his rich voice has gained him notice. Yet all his dreams are crushed when the sons of a neighboring lord cut out his tongue and kill his father. In a daze from his injury, Evyn doesn't realize right away that his uncle has sold him as a slave. Evyn tries to stay remote from the affairs within this new home, but luck is with him. His new mistress is beloved by Lord Harold, Earl of Wessex and the most powerful man in the land after King Edward. Not only does Evyn learn to read and write, he is able to serve as Lord Harold's squire.

And Evyn is so devoted to Lord Harold that he will follow him anywhere. The last days of Anglo-Saxon Britain come to life in Evyn's story.

Keywords: Eleventh Century; England; Performing; Physical Disability; Slavery

Banks, Lynne Reid.

The Dungeon. HarperCollins, 2002. 978-0-06-623782-4 (hardcover); 978-0-00-713778-7 (softcover). 279pp. **M** **J**

After a neighboring laird destroys what he loves most, Bruce MacLennan starts planning his revenge. He orders the creation of a castle with a dark dungeon underneath. While the castle is being built, MacLennan sets off on an adventure to far-off China. There, he impulsively buys a young girl named Peony, making her his tea slave. The little girl makes MacLennan remember the wife and children he lost during the war with the nearby laird, but he won't let himself go soft. He is focused on vengeance, no matter what. Matters come to a head after they return to Scotland. When Peony gets in his way, MacLennan takes brutal action against her.

Keywords: China; Family; Medieval; Scotland

Jones, Frewin.

Warrior Princess. HarperTeen, 2009. 978-0-06-087143-7 (hardcover); 978-0-06-087145-1 (softcover). 352pp. **J**

Peace has blessed the lands of Branwen's family, yet Saxons have been growing bolder in their raids. When her beloved older brother is killed by Saxons right before her, Branwen knows grief and thirsts for revenge. As her family's only heir, she must be protected. She is sent south and expected to marry her betrothed. Branwen hates to leave, but she understands why. Life in the court of her future husband is softer; she is dressed in rich clothes and eats fine food. Even though she is a princess, Branwen knows she is a warrior, especially when a woman in white predicts that she will lead her people against the invaders. But if Branwen fulfills her destiny, she will be disobeying her parents' wishes. What choice should she make?

Keywords: Family; Medieval; Wales; Women's Roles

Klein, Lisa.

Lady Macbeth's Daughter. Bloomsbury, 2009. 978-1-59990-347-7 (hardcover); 978-1-59990-522-8 (softcover). 304pp. **J** **S**

When she is born, Albia is seen as a double disappointment. First, she's an unneeded girl. Even worse, she has a damaged leg. Such a child is no advantage to Macbeth, Thane of Moray. Against the wishes of his wife, he tells a servant to abandon the baby. But instead, Lady Macbeth's maid takes the baby to her two sisters. They agree to raise the baby, name her Albia, and heal her damaged leg. As Albia grows up, her true parents gain power, but not enough for their ambitious natures. Macbeth is tearing Scotland apart, making a prophecy by the three sisters come true. Little does he know that his own daughter has the gift of second sight, and she has foreseen a terrible future. To save her potential happiness, Albia risks everything by taking a dangerous journey.

Keywords: Eleventh Century; Magic; Family; Multiple Voices; Scotland

McGraw, Eloise.

The Striped Ships. **Margaret K. McElderry, 1991. 978-0-689-50532-4 (hardcover). 224pp.** ▯

Juliana's life is unchanging. As a thane's daughter, she works on her embroidery and waits to marry her betrothed, yet has the freedom to run along the beaches near her home village. Then her whole world collapses when Norman ships sail across the English Channel and land near her village. The Normans burn homes and kill indiscriminately. Juliana finds herself a drudge, little better than a slave. She has no idea what happened to her mother and younger sibling—but then through luck, Juliana is reunited with her little brother Wulfric. Once they are reunited, Juliana cannot bear to be separated again. So when Wulfric insists on going to Canterbury instead of trying to find their mother in Winchester, Juliana gives in. The two young Saxons set off on the dangerous trip, unsure of what they may find.

Keywords: Brothers and Sisters; Eleventh Century; England

Moran, Katy.

Bloodline. **Candlewick, 2009. 978-0-7636-4083-5 (hardcover); 978-1-4063-0938-6 (softcover). 320pp.** ▯ ▮

Essa grew up as part of no tribe. He and his father Cai, a bard and storyteller, travel all over the country known as England. But on a visit to the land of the Wolf Folk, near East Anglia, Cai leaves Essa there, where Cai's foster sister Hild is the chief of the people called Wixna. Essa doesn't understand why his father has left him behind, especially since Essa is a half-breed. He doesn't fit in anywhere, not really. Years pass as Essa grows up and becomes mostly Wixna. At age fifteen he's nearly a man, with strange looks and the ability to sense animals' thoughts. Essa will be drawn into politics as the King of Mercia, the sworn enemy of the Wixna and the Wolf Folk, threatens the settlements of East Anglia. As he takes his place, the boy without a tribe discovers what his real role is and finds answers to many of his questions.

Keywords: Coming-of-age; England; Father and Child; Seventh Century

Sensel, Joni.

The Humming of Numbers. **Henry Holt, 2008. 978-0-8050-8327-9 (hardcover). 256pp. 🄹 🅂**

Aidan has a simple goal: He wants to take his final vows and become a monk, so he can begin to illuminate manuscripts. But something keeps holding him back, something that makes the other monks doubt his dedication. Aidan doesn't agree with them . . . and then he meets Lana. Sent to the monastery to hide her illegitimacy, Lana is bold and exciting. She makes Aidan begin to question his plan, for Lana hums of the number eleven. Aidan possesses a strange ability, to hear a number humming from any living thing—and until now, no one had ever hummed a number higher than ten. Aidan wants to learn more about this strange, compelling girl, but when Vikings raid the village, Aidan and Lana are the only ones who can save it.

Keywords: England; Political Rebellions; Tenth Century

Middle Ages: 1100–1500

The medieval period in Britain was marked by many invasions by outside groups. After William the Conqueror invaded England, some level of peace was achieved, although not without corruption. With figures such as Robin Hood, Britain before 1500 saw many of the most memorable events in its history.

Cadnum, Michael.

The King's Arrow. **Viking Juvenile, 2008. 978-0-670-06331-4 (hardcover). 224pp. 🄼 🄹**

The Norman Conquest of England is many years in the past, yet that doesn't mean relations are easy between the English natives and the Norman invaders. Sumien is an example of that tension. The son of a Norman nobleman and an English duke's daughter, he feels that there is no place for him, no way to gain power or riches. So the chance to join a royal hunt, even in a quasi-servant's role, seems like a great opportunity to Sumien. But even before the hunt begins, there are misgivings and vague rumblings of doom. At first the king plans not to join the hunt. But then he chooses to hunt, and no omens or warnings will deter William Rufus, King of England and Duke of Normandy. Yet perhaps he should have listened to those warnings . . . .

Keywords: Coming-of-age; England; Royalty; Twelfth Century

In a Dark Wood. **Scholastic, 1998. 978-0-531-30071-8 (hardcover); 978-0-14-130638-4 (softcover). 246pp. 🄼 🄹**

Tension is starting to form within Geoffrey, Sheriff of Nottingham. He doesn't care much for hunting and war stories—he'd rather study or spend time in gardens. But such a man is seen as soft and weak in late twelfth-century England. So Geoffrey hunts and listens to the stories because it is expected of him. And when the King becomes displeased about outlaws along the High Way, Geoffrey does as he's ordered, going after one particular outlaw. This outlaw robs travelers along the King's road, calling the money a toll. To keep his position and save his life, Geoffrey must capture the outlaw known as Robin Hood. But if he could find another way, allowing Robin to escape capture, Geoffrey might be able to break out of the path he has been following and do that which he truly wants to do.

Keywords: England; Robin Hood; Twelfth Century

Forbidden Forest: The Story of Little John and Robin Hood. **Orchard, 2002. 978-0-439-31774-0 (hardcover). 224pp. Ⓜ Ⓙ**

John Little is a giant of a man, tall, broad-shouldered, and strong. The death of his father has reduced him to a pickpocket and odd jobs like working on a ferry. But when he accidentally kills a man, he flees into the forest to hide. He falls in with an untrustworthy nobleman who plays outlaw, Red Roger. When John realizes whom he's working with, he runs again, making his way toward Nottingham. He's told that he need have no fear of robbery with the shadowy outlaw Robin Hood in the area, for Robin Hood is an easygoing, pleasant man, the opposite of Red Roger. Will John find success and happiness with Robin Hood and his followers, or will Red Roger makes good on his threats against John?

Keywords: England; Robin Hood; Twelfth Century

Cooney, Caroline B.

Enter Three Witches: A Story of Macbeth. **Scholastic Press, 2007. 978-0-439-71156-2 (hardcover); 978-0-439-71157-9 (softcover); 288pp. Ⓙ**

Macbeth and his wife were real people only known by scholars before Shakespeare wrote his dramatic play. But what really happened at Inverness Castle in the twelfth century? Were there really witches and murder and battles? Against the backdrop of the famous tragedy, a vast array of characters participate in the story of Macbeth's fall. There is the Lady Mary, ward of Lord and Lady Macbeth, a beautiful, godly maiden. There are servants and squires, like Swin and Seyton and Idred. Nobles like Banquo and Fleance, even the royal King Duncan, take their places. And front and center, drawing all eyes, are Macbeth and his lady. A fine soldier with great ambition, Macbeth is still no match for his wife in terms of pride and desire. And it is that desire—for power, for status, for more—that will doom this lord and lady.

Keywords: Magic; Political Rebellions; Scotland; Twelfth Century

Cushman, Karen.

Catherine, Called Birdy. Clarion, 1994. 978-0-395-68186-2 (hardcover); 978-0-06-440584-3 (softcover). 176pp. **M** **J**

Life as a minor nobleman's daughter isn't that exciting. Most days, the most interesting thing Birdy has to record in her diary is the number of fleas she's killed. Otherwise, she's just writing about the food she eats, the clothes she wears, and the religious services she attends. Then her parents begin introducing suitors to her, trying to find someone rich enough to marry her to. Of course none of them are who she wants to marry. So she has no choice but to try to get these suitors to leave on their own. And she'll tell how in her diary.

Awards: Newbery Honor Book

Keywords: Diary; England; Thirteenth Century; Women's Roles

Matilda Bone. Clarion, 2000. 978-0-395-88156-9 (hardcover); 978-0-440-41822-1 (softcover). 167pp. **M** **J**

Matilda is a very well-educated girl for her times. She's also pious and determined to get her heavenly reward. But her education and piety aren't much good to her new employer, Red Peg the bonesetter. Now, instead of intellectual pursuits, Matilda is expected to perform all kinds of menial labor as well as learn how to ease the sick and wounded. That's the last thing she wants to do—Isn't it a sin to interfere with God's plan? If a person is wounded, he deserves that wound and the suffering it creates. But slowly Matilda starts to look at the people she's expected to help. Facing a clash between her higher ideals and the real world, can Matilda find a balance between her conflicting desires?

Keywords: England; Fourteenth Century; Women's Roles

The Midwife's Apprentice. Clarion, 1995. 978-0-395-69229-5 (hardcover); 978-0-06-440630-7 (softcover). 128pp. **M** **J**

A girl named Brat is sleeping on a dung heap. She is awoken when the local midwife, Janet, kicks her and bids her to start working. Slowly Brat becomes Beetle, learning how to be a midwife, how to take care of herself, and how to help others. And then Beetle becomes Alyce, aware of her self-worth, strong enough to deal with failure and try again. When she fails during a difficult delivery, Alyce suffers a blow to her fragile self-confidence. Through time and thought, she will regain her strength and become more than the midwife's apprentice.

Awards: Newbery Medal

Keywords: Coming-of-age; England; Fourteenth Century

Dahme, Joanne.

The Plague. **Running Press Kids, 2009. 978-0-7624-3344-5 (hardcover). 272pp.** 🄹 🅂

A female spin on *The Prince and the Pauper*, set in the Middle Ages. Nell loses her parents to disease when she is a young teen, leaving her responsible for her younger brother George. By chance, she is spotted by King Edward III and recognized as a lookalike to his daughter, Princess Joan. To preserve his daughter's safety, the King takes in Nell and asks her to serve as the princess's decoy. For two years Nell and George live in Windsor Castle, serving the princess and enjoying life among royals and nobles. So attached is the princess to them that they will accompany her to far-off Castile when she marries. When the royal party reaches the French city of Bordeaux, plague is decimating the countryside. To Nell's horror, the princess dies of the pestilence. Her death leads to secret doings by Joan's brother Edward, the Black Prince. He forces Nell to take the princess's place to ensure the spread of the English Empire. Nell is no princess though—and she is determined to free herself from this falsehood.

Keywords: Brothers and Sisters; England; Fourteenth Century; France; Royalty

Goodman, Joan Elizabeth.

The Winter Hare. **Houghton Mifflin Books for Children, 1996. 978-0-395-78569-0 (hardcover); 978-0-7868-1242-4 (softcover). 272pp.** 🄼 🄹

England is torn between two ruling parties. The previous king had compelled the barons to accept his daughter Matilda and her son as next in line to the throne. But when the king died, his nephew Stephen took power and now rules. Some barons support Stephen, others support Matilda. In the midst of all this is Will Belet. Small for his years, he has arrived at the Earl of Oxford's castle to serve as a cup bearer. He dreams of becoming a knight, gaining riches and glory. Both Will's father and his new master support Matilda, fighting against Stephen. Even Will plays a role in this struggle. Will wants glory—Is this his chance?

Keywords: England; Political Rebellions; Twelfth Century

Grant, K. M.

The de Granville Trilogy. 🄼 🄹

Set in the same historical period so heavily mined by the Robin Hood legend, this series removes the myth and focuses on the struggles. The tension created in England by a vacant King Richard and the need to raise funds first for the Crusade and then for Richard's ransom easily lead to Richard's brother John taking over the throne. Against this backdrop, the story of one family's highs and lows is portrayed, in a mix of adventure and character drama.

Keywords: Animals; Brothers; Crusades; England; Political Rebellions; Romance; Twelfth Century

📖 *Blood Red Horse.* **Walker Books for Young Readers, 2005. 978-0-8027-8960-0 (hardcover); 978-0-8027-7734-8 (softcover). 288pp.**

As the younger brother, Will is allowed to do what he likes, as long as he doesn't cause too much trouble. Most of the time he's with Ellie, his father's ward and his brother's intended wife. But he's also preparing to become a knight, and the first step is choosing a horse. Will thinks he'll pick a large, solid, sturdy mount—but instead, he falls for a smaller but intelligent and tireless horse named Hosanna. He pours himself into training his horse, developing him into the perfect match for himself. Then a horrible event happens: Will's brother Gavin rides Hosanna to the brink of death, and Will must face the fact that Hosanna will never carry him into battle. It would take a miracle for Hosanna and Will to journey to the Holy Land . . . but perhaps there's a miracle waiting.

Green Jasper. Walker Books for Young Readers, 2006. 978-0-8027-8073-7 (hardcover); 978-0-8027-9627-1 (softcover). 256pp.

The Crusade both gave to and took from the de Granville brothers. While Will was honored by King Richard with a title and land, Gavin lost his arm in battle. Trying to put these events behind them, the brothers return to England, and Gavin prepares to marry Ellie. Yet on their wedding day, tragedy strikes. King Richard, held prisoner in far-off Austria, is believed dead, and his brother John seizes control. The new king sends his loyal knight—and the betrayer of the de Granvilles—to attack the castle, break up the wedding, and take Ellie away. Caught up in politics, Will and Gavin face difficult choices in a difficult time. Will they be able to rescue Ellie? Is King Richard really dead? And will the two brothers be able to stand together against those who would see them fail?

Blaze of Silver. Walker Books for Young Readers, 2007. 978-0-8027-9625-7 (hardcover); 978-0-8027-9737-7 (softcover). 272pp.

The castle of Hartslove and its residents are still recovering from the events of the past year. Will is now the master after the death of Gavin. Ellie still mourns for the man she was supposed to marry. Yet life goes on, and there are new people at Hartslove: Will's new squire, his Arab friend Kamil, and the twins Marie and Marissa. Some of these newcomers will join Will and Ellie on a new journey: traveling to Germany to deliver some of the money meant to ransom King Richard. It will be a dangerous trip, bound to attract thieves. Will trusts his horse Hosanna to carry him, and Ellie is learning about her new horse, Shihab. But it is people, not horses, that attempt to betray Will and Ellie.

Hunter, Mollie.

The King's Swift Rider: A Novel on Robert the Bruce. HarperTeen, 2006. 978-0-06-447216-6 (softcover). 336pp. ⬛

> One day, Martin chooses to help a man fleeing a group of armed pursuers. To his surprise, the man he has rescued is Robert the Bruce, King of Scots. The king has need of strong men, like Martin's older brother Sean—but he also needs intelligent men like Martin. So both brothers join Bruce's army, with Martin taking on the role of the King's swift rider, planting gossip and carrying news. As the sixteen-year-old rides across Scotland, he learns techniques of espionage, which he will use to help the Bruce in a critical event, the Battle of Bannockburn.
>
> **Keywords:** Fourteenth Century; Political Rebellions; Scotland; Spies

Springer, Nancy.

Rowan Hood: Outlaw Girl of Sherwood Forest. Philomel, 2001. 978-0-399-23368-5 (hardcover); 978-0-698-11972-7 (softcover). 170pp. ⬛ ⬛

> Rosemary has lived her whole life in a small glade with her mother, Celandine. Part-elf, Celandine performs small bits of wood-magic for the local villagers. When Rosemary feels her mother putting a strong protection spell on her one day, Rosemary knows something is wrong. Finding their cottage burned down and her mother dead, Rosemary flees into the forest. Disguising herself as a boy, she sets off to find her father. But this is no ordinary quest, for her father is Robin Hood, famous outlaw. Once she finds him, she continues to conceal her identity, posing as the boy Rowan, because it's as a boy that she'll be able to help her father in his struggle against Guy of Gisbon.
>
> **Keywords:** Disguised as Boy; England; Father and Child; Robin Hood; Twelfth Century; Women's Roles

Tomlinson, Theresa.

Women of Robin Hood. ⬛ ⬛

> These interesting novels take a more feminist slant on the stories surrounding Robin Hood and his followers. By focusing on the females in the stories, Tomlinson highlights other aspects of King John's repression of the English.
>
> **Keywords:** England; Robin Hood; Twelfth Century; Women's Roles

> *The Forestwife.* Orchard Books, 1995. 978-0-531-09450-1 (hardcover); 978-0-440-41350-9 (softcover). 170pp.
>
>> Mary de Holt is a young noblewoman, naïve and untested. When her uncle tells her she will be married to a fat, old man, she decides to run away. Thanks to her nurse Agnes, they're able to find safety in the forest. There, Agnes takes on the mantle of the Forestwife, a healer and wise woman consulted by those who have no other choice. Mary is renamed Marian, the

Green Lady. Her new name suits her, for Marian soon learns the ways of the forest, able to spy food and herbs and hidden paths. Together the Forestwife and the Green Lady care for all who come to them, whether a convent of rebellious nuns or outlaws from the harsh laws of the nobles. And Marian will find herself caring for one particular outlaw, a young man named Robert of Loxley, better known as Robin Hood.

Child of the May. Orchard Books, 1998. 978-0-531-30118-0 (hardcover); 978-0-440-41577-0 (softcover). 144pp.

Life with the Forestwife might be free, but it's also hard. Magda, young and strong, is expected to perform difficult tasks like digging latrine trenches. She's tired of all this and wants to leave the forest. She can survive on her own better than other women. So when Magda has the chance to help the poverty-stricken Lady Matilda and her daughter Isabel, she takes it. Magda joins the band of outlaws that her father Little John is part of. With them, and under the leadership of Robert, or Robin Hood, Magda will have to use all her skills to help save the women.

Williams, Laura E.

The Executioner's Daughter. Henry Holt, 2000. 978-1-4223-9205-8 (hardcover); 978-0-8050-8186-2 (softcover). 134pp. **J** **S**

Being the daughter of the village's executioner makes Lily an outsider. She doesn't really mind—she's happier hunting for herbs, caring for her animals, and spending time with her mother. Lily has nothing to do with her father's work because her mother has kept Lily away from it. But when Lily's mother falls ill and is unable to help her husband, it falls to Lily. She dreads having to go among the villagers, having their eyes on her. And even worse are the executions. Lily's soft heart and caring nature is beaten down by the pain of watching the executions and helping her father. She can either let her spirit be crushed . . . or she can try to rise above her place in the village.

Keywords: England; Father and Child; Fifteenth Century

Yolen, Jane, and Robert J. Harris.

Girl in a Cage. Philomel, 2002. 978-0-399-23627-3 (hardcover); 978-0-14-240-132-3 (softcover). 240pp. **M** **J**

Imagine you're a princess. But you're a princess of Scotland, a country that is struggling to keep its freedom and independence from England. One day, you're captured by English forces and you fear for your life. The King of England rules that you will be taken to a town in the north of England and put in an iron cage, outdoors. And you will stay in that cage, day and night, while people throw food at you and you shiver and roast. That's what's faced by Marjorie, the daughter of Robert the Bruce, the declared King of Scotland. How will she face this horrible fate? And what will happen to her?

Keywords: Fourteenth Century; Political Rebellions; Royalty; Scotland

The Tudor Era: 1500–1600

The Tudor period is one of the most popular ones for historical fiction, thanks to real events being as dramatic as fiction. From Henry VII's struggle to claim the English throne to Henry VIII's six wives and the religious turmoil of these marriages, British history of this time is full of drama.

Crowley, Suzanne.

The Stolen One. **Greenwillow Books, 2009. 978-0-06-123200-8 (hardcover); 978-0-06-123202-2 (softcover). 416pp. ⑤**

There is something different about Kat—something that has set her apart since she was young. In her village, people whisper that Kat, her deaf sister Anna, and their mother Grace are witches. It's not true; they earn their living by sewing and embroidering clothes for the rich. Kat has a real talent and skill for this work, and she dreams of escaping the quiet valley, perhaps going to London and unraveling the mystery of her birth. She knows that Grace is not her true mother, but Grace is the only one who ever wanted Kat. At least that's what Grace claims. When Kat finally journeys to London, she discovers that there was someone else looking for her.

Keywords: England; Magic; Women's Roles

Cushman, Karen.

📖 *Alchemy and Meggy Swann.* **Clarion Books, 2010. 978-0-547-23184-6 (hardcover). 176pp. ⓜ ⓙ**

Young Meggy Swann has been sent to London by a mother who doesn't want her. When she arrives, she finds that her father doesn't want her either. In 1573, no one would want a crippled teenage girl like Meggy. Used to taunts and jeers, Meggy returns the insults and relies on her goose Louise for friendship. But slowly, Meggy realizes that you can't go through life with clenched fists, ready for a fight. The kindness of new friends like Roger and Mistress Grimm let Meggy blossom. Yet when she learns a secret about her father the alchemist, Meggy will need both her old attitude and her new friends to accept the truth.

Keywords: Animals; England; Physical Disability

Hassinger, Peter.

Shakespeare's Daughter. **Laura Geringer, 2004. 978-0-06-028467-1 (hardcover). 320pp. ⓙ ⑤**

At age thirteen, many young girls in the late 1500s were expected to act like adult women. For Susanna Shakespeare, though, becoming a mature woman is a challenging process. She prefers to spend time with her wild brother Hamnet and wishes she could join choirs or compose music as men can. She can't even go to London and hear music. But her life changes with the death of her brother. Allowed to go to London, Susanna finds that her dreams of singing and her relationship with her father don't exist as she expected. But with the love of a fellow singer and a religious choice, Susanna can find the place that will let her dreams come true.

Keywords: England; Religious Conflicts; Romance; Shakespeare, William; Women's Roles

Holmes, Victoria.

The Horse from the Sea. **HarperCollins, 2005. 978-0-06-052028-1 (hardcover); 978-0-06-052030-4 (softcover). 320pp.** 🅜 🅙

Nora would rather spend time with her horse than at a noisy party. She also likes running along the beach, chasing the wild ponies on Ireland's west coast. It's 1588, and the war between England and Spain is about to affect Ireland. A Spanish ship sailing around Ireland to return to Spain founders and wrecks. While walking along the beach, Nora discovers a beautiful Andalusian stallion. For a horse-crazy fourteen-year-old, there's only one choice: hide the horse and help it recover. But when she takes the stallion to a nearby cave, she finds a wounded Spanish soldier. It's treason to help a Spaniard, but Nora can't keep herself from helping.

Keywords: Animals; Ireland

Kolosov, Jacqueline.

A Sweet Disorder. **Hyperion, 2009. 978-1-4231-1245-7 (hardcover). 432pp.** 🅢

The death of her kind, restless father leaves Miranda's family deeply in debt. No longer wealthy, Miranda's engagement is broken and she is sent to live with the Earl and Countess of Turbury. Miranda finds herself in a gray, colorless house, instructed by the Countess in spiritual devotion. For any sixteen-year-old, such a life would be dull. Miranda, who is used to color and beauty, does her best to adapt. When she learns that she will go to Queen Elizabeth's court, she is excited, until she learns her guardians are arranging a marriage for her. Miranda's future husband is loud and rude, and their marriage would benefit the Earl and Countess more than Miranda. Her only hope is her skill in sewing and embroidery. If Miranda can become the Queen's seamstress, she will have riches and freedom enough to marry whomever she likes. But it all rests on gaining the Queen's favor.

Keywords: England; Women's Roles

Lawlor, Laurie.

The Two Loves of Will Shakespeare. Holiday House, 2006. 978-0-8234-1901-2 (hardcover). 278pp. **J** **S**

> Will Shakespeare is a true rabble-rouser. He drinks, carouses with barmaids, and watches any play he can. He's a disappointment to his parents, but eighteen-year-old Will can't help being what he is. But love makes Will reconsider his behavior. Writing sonnets for a love-struck friend, Will falls in love with the same woman. To win Anne Whateley, Will vows to change. That's easier said than done, though, and Will finds himself spending time with the more mature Anne Hathaway. Finally, Will makes a decision about whom he will marry, only for a pregnancy to force another decision. An unwanted marriage then leads to Will beginning the life that made him famous.
>
> **Keywords:** Coming-of-age; England; Romance; Shakespeare, William

Libby, Alisa.

The King's Rose. Dutton Juvenile, 2009. 978-0-525-47970-3 (hardcover). 320pp. **J** **S**

> In Tudor England, the closer you were to the King, the closer you were to power. No position has more potential than the wife of the King. Catherine Howard was just a girl, but now she is Queen, married to King Henry VIII. It is a great moment for her family, and they are all scheming about how Catherine, with the King's ear, will be able to advance them. In the middle is Catherine, a fifteen-year-old girl, barely noticed by her family until the King singled her out. Catherine grew up unrestrained, seeking love. She found it with Thomas Culpepper, a groom in service to the King. Even after she marries the King, Catherine still loves Thomas. That love will be her doom, for a queen who gives any sign that her heart belongs to someone other than the King is committing treason, and the punishment for treason is death.
>
> **Keywords:** England; Romance; Royalty; Women's Roles

Meyer, Carolyn.

Young Royals. **M** **J**

> One of the most dynamic, intriguing periods of history is covered in this series. The early sixteenth century saw great turmoil in England, revolving around several women and one man: Henry VIII and his wives and daughters. These novels cover the women, highlighting their interactions and relationships and imagining the inner thoughts of the women who would be queen by marriage or birth.
>
> **Keywords:** England; Mother and Child; Royalty; Sisters; Women's Roles

> *Mary, Bloody Mary*. Harcourt Children's Books, 1999. 978-0-15-201906-8 Hardcover); 978-0-00-715029-8 (softcover). 240pp.
>
> > The life of Princess Mary has been full of intrigue ever since she was an infant. By the time she was eleven, she had been betrothed three times,

crowned Princess of Wales, and separated from her parents and sent to a far-off castle. Mary is proud of her parents, King Henry and Queen Catherine, and believes she will one day rule England. But Mary's father has a different idea. He feels that no woman is strong enough to rule England alone. He must have a son, even if it means casting off his wife and daughter. Mary will have to prove that she has the courage and strength to be queen, even as her father makes Anne Boleyn his next queen.

Beware, Princess Elizabeth. Gulliver, 2001. 978-0-15-202659-2 (hardcover); 978-0-15-204556-2 (softcover). 224pp.

With the death of her father, the position of the Princess Elizabeth becomes even more perilous. The new king, her half-brother Edward, is young and sickly, and it's not long before he dies as well. The new monarch is Mary, King Henry VIII's oldest daughter. Mary is old and tired, but finally being queen and having the love of the English people lifts her spirits. She cannot help but loathe Elizabeth, the daughter of Anne Boleyn. Elizabeth, with her great intelligence and strategic mind, knows how dangerous this situation is for her. She will do whatever necessary to survive by not angering Mary. So Elizabeth remains in the country, studying in quiet surroundings. She is determined to remain as free and independent as she can and wait for the day that she might become queen.

Doomed Queen Anne. Harcourt Children's Books, 2002. 978-0-15-216523-9 (hardcover); 978-0-15-205086-3 (softcover). 240pp.

At the court of King Henry VIII, a beautiful woman has fair hair, blue eyes, skin that blushes pink, and generous curves. Anne Boleyn has none of these features. She's thin and dark of hair and eyes, with milk-white skin. Even worse, she has an ill-formed sixth finger on one hand and a mole at the base of her neck. Her parents, hoping she can acquire wit and grace, pack Anne off to foreign lands, serving the Austrian archduchess and the French Queen. As she grows up, Anne gains a reputation for charm and her own particular beauty. She attracts young men and even gains the attention of King Henry. But Anne is not content to be the king's mistress—she will be queen, nothing else, even if her ambition will lead to her downfall.

Patience, Princess Catherine. Harcourt Children's Books, 2004. 978-0-15-216544-4 (hardcover); 978-0-15-205447-2 (softcover). 208pp.

Since the age of two, Catherine has known what her future holds. As the daughter of the Spanish King Ferdinand and Queen Isabella, she is betrothed to the son and heir of the King of England. As she grows up, she waits for the day she will set sail for England. But once she arrives there, her new husband, Arthur, is too weak to live with her as man and wife. Catherine is content to wait, but her husband's sudden death dashes all her hopes and dreams. Adrift among the English nobility, Catherine spends each day worrying over her fate. Then a ray of hope appears: Her husband's younger brother Henry, dashing and charming, declares that he will marry her. Yet there are those at court who don't want this marriage to happen. Can Catherine summon up even more patience to get all she longs for?

Rinaldi, Ann.

Nine Days a Queen: The Short Life and Reign of Lady Jane Grey. HarperTeen, 2005. 978-0-06-054923-7 (hardcover); 978-0-06-054925-1 (softcover). 192pp. **Ⓜ Ⓙ**

The 1540s in England was a time of turmoil. Questions about religion, about Catholicism vs. the new Protestantism, invaded every aspect of life. Politics were jumbled, with the death of Henry VIII, the rule of the child-king Edward VI, and the uncertain status of the former princesses Mary and Elizabeth. In the midst of all this is Lady Jane Grey, a granddaughter of Henry VII and fourth in line to the throne. Jane is a quiet, plain girl, devoted to her studies. She's one of the best-educated women in England as a teenager. She still likes playing games or talking with her cousins. But with the death of Queen Katherine Parr, her guardian, Jane's happy times comes to an end, and she becomes the center of a treacherous plot. Thanks to a group of greedy noblemen, Jane Grey will be named Queen of England. But she will only reign nine days.

Keywords: England; Political Rebellions; Religious Conflicts; Royalty; Women's Roles

The Red-Headed Princess. HarperCollins, 2008. 978-0-06-073374-2 (hardcover). 224pp. **Ⓙ**

As the daughter of King Henry VIII, Elizabeth should expect to have status, riches, and the hope of being queen someday. But nothing is as expected when it comes to Henry VIII. Elizabeth has spent most of her life not under suspicion because of her mother's actions. She's not even called Princess Elizabeth, but the Lady Elizabeth. But she can't help hoping that some day her father will restore her to her rightful position. She strives hard, learning as much as she can. On the happy day that she is restored to the line of succession, Elizabeth feels that everything is looking up. But a series of events, including her father's death and rumors of a scandalous affair, could jeopardize her future.

Keywords: England; Royalty; Women's Roles

Thomas, Jane Resh.

The Counterfeit Princess. Clarion, 2005. 978-0-395-93870-6 (hardcover). 208pp. **Ⓜ Ⓙ**

Religion and politics combine to create danger for a young girl. Iris's parents, the Earl and Countess of Bentham, have been arrested by the scheming Duke of Northumberland. The duke wants to eliminate King Edward's heirs, the Ladies Mary and Elizabeth, and rule England through a puppet. Iris's parents have supported Elizabeth—and for that support, they are arrested and later die while in the Tower of London. When she learns this, Iris vows revenge and is trained as a spy. To protect Princess Elizabeth, she will act as a kitchen maid, a lady-in-waiting, and even as the princess's double. But by acting in these different roles, she risks losing herself. Iris will have to find a way to remember who she is in a world of make-believe.

Keywords: England; Religious Conflicts; Spies

Revolution and Recovery: 1600–1800

In the 1600s England was such a hotbed of radical political thought that Parliament executed King Charles I, an action that sent shock waves throughout Europe and its other monarchies. Its republican government, led by Oliver Cromwell, only lasted a decade before the restoration of the monarchy. During the 1700s England was ruled by a string of Germanic kings, whose actions and decisions resulted in the loss of the profitable and valuable colonies in America.

Forrester, Sandra.

Wheel of the Moon. HarperCollins, 2000. 978-0-688-17149-0 (hardcover). 167pp. **M J**

Pen is happy living with her mother in their small cottage. But when her mother dies, the villagers turn against Pen because she is illegitimate. Escaping to London, Pen experiences a rude awakening to how different the city is from the country. Luckily, she is taken in by a group of orphans, and together they scrounge up enough food to survive. Even better, her fellow outcasts become like a family to Pen. Beggars and orphans, however, are not welcome in London, and one day the whole group is thrown into jail. Pen is separated from them and sent to the New World as an indentured servant. Will Pen find a home for good in Virginia?

Keywords: America; England; Seventeenth Century; Women's Roles

Forsyth, Kate.

Gypsy Crown. Hyperion, 2008. 978-1-4231-0494-0 (hardcover); 978-1-4231-0495-7 (softcover). 400pp. **J**

Emilia and Luka live a life of pure freedom. They are members of the Rom—Gypsies, roaming from towns to forests, enjoying their music and stories. But in Commonwealth England, the Puritans see Gypsies as criminals. Baba, the oldest female in the family, warns everyone against going into town during the fair. But the family goes, and disaster strikes. They are arrested and accused of murder. Emilia and Luka, though, are able to escape. It is up to them to save their family. Will it be practical Luka or traditional Emilia who finds the way to outwit the Puritans?

Keywords: England; Family; Religious Conflicts; Seventeenth Century

Gavin, Jamila.

Coram Boy. **Farrar, Straus & Giroux, 2000. 978-0-374-31544-3 (hardcover); 978-0-374-41374-3 (softcover). 336pp.** **S**

Four very different young men's lives intertwine in eighteenth-century England. When unwanted children are abused or abandoned, an institution that cares and provides for such children is seen as a beacon of hope. Such a place is the Coram Hospital in London. But unscrupulous people, Coram men, take children and sell or kill them instead of escorting them to the hospital. Otis Gardiner is one of these men, helped by his simple-minded son Mishak. When Mishak saves a baby, born to a well-off girl named Melissa, he starts a chain reaction that will change their lives, as well as the baby's unknowing father Alexander and Alex's friend Thomas.

Awards: Carnegie Medal Finalist

Keywords: Eighteenth Century; England; Multiple Voices; Parallel Narratives

Hearn, Julie.

📖 *The Minister's Daughter.* **Ginee Seo Books, 2005. 978-0-689-87690-5 (hardcover); 978- 0-689-87691-2 (softcover). 272pp.** **J** **S**

A novel about three girls in Civil War–era England reveals how hard the old ways die. In a small village, a new minister has arrived, a staunch Puritan who is drumming out both Catholic and pagan beliefs. His two daughters, Grace and Patience, give every appearance of goodness. Meanwhile Nell, the granddaughter of the cunning woman, is trying to learn all that her grandmother knows. It is up to Nell to provide healing and other help to the villagers, especially pregnant women. For this reason, Grace comes to Nell. Grace trysted with the blacksmith's son and is now pregnant. But when Nell refuses to help her abort the baby, Grace influences Patience to act like they are victims of witches. Spitting out pins and speaking in tongues, the girls strike fear into the villagers—and they turn against Nell and her grandmother. The fate of these three girls will be forever changed. As Patience looks back on her past actions to tell this story, a similar witch hunt is going on in 1692 Salem.

Keywords: England; Seventeenth Century; Witch Trials

Holmes, Victoria.

Rider in the Dark: An Epic Horse Story. **HarperCollins, 2004. 978-0-06-052025-0 (hardcover); 978-0-06-052027-4 (softcover). 320pp.** **M** **J**

Lady Helena has an ideal life. She lives on a fine estate, and her father is a highly regarded magistrate. Her favorite activity is riding her father's powerful horses, aided by her friend, the stable boy Jamie. One day two events occur that will have a major impact on her life: A new customs agent arrives to crack down on local smugglers, and her father brings home a new stallion. Helena can't help being drawn to this new horse, yet it may be too powerful for a fifteen-year-old girl. But Helena persists, taking the horse out on a midnight ride to warn the smugglers. To her surprise, Helena discovers that the band of thieves are actually locals, including Jamie and his father. And her ride of warning might yield other surprises.

Keywords: Animals; Eighteenth Century; England; Father and Child

Hooper, Mary.

Newes from the Dead: Being a True Story of Anne Green, Hanged for Infanticide at Oxford Assizes in 1650, Restored to the World and Died again 1665. **Roaring Brook Press, 2008. 978-1-59643-355-7 (hardcover); 978-0-312-60864-4 (softcover). 272pp.** 🔳 🔳

Life for a poor scullery maid isn't very happy, especially when she is seduced by the heir to a noble family. Deluded into thinking the young master will marry her, Anne Green finds herself pregnant. After getting her with child, Master Geoffrey will have nothing to do with her. Alone and confused, Anne hides her pregnancy for several months but delivers early, giving birth to a stillborn child. When she is found with a dead baby, she is quickly accused of infanticide, tried, and convicted. Sentenced to hang, Anne keeps protesting that the baby's death was not caused by her. But the courts will not hear her, and Anne is executed, kept swinging on the gallows for a full half-hour. As a criminal, her body is given to a group of doctors and medical students for dissection. The first to arrive is Robert, a young, stuttering student. While he waits to view the dissection, the strangest thing happens. His eyes could have deceived him . . . but he thought he saw its eyelids flutter.

Keywords: England; Seventeenth Century; Women's Roles

The Remarkable Life and Times of Eliza Rose. **Bloomsbury, 2006. 978-1-58234-854-4 (hardcover); 978-0-7475-7582-5 (softcover). 336pp.** 🔳 🔳

Thrown out by her stepmother, Eliza heads to London to search for her father. It's not long before Eliza finds herself in Newgate Prison, arrested for stealing a meat pastry. It's a horrible, dirty, smelly place—one that people try to get out of as quickly as possible. Thanks to her new friend Elinor, Eliza learns to smile at noblemen who throw coins to the prisoners. Soon she's rescued by Ma Gwynn and taken in. Expected to be a prostitute, Eliza manages to escape such a fate thanks to Ma's daughter, Nelly, an actress. Nelly is happy in the theater, although she has set her sights on higher positions. Eliza is still searching for her place—and to learn the secret of who she is.

Keywords: Eighteenth Century; England; Women's Roles

Plague and Fire. 🔳

These novels draw the reader into the world of England in the mid-seventeenth century. From the smells and sounds to the attitudes and knowledge, the life lived by Hannah is fully realized.

Keywords: Disasters; England; Illness; Seventeenth Century; Sisters

At the Sign of the Sugared Plum. **Bloomsbury, 2003. 978-1-58234-849-0 (hardcover); 978-0-7475-6124-8 (softcover). 169pp.**

Hannah is very excited to travel to London and work in her sister's sweetmeat shop. Learning how to make candied lemons and sugar violets is much more interesting than helping take care of her brothers and sisters in the village. London in 1665 is full of activity and new joy, with the recent return of the monarchy. But Hannah doesn't realize that a sickness is spreading through London, putting herself, her sister Sarah, and all her friends at risk. The plague is here, and it will take anyone.

Petals in the Ashes. Bloomsbury, 2004. 978-1-58234-936-7 (hardcover); 978-1-58234-720-2 (softcover). 200pp.

It is a year after the events of the terrible plague, and although Hannah and Sarah were able to survive, there are still risks in London. Sarah chooses to stay in their village, but Hannah, now with her younger sister Anne, goes back to the city to reopen the sweetmeats shop. At first things are good; Hannah reconnects with her friend Tom, whom she thought had died in the plague, and business is steady. But then, on a terrible day, a fire starts in Pudding Lane. And this fire is different from other fires; it keeps spreading. Soon all of London is in danger, and Hannah and Anne must find a way to escape.

Rees, Celia.

The Fool's Girl. **Bloomsbury, 2010. 978-1-59990-486-3 (hardcover). 304pp.** 🔳 🔳

Like many others, Violetta and her protector Feste have come to London. Their country was swallowed up by invaders, and now Feste works as a clown while Violetta is his assistant. But they are more than just refugees; they are seekers. Before the fall of the kingdom, a priceless artifact was stolen. The man who stole it is in London, and Feste and Violetta will stop at nothing to confront the thief and regain the relic. But they are poor and without connections. They live with Violetta's distant relation, Sir Toby, in a decaying brothel. Only when they start to tell their story to William Shakespeare, playwright and producer, does their quest become more possible. Through luck and talent, the clown and the fool's girl just might succeed.

Keywords: England; Performing; Seventeenth Century; Shakespeare, William; Theft

Sturtevant, Katherine.

The Brothers Story. Farrar, Straus & Giroux, 2009. 978-0-374-30992-3 (hardcover). 288pp. **I** **S**

For his whole life, Kit has been responsible for his twin brother, Christy. Born simple, Christy is forgetful and unreliable, but he's also good-natured and kind. The winter of 1683 has been the coldest in living memory, and poor families like Kit's are even more affected. After his youngest brother dies from starvation and cold, Kit's mother takes a position as a maid, and Kit and Christy are sent as servants to a well-off but cruel villager. After Christy is abused, Kit takes a risk: He leaves for London and an apprenticeship, rather than stand by and watch his brother be beaten. London opens Kit's eyes to wonders and lets him make a new life. But he still has Christy to protect. Will he return to poverty to take care of his brother, or stay in London with his dreams of success?

Keywords: Brothers; England; Mental Disability; Seventeenth Century

A Young Woman Writer. **M** **I**

The effort to have a career is difficult for a young woman, especially in the seventeenth century. Yet Meg is determined, stubborn, and resourceful. She will find a way to use her pen.

Keywords: England; Father and Child; Seventeenth Century; Women's Roles; Writing

At the Sign of the Star. Farrar, Straus & Giroux, 2000. 978-0-374-30449-2 (hardcover); 978-0-374-40458-1 (softcover). 140pp.

Since the death of her mother, it has just been Meg and her father. She spends a lot of time in the bookshop that her father runs, reading and talking with customers. When Meg gets older, she'll get to pick her husband from a range of suitors, men eager to marry a well-off young woman. But Meg won't just be a trophy wife; she intends to work in the shop with her husband. That's all that Meg wants, but then her father's news throws this future into doubt. He has decided to remarry, a young, rich woman. Meg is shocked and worried, especially when her new stepmother becomes pregnant. Will this new child take her place as her father's heir? Meg tries different schemes to stop these changes, but gradually she realizes that it's up to her to change as well.

A True and Faithful Narrative. Farrar, Straus & Giroux, 2006. 978-0-374-37809-7 (hardcover). 256pp.

At sixteen, Meg knows that the time for marriage is approaching. But she didn't expect to have Edward, the brother of her best friend Anne, make overtures to her! Very bewildered by this, Meg makes a joke of his offer. Edward leaves, heading toward the Mediterranean as part of his apprenticeship, and Meg continues in her daily life, visiting Anne and worrying about her future. Most of all Meg wishes her father would let her write, using her pen to improve poorly written manuscripts or even write her own stories. And then Meg gets her chance in an unexpected way. Edward is captured by pirates and held for ransom. His family can't pay for his return, so Meg starts writing and incites all of London to contribute to Edward's ransom. Will this be enough to make up for her thoughtless behavior? And will Meg discover what the best future for her is?

Turnbull, Ann.

Quaker Love. ⑤

Turnbull dramatically shows how the concerns of teenagers are somewhat universal. Regardless of the time period, there is a desire to express themselves, to set their own goals, and to find love.

Keywords: Eighteenth Century; England; Multiple Voices; Religious Conflicts; Romance

No Shame, No Fear. Candlewick, 2004. 978-0-7636-2505-4 (hardcover); 978-0-7636-3190-1 (softcover). 304pp.

Every day, teenagers fall in love. Yet when there are great differences in their class and position, it's difficult to make love work. William is the son of the mayor and an Anglican. Susanna is poor and a Quaker. Being a Quaker has been outlawed by Parliament, leading to arrests of many adult Quakers. Susanna wants to remain true to her faith, but she would face persecution, imprisonment—maybe even death. William finds himself intrigued by the Quaker faith, but he risks being cut off by his father and left penniless, without any way to support himself. Add to that the fact that falling in love with each other is equally forbidden, due to Susanna's lack of wealth and William's higher class. Will their love survive these challenges?

Forged in the Fire. Candlewick, 2007. 978-0-7636-3144-4 (hardcover). 320pp.

Three years have passed since William and Susanna fell in love. They have both been working and saving money until they have enough to get married. They've remained true to each other and to their shared faith. Yet conditions are getting even worse for Quakers, and there are other dangers afoot. William is imprisoned for protesting about the outlawing of the Quaker faith, and while in prison, he becomes ill. Susanna comes to take care of him, yet William has been moved to a rich merchant's house to recuperate—a merchant who has a very attractive daughter. Together and separately, William and Susanna have to find a way to share their faith and their lives.

Yolen, Jane, and Robert J. Harris.

Prince Across the Water. Philomel, 2004. 978-0-399-23897-0 (hardcover); 978-0-14-240645-8 (softcover). 304pp. **M** **J**

All his life Duncan has heard his grandfather's stories about fighting to restore a Stuart to the British throne in 1715, thirty years ago. Now a Stuart has returned to lead the Scottish clans against King George II. Duncan's father doesn't want him to fight because Duncan is prone to strange fits. In addition, he's only thirteen. But Duncan feels he's man enough to fight for his clan, his king, and Scotland. He and his cousin Ewan manage to sneak away, heading toward the battlefield. But the battle they enter is Culloden, a bloody disaster for the Scots. Bonnie Prince Charlie will be left criss-crossing the Highlands until he can escape back to Europe. And for Duncan and his family, their way of life will come to an end.

Keywords: Eighteenth Century; Family; Political Rebellions; Scotland

The Rogues. Philomel, 2007. 978-0-399-23898-7 (hardcover); 978-0-14-241206-0 (softcover). 288pp. **M** **J**

The saddest day for a Scot is the day his laird clears him from his land. The lairds realize that it's more profitable to graze sheep on their lands rather than rent small parcels to farmers, so they burn the villages and send the peasants on their way. Men like Roddy Macallan protest against this cruelty. He sneaks into his burned village to recover a family heirloom, a brooch that was a gift from Bonnie Prince Charlie himself. But Willie Rood, the laird's right hand man, steals the brooch from him. Furious, Roddy plots revenge, but his attempt ends with him being beaten nearly to death by Rood. He survives thanks to Alan Dunbar, an outlaw who takes Roddy as an apprentice. Together the two young men ride across the Highlands, stealing the brooch back and causing trouble for the lairds and groups of English soldiers. Roddy then has to choose whether to labor in Scotland or risk a journey to the New World. Can he leave his home, even though there is little there for him?

Keywords: Eighteenth Century; Political Rebellions; Scotland

The Regency and the Victorian Era: 1800–1900

The incapacitation of King George III, afflicted with a strange illness that caused madness, led to a regency by his son, the future George IV. During this period there was a new vitality and spirit in British life, as seen in the works of such writers as Jane Austen. Yet the truly dominant force of the 1800s in Britain was Queen Victoria. Coming to the throne in 1837, she ruled the nation for the rest of the century and left an indelible mark on more than just Britain.

Barratt, Mark.

Joe Rat. Eerdmans Books for Young Readers, 2009. 978-0-8028-5356-1 (softcover). 320pp. 🅜 🅙

For the orphan boy known as Joe Rat, looking out for himself is the first priority. He scavenges in the London sewers, gathering metal objects like nails and coins. He gets money for these finds from Mother, a grasping old woman who exploits orphans. It's a dirty, cold, hungry life, but he can't find much better in the East End of Victorian London. Then Joe's path crosses that of Bess Farleigh, a country girl newly arrived in London. Her own mother had tried to sell Bess into prostitution, but Bess escaped. Now hunted, Bess needs help to survive. Joe helps her, even though friendship doesn't amount to much normally. The two of them stay with the local madman, who gives Bess and Joe help when they need it. But the question remains: Can Joe learn to trust his new friends, or will he put himself first as always?

Keywords: Coming-of-age; England; Friendship

Frost, Helen.

The Braid. Farrar, Straus & Giroux, 2006. 978-0-374-30962-6 (hardcover). 112pp. 🅙

In 1850 the landowners decided that on the Outer Islands of Scotland it would be better to raise sheep than to rent the land to farmers. So the tenant farmers were evicted—sometimes with only the clothes on their backs. The people scattered to mainland Scotland, America, Canada, and even far-off Australia. Jeannie and Sarah's family decide to travel to Canada. But Sarah can't leave the islands. On the day the family is to leave, she hides, and she eventually joins her grandmother on another safe island. On the long, dangerous sea crossing, all Jeannie has to remember her sister by is a braid, made up of both sisters' hair. In intertwining poems, Jeannie and Sarah tell their stories, each hoping to one day hear news from the other.

Keywords: Canada; Multiple Voices; Novel in Verse; Scotland; Sisters

Grant, K. M.

How the Hangman Lost His Heart. Walker Books for Young Readers, 2007. 978-0-8027-9672-1 (hardcover). 256pp. 🅙

A story from the author's family history is re-created as a novel. Alice's Uncle Frank, dashing and charming, has just been executed for attempting to overthrow King George II. Alice is the only one in her family willing to attend the execution and make arrangements for her uncle's remains. But Alice doesn't realize that Dan Skinslicer, the executioner, has to mount her uncle's head on a pike and put it up at Temple Bar. Horrified, Alice goes back the next day and tries to steal back the head. Unfortunately she fails, but she manages to escape with the help of Dan and Captain Hew French. The three of them, now targeted by Justice Peckersniff, do their best to stay one step ahead of the soldiers chasing them. There are twists and turns, romance and action, as Alice tries to reunite Uncle Frank's head with his body.

Keywords: England; Family; Romance

Harrison, Cora.

I Was Jane Austen's Best Friend: A Secret Diary. **Delacorte Books for Young Readers, 2010. 978-0-385-73940-5 (hardcover). 352pp.** Ⓜ️ Ⓙ

Jenny Cooper knows that her cousin's life is in her hands. Jane is very sick, and the cruel headmistress won't send for Jane's parents. So Jenny sneaks out and sends a letter to her aunt Austen. Mr. And Mrs. Austen come and rescue both Jane and Jenny, bringing them to the Austen country home. Jenny is very happy to be living with the Austen family. Together with Jane, she has good times at family meals and small parties in town. Jane even helps Jenny find true love with the handsome naval Captain Williams. Through it all, Jenny records these events, as well as her feelings and sketches, in her journal. And it's only there that Jenny can confess the secret she carries.

Keywords: Diary; England; Family; Friendship; Romance

Hearn, Julie.

Ivy. **Ginee Seo Books, 2008. 978-1-4169-2506-4 (hardcover); 978-1-4169-2507-1 (softcover). 368pp.** Ⓙ Ⓢ

Red hair makes Ivy different. In her family of thieves and ruffians, Ivy is considered worthless. As she grows up, she becomes addicted to laudanum, a common drug in Victorian England. But Ivy, with her red hair and hazel eyes, has something about her—something that draws people's eyes. Ivy catches the eye of Oscar Aretino Fosdick, an artist who makes Ivy his muse. Posing for paintings helps her family, but her drug addiction and her sadness remain. Subjected to cruelty by Oscar's mother, Ivy realizes that if she is to achieve a happy ending for herself, she must conquer her addiction and make her own way in the world. The Pre-Raphaelite art movement is explored in this novel akin to Dickens's works.

Keywords: Art; England; Women's Roles

Jocelyn, Marthe.

Folly. **Wendy Lamb Books, 2010. 978-0-385-73846-0 (hardcover); 978-0-375-85543-6 (softcover). 256pp.** Ⓙ

Mary Finn is a fifteen-year-old country girl. After her father remarries, her stepmother manages to get Mary sent away. Mary finds herself working in a lord's house as a scullery maid. She's practical and full of common sense until she meets Caden Tucker. He's a scoundrel and a braggart, but he's also her heart's delight. Mary's relationship with Caden changes her life, making her wish that she knew then what she knows now. While Mary tells her story, young James Nelligan leaves his foster family and is sent to a foundling hospital. These two stories come together in unexpected ways, revealing the role that luck played in Victorian England.

Keywords: England; Multiple Voices; Parallel Narratives

Morgan, Nicola.

Fleshmarket. **Delacorte, 2004. 978-0-385-73154-6 (hardcover). 224pp.** 🔲 🔲

The death of his mother is the end of Robbie's childhood. Suffering from a tumor in her breast, she goes to Dr. Knox, a prominent surgeon, to be operated on. But in five days she is dead—and Robbie blames the doctor. Six years later, fourteen-year-old Robbie struggles to survive, to provide for himself and his sister. In the wake of their mother's death, their father became a drunkard, so it's all up to Robbie. Through it all, he longs for revenge against Dr. Knox. When he gets the chance to provide dead bodies to the doctor, he takes it, even though he knows that people are killed to provide fresh bodies. But slowly, Robbie's morals—and his sister's love—cause him to take a stand. Can Robbie speak out against this outrage and save others? If he does, he might just save himself as well. The grim world of early nineteenth-century Edinburgh is vividly imagined, with its horrible sights and smells.

Keywords: Family; Scotland

The Highwayman's Footsteps. **Candlewick, 2007. 978-0-7636-3472-8 (hardcover); 978-1-4063-0311-7 (softcover). 368pp.** 🔲 🔲

As civil war looms in England, Will has run away from home. He seems to be a constant disappointment to his father because he's not like his older brother. Having set off with no money and only a highborn education, Will is soon reduced to theft so he can eat. But soon after lifting a purse full of money, Will is assaulted by a highwayman. The criminal is ready to take Will's money, but then faints, suffering from a previous injury. That's when Will realizes the highwayman is a girl, just about his age. Bess is the daughter of a highwayman, forced to follow his profession after his death. Will and Bess will slowly grow to trust each other—and with that trust, they attempt a great adventure.

Keywords: England; Romance

Pignat, Caroline.

Greener Grass. **Red Deer Press, 2009. 978-0-88995-402-1 (softcover). 278pp.** 🔲

Times are hard in Ireland, with blight wiping out potato crops and most of the jobs. Still, Kit's family is doing all right, thanks to her job at the Big House—the local lord's home. As soon as her father starts sending his wages from his job in England, they'll have some breathing room before the new baby comes. But Kit has a sense of foreboding. It seems like things are going to go very, very wrong. When the blight becomes worse and totally destroys the potato crop, Kit's father dies, and Kit loses her job, they suddenly are one of the poorest families in the village. With the landlord's decision to evict them, Kit is unable to see how her family will survive. How far must she go to save her family?

Keywords: Disasters; Family; Ireland

Rinaldi, Ann.

Mutiny's Daughter. HarperTeen, 2004. 978-0-06-029638-4 (hardcover); 978-0-06-441010-6 (softcover). 218pp. **M J**

Keeping the family honor intact has been drilled into Mary Christian. She's the daughter of the notorious Fletcher Christian, the man who led the mutiny on the HMS *Bounty*. Fletcher and his fellow mutineers settled on Tahiti, and Fletcher married a local woman. On the day Mary was born, a rebellion within the settlement resulted in Fletcher's death—or at least that's what the Christian family has said. Actually, Fletcher brought Mary to England, to his ancestral home on the Isle of Man. Mary has grown up as the daughter of her uncle Charles, and now at fourteen she's getting ready to go to an exclusive boarding school. Mary will have to keep the secret of her father's identity at school, because revealing it would not just damage the school; it would hurt the family she can't help loving.

Keywords: England; Family

Updale, Eleanor.

Montmorency Series. **J S**

Giving new meaning to starting over, the man known as Montmorency begins as a criminal, then uses his wealth and his knowledge to work for the British government in a series of political and physical intrigues.

Keywords: England; Europe; Political Rebellions; Spies

Montmorency: Thief, Liar, Gentleman? Orchard, 2004. 978-0-439-58035-9 (hardcover); 978-0-439-58036-6 (softcover). 240pp.

Before the accident, the prisoner now known as Montmorency was just a common thief. But while trying to escape after a heist, he falls through a skylight, leaving his body broken and mangled. He's rescued from death by Doctor Farcett, who believes that saving Montmorency will make his career. The doctor is right—and what's more, he saves Montmorency's career. Exposed to new ideas and the privileged elite, Montmorency hatches an elaborate plan. Using the new sewer system, he will rob from the rich, creating a double life to make it work. He will be Montmorency, fine gentleman, and Scarper,

Montmorency's low-born servant. The big question is, just how long can he keep this up? The smallest mistake could bring everything crashing down—and that's the last thing Montmorency wants.

Mountmorency on the Rocks: Doctor, Aristocrat, Murderer? Orchard, 2005. 978-0-439-60676-9 (hardcover); 978-0-439-60677-6 (softcover). 368pp.

Five years have passed since Montmorency left prison and began his new life as a well-to-do gentleman. This life was only possible thanks to his alter ego, Scarper, but Scarper has been put to rest, it seems. But on a trip through Europe with his companion, Lord George Fox-Selwyn, Montmorency comes under the influence of powerful drugs during their time in Turkey. These drugs threaten not just Montmorency but also the state secrets he knows. Lord Fox-Selwyn resolves to beat the drugs' hold on Montmorency with the help of Doctor Farcett—the same doctor who saved Montmorency's life six years before. As Montmorency fights withdrawal, a series of bomb attacks in London calls for the skills of Fox-Selwyn and Montmorency. It will take all his strength not to fall into Scarper's dark underworld, but Montmorency must stay clean, in many different ways, to catch the bombers and preserve his self-respect.

Montmorency and the Assassins: Master, Criminal, Spy? Orchard, 2006. 978-0-439-68343-2 (hardcover); 978-0-439-68344-9 (softcover). 416pp.

After working for the British government for more than ten years, Montmorency and his friend and colleague, Lord George Fox-Selwyn, are looking forward to a simple detective case. When a wealthy naturalist is robbed of several specimens, it's recommended he contact Montmorency and Fox-Selwyn. Setting off for Florence, the two men plan to pose as amateur naturalists, suspecting that another collector had arranged the thefts. Their arrival in Florence lets them spend time with Fox-Selwyn's brother and nephews, as well. But quickly all five men become drawn into this case. What appeared to be a simple robbery leads Montmorency and Fox-Selwyn to a network of anarchist terrorists, who are determined to overthrow the current political order. It's up to the British agents to stop them.

Montmorency's Revenge. Orchard, 2007. 978-0-439-81373-0 (hardcover); 978-0-439-81374-7 (softcover); 304pp.

The Italian adventure of Montmorency and Fox-Selwyn has ended in tragedy. Fox-Selwyn's friends and family are set on revenge against his killer, Moretti. But even more important is punishing Malpensa, the head of the anarchist group, who ordered George's death. When Montmorency and the Fox-Selwyn family learn that Malpensa is readying his plot against the Royal Family, they will have to risk their reputations to stop Malpensa. Montmorency will face several dangerous, difficult tasks. Can he protect Frank Fox-Selwyn from the anarchists? Can he help Doctor Farcett regain his sanity? And will he be able to stop Malpensa from harming the Royal

Family, still mourning the death of Queen Victoria? Only Montmorency could achieve all this.

Wallace, Karen.

The Unrivalled Spangles. **Atheneum, 2006. 978-1-4169-1503-4 (hardcover); 978-0-689-87282-2 (softcover). 219pp. ⓜ ⓙ**

Circus life is full of rules and codes; it's a life that turns one into an outsider. For Ellen Spangle, daughter of a circus owner, it's not the life she wants. It may be exotic and exciting to be part of a horse-riding act with her sister Lucy, but Ellen wants something different. Now that she's sixteen, her secret tutoring has educated her enough so that she can get a job as a teacher or governess and leave circus life. Fourteen-year-old Lucy doesn't know why Ellen wants to leave; the circus is all Lucy wants—except for Joe Morgan, the son of a rival circus owner. Lucy, behind their father's back, starts a romance with Joe, with Ellen's help. Ellen isn't without a romantic interest of her own: a gentleman, no less. But when bad times come for Spangle's Circus, one of the sisters will have to sacrifice her dreams for the show to go on.

Keywords: England; Romance; Sisters

Modern Times: 1900–1980

Britain stood strong to combat the threats of both world wars. Yet its resistance brought much hardship, particularly during World War II. And the end of the war didn't immediately end the hardships.

Almond, David.

The Fire-Eaters. **Delacorte, 2004. 978-0-385-73170-6 (hardcover); 978-0-440-42012-5 (softcover). 224pp. ⓜ ⓙ**

It's a time of transition for Bobby. Cuba and the United States are facing off, his father is ill, and he's getting ready to start at a new school. Also, now that he's twelve, he's looking at his friendships with Joseph and Ailsa with new eyes. His school is a cold place, very different from his cozy seaside village. Symbolizing all this change—and a catalyst for more changes—is McNulty, a fire-eater and illusionist. A World War II veteran like Bobby's father, McNulty saw too much and can't escape the past. He opens Bobby's eyes to the world around him, showing him how to take in all its glories. Northern England in the 1960s is the background for one boy's coming-of-age.

Keywords: 1960s; Cold War; Coming-of-age; England

Bunting, Eve.

SOS Titanic. Harcourt Children's Books, 1996. 978-0-15-200271-8 (hardcover); 978-0-15-201305-9 (softcover). 256pp. **J**

Barry O'Neill is a well-to-do young man, without many traces of his Irish heritage. But he loves Ireland and is miserable about moving to New York. Even making the trip on the new liner *Titanic* hasn't eased his discomfort. Not only are two toughs from his home village on the ship, but Barry can't help feeling superstitious. The *Titanic* is unsinkable—but what about the premonitions and logic that say no ship is unsinkable? When the ship hits an iceberg, Barry's first thought is helping the Flynns. They may be his enemies, but they're also part of him. The Flynns seem to be trapped in steerage, but Barry can't let them perish.

Keywords: 1910s; Atlantic Ocean; Disasters; Ireland

Hearn, Julie.

Hazel. Atheneum, 2009. 978-1-4169-2504-0 (hardcover); 978-1-4169-2505-7 (softcover). 389pp. **J** **S**

The life of Hazel Mull-Dare is that of a pampered, respectable girl. She spends time with her beloved father and attends a school that teaches the daughters of gentlemen. But Hazel doesn't realize how her life is going to change right before her thirteenth birthday. First she sees a suffragette get run down by a racehorse during the Epsom Derby while demonstrating for the right to vote. The new girl at school, Gloria, is full of unconventional ideas and saucy language. But worst of all, her father has a breakdown and is sent away for rest. Hazel is left adrift, full of all kinds of questions. When she stages a suffragette protest at Madame Tussaud's wax museum, she is sent away, to the family sugar plantation in the Caribbean. In this tropical land, Hazel discovers even more questions and attempts to find the answers.

Keywords: 1910s; Caribbean; Coming-of-age; England

Hinton, Nigel.

Time Bomb. Tricycle Press, 2006. 978-1-58246-186-1 (hardcover); 978-1-58246-237-0 (softcover). 288pp. **M** **J**

Now that school is out, Andy and his friends are looking forward to a summer of play and good times. Now that World War II has been over for four years, things like sweets are becoming more available. But there are still plenty of reminders of the war—including the ruined houses, bombed out and now a playground of sorts for the neighborhood kids. It's a dangerous spot, but Andy and his friends love playing there. This summer, though, changes are coming—and when the boys discover an unexploded bomb on Big Brown Hill, they decide to keep it secret to protect the Hill from being turned into houses. But keeping this secret will turn out to have major consequences.

Keywords: 1940s; Coming-of-age; England

Kent, Trilby.

Medina Hill. **Tundra Books, 2009. 978-0-88776-888-0 (hardcover). 176pp. Ⓜ**

One day Dominic stopped talking. Nothing traumatic happened; he just couldn't speak. In London's docklands neighborhood in 1935, that makes Dominic a target for bullies, just like his chubby sister Marlo. The only thing that gets Dominic through is his guidebook for boys, with advice from Lawrence of Arabia himself. But then Uncle Roo arrives and invites Dominic and Marlo to visit him in Cornwall. Wild and windswept, Cornwall is full of a different energy. The boarding house they stay in is full of unusual people, and slowly Dominic regains his voice. When he decides to use it to help a group of Travelers—Gypsies that are seen as a menace— it will take all of Dominic's courage, and his faith in Colonel Lawrence's methods, to protect them.

Keywords: 1930s; Brothers and Sisters; England; Family

Morpurgo, Michael.

Private Peaceful. **Scholastic, 2004. 978-0-439-63648-3 (hardcover); 978-0-439-63653-7 (softcover). 208pp. Ⓙ Ⓢ**

Thomas Peaceful is standing night watch. A soldier in the British army during World War I, he lied about his age so he could follow his older brother Charlie into the military. To stay awake through his watch, Thomas—or Tommo—looks back over his life, spent with his family in a cottage on a big estate. Tommo worshipped Charlie, and they both stood up for their mentally handicapped brother Big Joe. Times are hard after their father dies, but they find a new friend, Molly. Tommo loves Molly, but she marries Charlie. When World War I starts, Charlie enlists and Tommo, only fifteen, knows he will enlist, too. Two years later, when Tommo is injured, Charlie stays with him despite orders. The consequences of disobeying those orders have a great impact on both Charlie and Tommo.

Awards: Carnegie Medal Finalist

Keywords: 1910s; Brothers; England; Mental Disability; World War I

Westall, Robert.

The Machine Gunners. **HarperCollins, 1976. 978-0-688-80055-0 (hardcover); 978-0-330-39785-8 (softcover). 186pp. Ⓜ Ⓙ**

It's 1941, and German bombers are carrying out the bombing flights known as the Blitz. For Chas and his family, every day brings the chance of an air raid, forcing them to hide in a shelter and hope their house remains standing. Like many of the other boys, Chas collects spent bullets, damaged airplane parts, and other war souvenirs. He has the second-best collection in town—and he'll have the best when everyone learns he has a German machine gun, complete with ammunition. Helped by his friends, Chas hides the machine gun and makes plans to use it against the Nazis. The authorities know something's up, but they don't know where the gun is—until Chas and his friends use it one day, with disastrous results.

Keywords: 1940s; Coming-of-age; England; World War II

Chapter 3

Traditional Historical Fiction: History of the Americas

American history is perhaps the most popular topic for historical fiction for children and young adults in the United States. For a country that has existed for fewer than 300 years, the United States has spawned a remarkable number of novels. Like the previous chapter, this one covers works of traditional historical fiction, novels that do not cross into other genres.

Also included in this chapter are titles that cover other countries and regions within the Americas. Ranging from Canada to the Caribbean, Mexico to South America, these novels highlight the differences and similarities between these areas and the United States.

United States

Beginning with the earliest explorations in the 1500s, America was seen as a land of opportunity. The vast, untamed lands were so different from Europe that they drew millions of people to its shores. Once they settled in this new world, these people were no longer Europeans but Americans. Beginning with a successful revolution against the mother country, the American colonies became their own nation, one that has a rich history in spite of its relative youth.

Early Exploration: 1500–1800

Those who explored America found great danger and great beauties on their journeys. Through their explorations, these people were tested to their limits and emerged with a new understanding of themselves and this new land.

Bruchac, Joseph.

Pocahontas. Harcourt Children's Books, 2003. 978-0-15-216737-0 (hardcover); 978-0-15-205465-6 (softcover). 192pp. **M**

> What the Europeans call the New World is simply their home to the Powhatan. They have seen Coatmen come before, white men who are often cruel, whether wielding their thunder sticks or spreading diseases. Yet when a new group of white men arrive, the Powhatan chief acts cautiously, hoping for peace but preparing for war. His favorite daughter, Pocahontas, wishes to visit these men, but her father does not allow her. Pocahontas is curious about these men with their strange ways. The white men for the most part see the natives as a nuisance. Only John Smith, in disgrace with his fellow settlers, is willing to consider other viewpoints. A well-known story is told in two voices.
>
> **Keywords:** Multiple Voices; Native American Issues; Seventeenth Century

Duble, Kathleen Benner.

Quest. Margaret K. McElderry, 2008. 978-1-4169-3386-1 (hardcover). 256pp. **J** **S**

> Four stories are interwoven to re-create the full experience of a sea voyage during the Age of Discovery. Henry Hudson has set off to find the Northwest Passage, the route that will connect Europe with Asia via the sea. With him is his son John, who describes his excitement at the trip, as well as his sadness at leaving behind his family and friends. John's younger brother Richard misses his brother and father, but he's happy to stay with his mother, listening to her stories about romance. For some people romance is just stories. Isabella Digges, as infatuated with John Hudson as he is with her, can't help being thankful that he's gone. Maybe that way it'll be easier for her to focus on the task before her: regaining wealth for her family, either through marriage or by spying on the Dutch East Indies Trading Company. Finally, there's the last one to tell his story—Seth Syms, a member of the crew of Henry Hudson's ship, who will return from the New World, unlike John Hudson and his father. The race to the East is presented with all its adventure and danger.
>
> **Keywords:** Atlantic Ocean; Multiple Voices; Sixteenth Century

Durbin, William.

Voyageur. **M** **J**

> A young boy learns how to be a man through danger, work, and friendship. Pierre's story was reality for hundreds of men who followed the rivers of America and Canada to adventure.
>
> **Keywords:** America; Canada; Coming-of-age; Nineteenth Century

The Broken Blade. Delacorte Books for Young Readers, 1997. 978-0-385-32224-9 (hardcover); 978-0-440-41184-0 (softcover). 176pp.

> Pierre, at age thirteen, is responsible for several small chores, like splitting kindling. When his father injures himself while doing Pierre's work, Pierre feels guilty. To help his family, he impulsively signs on as a voyageur, serving as a paddler on a canoe traveling from Montreal into the wilderness. Pierre isn't used to such hard work; after one day he's sore and blistered. How will he manage paddling for 2,400 miles? And will he ever gain the respect of the other men when he's the youngest? Pierre has a lot to prove, and he's determined to succeed for his family's sake.

Wintering. Delacorte Books for Young Readers, 1999. 978-0-385-32598-1 (hardcover); 978-0-440-22759-5 (softcover). 208pp.

> Two summers of paddling have helped Pierre grow larger and stronger. Now fourteen, he's planning to spend the winter as a hivernant, living in the north and trapping furs. The only difficulty is Beloit, the scarred, crude voyageur who's wintering over also. There are other tensions as well, like other companies competing with the North West Company, Pierre's employer. And although Pierre has talked—well, joked—about marriage with a rich girl back home, he's grieving for Kennewk, the Ojibwe girl he became friends with last summer. Pierre may now be a man of the north, but being a man means facing all these problems and more.

Goodman, Joan Elizabeth.

Paradise. **Houghton Mifflin Books for Young Readers, 2002. 978-0-618-11450-4 (hardcover); 978-0-618-49481-1 (softcover). 224pp.** ▪

In the 1500s, the New World was seen as being a land full of gold and diamonds. Yet many came to the vast lands for other reasons. For Marguerite de la Rocque, sailing with her uncle to Canada gives her the chance to love as she wants. Marguerite is from a family of Protestants, but her love, Pierre, is Catholic. Unable to marry, they hatch a plan and Pierre joins the ship when Marguerite is ordered to accompany her uncle. But when they are discovered, the pair, along with Marguerite's maid, are marooned on the small Island of Demons. At first they are able to survive, for it is summer. But winter is coming.

Keywords: Romance; Sixteenth Century

O'Dell, Scott.

The Serpent Never Sleeps: A Novel of Jamestown and Pocahontas. **Houghton Mifflin Harcourt, 1987. 978-0-395-44242-5 (hardcover); 978-0-449-70328-1 (softcover). 240pp.** 🄼 🄹

Young Serena is very timid. She's not one to take a risk—except on Anthony Foxcroft, the nobleman she's loved for years. She convinces King James I to free Anthony from the Tower of London, then turns down a court position to follow Anthony to the New World. They sail on a ship carrying supplies for the colony in Virginia. But a shipwreck lands them on Bermuda. It's a hard struggle to survive, but Serena and Anthony manage to make it to Jamestown. There, conditions are even worse than reported. It's only thanks to the help of Indian princess Pocahontas that the colony is able to continue, again thanks to Serena's pleas. But when a tragedy strikes at what she holds most dear, Serena must determine whether her place is in England or America.

Keywords: Native American Issues; Romance; Seventeenth Century

Trottier, Maxine.

Sister to the Wolf. **Kids Can Press, 2004. 978-1-55337-519-7 (hardcover); 978-1-55337-520-3 (softcover). 352pp.** 🄹 🅂

Life in the city of Québec doesn't suit Cécile or her father. So they make plans to leave and travel to the new settlement of Détroit, located in the wilderness around Lake Erie. But before they leave, Cécile makes a rash, spur-of-the-moment decision: She buys an Indian pani, a slave, named Lesharo. She wants to set him free, but Lesharo insists on accompanying Cécile and her father to Détroit. On their journey, the three of them learn to respect one another, and Lesharo and Cécile grow close. But in Détroit, Lesharo is expected to be a slave and nothing more. Cécile will make another life-changing decision—only this one doesn't affect just her.

Keywords: Native American Issues; Romance; Seventeenth Century; Slavery

Colonial Life: 1600–1776

After decades of wheeling and dealing, eventually Britain was the country most able to support colonies in the New World. The thirteen colonies along the Eastern Seaboard drew people seeking land, religious toleration, and freedom. Yet as Britain leveled higher and higher taxes upon them, the colonies began to chafe under this burden.

Draper, Sharon.

Copper Sun. **Atheneum, 2006. 978-0-689-82181-3 (hardcover); 978-1-4169-5348-7 (softcover). 302pp.** 🄹 🅂

The misery of slavery is vividly, horribly portrayed. Amari and the rest of her village welcome the strange men with their pale faces. But then the strangers turn on them, killing many and chaining the young and strong. Dazed and sickened,

Amari manages to survive the journey to the coast, where she and other slaves are loaded on a ship. When she arrives in the strange new land, she is sold to a man who gives her to his sixteen-year-old son as a birthday present. Amari suffers in the fields and in her master's bedroom. Her only friend is Polly, an indentured servant who is fifteen like Amari. Soon the two girls will create a plan to escape to Florida. But the plan won't be enough—they'll need luck, too.

Keywords: Friendship; Multiple Voices; Slavery

Duble, Kathleen Benner.

The Sacrifice. **Margaret K. McElderry, 2005. 978-0-689-87650-9 (hardcover); 978-0-689-87651-6 (softcover). 224pp.** 🅜 🅙

In Abigail's small village, everyone watches everyone else. For the Puritans, such vigilance is necessary to keep the Devil at bay. When Abigail is caught racing, she's put in the stocks. She expects even more punishment, but instead news arrives from Salem Village that witches are at large, acting through those seen as outsiders. This news causes fear within Abigail's whole family. Not only has Abigail flouted conventions, but her father suffers from strange fits. As witch fever sweeps through their settlement, Abigail and her older sister Dorothy will do everything they can to keep their family safe.

Keywords: Family; Illness; Religious Conflicts; Seventeenth Century; Witch Trials

Fleischman, Paul.

Saturnalia. **HarperCollins, 1990. 978-0-06-021912-3 (hardcover); 978-0-06-447089-6 (softcover). 113pp.** 🅙

Boston in 1681 was a small colonial outpost, full of Puritans and still recovering from the Indian wars that ended years before. Against this backdrop, a cast of characters take the stage over the course of a few days in late December. There is the pompous wig maker courting a rich widow. There's the wig maker's indentured servant, nearing the end of his bondage. Watchmen and guards stalk the streets, maintaining order in all senses of the word. And then there's William, a captured Indian boy who is now the ideal apprentice. Just as William struggles with his two sides, Indian and English, we see the struggle between day and night, master and servant.

Keywords: Eighteenth Century; Multiple Voices; Native American Issues

Lyons, Mary E.

The Poison Place. **Atheneum, 1997. 978-0-689-81146-3 (hardcover); 978-1-4169-6842-9 (softcover). 160pp.** 🅜 🅙

In early America, slaves were an important part of many households. Moses, a young slave, is brought up in the home of Charles Willson Peale and his family. Peale, a gifted artist but also a dabbler in scientific subjects, claims to dislike slavery but has several slaves among his possessions. Moses is more focused on playing with his closest friend, Peale's oldest son Raphaelle. Together, the boys grow up—but slowly, the differences in their stations start to pull them apart. While Moses works, Raphaelle studies and gets into mischief. This pattern continues into adulthood, with both young men trying to gain favor with Charles Willson Peale. For Raphaelle, it's about gaining his father's love. But for Moses, it's about gaining his freedom.

Keywords: Art; Eighteenth Century; Family; Slavery

Myers, Anna.

Time of the Witches. **Walker Books for Young Readers, 2009. 978-0-8027-9820-6 (hardcover). 208pp. 🄼 🄹**

Life for orphans could be very difficult in the late seventeenth century. Drucilla's mother dies in childbirth, and her father a few years later. She has lived since birth with the Masons and their son Gabe. Dru and Gabe were born at the same time and have been friends their entire lives. It's almost like they're two peas in a pod, because they're happiest when they're together. The death of Gabe's parents, though, starts years of moves for both of them. They manage to stay together until they are twelve, when they are taken in by two branches of the Putnam family. At first Dru is impressed by the fine Putnam house and is warmed by Mistress Putnam's kindness. But Mistress Putnam begins to act strangely, and Ann Putnam seems to harbor some secret. Could it be connected to the new minister's slave, Tituba? Just why are so many young girls in Salem falling ill? Dru finds herself caught in the middle of the hysteria, and the only way to stay safe might mean speaking a lie.

Keywords: Family; Orphans; Seventeenth Century; Witch Trials

Rees, Celia.

📖 *Witch Child.* **Bloomsbury, 2000. 978-0-7475-4639-9 (hardcover); 978-0-7475-5009-9 (softcover). 240pp. 🄹 🅂**

Being accused of witchcraft is often a death sentence. That's what happens to Mary's grandmother, who is tortured to draw out a confession. When she refuses to speak, she's hanged. Mary is left alone and without resources. Then a noblewoman provides Mary with money and passage to the New World. Mary tries to put her true feelings away and act like a good Puritan. Once she arrives in America, there are so many things to explore: the woods, the Native American beliefs. But her fellow colonists, who avoid the woods and look down on the Indians, do not share Mary's enthusiasm. Mary soon finds herself an object of suspicion and accused of being a witch. She must choose whether to value her beliefs or her survival.

Keywords: Native American Issues; Seventeenth Century; Witch Trials

Rinaldi, Ann.

A Break with Charity: A Story About the Salem Witch Trials. **Harcourt Children's Books, 1992. 978-0-15-200353-1 (hardcover); 978-0-15-204682-8 (softcover). 272pp. ⓜ ⓙ**

> Among the people of Salem, Susanna English and her family are outsiders. Fourteen-year-old Susanna knows why: They are the gentry, rich and respected. But that doesn't mean she's part of the friendship circle that the local girls share. Susanna is left out, as the girls spend time at the home of the local minister. The girls visit to hear the stories of Tituba, the minister's slave. What's more, Tituba practices magic, like reading tea leaves and using a poppet. And Susanna, whose brother William is lost at sea, is drawn to Tituba and the hope she can offer. But in 1692 Salem, such things are the work of the Devil and not to be encouraged. As hysteria sweeps through the townspeople, Susanna watches and struggles with whether to break charity: to confess what she knows.
>
> **Keywords:** Seventeenth Century; Witch Trials

The Color of Fire. **Hyperion Books, 2005. 978-0-7868-0938-7 (hardcover); 978-0-7868-1825-9 (softcover). 208pp. ⓜ ⓙ**

> A tough choice must be made during a time of hysteria. Phoebe lives in New York City, a slave to the Philipse family. She's been well-treated by her owners, taught to read and allowed to run errands on her own. But in 1741 Britain and Spain are at war, and the American colonies are also involved. Everyone's looking for spies and Catholics, and suspicion is falling on Phoebe's tutor, Mr. Ury. Even worse, her friend and fellow slave Cuffee has gotten drawn into a group of slaves who are accused of causing trouble. Fires are breaking out all over New York, and whites suspect their slaves as the firebugs, acting under orders from Spanish agents. Phoebe has the chance to help Cuffee, but that choice would end her dreams.
>
> **Keywords:** Coming-of-age; Eighteenth Century; Slavery

The Family Greene. **Harcourt Children's Books, 2010. 978-0-547-26067-9 (hardcover). 256pp. ⓜ ⓙ**

> How much of our personality is set by our parents? Cornelia Greene sees how her mother, Caty Littlefield Greene, flirts with other men. Gossip says that Mrs. Greene doesn't stop at flirting—and Cornelia knows that her mother's behavior hurts her father, General Nathanael Greene. Caty, who was taught how to flirt by her aunt, claims that flirting is the only way women have power. That's what Caty's aunt told her, and what Caty knows firsthand. But Cornelia loves her father so much, she can't bear the thought of his sadness. Then a rumor reaches Cornelia that her father is not General Greene. Is the rumor true? Did her mother betray her father? Finding the answer to that question will lead Cornelia to many lessons about her family and herself.
>
> **Keywords:** Eighteenth Century; Family; Women's Roles

The Fifth of March. **Harcourt Children's Books, 1993. 978-0-15-200343-2 (hardcover); 978-0-15-227517-4 (softcover). 352pp.** 🅜 🅙

Even for an observant girl like Rachel, there are still many questions about what is going on in Boston. It's 1768, and the tensions between Loyalists and Patriots are growing. Patriots protest against the taxes and restrictions on liberty, while Loyalists defend the Crown and believe in law and order. Although her friend Jane is a Patriot, Rachel isn't sure which side she's on. After all, her master, John Adams, is trying to stay neutral, so Rachel attempts to do the same. She's more torn when she becomes friends with a British soldier. But when the British open fire on a group of Patriots—an attack called the Boston Massacre—Rachel finds she will have to determine which cause is just.

Keywords: Eighteenth Century; Political Rebellions

Hang a Thousand Trees with Ribbons: The Story of Phillis Wheatley. **Gulliver Books, 1996. 978-0-15-200876-5 (hardcover); 978-0-15-205393-2 (softcover). 352pp.** 🅙

Phillis Wheatley is something unique. Not because she's a slave in 1770s Boston, and not because she was sold by another African into slavery. What makes Phillis unique is that she is the first black poet in America. She arrived in America as a young girl, orphaned and lonely. When she is bought by the wealthy Wheatley family, she is treated well—better than well. Nathaniel, the son of her owner, helps her learn how to read and write. When Phillis displays a talent for expressing herself, Nathaniel and the rest of the Wheatleys encourage her to write down her thoughts. She creates such beautiful poems that many white men don't believe they were written by a slave. Phillis will have to prove herself, even though she dreads providing such proof. for a slave with skills like hers is still a slave.

Keywords: Eighteenth Century; Romance; Slavery; Writing

Or Give Me Death: A Novel of Patrick Henry's Family. **Harcourt Children's Books, 2003. 978-0-15-216687-8 (hardcover); 978-0-15-205076-4 (softcover). 240pp.** 🅜 🅙

The family of Patrick Henry is keeping a horrible secret. With their father riding around Virginia to defend the accused, the children are left with their mother. And their mother is slowly losing her mind. She tries to drown the newest baby, accuses one of the slaves of poisoning her, and seems to see the future. Patsy, the oldest, takes charge of the household, caring for her mother and protecting the children. For Anne, stubborn and plain, being bossed around by Patsy is no fun. Anne spends much time with the slaves, learning to see signs in nature. But slowly Anne starts to see other things, like how her mother's condition is deteriorating. When she learns that one of her siblings apparently shares their mother's madness, Anne will do all she can to keep this secret.

Keywords: Eighteenth Century; Family; Illness; Multiple Voices

Taking Liberty: The Story of Oney Judge, George Washington's Runaway Slave. **Simon & Schuster Children's Publishing, 2002. 978-0-689-85187-2 (hardcover); 978-0-689-85188-9 (softcover). 272pp.** ⬛

> Since she was a very small child, Oney Judge has been a pet of Martha Washington. Lady Washington lets Oney read and do sums, gives her pretty new clothes, and treats her kindly. Oney's mother tries to keep her in check, but as Oney rises in the household, she becomes less like a slave. Soon she is Lady Washington's personal servant, with more power than most of the plantation's servants, either black or white. She's practically part of the family. Yet slowly, Oney begins to realize that even though she feels like a member of the family, she is really a slave. Oney finds herself pondering the most difficult decision of her life: to stay with people who love her, but not as a person, or to escape and find her liberty.
>
> **Keywords:** Eighteenth Century; Family; Slavery

Shaik, Fatima.

Melitte. **Dial, 1997. 978-0-8037-2106-7 (hardcover); 978-0-14-130420-5 (softcover). 160pp.** ⬛

> Young Melitte is a slave. Not on a grand plantation, but on a small farm with a one-room cabin. Her owners, Monsieur and Madame, eke out an existence in eighteenth-century Louisiana as their land changes hands from France to Spain. And they only manage to survive thanks to Melitte. Although Monsieur is patient with her, Madame is cold and haughty, without any kindness. Melitte is starved for love and affection. It's only when Madame has a baby that Melitte finds love. Marie is fair-skinned and blonde, but she loves Melitte and sees her as a friend and a sister. Melitte promises Marie to always be her sister, but a chance for freedom will make Melitte consider how to break away from slavery without breaking her promise to Marie.
>
> **Keywords:** Eighteenth Century; Sisters; Slavery

Speare, Elizabeth George.

The Witch of Blackbird Pond. **Houghton Mifflin, 1958. 978-0-395-07114-4 (hardcover); 978-0-00-714897-4 (softcover). 249pp.** ⬛

> This historical fiction classic is the story of Kit Tyler, newly arrived in the colony of Connecticut after living most of her life in Barbados. Living in the cramped home of her aunt and uncle, forbidden to wear her beautiful silk and satin gowns, and constantly reminded to hold her tongue, Kit is miserable at first. But her friendship with Hannah, a Quaker, helps her to adjust, as well as her cousins, the beautiful Judith and the saintly Mercy. Kit cannot seem to curb her impulsive ways, like helping Prudence, the

shrinking, abused daughter of Goody Cruff. Yet when Hannah is accused of being a witch, Kit risks the safety of her new life to help her friend.

Awards: Newbery Medal

Keywords: Eighteenth Century; Family; Religious Conflicts; Witch Trials

Native Americans, Captives, and Conflicts: 1700s

As Native Americans were dispossessed of their ancestral lands and forced west, some struck back against the settlers. There were attacks on villages, with men scalped and women and children captured. Though many of the captives longed to return home, some found that life among the Indians gave them new and greater freedoms.

Cooney, Caroline B.

The Ransom of Mercy Carter. **Delacorte, 2001. 978-0-385-32615-5 (hardcover); 978-0-440-22775-5 (softcover). 249pp. ⓜ**

It is a bitterly cold night. In your small house, seventeen people are living and sleeping, but all those people aren't enough to fight back the cold. It is the year 1704, in a Massachusetts settlement that is at the edge of the wilderness. Eleven-year-old Mercy Carter's life is about to change forever. A large force of Indians and French attack and carry off nearly a hundred settlers. The English are marched 300 miles to an Indian village in Canada. Some will fall on the way, and unbelievable horrors wrack the minds of others. In the Indian village, Mercy's only hope is that the British government will pay to ransom her and the other settlers out of their captivity. Yet as she grows used to life in the village, experiencing new freedoms, Mercy begins to wonder if she really wants to be ransomed.

Keywords: Identity

Durrant, Lynda.

The Beaded Moccasins: The Story of Mary Campbell. **Clarion Books, 1998. 978-0-395-85398-6 (hardcover); 978-0-440-41591-6 (softcover). 192pp. ⓜ ⓙ**

Making a home out of the wilderness is a long, difficult task. All the members of Mary's family are expected to help, but twelve-year-old Mary is having a hard time adjusting to uncivilized central Pennsylvania. She longs to return to Connecticut, to live the life of a proper young lady. But on the morning of her twelfth birthday, Mary is captured by a group of Delaware Indians. Along with her neighbor, Mrs. Stewart, Mary is marched west. She has been picked as the replacement granddaughter for the tribe's sachem and will join the Delaware as they move from Pennsylvania into Ohio. Mary is determined to remain true to herself and return to her real family. But the longer she remains among the

Delaware, the more she adapts. Mary will have to find a way to survive—the only question is whether she will become Indian or remain English.

Keywords: Identity

The Turtle Clan. 🄼 🄹

An Indian captive grows to appreciate his true roots, while choosing to stay with his adoptive family. Several children who were captured by Native Americans made a similar choice.

Keywords: Brothers; Father and Child; Identity

Echohawk. Clarion Books, 1996. 978-0-395-74430-7 (hardcover); 978-0-440-41438-4 (softcover). 192pp.

> Many moons ago Echohawk had a different name. When he lived with his white parents, his name was Jonathan. But since he was four years old he has lived as a Mohican. Now at thirteen, Echohawk is like any other Mohican boy, with a talent for hunting. He lives with his father Glickihigan and his younger brother Bamaineo, their family grieving for the loss of the boys' mother. More and more whites are moving into the Mohican lands, chasing away the deer. Some within the Mohican settlement think their misfortunes are due to Echohawk bringing bad luck. Echohawk is caught between those who want to preserve the old ways and those who want to adapt and survive. Glickihigan decides to send Echohawk and Bamaineo to be educated among whites, hoping it will help the Mohicans. As Echohawk's earliest memories reawaken, he will have to make a choice between two different lives.

Turtle Clan Journey. Clarion Books, 1999. 978-0-395-90369-8 (hardcover). 192pp.

> The Turtle clan has been reduced to three members after a white man's sickness swept through their Mohican settlement. Now Glickihigan and his sons Echohawk and Bamaineo are traveling west, toward the Three Sisters. Known to the whites as the rivers that meet near Fort Pitt, this area is where many Native American are traveling in search of new hunting grounds. But the journey is not just long and difficult; there is a new danger. Colonial governments are now sponsoring ransoms for white captives. People like Echohawk, who was captured as a child and now living as a native, could be turned in for a reward. This news makes Echohawk cautious. Even though life among the whites has great luxuries, he knows he is a Mohican. And he will not leave his father and brother. Will Echohawk be able to stay a Mohican, or will he be returned to a life as a white?

Ketchum, Liza.

Where the Great Hawk Flies. **Clarion, 2005. 978-0-618-40085-0 (hardcover). 272pp. ◾J**

In the wilderness of Vermont just after the American Revolution, two boys try to find common ground. Daniel sees two paths before him: either being true to the Pequot blood of his mother or being English like his father. When a family moves into the neighboring cabin, Daniel hopes for a friend. Instead, he finds an enemy. Hiram is two years younger than Daniel and full of hate for the dirty Injun. Hiram is still shaken by the Indian raid that happened two years ago and drove his family out of Vermont. Looking at Daniel takes Hiram back to that horrible day and prevents him from acting logically. Will the old grudges between Indian and white, thought to have been laid to rest by the war, flare up again between these two boys?

Keywords: Friendship; Multiple Voices

Rinaldi, Ann.

The Second Bend in the River. **Scholastic, 1997. 978-0-590-74258-0 (hardcover); 978-0-590-74259-7 (softcover). 280pp. ◾J**

Living in Ohio Territory, on the very edge of the frontier, means that Rebecca Galloway has a lot of chores. The only girl in a family of boys, Rebecca helps her mother, loves books, and is afraid of Indians. Her opinion slowly changes as she gets to know one Indian—the Shawnee chief Tecumseh. He first visits Rebecca's home when she is seven, because the Galloway home is on the land that was Tecumseh's childhood village. Over the years Tecumseh keeps visiting, bringing gifts for everyone in the family but particularly Rebecca. She learns about Indian ways and beliefs, and Rebecca teaches Tecumseh about grammar and literature. By the time Rebecca is sixteen, Tecumseh has become more than a friend to her. Choosing Tecumseh would change her whole life. But can she turn her back on the man she loves?

Keywords: Family; Romance

Speare, Elizabeth George.

The Sign of the Beaver. **Houghton Mifflin, 1983. 978-0-395-33890-2 (hardcover); 978-0-440-47900-0 (softcover). 144pp. ◾M ◾J**

After helping his father build their family a cabin in the remote Maine woods, Matt is a little nervous about being left there to guard it. While his father sets off to bring his mother and sister from Massachusetts, thirteen-year-old Matt passes the days at first doing chores and hunting with his father's gun. He feels safe knowing he has the gun for protection. But then a wandering traveler steals the gun, and a bear breaks into the cabin and destroys most of Matt's supplies. Desperate, he risks climbing a bee tree for some honey, only to receive many bee stings. He's rescued by an Indian named Saknis, who takes care of Matt and brings him food. In payment for this debt, Saknis asks Matt to teach his grandson,

Attean, how to read English. It's slow going at first, but eventually the boys become friends. As Matt learns Indian ways, he begins to see how Attean's way of life is slowly fading away.

Awards: Newbery Honor Book; Scott O'Dell Award for Historical Fiction

Keywords: Friendship; Survival

American Revolution: 1776–1800

Eventually the colonies refused to pay taxes that they had not agreed to, despite what Britain said. Launching a revolution against Great Britain created great upheaval in the lives of all colonists, regardless of which side of the conflict they supported. Yet in the end, the colonists would become free and independent.

Anderson, Laurie Halse.

Chains. **Simon & Schuster Children's Publishing, 2008. 978-1-4169-0585-1 (hardcover); 978-1-4169-0586-8 (softcover). 320pp. 🄜 🄙**

The death of her owner was supposed to bring freedom for Isabel and her sister. Instead, the two girls are split up and sold to different owners. Isabel ends up in New York City, working with a family that is loyal to Great Britain. The colonies have just begun their revolt against Britain, but New York is full of Tories. Angry and betrayed, Isabel longs for a way to escape, find her sister, and gain their freedom. Curzon, the young Patriot she meets, says that freedom can be had if the rebels win their fight. He urges Isabel to spy on the family she works for. But Isabel isn't sure. Perhaps instead of choosing a side, she should just do whatever will benefit herself.

Awards: National Book Award Finalist; Scott O'Dell Award for Historical Fiction

Keywords: Political Rebellions; Sisters; Slavery; Spies

Fever 1793. **Simon & Schuster's Children's Publishing, 2000. 978-0-689-83858-3 (hardcover); 978-0-689-84891-9 (softcover). 251pp. 🄜 🄙**

Philadelphia, the capital of the young United States of America, is a busy, thriving city. Mattie and her mother, helped by Mattie's grandfather, run a popular coffee house, a place where people gather to exchange news and gossip. Mattie resents the work that she has to do, especially as a strange sickness starts spreading through Philadelphia and she has to work even harder. But as more and more people get sick, many of them dying, Mattie has to shoulder more and more burdens. How will she get through this horrible summer?

Read-alike: For a nonfiction take on the history in this book, you might also like *An American Plague: The True and Terrifying Story of the Yellow Fever Epidemic of 1793* by Jim Murphy.

Keywords: Coming-of-age; Family; Illness

Anderson, M. T.

The Astonishing Life of Octavian Nothing, Traitor to the Nation. Ⓢ

Anderson's vivid reimaging of the life of one young slave boy is set against the backdrop of the American Revolution. Written in a late eighteenth-century style, these two books will reward patient readers.

Keywords: Identity; Political Rebellions; Slavery

Volume I, The Pox Party. **Candlewick, 2006. 978-0-7636-2402-6 (hardcover); 978-0-7636-3679-1 (softcover). 368pp.**

A genre-defying first volume of an epic story. For as long as he can remember, young Octavian has been forbidden to enter one room in the vast house he lives in. He doesn't think much of it, because he has other occupations. The estate he lives on is part of the Novanglian College of Lucidity. The college is made up of a group of philosophers and thinkers, applying their concepts from the Age of Reason in various experiments. While all the philosophers are identified by numbers, Octavian and his mother have names. Cassiopeia, his mother, is an African princess, full of charm and very beautiful. Octavian is given a complete classical education, not realizing that he and his mother are part of the philosophers' experiments. And when he learns just what this experiment is, it will force him to open his eyes to the reality of the outside world.

Awards: Printz Honor Book; National Book Award

Volume II, The Kingdom on the Waves. **Candlewick, 2008. 978-0-7636-2950-2 (hardcover); 978-0-7636-4626-4 (softcover). 592pp.**

The College of Lucidity is broken up, many of its members victims of a failed smallpox inoculation. Among the dead is Octavian's mother. With his mother gone, Octavian and his kind tutor, Dr. Trefusis, have fled the countryside for the town of Boston. Freed from his masters but still a slave, Octavian seeks a method to become fully free. At first he just struggles to survive, supporting himself and Dr. Trefusis by playing the violin. But soon he cannot ignore the conflict engulfing the American continent, pitting the colonies against the British. Focused on a future for himself and his fellow slaves, Octavian enlists in a British regiment, having been promised freedom after his service is completed. Will Octavian gain the prize he covets?

Awards: Printz Honor Book

Blackwood, Gary.

📖 *The Year of the Hangman.* **Dutton Juvenile, 2002. 978-0-525-46921-6 (hardcover); 978-0-14-240078-4 (softcover). 196pp. Ⓜ Ⓙ**

History is the past; how it happened was what happened. But what if something had changed? What if the British had won the American Revolution? In such a world, Creighton Brown is a wild young British man, spending his money on drinks and gambling. Frustrated with his behavior, his mother arranges to have him shipped off to the colonies, into the care of Creighton's uncle. His arrival is only the beginning of Creighton's adventures in America. Eventually he crosses paths with Benjamin Franklin, the publisher of the treasonous newspaper *Liberty Tree*. It's expected that Creighton will be a British spy, passing information about the American rebels to the British Army. But perhaps Creighton won't make the obvious choice. Perhaps he'll choose to turn his back on Britain and make his stand as an American.

Keywords: Alternate Universe; Political Rebellions; Spies

Collier, James Lincoln, and Christopher Collier.

My Brother Sam Is Dead. Scholastic, 1977. 978-0-590-40666-6 (hardcover); 978-0-439-78360-6 (softcover). 182pp. 🄼 🄹

It seems as though for Tim's whole life, people have been arguing about life in the colonies. It's not a simple debate with two sides; people take lots of different positions. Tim doesn't really understand it all, so he'd rather think about his own life: playing with his friend Jerry, doing his chores, and wanting to be like his big brother Sam. Sam is smart and brave and stubborn—perhaps too stubborn. Sam is convinced that the time has come to fight the Lobsterbacks, to show the King and Parliament that they can't tax the colonies without restraint. But Sam and Tim's father doesn't see the political situation like that. He's an Englishman, who owes loyalty and respect to the King. Most people in their Connecticut town feel that way. When Sam steals his father's gun and runs off to join the Patriots, he does more than risk his life. He brings the conflicts of the American Revolution into his town and his family.

Awards: Newbery Honor Book

Keywords: Brothers; Coming-of-age; Family; Political Rebellions

War Comes to Willy Freeman. Delacorte, 1983. 978-0-385-29235-1 (hardcover); 978-0-440-49504-8 (softcover). 192pp. 🄼 🄹

Her real name is Wilhelmina, but everyone calls her Willy. She's a free black, living on Long Island Sound near the village of Groton, Connecticut. Seeing her father killed by Redcoats sends Willy running. Her mother has been taken by the British to New York, and Willy has no place safe to stay. Going to New York would be incredibly dangerous; without her freedom papers, Willy is likely to be sold to the West Indies as a slave. But she has to find her mother. Disguising herself as a boy, Willy makes the journey to the city and finds help at the Fraunces Tavern. But even with the help of her new friends, it'll take a miracle to find her mother.

Keywords: Disguised as Boy; Political Rebellions; Slavery

Fast, Howard.

April Morning. **Crown Publishing Group, 1961. 978-0-517-50681-3 (hardcover); 978-0-553-27322-9 (softcover). 204pp. ⓂⒿ**

> Adults have always complained about teenagers. It's no different in 1775 in the village of Concord. Adam Cooper questions and doubts his father, religion, and other aspects of life. He kisses a local girl and curses. To his stern father, all this makes Adam a child, not a man. Adam keeps looking for something that will make his father see how mature he really is. Will his chance come as tensions between Britain and the colonies reach the boiling point? Adam will get the answer when the redcoats march into the village on April 19, and the shot heard 'round the world is fired.
>
> **Keywords:** Father and Child; Political Rebellions

Forbes, Esther.

Johnny Tremain. **Houghton Mifflin, 1943. 978-0-395-06766-6 (hardcover); 978-0-440-94250-4 (softcover). 288pp. ⓂⒿ**

> In the world of 1773 Boston, Johnny Tremain was one of the most talented silversmiths in town. Although only an apprentice, he basically runs the shop, handling all the difficult assignments. However, when his hand is injured in an accident, Johnny's future is in jeopardy. Released from his apprenticeship, he finds a new job as a delivery boy for the *Boston Observer*, a weekly newspaper that promotes the idea of the American colonies' freedom from British oppression. As Johnny gets caught up in revolutionary causes, he slowly finds a new place for himself. No longer a spoiled, cocky boy, Johnny becomes a strong, steady young man, just in time to play a major part in the early days of the American Revolution.
>
> **Awards:** Newbery Medal
>
> **Keywords:** Coming-of-age; Political Rebellions

Klass, Sheila Solomon.

Soldier's Secret: The Story of Deborah Sampson. **Henry Holt, 2009. 978-0-8050-8200-5 (hardcover). 224pp. ⓂⒿ**

> For a strong, smart woman in the America of the late 1700s, there were no more choices than for any other woman. The only choice, the only respectable choice, was marriage, running a household, and raising children. Although some women were independent, they were viewed as odd or of questionable morals. Deborah Sampson, a masterless woman, is as independent as any woman could be. She works as a teacher and earns her keep. But it isn't enough for Deborah. So she makes herself a suit of men's clothes, creates a corset that flattens her breasts, and joins the army. It's after the British defeat at Yorktown, but even though the

American Revolution is over, there is still guerrilla fighting and a need for soldiers. Deborah, now known as Robert Shurtliff, agrees to serve two years. As Shurtliff, she is wounded twice, fights bravely, and is discovered by a doctor who treats her during a yellow fever epidemic. But when the doctor keeps her secret, Deborah is able to continue her deception, until she reaches the point when she is ready to be Deborah Sampson again.

Keywords: Disguised as Boy; Political Rebellions; Women Soldiers

Lavender, William.

Just Jane: A Daughter of England Caught in the Struggle of the American Revolution. Gulliver Books, 2002. 978-0-15-202587-8 (hardcover); 978-0-439-81070-8 (softcover). 288pp. ⬛

She may be the daughter of an English earl, but Lady Jane Prentice is left penniless when he dies. So she sails to America, settling with her family in South Carolina. It is 1776, and unrest is stirring in the colonies. Patriots and Loyalists are finding it harder and harder to discuss politics, which divides friend from friend and family from family. Jane is dismayed to find this is the case within her family. Her uncle Robert, a Loyalist, even refuses to let her visit his cousin Hugh, a staunch Patriot. Curious and intelligent, Jane seeks out Simon Cordwyn, the schoolmaster, for answers to her questions. As the dispute between Britain and the colonies edges closer to war, Jane feels caught in the middle. And if she picks a side, she might lose more than a war: the new family and life she has found.

Keywords: Family; Political Rebellions

O'Dell, Scott.

Sarah Bishop. Houghton Mifflin Harcourt, 1980. 978-0-395-29185-6 (hardcover); 978-0-590-44651-8 (softcover). 192pp. ⬛ ⬛

The American Revolution, like the Civil War, also divided families. The Bishop family of Long Island, in the colony of New York, were Tories and loyal to King George. Yet they were outnumbered in their village; most families were Patriots. When Sarah's brother Chad joins the Patriot militia, it splits the family in two. Even worse, it's not enough to protect Sarah and her father from Patriot raiding parties. One of those groups of marauders runs off their animals, burns their crops, and tars and feathers Sarah's father. When he dies, fifteen-year-old Sarah is left on her own. She is determined to stay free and keep her independence, even as her brother is a British prisoner. Sarah journeys to many places, including New York City and the wilderness, all with the British chasing her seeking to arrest her. But through it all, she finds she has the strength to win her own independence.

Keywords: Brothers and Sisters; Political Rebellions; Women's Roles

Paulsen, Gary.

Woods Runner. **Wendy Lamb Books, 2010. 978-0-385-73884-2 (hardcover); 978-0-375-85908-3 (softcover). 176pp. Ⓜ Ⓙ**

> The wooded land of Pennsylvania is far away from the conflicts of the eastern cities. When news reaches Samuel and his family of the skirmishes at Lexington and Concord, they don't think much of it. But then Samuel's parents are captured by a band of British soldiers and Iroquois. Samuel escapes their fate because he was hunting in the forest. Now, with his parents gone, he will use all his skills for tracking and survival to rescue them. But when the trail leads to the city of New York, how will a fourteen-year-old frontier boy cope with the big city?
>
> **Keywords:** Family; Native American Issues; Survival

Rinaldi, Ann.

Cast Two Shadows: The American Revolution in the South. **Gulliver Books, 1998. 978-0-15-200881-9 (hardcover); 978-0-15-205077-1 (softcover). 288pp. Ⓜ Ⓙ**

> Caroline's heart is hardened against the British soldiers when they hang her best friend. When you attack a column of British troops, punishment is expected—but perhaps not as severe when the attacker is a fourteen-year-old boy. With British troops taking over her home and imprisoning her father, Caroline is even more loathful of the British and what this war is doing. In 1780 South Carolina, war between the British and the colonists gives the locals plenty of chances to switch sides and attempt to settle old scores. Caroline thinks this is all madness, but then, she's an outsider with a secret: Although her father is white, her mother is black and one of her father's slaves. Brought up in the plantation house as a daughter of her father's white wife, Caroline is restricted from spending time with her secret grandmother, Miz Melindy. But when her older brother Johnny is injured, it is up to Caroline and Miz Melindy to save him.
>
> **Keywords:** Family; Political Rebellions; Slavery

Finishing Becca: A Story About Peggy Shippen and Benedict Arnold. **Harcourt Children's Books, 1994. 978-0-15-200880-2 (hardcover); 978-0-15-205079-5 (softcover). 384pp. Ⓙ**

> Fourteen-year-old Becca feels like there are pieces of herself missing—pieces that once found will let her be the person she's meant to be. Perhaps her new job working for the Shippen family will help with her quest. But Becca's eyes are opened to a new world when she serves as a maid to young Peggy Shippen. Peggy is rich, spoiled, and beautiful, the jewel of her Quaker family. Peggy is supposed to help educate Becca, to finish her off and turn her into a lady. Becca finds that the education she receives only prepares her to be deceitful and duplicitous. As Becca watches Peggy move through a Philadelphia split between Patriots and Loyalists, she wonders how it will all end. When Peggy marries the Patriot general Benedict Arnold, Becca is there as Peggy leads her husband to his destruction.

Read-alike: *The Real Benedict Arnold* by Jim Murphy lets you discover the man that Peggy Shippen married.

Keywords: Identity; Political Rebellions

A Ride into Morning: The Story of Tempe Wick. **Harcourt Children's Books, 1991. 978-0-15-200573-3 (hardcover); 978-0-15-204683-5 (softcover). 368pp. Ⓜ Ⓙ**

Mary Cooper is caught between several powerful people. When she declares that she's a Patriot, her Loyalist family ship her off to various relatives until she ends up in the home of her Aunt Mary and her cousin Tempe. Tempe Wick is beautiful, stubborn, and witty, and Mary knows she can't compare to her. It's the winter of 1781–1782, and the colonial troops are camped for the winter in Morristown, New Jersey, on the Wick family farm. To escape all the stress, Tempe takes rides on her beloved horse— and might be helping stir up mutiny. Can Mary prevent her cousin from making a mistake she'll regret? And what fate awaits Mary? Can she find someplace to belong?

Keywords: Family; Political Rebellions

The Secret of Sarah Revere. **Harcourt Children's Books, 1995. 978-0-15-200393-7 (hardcover); 978-0-15-204684-2 (softcover). 336pp. Ⓙ**

Thirteen-year-old Sarah is struggling with questions that confuse adults. Many people wonder about Sarah's father, Paul Revere. Did he see who fired the first shot at Lexington? Was his answer the reason his deposition was returned rather than sent to England? Many people visit the Revere home, wanting these answers. Sarah is more worried about her stepmother, Rachel. When Rachel arrived, she pulled Sarah's father out of his grief over the death of his first wife. And she's been a good mother to Sarah and her siblings. But Sarah's father is often away on independence matters, and his friend Dr. Warren, who often visits, seems too close to Rachel. Sarah must decide if the truth is more important than the appearance of the truth.

Keywords: Family

Time Enough for Drums. **Laurel Leaf, 2000. 978-0-440-22850-9 (softcover). 256pp. Ⓙ**

The Battles of Lexington and Concord occurred only last spring, but Jemima Emerson's family was already split before those battles. Her grandfather and older sister are Tories; her older brothers and parents are Patriots. Jemima may only be fifteen, but she's a staunch Patriot, too. She can't understand why her parents remain friends with John Reid, her tutor, as well as the local schoolmaster. John Reid is a definite Tory, loyal to the King of England. What's more, he's aggravating and stern with Jemima, frustrating her even as she wonders why she cares. As the American Revolution begins to coalesce, Jemima's brothers lead their militias into battle, and Jemima learns that her mother has written Patriot essays for a

Philadelphia newspaper. But most surprising of all is what Jemima learns about John Reid.

Keywords: Family; Political Rebellions; Romance

Sterman, Betsy.

Saratoga Secret. **Dial, 1998. 978-0-8037-2332-0 (hardcover); 978-0-439-28230-7 (softcover). 176pp. ◘**

The people who live in the wilderness of northern New York had counted on the lack of roads to keep them safe. The battles between the colonists and the British were all happening in Pennsylvania and New Jersey. Then General Burgoyne invades from Canada, cutting across New York for Albany. If he succeeds, the United States will be cut in two. The British threat strikes fear into Amity Spencer. Her father and the other men of the valley march off to fight the British, leaving behind women and children. At age sixteen, Amity knows she shouldn't be scared, but she can't help worrying. What's more, the only man left is Cheppa John, a peddler Amity had begun to develop feelings for. When Cheppa John disappears, Amity wonders why he left and finds herself in possession of a secret of her own. The Battle of Saratoga might rest on Amity getting her information to the Continental Army.

Keywords: Political Rebellions; Romance

Walter, Mildred Pitts.

Second Daughter: The Story of a Slave Girl. **Scholastic, 1996. 978-0-590-48283-7 (softcover). 211pp. Ⓜ ◘**

In the days leading up to the American Revolution, some slaves were inspired by the ideas of freedom being debated by the Patriots. Perhaps if the colonies were their own nation, all people would be free, including slaves. That's what Bett, a slave in Massachusetts, thinks. With her younger sister Lizzie watching, Bett will wait for freedom, thinking that it will come as revolution begins. Lizzie, stubborn and determined to hang onto her heritage and past, finds it difficult to wait for freedom. One sister will gain her freedom through a most unusual method. In 1781 Bett is able to win her freedom by taking her master to court. By winning her case, Bett's name will be remembered for all time. Based on a real story, a rich story about love and freedom explores life in late eighteenth-century America.

Keywords: Sisters; Slavery

A New Nation: 1800–1900

At the beginning of the nineteenth century, America was still a new country, finding its way internationally and within its borders. By the end of the century it had survived a horrible civil war, expanded its borders from sea to sea, and was positioned as one of the greatest countries in the world. It is a boggling transformation to have occurred in just a hundred years.

Blankslee, Anne R.

A Different Kind of Hero. **Marshall Cavendish, 1997. 978-0-7614-5000-9 (hardcover); 978-0-7614-5147-1 (softcover). 143pp. ⓜ ⓙ**

In the rough and tumble settlement of Miner's Chance, Renny's dad is the unofficial leader. He's big and strong and tough, and he expects Renny to be the same. Although he tries, Renny can never live up to his dad's expectations. Things get even worse when Mrs. Maynard, the owner of one of the mines, insists that her Chinese houseboy be enrolled in school. The miners don't like the Chinese, because the exotic foreigners work jobs at lower pay. If more Chinese come, the miners could lose their jobs, meaning misery for their families. But Renny can't help giving Wong Gum Zi a hand. The tensions in the camp explode when the local priest is unfairly jailed. The miners take matters into their own hands, led by Renny's father, with devastating results. And it's up to Renny to stop the violence—even if it means he'll lose his family.

Keywords: Coming-of-age; Family; Immigrants

Blos, Joan W.

A Gathering of Days: A New England Girl's Journal, 1830–1832. **Charles Scribner's Sons, 1979. 978-0-684-16340-6 (hardcover); 978-0-689-71419-1 (softcover). 144pp. ⓜ ⓙ**

Life in New England is full of work, but also has simple pleasures. Catherine details how much her life changes in two years. Her father remarries, bringing home not just a new mother for Catherine and her sister Matty, but a brother as well. The question of slavery vs. abolition comes to their small New Hampshire village, and Catherine helps a young runaway slave boy. The biggest and worst change is the death of her best friend Cassie. Catherine starts to think, with all these changes, that it'd be better to never grow up. But Catherine can't stop getting older. As the days pass, filled with tasks like quilting and berry-picking, sugaring and breaking out, Catherine records it all in her journal, creating a record that will bring the past to life for Catherine's future great-granddaughter.

Awards: Newbery Medal

Keywords: Coming-of-age; Diary; Slavery

Carvell, Marlene.

Sweetgrass Basket. **Dutton Juvenile, 2005. 978-0-525-47547-7 (hardcover). 256pp. ⓙ**

Mattie and Sarah tell their stories of the way their lives changed. After their mother dies, their father splits up the family, sending all the children to various schools. Mattie and Sarah have been sent to the Carlisle Indian

School in Pennsylvania, where they will be educated and trained for a future career. Although some teachers are kind, others are mean, using physical punishment for small mistakes. Mattie begins to develop her writing ability, nurtured by a caring teacher. But Sarah doesn't like this strange place with all its rules. The two sisters seem to be on different paths, yet they are still sisters. Mattie and Sarah illustrate the experiences of many Native American children who were sent to off-reservation schools.

Keywords: Multiple Voices; Native American Issues; Novel in Verse; Sisters

Donaldson, Joan.

On Viney's Mountain. **Holiday House, 2009. 978-0-8234-2129-9 (hardcover). 231pp. ◑ ⑤**

Viney is stubborn and opinionated, and she's determined to stay free of any man. If she became a wife and mother like all the other girls—as her sister Lizzie wants—she wouldn't be free to weave or to tramp all over the mountain that she loves. But change is coming to Viney's mountain. A group of Englishmen have come to establish a colony, cutting trees and destroying nature. It makes Viney madder than a hornet to see what they're doing, especially because one of the foreigners doesn't leave her alone. Charlie wants to learn how to farm, but he knows more about Latin and science than about practical things. Viney would like to learn what Charlie knows . . . and maybe if she's seen with him, people will stop talking about her unnatural ways. But when playacting becomes reality, how will Viney deal with the choice in front of her? She can choose Charlie or freedom. Viney learns a hard lesson: Perhaps freedom is meaningless if you are unhappy.

Keywords: Coming-of-age; Identity; Romance

Duble, Kathleen Benner.

Hearts of Iron. **Margaret K. McElderry, 2006. 978-1-4169-0850-0 (hardcover). 256pp. ⓜ ◑**

Ever since Lucy's father brought her to the mountains, she has loved it there. The small community revolves around the work of the iron furnace; most boys and men work there, including Lucy's best friend Jesse. It's the last job that Jesse wants, though; he wants to join the navy. But in 1820 Connecticut, children are expected to obey their parents. So Jesse is supposed to work at the furnace like his father and brothers, and Lucy is expected to get married and leave the mountains. However, neither Lucy nor Jesse is able to meet these expectations, especially once years of friendship turn into love. Jesse and Lucy find out if their love is strong enough to survive a major test.

Keywords: Coming-of-age; Romance

Durrant, Lynda.

Imperfections. **Clarion Books, 2008. 978-0-547-00357-3 (hardcover). 176pp.** Ⓜ Ⓙ

Coming to the Shaker community in Pleasant Hill, Kentucky, is a chance for Rosemary Elizabeth to escape her abusive father, keep her family together, and stay safe during the Civil War. For that she's willing to learn Shaker ways. Some of them are good: the simple but delicious food, the clean rooms in the white buildings. Others, though, like the separation of the sexes, are very hard to follow. Rosemary Elizabeth wants to stay at Pleasant Hill, even though she's kept away from her brother and she learns her mother has left them there. She tries very hard to be perfect like all the other Shakers. But it seems that Rosemary Elizabeth just can't be perfect, no matter how hard she tries. If she can't be the perfect Shaker, Rosemary Elizabeth will have to find a new home.

Keywords: Family; Shakers

Fletcher, Susan.

Walk Across the Sea. **Atheneum, 2001. 978-0-689-84133-0 (hardcover); 978-0-689-85707-2 (softcover). 214pp.** Ⓜ Ⓙ

On the California coast, the ocean is never far away. That's especially true for Eliza Jane, who lives with her parents in a lighthouse. The lighthouse is separated from land except during low tide. One day Eliza sees a boy—a China boy—on the rocks. When he helps save her life, she becomes curious about him. Many people think the Chinese are good-for-nothing heathens. They work longer, and for less money, than white people, but in many nearby towns, the Chinese have been driven away. Will that happen in Eliza's hometown? Or will Eliza and Wah Chung form a friendship that could make a difference?

Keywords: Friendship; Immigrants

Gaeddert, Louann.

Hope. **Atheneum, 1995. 978-0-689-80128-0 (hardcover); 978-0-689-80382-6 (softcover). 160pp.** Ⓜ

Life in a Shaker community is the last thing Hope wanted. They have strange rules and strange ways. But worst of all, Hope is separated from her brother, John. All Hope wants is for their father to return for them. On the other hand, John likes living with the Shakers. There's always plenty of food and warm rooms, and the Shakers are kind and never hit children. Full bellies, easy chores, and no corporal punishment are not things known to many children in 1851. Even though Hope finds things to like about the

Shakers, she can't give up on her dream of being a family again—a family of Pa, Hope, and John.

Keywords: Family; Multiple Voices; Shakers

Godbersen, Anna.

The Luxe Series. ⬛ ⬛

Melding Edith Wharton morals with natural teenage instincts, Anna Godbersen shows that wealthy teens have always misbehaved, according to their elders.

Keywords: Family; Multiple Voices; Romance; Sisters; Women's Roles

The Luxe. HarperCollins, 2007. 978-0-06-134566-1 (hardcover); 978-0-06-134568-5 (softcover). 448pp.

> All of New York is distraught at the death of Elizabeth Holland. She was a perfect example of a well-brought-up daughter of an established family. She left behind many mourners: her mother, her bohemian sister Diana, her charmingly devious friend Penelope, and her fiancé, the playboy Henry. But while everyone says the right things, people can't help talking about the strange circumstances of Elizabeth's death. Was it an accident—or murder? As the nineteenth century draws closer to its end, New York society will ask how Elizabeth died, yet few will realize that the real question is why Elizabeth wanted everyone to think she *had* died.

Rumors. HarperCollins, 2008. 978-0-06-134569-2 (hardcover); 978-0-06-134571-5 (softcover). 432pp.

> As 1899 draws to a close, New York's finest families look forward to the new year, which will hopefully be free of this year's sadness. But now that Elizabeth Holland has been gone two months, people are moving on. Penelope Hayes, her best friend, is painting herself as a respectable society daughter, angling for marriage. Her intended fiancé is Henry Schoonmaker, Elizabeth's former betrothed, who at one time had a sizzling chemistry with Penelope. Meanwhile, Lina Broud is trying to establish herself in society, but it's difficult without a family name or riches. And then there's Diana Holland, who knows that her sister is not dead, but in California with the man she loves. Will Diana be as lucky as her sister and get the man she loves? That's the question, and Diana will have to go toe-to-toe with Penelope Hayes to be with Henry.

Envy. HarperTeen, 2009. 978-0-06-134572-2 (hardcover); 978-0-06-134574-6 (softcover). 416pp.

> The start of a new year has redrawn New York society. Elizabeth Holland returns to New York, keeping her marriage to the lower-class Will Keller a secret. But the baby that was created out of their love must have a father, because no one knows that Elizabeth is a widow. Diana, Elizabeth's sister,

has to face the loss of Henry Schoonmaker—but to marriage, not death. Diana tries to be the perfect society debutante, but the chance to really be with Henry will inspire a return to her impulsive ways. Carolina Broad is now the most popular girl in New York. Only a few people know her true background . . . and one of those people is trying to reveal it. Then there's Penelope Hayes Schoonmaker, finally in possession of the status she coveted. But her marriage is only a façade, one that could easily crumble. Upper-class life in New York remains fuel for gossip, even in 1900.

Splendor. HarperCollins, 2009. 978-0-06-162631-9 (hardcover); 978-0-06-162633-3 (softcover). 400pp.

As the first summer of the twentieth century begins, the citizens of Manhattan find their lives are heating up. Diana Holland, after following her heart—and Henry Schoonmaker—to Cuba, finds out just how deeply she loves. Henry sees finding Diana as evidence of the rightness of their love, even though his wife remains in New York. But Penelope Hayes Schoonmaker isn't suffering, for a real prince has arrived in the city, and Penelope dreams of becoming royalty. Elizabeth Holland, now married to Snowden Cairns in a marriage of protection, discovers her feelings for her husband are changing and growing. And for Carolina Broad, formerly Elizabeth's maid, her world of riches is vastly improved with a new love. As these six young people strive for love, power, or security, they determine whether the splendor is worth the risk.

Gray, Dianne E.

Together Apart. **Houghton Mifflin Harcourt, 2002. 978-0-618-18721-8 (hardcover). 208pp.** 🅜 🅙

After a natural disaster, it can be difficult to carry on. Fourteen-year-old Hannah is still dealing with her guilt and grief over the loss of her two brothers in the Blizzard of 1888. Her brothers perished in their schoolhouse while Hannah survived, all because she was out on the prairie. She sheltered inside a haystack with Isaac, the fifteen-year-old stepson of the local ne'er-do-well. They weren't friends before the blizzard—although Isaac was sweet on her—but surviving the storm together created a connection between them. Now, a few months later, they are brought together when they are both hired by the widow Eliza Moore. Mrs. Moore, who has progressive ideas, encourages both of them in different ways. Hannah and Isaac see Mrs. Moore's house as a sanctuary. But someday soon, they will have to leave and see if they're strong enough to survive again.

Keywords: Disasters; Romance

Tomorrow, the River. **Houghton Mifflin, 2006. 978-0-618-56329-6 (hardcover). 240pp. Ⓜ Ⓙ**

> In the Midwest of 1896, a fourteen-year-old girl might be too young to travel on her own. Megan is sent to spend the summer with her older sister, serving as a mother's helper. Her train journey, with unusual characters and new scenery, makes Megan contemplate just who she is. She would seem to have only one talent—being good. Her mother has made sure of that, with all the rules she has drummed into Megan. But in reality, Megan is also good at seeing things and finding that the unexpected is beautiful. As she spends time with her sister Hannah and Hannah's family, Megan begins to throw away all those rules that didn't help her at all. And as they travel along the Mississippi River in a paddle wheel steamboat, Megan's eyes will find many things to see.
>
> **Keywords:** Coming-of-age; Family

Heuston, Kimberly.

The Shakeress. **Hand Print, 2002. 978-1-886910-56-0 (hardcover); 978-1-59078-575-1 (softcover). 208pp. Ⓜ Ⓙ**

> To prevent their family from being completely separated, Naomi and her orphaned siblings join a Shaker community. Naomi and her sister are apart from their brothers, but they are well-fed and prepared for good careers. Naomi, who has a talent for healing, is trained in the making of herbal cures and potions. Life among the Shakers is peaceful, yet Naomi finds herself looking for more. At age sixteen she leaves the Shakers, finding herself a position as a herbalist. She struggles to hear God's voice, to be shown her path. Is it in the arms of Joseph Fairbanks, as a wife and mother? Is it being an independent woman, healing others? Or is there a third choice for Naomi? Only by searching her heart will she find the answer.
>
> **Keywords:** Family; Nineteenth Century; Shakers; Women's Roles

Hill, Donna.

Shipwreck Season. **Clarion, 1998. 978-0-395-86614-6 (hardcover). 224pp. Ⓙ**

> The death of his father has allowed Daniel to fall in with a bad crowd. He failed his classes, started drinking, and gambled with his friends. Desperate, his mother sends him to spend the winter with her brother, Captain Alder. Daniel, a conceited young man, is determined not to perform duties unbefitting a gentleman. Working with his uncle and the other men of the Life Saving Service is hard, physical, demanding work. Daniel butts heads with his uncle and thinks the other men are ruffians. But slowly Daniel begins to respect these men who risk their lives to save people from shipwrecks. As Daniel begins to fit in, using his athletic skills, he will slowly learn how to change from wild boy to honest man.
>
> **Keywords:** Coming-of-age; Family

Hostetter, Joyce Moyer.

Healing Water: A Hawaiian Story. Calkins Creek Books, 2008. 978-1-59078-514-0 (hardcover). 217pp. **J** **S**

Hawaii in the 1860s is a paradise on Earth. Pia has grown up there, living with his mother and little sister. He doesn't know who his father is, but at least he has Kamaka. Seven years older than Pia, Kamaka has taught him the things he needs to know. But at age thirteen everything changes for Pia when he displays the sores of leprosy. Due to the law and public opinion, those with leprosy must be isolated. Staying in a hospital, Pia waits for Kamaka to come visit, but he never does. His mother cries over losing her son, because a leper is like someone dead. Soon Pia is taken along with other afflicted people to the leper colony on Molokai. There, among people disfigured by disease, Pia lets his anger make him hard and solitary. It is only thanks to a kindly priest that Pia begins to let go of his pain and form a new family.

Keywords: Coming-of-age; Friendship; Illness

Ingold, Jeanette.

Mountain Solo. Harcourt, 2003. 978-0-15-202670-7 (hardcover); 978-0-15-205358-1 (softcover). 320pp. **J**

Tess showed signs of being a musical prodigy early. By the time she was six, her mother had pushed her into leaving their Montana home for a better violin teacher, starting Tess on a merry-go-round of competition and lessons. But at age sixteen it all falls apart when Tess plays badly during a symphony performance. She leaves New York and returns to Montana, staying with her dad and his new family. As she tries to rediscover her love for music, Tess helps her stepmother with a project. A historian, her stepmother is exploring a homestead site along the Rattlesnake River. The homesteader, Frederik Bottner, was a German orphan who also played the violin. As Tess learns about Frederik, his story of hardship and struggle is also told. Through it all, he still had his fiddle. Can Frederik's example teach Tess something important, something that she needs to know?

Keywords: Multiple Voices; Music

Ives, David.

Scrib. HarperCollins, 2005. 978-0-06-059841-9 (hardcover). 208pp. **M** **J**

The day before he turned thirteen, William Stanley Christmas set out for the West, leaving behind a letter for his mother. He was tired of being scolded for bad spelling and grammar, tired of feeling hemmed in, and tired of all his mother's rules. Becoming Billy Christmas, he starts traveling in the West, writing letters for those who can't. His clients range from

Pierre the Paiute Indian to the lovestruck Romulus, even Crazy James Kincaid the murderer. As the War Between the States goes on, Billy travels through the West. With language that captures the feel of the time and the people, follow along on Scrib's journey.

Keywords: Humor; Writing

Karr, Kathleen.

The Boxer. **Farrar, Straus & Giroux, 2000. 978-0-374-30921-3 (hardcover); 978-0-374-40886-2 (softcover). 144pp.** 🔲

The Lower East Side of New York City in the late 1800s is the original hard-knocks life. Johnny needs to find a job to help support his family, but the only jobs pay almost nothing. Then he sees a sign advertising for bare-knuckle fighters. After a slow start, Johnny finds success in the ring, making money and plans. He's moved his family to a house in Brooklyn and has put aside some money. He's even starting to think about his future . . . and then his father and his past come back to haunt him.

Keywords: Family; Sports

Kelly, Jacqueline.

The Evolution of Calpurnia Tate. **Henry Holt, 2009. 978-0-8050-8841-0 (hardcover); 978-0-312-65930-1 (softcover). 352pp.** 🅜 🔲

Summer in Texas is hot. The summer of 1899 is particularly hot, leaving Calpurnia—or Callie Vee, as most of her family calls her—reduced to cutting her hair off an inch at a time to escape the heat. Calpurnia doesn't have many other ways of distracting herself from the woes of being the only girl among six brothers, until she starts spending time with her grandfather. A naturalist, he opens Calpurnia's eyes to the world around her. As she starts to observe, she realizes how much she can see if she just waits and watches. And if she goes looking, there's even more to learn, like when her grandfather helps her examine river water, discovering all the tiny creatures that exist in one drop. Callie learns about Darwin's *The Origin of Species*, forms a close relationship with her grandfather, and learns how to set her own path into the new century.

Read-alike: Discover how Charles Darwin wrote *The Origin of Species* in Deborah Heiligman's *Charles and Emma: The Darwins' Leap of Faith.*

Awards: Newbery Honor Book

Keywords: Coming-of-age; Family

Krisher, Trudy.

Uncommon Faith. **Holiday House, 2003. 978-0-8234-1791-9 (hardcover). 263pp.** 🔲 🅢

Times are changing in Millbank, Massachusetts, because of two things: a fire that kills six people and a headstrong girl named Faith Common. After the fire, people are grieving and questioning the nature of their lives. Celia's mother runs off after suffering years of abuse from her husband. Some people wonder how the fire started, while Biddy Bostick thinks she knows. But the fire is just one agent for change. Faith refuses to be pigeonholed into what's proper for a woman. Instead, the fourteen-year-old wants everyone to do what they're best suited for. She starts her campaign by speaking out against a sexist schoolteacher, and she keeps going. What changes can one girl create?

Keywords: Disasters; Multiple Voices; Women's Roles

Landman, Tanya.

I Am Apache. **Candlewick, 2008. 978-0-7636-3664-7 (hardcover); 978-0-7636-4375-1 (softcover). 320pp.** ◑

Seeing her beloved brother be killed changes Siki's life. When a group of Mexican warriors rides into her village, they attack women and children. Siki sees her little brother be run through by a warrior whose face she cannot forget. As a fourteen-year-old, Siki is practically a woman, although she poorly performs female tasks. Her brother's death makes her start on the warrior path. Determined to avenge her brother, Siki learns to make her own weapons and improve her hunting skills. Helped by her tribe's greatest warrior, Siki slowly gains the respect of other warriors—all except Keste, who wants to see Siki fail and be humiliated. He begins to spread rumors about the death of Siki's father, claiming he died dishonorably. Siki faces a challenge that her warrior skills cannot help her with. Can she find a place in her tribe?

Awards: Carnegie Medal Finalist

Keywords: Brothers and Sisters; Native American Issues; Women Soldiers; Women's Roles

Love, D. Anne

I Remember the Alamo. **Holiday House, 1999. 978-0-8234-1426-0 (hardcover); 978-0-440-41697-5 (softcover). 156pp.** ◐ ◑

Jessie's father is full of dreams and grand plans. But none of those plans has worked out, so eleven-year-old Jessie is particularly angry about his newest idea. Moving from Kentucky to Texas sounds like the worst plan yet, but Jessie goes along with the rest of her family. It's a long, hard journey, and Jessie's little sister dies during it. Heartbroken, the family settles down in San Antonio. Jessie makes a new friend, a Mexican girl named Angelina. But her father forbids her to have a Mexican friend, because soon Texas will be at war with Mexico. Jessie defies him, though, too angry at him to obey. When her father, along with her older brother, joins the Texian army, Jessie is left to help her mother survive. Soon, as the battle comes closer to the town, the only safety for the women and children is inside the old mission known as the Alamo.

Keywords: Family; Political Rebellions

McMullan, Margaret.

When I Crossed No-Bob. **Houghton Mifflin Books for Children, 2007. 978-0-618-71715-6 (hardcover); 978-0-547-23763-3 (softcover). 209pp.** 🅜 🅙

Addy is an O'Donnell. In Smith County, Mississippi, that makes her the lowest of the low. Nobody trusts an O'Donnell. So when Addy's mother abandons her during the wedding of Frank Russell, Addy doesn't have anywhere to go. Mr. Frank and his new bride Miss Irene take her in—grudgingly on Frank's part. But Addy likes living with them after just a day, so she works hard to prove herself, to show that an O'Donnell can be good. And she does prove herself, being rewarded with schooling. But then her father returns, and Addy has to go back to No-Bob with him. As she feels herself drawn back into a life she doesn't want, Addy learns whether she's strong enough to fight for the life she wants.

Keywords: Coming-of-age; Family

Napoli, Donna Jo.

📖 *Alligator Bayou.* **Wendy Lamb Books, 2009. 978-0-385-74654-0 (hardcover); 978-0-553-49417-4 (softcover). 288pp.** 🅙 🅢

Being Sicilian in Louisiana makes one an outsider, especially in 1899. Fourteen-year-old Calogero lives with five of his male relatives, working in their grocery store and on their farm stand. They grow and import wonderful fruits and vegetables, and they treat all their customers the same. But because they don't make black customers wait at the back door, the town's whites don't want to buy their produce. Calogero, like the rest of his family, doesn't understand this tension between white and black. And Sicilians aren't as good as whites, but they're not black, either. Calogero is more interested in going on an alligator hunt or being friends with Patricia, a smart black girl. When a misunderstanding sparks a fight between the whites and the Sicilians, Calogero will have to set his own course.

Keywords: African American Issues; Civil Rights; Family; Immigrants

Paterson, Katherine.

Lyddie. **Dutton Juvenile, 1991. 978-0-525-67338-5 (hardcover); 978-0-14-037389-9 (softcover). 192pp.** 🅜 🅙

Vermonters are made of stern stuff. They're stubborn and self-reliant—and no one is more stubborn than Lyddie. She has tried to hold together the family farm even after her mother takes Lyddie's youngest sisters and joins a commune. But when her mother rents the farm to pay debts, Lyddie has to leave. She toils in the local tavern, but then she has an idea. She will travel to Lowell, Massachusetts, and find work in one of the textile mills. A hard-working girl like Lyddie could clear two dollars a week. With those kinds of riches, she could pay the debts on the farm and have it as her own. But working conditions in the mill are brutal, and some workers want to lobby for a union, including Lyddie's new friend Diana. Should Lyddie risk it all and join with Diana, or value her security?

Keywords: Coming-of-age; Family; Friendship

Peck, Richard.

Fair Weather. **Dial, 2001. 978-0-8037-2516-4 (hardcover); 978-0-439-43034-0 (softcover). 140pp.** ⓜ

It's shaping up to be another hot, dusty summer for the Becketts. Lottie is seventeen and in love, Buster is seven and always chasing critters, and Rosie is thirteen and watching it all. One day their mother gets a letter from her sister. Aunt Euterpe has invited them to the World's Columbian Exposition in Chicago: the biggest, brightest, most exciting fair ever to be held! Accompanied by their crotchety, lively grandfather, the children leave for the big city. Once they arrive, they experience all the marvels of Chicago and the fair. There are lectures designed to educate, and beautiful grounds to stroll through. Best of all, there's the Midway, with games and food and celebrities like Buffalo Bill! It's the trip of a lifetime, and Rosie will remember every minute of it.

Keywords: Family; Humor

Reich, Susanna.

Penelope Bailey Takes the Stage. **Marshall Cavendish Children's Books, 2006. 978-0-7614-5287-4 (hardcover). 198pp.** ⓜ ⒥

When her mother has to travel to Hawaii to help her father, Penny finds that she will have to stay in San Francisco. An aspiring actress, Penny hopes that she might get to attend the theater. But her Aunt Phyllis is very proper, and the stage is the last place for a young lady. Prone to blurting out anything she thinks, Penny finds it difficult to adapt to such a formal household. At least she has her cousin Aldy to play with—and there are actual actors living next door! Mr. and Mrs. Prenderwinkel give Penny support, helping her learn more about acting. Penny lets her dreams grow bigger and bigger, imagining performing in front of thousands of people. But Aunt Phyllis is more than ready to squash Penny's dreams; in fact, she thinks it's the moral thing to do. Will Penny become an actress or be forced to live her life by the standards of the day?

Keywords: Coming-of-age; Family; Performing; Women's Roles

Richards, Jame.

Three Rivers Rising: A Novel of the Johnstown Flood. **Knopf Books for Young Readers, 2010. 978-0-375-85885-7 (hardcover). 304pp.** 🔲 🔲

> The love of a separated couple is made more poignant by a natural disaster. Celestia, the sixteen-year-old daughter of one of Pittsburgh's newly rich families, meets Peter at the clubhouse perched by Lake Conemaugh. The lake is actually a reservoir, thousands of gallons of water held back by an earthen dam. Peter lives in the valley below the lake and works as the hired boy at the club. Because of their different status, Celestia and Peter cannot be together without destructive consequences. In the spring of 1889, the rains fall and Peter and Celestia try to find a way to preserve their love. The failure of the dam changes not just their lives, but the lives of everyone in Johnstown.
>
> **Keywords:** Disasters; Multiple Voices; Novel in Verse; Romance

Rinaldi, Ann.

The Coffin Quilt: The Feud Between the Hatfields and the McCoys. **Harcourt Children's Books, 1999. 978-0-15-202015-6 (hardcover); 978-0-15-216450-8 (softcover). 228pp.** 🔲 🔲

> The infamous conflict between the Hatfields and McCoys is re-created in a story about family. Fanny McCoy is the youngest in her family, especially attached to her older sister Roseanna. There's been tension between the McCoys of Kentucky and the Hatfields of West Virginia since the Civil War. When the Hatfields steal McCoy pigs, it sets the stage for a final match to the gasoline of emotions. And the match is lit when Roseanna McCoy runs off with Johnse Hatfield. Nine years of warfare begin between the two families as Fanny watches helplessly. She grows up, becoming a good student and encouraged to consider further schooling by her teacher. But until she can figure out her sister's actions, Fanny won't have the peace to make her own life.
>
> **Keywords:** Family

The Staircase. **Gulliver Books, 2000. 978-0-15-202430-7 (hardcover); 978-0-15-216788-2 (softcover). 240pp.** 🔲 🔲

> Lizzy Enders can't believe her father has left her with the Sisters of Loretto in Santa Fe. Her mother died on the journey west, and her father leaves Lizzy with the nuns while he travels to Colorado. For a determined thirteen-year-old, being left behind is a bitter pill, especially because that means spending more time with stuck-up Elenora. At least she has her horse, Ben. And soon Lizzy will have a new friendship, with the carpenter who is building a spiral staircase in the chapel. His friendship shows Lizzy a new way to look at her situation, just as the carpenter creates something that makes people reexamine the meaning of the word "miracle."
>
> **Keywords:** Coming-of-age; Family

The Quilt Trilogy. 🄜

Following the evolution of one family over several tumultuous decades, this trilogy also shows the power of love and the family bond. Through the quilt pieces the Chelmsfords share, they remember their family.

Keywords: Family; Native American Issues; Romance

A Stitch in Time. Scholastic, 1995. 978-0-590-46056-9 (softcover). 320pp.

> The death of Hannah's mother and the American Revolution had a disastrous effect on her family. Her father is distant and controlling, and as Hannah and her siblings grow up, they find they have to find a way to deal with their father. But it's becoming harder and harder for all of them. Hannah may be only sixteen, but she has held the family together for many years. Now that the family is starting to separate, Hannah wants something that they can each hold on to, to remind them of the power of family. That object will be a quilt. Pieces of it will go with Hannah and her sisters, Abby and Thankful, wherever they go.

Broken Days. Scholastic, 1997. 978-0-590-46054-5 (softcover). 288pp.

> It's a time of upheaval for the Chelmsford family. At the center of it all is Ebie Chelmsford, a confused fourteen-year-old. She doesn't understand why her Aunt Hannah hasn't chosen between her two suitors, the men Ebie knows as Uncle Louis and Uncle Richard. She wishes her mother hadn't left her father, leaving her father without any self-esteem. And most of all, she wishes her cousin Georgie, who is part-Indian, wasn't so crazy. When news arrives that Ebie's Aunt Thankful, captured by Indians years before, has just died, there is sadness. But Thankful's daughter Walking Breeze is coming to live with the Chelmsfords in Salem. Ebie's not sure how to feel about Walking Breeze, and Walking Breeze is equally unsure about her white relatives. Together, the two girls will learn a new definition of family.

The Blue Door. Scholastic, 1999. 978-0-590-46052-1 (softcover). 288pp.

> Being a headstrong, talkative girl in the South could be a detriment to a family. That's what Amanda Videau sees, as the stubborn girl in her family. After disagreeing with her stepmother and making problems, Amanda's grandmother makes plans. First she asks Amanda to stay silent for two weeks, to see the power in not talking. Then she arranges for Amanda to go north, to visit with the Chelmsford family in Massachusetts. Amanda's grandmother wants her to learn independence, but how independent can a fourteen-year-old girl be in 1841? Amanda will find out when she has to work in her great-grandfather's textile mill, hiding from people who wish her ill. Amanda will have to learn how to take care of herself and how family can help with that goal.

Taylor, Kim.

Bowery Girl. Viking Juvenile, 2006. 978-0-670-05966-9 (hardcover); 978-0-14-240903-9 (softcover). 240pp. **S**

The whole of the Bowery, in New York City, has everything that Mollie and Annabelle need. They may make money by picking pockets or having sex, and they only have a one-room tenement apartment. But Mollie and Annabelle are happy, because they are together to share good times and look out for each other. And there are plenty of good times, like drinking in Lefty's saloon and betting on the rat baiting. Best of all is walking down toward the water, seeing how far the construction on the new Brooklyn Bridge has come. But then the girls meet the latest do-gooder to come to the Bowery, who makes rules about what people have to do before they can get a bath at the settlement house. Miss DuPre really means what she says; she really does want to help girls like Mollie and Annabelle. At first Mollie and Annabelle give it a try, with different levels of interest, but maybe, just maybe, they can acquire skills that will let them escape the Bowery and head to Brooklyn. When tragedy strikes, Mollie finds her own way out of the Bowery.

Keywords: Friendship

Wait, Lea.

Wintering Well. Margaret K. McElderry, 2004. 978-0-689-85646-4 (hardcover); 978-0-689-85647-1 (softcover). 192pp. **M J**

An accident changes the lives of Cassie and her brother Will. At age eleven, Cassie should be a young lady, helping her mother in the house. But she'd rather be out in the fields like Will. One day Will's axe slips and cuts deeply into his leg. Will's leg must be amputated, ending his dreams of being a farmer. Once he is healed, Will and Cassie go to the nearby town of Wicasset to live with their older sister. In 1820 Maine, a boy without a leg is an object of stares and whispers. Will slowly tries to find a new occupation. Cassie gets swept up by thoughts of her own future. Could she have something more than a life as a wife and mother? The early days of Maine's statehood, gaining independence and standing on its own, are reflected in the story of Will and Cassie.

Keywords: Brothers and Sisters; Coming-of-age; Physical Disability

Wemmlinger, Raymond.

Booth's Daughter. Calkins Creek Books, 2007. 978-1-932425-86-4 (hardcover). 210pp. **J S**

Edwina Booth is a well-educated, genteel, supportive young lady. She spends time with her friends, develops a relationship with a young artist, and gives comfort to her father, the great actor Edwin Booth. Only one issue brings out her bad side: her uncle, John Wilkes Booth. The assassination of President Garfield reignites interest in her family's past just as her stepmother is dying and her father is planning to travel abroad again. Edwina worries that her absence will cause Downing Vaux, the man she loves, to lose interest in her. As a woman who has planned to support her future husband's artistic career, should she be patient and wait? Or perhaps Edwina needs to find and use her own artistic gifts.

Keywords: Family; Performing; Women's Roles

Wilson, Diane Lee.

Firehorse. **Margaret K. McElderry, 2006. 978-1-4169-1551-5 (hardcover); 978-1-4424-0331-4 (softcover). 336pp.** 🄹 🅂

When her family moves to Boston, Rachel has to give up the thing she loves most: her horse, Peaches. Peaches was more than a horse—she was Rachel's freedom. Now, though, Rachel is in a corset and weighed down by her father's rules and restrictions. But then she gets something to live for in the Governor's Girl. A famous firehorse, Governor's Girl was badly burned in the latest fire to sweep through Boston. Rather than let the horse be destroyed, Rachel begs for the chance to care for her. As Rachel, who dreams of being a veterinarian, cares for the horse, it sparks fights with her autocratic father. But he's also busy chasing down a story about Boston's suspicious fires and inadequate firefighters. When Rachel learns about an illness that's affecting firehorses, it may be that there's a connection between these two stories. But Rachel needs to learn how to deal with her father if she is to save the horses.

Keywords: Animals; Disasters; Father and Child; Women's Roles

Slavery: 1800–1863

As the nineteenth century progressed, the arguments over slavery became more and more heated. The addition of Missouri and Kansas to the Union led to a time known as Bleeding Kansas, when the violence of anti- and pro-slavery groups resulted in the Missouri Compromise. This law said that the balance between slave and free states in the United States had to remain equal. But this solution grew more unworkable as time passed, especially with events like John Brown's raid.

Ayres, Katherine.

North by Night: A Story of the Underground Railroad. **Delacorte Books for Young Readers, 1998. 978-0-385-32564-6 (hardcover); 978-0-440-22747-2 (softcover). 192pp.** 🄼 🄹

In 1850s Ohio, the Fugitive Slave Law turned quiet farms and villages into outposts of rebellion. Quakers and abolitionists opened their homes to slaves fleeing to freedom, serving as stations on the Underground Railroad. Lucy Spencer has been helping her parents hide slaves for several years; now, at age sixteen, she's ready to do more. When a large group of slaves, including a sick pregnant woman, arrives at the Widow Mercer's place, Lucy goes to help. Between Cass, the pregnant slave, and the dynamic Widow Mercer, Lucy finds herself learning a great deal. Will this knowledge be enough to help her choose between two young men—and make her strong enough to keep helping the less fortunate?

Keywords: Coming-of-age; Romance

Ferris, Jean.

Underground. **Farrar, Straus & Giroux, 2007. 978-0-374-37243-9 (hardcover). 176pp.** Ⓜ Ⓙ

Kentucky's Mammoth Cave is a popular tourist spot in the late 1830s. The head guide, Stephen Bishop, may be a slave, but he's well-known and highly regarded for his knowledge of the cave. Deep in the earth, black or white doesn't matter; Stephen is the expert, and he feels a freedom in the cave that he doesn't have above ground. For Charlotte, the new maid at the Mammoth Cave Hotel, Stephen is foolish in spite of all his knowledge. They're both slaves, and freedom is just an illusion. But sixteen-year-old Charlotte can't help being drawn to Stephen, who opens her eye to a larger world. But then Charlotte and Stephen face a dilemma: Runaway slaves, looking for help, come to the Mammoth Cave Hotel. Charlotte wants to help them, but she can't do it on her own. Will Stephen be willing to risk the work he loves to help others find their own freedom?

Keywords: Multiple Voices; Romance

Lester, Julius.

Day of Tears: A Novel in Dialogue. **Hyperion Book, 2005. 978-0-7868-0490-0 (hardcover); 978-1-4231-0409-4 (softcover). 92pp.** Ⓙ

In 1859, what was billed as the largest slave auction in America took place. Over two days, as rain poured down, more than 400 slaves were sold by Pierce Butler. He had to sell them to pay his gambling debts. He regretted having to do it, mostly because of what he was losing. But there were others who knew how wrong it was. People like Butler's daughter, Sarah, not to mention the slaves like Mattie, the cook, and Emma, the nursemaid. The selling of the Butler slaves will echo through time, sending ripples through the lives of everyone involved. The stories of these people are told in multiple voices.

Keywords: Family; Multiple Voices

Paulsen, Gary.

Nightjohn and Sarny. Ⓜ

A stirring look at the pain created by slavery. Though not all slaves were physically abused, all African Americans in bondage knew the emotional pain of being separated from loved ones.

Keywords: Coming-of-age; Family

Nightjohn. Delacorte, 1993. 978-0-385-30838-0 (hardcover); 978-0-440-21936-1 (softcover). 96pp.

> When John is brought to the plantation, Sarny and all the other slaves know he must be a troublemaker. They can tell because his back is covered in scars from whippings. But John is there for a reason, because the Waller plantation is full of misery for the slaves. He's there to teach reading, to show them that their story needs to be told someday. Sarny is the only one to take the chance. If the master finds out she can read, she could be whipped or even lose her thumbs. But Sarny likes learning, especially from John. She's excited at what learning the letters means. But she's young. When her secret is discovered, it means heartache for Sarny and pain for the ones she cares about. Is that enough to make Sarny stop learning?

Sarny. Delacorte, 1997. 978-0-385-32195-2 (hardcover); 978-0-440-21973-6 (softcover). 192pp.

> Sarny has lived to age ninety-four. The current generation has never known slavery, never known the whip or the pain of having their loved ones sold away. In this volume she tells them her story. Sarny grew up, still teaching her fellow slaves to read. She got married, had two children, and saw her husband die from overwork. That was bad enough—but worse was her master selling her children, a week before Union soldiers came and freed all the slaves. So Sarny took off, desperate to find her children. Once she learned that they were in far-off New Orleans, she could not stay on the plantation. She fought her way through deserting Confederates, bounty hunters, and battles to find her children. And once in New Orleans, she found more than her family—she found a mentor and a teacher, the first she had known since Nightjohn.

Rinaldi, Ann.

Come Juneteenth. Harcourt Children's Books, 2007. 978-0-15-205947-7 (hardcover); 978-0-15-206392-4 (softcover). 256pp.

> Is telling a lie ever a kindness? Slave owners in Texas managed to hide the truth about their freedom from their slaves for over two years. That lie would have repercussions for many people, like Luli's family. Ever since she was a baby, Sis Goose has been part of the family. Half-white, she's still a slave technically, but Luli's parents treat her like a daughter. By the time Luli is born and begins to grow up, Sis Goose is her older sister. Luli grows up with Sis Goose and her older brother Gabe, learning how to shoot and spending a lot of time laughing. But as news about the Emancipation

Proclamation begins reaching Texas, whites have to lie to keep their slaves and maintain their way of life. When Sis Goose learns the truth, tragedy unfolds.

Keywords: Sisters

The Letter Writer. **Harcourt Children's Books, 2008. 978-0-15-206402-0 (hardcover); 978-0-547-32785-3 (softcover). 224pp. Ⓜ Ⓙ**

Eleven-year-old Hannah has never fit in with her family. That's because she is the product of an adulterous affair between her father and an English woman. When she was two he brought her to the Southern plantation that his wife and other two children lived on. His death at sea left Hannah adrift. She wants to belong, so when her half-brother Richard orders her to write letters for his blind mother, Hannah happily complies. It's through writing letters that Hannah learns about Nat Turner, a slave who can read and write, make fine furniture, and preach the Gospel. Meeting Nat exposes her to a gentle, loving God, so different from the one Richard preaches about. When Nat asks a favor of Hannah, she does it, not realizing that she has helped set in motion a bloody slave revolt. How will Hannah accept what she has done?

Keywords: Coming-of-age; Family

An Unlikely Friendship: A Novel of Mary Todd Lincoln and Elizabeth Keckley. **Harcourt Children's Books, 2007. 978-0-15-205597-4 (hardcover); 978-0-15-206398-6 (softcover). 243pp. Ⓜ Ⓙ**

Two women are drawn together in spite of their differences and form the friendship of a lifetime. Mary Todd Lincoln was a Southern belle brought up in luxury in Kentucky, in a household that owned slaves. Mammy Sally was a source of love and comfort after the death of her mother and the cruelty of her stepmother. After marrying Abraham Lincoln, Mary Lincoln comes to Washington, D.C., and the White House, joining the social whirl of the nation's capital. There she meets Elizabeth Keckley, an African American woman who is the most successful seamstress in the city. Thanks to her skill with her needle, she had gained freedom for herself and her son. When she meets Mary Lincoln, they realize that there's a connection between them. Together, their friendship helps them survive a climactic, tragic event.

Keywords: Friendship

Wolf by the Ears. **Scholastic, 1993. 978-0-590-43412-6 (softcover). 272pp. Ⓙ**

For young Harriet Hemings, there's no reason to leave Monticello, her mother's opinion notwithstanding. She's taken care of, given good clothes, and well fed. She even has a tutor who has taught her to read and write. But even though she's called a servant, Harriet is actually a slave. And she may be the daughter of Thomas Jefferson. Harriet doesn't want to leave the comfort of Monticello, where the master's shadow touches everything. But in two years, when she turns twenty-one, Harriet will have to make her decision: to stay a slave and be looked after or take her freedom and be responsible for herself. It's a difficult decision, which will require much thought and writing in her journal.

Keywords: Coming-of-age; Family

Westward Expansion: 1848–1920

The discovery of gold in California in 1848 prompted many men to take a risk at acquiring great riches—even though the journey and the work were both long and back-breaking. Miners, on the whole, weren't interested in forming towns and civilizing the West; that was left to the pioneers and the homesteaders. Beginning in 1862, with the Homestead Act, Americans could lay claim to up to 160 acres of land. This sparked an explosion of the population in the vast expanses of the American West. As homesteaders moved west, so did merchants and professionals—not to mention adventurers and con men.

Bruchac, Joseph.

Geronimo. Scholastic, 2006. 978-0-439-35360-1 (hardcover). 240pp. **J**

In 1908 the great warrior Geronimo approaches the end of his life. He has spent twenty years at Fort Sill, after decades spent fighting against the white man, other tribes, and even his own people. But now he is old, and it is up to other people to remember him. So his grandson will tell of how the Apaches were moved from their lands. How the white men sought help from Apache scouts to find hidden settlements, and then went back on their promises to the scouts. How the Apaches escaped and were sometimes caught. But through it all, Geronimo kept leading his people, fighting against the soldiers who treated them all cruelly.

Keywords: Family; Native American Issues

Burks, Brian.

Soldier Boy. Harcourt Children's Books, 1997. 978-0-15-201218-2 (hardcover); 978-0-15-201219-9 (softcover). 160pp. **M J**

Johnny McBane is known as the Kid in Chicago's alleys and back rooms. He's one of the best bare-knuckle boxers in the city, but when he's ordered to throw a fight and refuses, his career comes to an abrupt end. On the run, he joins the army for the money and the chance to see the West. It takes a bit of time to adjust to army life, especially when Johnny sees that not all the promises made to him will be kept. But being assigned to General Custer's regiment is exciting: to serve under Custer, the hero of the Civil War and the scourge of the Indians! What does it matter that Johnny can't ride a horse or fire a gun? Unfortunately, Johnny discovers that this life depends on those skills.

Keywords: Army; Native American Issues

Carbone, Elisa.

📖 *Last Dance on Holladay Street*. **Knopf Books for Young Readers, 2005. 978-0-375-82896-6 (hardcover); 978-0-553-49426-6 (softcover). 208pp.** 🔳

Living on the Colorado prairie in the 1870s is difficult. Thirteen-year-old Eva and her family have had a hard year. First Daddy Walter died of tetanus, and then Mama Kate's consumption got worse. When Mama dies, Eva has no choice but to go to Denver. She knows that her real mother lives on Holladay Street. Eva's mother Sadie always sent money once a year for her—but why did she send Eva away while keeping her other daughter? It's only when she arrives at the house on Holladay Street that Eva realizes two facts. First is that Holladay Street is Denver's red light district, and Sadie is a prostitute. But even more shocking is that Sadie, and all the other women in the house, are white. Eva wasn't prepared for that, because she grew up with black parents and thought she was also black. Now Eva must decide what she is willing to do to be close to the only family she has left.

Keywords: African American Issues; Family

Ferris, Jean.

Much Ado about Grubstake. **Harcourt Children's Books, 2006. 978-0-15-205706-0 (hardcover); 978-0-545-07467-4 (softcover). 272pp.** 🔳

What happens to a mining town when the mines start petering out? In Grubstake, many of the services have closed down in the years since the last big strikes. Now, its population is only sixty-two, and sixteen-year-old Arley is one of Grubstake's residents. She runs a boarding house, scrimping to make ends meet. Arley makes her penny dreadful novels last between the monthly deliveries by train and hopes that Duncan McKenzie, the newspaper editor, will notice her. But life in Grubstake is totally upended when a stranger comes to town. This city slicker is buying up mines, offering cash for claims. This raises Arley's suspicions. Does Mr. Randall really represent someone who wants to turn Grubstake into a mountain resort? Or is it something more unethical? Arley seems to be the only one asking these questions, so she's the only one to get the answers.

Keywords: Coming-of-age; Romance

Lawlor, Laurie.

He Will Go Fearless. **Simon & Schuster Children's, 2006. 978-0-689-86579-4 (hardcover). 205pp.** 🔳 🔳

Life in St. Joseph, Missouri, is like a prison for Billy. He's a tall, strapping boy who looks more like he's nineteen, not fifteen. His stepfather beats him often for laziness, which makes Billy even more eager to run away. Taking some money from the safe in his stepfather's store, Billy plans to head to Virginia City in

Montana Territory. That's where his father is, and Billy will find adventure on the journey. Billy falls in with two fellow adventurers, Rock and Jackson, who are seeking gold in Montana Territory. Will Billy find his fortune or his father? The journey to the frontier is full of challenges for Billy.

Keywords: Coming-of-age; Father and Child

McKernan, Victoria.

The Devil's Paintbox. **Knopf Books for Young Readers, 2009. 978-0-375-83750-0 (hardcover); 978-0-440-23962-8 (softcover). 368pp. ⒥ Ⓢ**

Left alone on their family farm, Aidan and Maddy are slowly starving to death when they're found by Jefferson J. Jackson. Jackson is looking for men to go to Washington Territory, where there are plenty of logging jobs for a strong man. Something about Aidan and Maddy—his pride, her talkativeness—convinces Jackson to bring them along. It'll be a long, difficult journey, one that could end in death for either of them. But thanks to food and respect, Aidan and Maddy begin to grow strong. Aidan learns how to drop some of his pride, how to get along with other men. Thanks to his skill with a bow and arrow, he makes a place for himself in Jackson's wagon train. And that skill will also make Aidan befriend a community of Indians. When those friends are threatened with smallpox, Aidan must find out if he is strong enough now to help someone else.

Keywords: Brothers and Sisters; Native American Issues

Paulsen, Gary.

The Legend of Bass Reeves. **Wendy Lamb Books, 2006. 978-0-385-74661-8 (hardcover); 978-0-553-49429-7 (softcover). 160pp. Ⓜ**

In the Wild West, many of the men who are now called heroes were actually pretty despicable. A notable exception was Bass Reeves, a marshal who lived by a particular code. He didn't shoot first, he served with honor, and he even hunted down his own son when he murdered his wife. And the most unusual thing about Bass Reeves was that he was black. Born into slavery, he gained his freedom and grew up to be of the West's greatest unknown men. It was the lessons he learned from his mother that turned him into that great man. He had to leave her behind to gain his freedom, but that was the last time he ran from the law.

Read-alike: Try another take on Bass Reeves in the illustrated nonfiction book *Bad News for Outlaws: The Remarkable Life of Bass Reeves, Deputy U.S. Marshal* by Vaunda Micheaux Nelson, illustrated by R. Gregory Christie.

Keywords: African American Issues; Slavery

Wilson, Diane Lee.

Black Storm Comin'. **Margaret K. McElderry, 2005. 978-0-689-87137-5 (hardcover); 978-0-689-87138-2 (softcover). 304pp.** ◧

When his father accidentally shoots him in the leg, it's the start of some low times for Colton. His father runs off in shame, leaving Colton with his mother and two sisters. They were heading to California as part of a wagon train, but no one does much to help them, because Colton and his family are mixed race. Soon Colton's mother is sick, and it's up to him to find a doctor and get them to California. But for that, he'll need money . . . and the only way he can get it is by joining the Pony Express. Of course the service doesn't take colored boys, so Colton will not only face a lot of difficult, dangerous riding; he'll have to pass for white. That's a tough job in 1860, as the nation is on the verge of tearing itself apart over slavery. But Colton will face any challenge to save his family.

Keywords: African American Issues; Family

The Gold Rush: 1848–1900

Although gold rushes happened several times before 1848, the California Gold Rush of 1848–1852 was perhaps the first to be widely reported, sparking a free-for-all by people looking to strike it rich. Not only did the Gold Rush make a few fortunes—while destroying many lives—but it was instrumental in California becoming part of the United States. In addition, any future strike of gold would set off another rush, from the Black Hills of Montana to Alaska.

Blos, Joan W.

Letters from the Corrugated Castle: A Novel of Gold Rush California, 1850–1852. **Ginee Seo Books, 2007. 978-0-689-87077-4 (hardcover); 978-0-689-87078-1 (softcover). 320pp.** ◧

Imagine making a long, difficult journey to California. That's what Eldora has done, accompanied by the adoptive parents who have raised her. San Francisco is full of people who have followed the Gold Rush, searching for riches. Eldora is searching for something as well: a feeling of home, someplace that she belongs. And Eldora finds that home, in unexpected ways. She makes friends among fellow emigrants and local Mexicans. Even better, Eldora finds her mother, who had fallen ill years before and had to let Eldora continue on the family's journey without her. The reunion with her mother opens up a new world. But there are many other choices, like seeing the mining camps with her friend Luke. Will Eldora have to make a choice? And what will she choose?

Keywords: Family; Identity

Cadnum, Michael.

Blood Gold. **Viking Juvenile, 2004. 978-0-670-05884-6 (hardcover). 224pp.** 🄹 🅂

William, like many other men in 1849, has set off for the gold fields of California. But although he's interested in striking it rich, it's not his main reason for going. William is on the trail of Ezra Nevin, his former friend, who abandoned William's friend Elizabeth. William is determined to find Ezra and bring him back to make an honest woman of Elizabeth. To do this, William has sailed from New York to the jungles of Panama. After crossing the narrow but treacherous isthmus, trying to avoid dangerous creatures and diseases, reaching the western coast means the journey is only half-over. William will have to gather all his strength and skill to make it to California and find Ezra.

Keywords: Coming-of-age; Panama

Cushman, Karen.

📖 *The Ballad of Lucy Whipple.* **Clarion Books, 1996. 978-0-395-72806-2 (hardcover); 978-0-06-440684-0 (softcover). 208pp.** 🄼 🄹

Some people are designed to stay in one place, and others are destined to roam to new places. California Morning Whipple, contrary to her name, is the former. She'd be much happier if she were in Massachusetts with her grandparents. But her mother has transplanted the whole Whipple family to the settlement of Lucky Diggins, California. Once there, California Morning renames herself Lucy, writes letters to her grandparents, and dreams of going home. Lucy's mother doesn't think much of her dreams or her new name and insists that Lucy earn her keep. As Lucy sells pies to miners, shoots game, and begins to become friends with the boarders, she finds her place. Soon Lucy begins to realize that California is the home she wants.

Keywords: Family; Identity

Hobbs, Will.

Jason's Adventures. 🄼 🄹

Life on the northern frontier, where Canada meets Alaska, was full of adventures and challenges. For Jason, the far north gives him enough excitement to keep his wandering feet firmly planted.

Keywords: Brothers

Jason's Gold. HarperCollins, 1999. 978-0-688-15093-8 (hardcover); 978-0-380-72914-2 (softcover). 240pp.

> The news of a gold strike in the Yukon lights a fire under Jason. He may be only fifteen, but he knows how to survive. Like so many others, he sets off for the north, relying on a $500 inheritance from his father to buy his supplies. Discovering that his older brothers have borrowed his money to use for their own supplies, Jason sets off after them. Through luck, hard work, and an occasional helping hand, Jason makes it to Skagway, the gateway to the Klondike. It's the start of the most dangerous leg of his journey, and Jason's only companion is a husky named King. Can they make it up the Yukon River before winter sets in? And will Jason find his brothers and strike it rich?

Down the Yukon. HarperCollins, 2001. 978-0-688-17472-9 (hardcover); 978-0-380-73309-5 (softcover). 208pp.

> Life in Dawson City for Jason and his brothers is full of hard work. In their sawmill, they turn timber into lumber to supply the city's booming construction. Meanwhile, news of a new gold strike near the city of Nome sets Jason's feet itching. Who cares that Nome is nearly 2,000 miles away in Alaska Territory? After the brothers are cheated out of their sawmill, Jason decides to set out for Nome. If he wins the newly announced race to Nome, the prize is $20,000—a prize that would let him reclaim the sawmill. Together with Jamie, the girl he loves, Jason sets out in a canoe for Nome, traveling down the Yukon River. Jason has a lot riding on this trip; it will take all his survival skills to reach the finish line.

Wood, Frances.

Daughter of Madrugada. **Delacorte, 2002. 978-0-385-32719-0 (hardcover); 978-0-440-41644-9 (softcover). 163pp.** 🅼 🅹

> Her nickname is short for princess, because that's practically what Cesa is. She's the only girl and the eldest child in the de Haro family. Her family lives on a beautiful ranch named after the dawn, *la madrugada*, and Cesa thinks that her life, like the dawn and the land, will be never-changing. But it is 1846, and life in California is changing. After Mexico lost its war with the United States, Californios can now become American citizens, and their land is part of America. This means that Americans are coming in greater numbers to California. They're looking for land and gold—and they will sometimes take what is not theirs. As Cesa sees her world crumbling around her, she must find a way to become a woman in this new world.

> **Keywords:** Coming-of-age; Family; Politics

Pioneers on the Frontier: 1854–1920

Once the news of the breadth of the American continent began to spread, adventurers found their eyes turning westward. Facing the wilds of untamed lands, these settlers found excitement, danger, and freedom. Once the Homestead Act became law in 1862, a land rush began, with settlers hurrying to find the perfect claim.

Holm, Jennifer L.

Boston Jane Adventures. ◨

In 1854 Jane sets out on a five-month journey to Oregon Territory to join her fiancé. A proper young lady like Jane is in for many surprises when she arrives on the untamed frontier, surrounded by unwashed, hairy men and Indians, and no fiancé in sight. But slowly Jane will develop the courage and self-reliance to survive on the frontier—skills that don't negate all her training as a lady.

Keywords: Native American Issues; Nineteenth Century; Romance; Women's Roles

   📖 *Boston Jane: An Adventure.* HarperCollins, 2001. 978-0-06-028738-2 (hardcover); 978-0-375-86204-5 (softcover). 288pp.

     The Chinook Indians of Oregon Territory call her Boston Jane. She's actually Miss Jane Peck of Philadelphia. After a tomboy childhood, Jane decides to become a proper lady by entering Miss Hepplewhite's Young Ladies Academy. She has loved William Baldt since she was eleven, and now that she's sixteen, she has come out to Oregon Territory to marry him. When she arrives, William has been delayed, and Jane will have to find shelter and food from supplies that don't live up to her standards. She discovers that all the rules from the academy don't really apply on the frontier among a group of rough, uncouth men. But perhaps Jane shouldn't be following those rules at all . . . .

   Boston Jane: Wilderness Days. HarperCollins, 2002. 978-0-06-029043-6 (hardcover); 978-0-375-86205-2 (softcover). 244pp.

     Jane is ready to return to Philadelphia—her former fiancé has deserted her, and Oregon Territory is no place for a proper young lady. But then Jane receives the news that her father is dead, and she is now an orphan at sixteen. So she settles in again at Shoalwater Bay, the only white woman among Chinook Indians, white men, and sailors. Doing laundry and mending, baking pies, and other female tasks fall to Jane and help her make money. But she's also able to bargain for services and owns part of an oyster bed. Jane's happy with her new life, even with the frustration of Jehu, the sailor who's in love with her—and she's falling in love with him. Will Jane realize that Shoalwater Bay is not just where she lives, but where her heart is?

Boston Jane: The Claim. HarperCollins, 2004. 978-0-06-029045-0 (hardcover); 978-0-375-86206-9 (softcover). 240pp.

> In Shoalwater Bay, Jane Peck has found her place. She has friends, a job, and a house that's nearly ready for her. Best of all, she has Jehu. The arrival of her archnemesis from Philadelphia, however, sends her whole life into disarray. Sally Biddle is beautiful, charming, and manipulative. She worms her way into the ladies' sewing circle, convincing everyone that Sally and Jane were old friends. But Jane doesn't trust Sally. It's bad enough when Sally makes Jane look unfriendly and jealous, but when Sally starts to play with Jehu, Jane realizes that once and for all, she'll have to stake her claim.

Ketchum, Liza.

Newsgirl. Viking Juvenile, 2009. 978-0-670-01119-3 (hardcover). 336pp. **M** **J**

> Arriving in California leaves Amelia, her mother, and their friend flat broke. Amelia takes advantage of an opportunity and sells the newspapers they used to pack their trunks. These papers have more recent news than the local newsboys' papers, and people in California are desperate for news. But this makes Amelia some enemies: the newsboys, who don't like a girl horning in on their business. With her family's survival depending on her, Amelia takes action. She cuts off her hair, dresses as a boy, and joins the newsboy ranks. Slowly Amelia becomes part of the gang, discovering the freedoms of being a boy and roaming around the city. But what would it be like to be even freer? Stumbling into a hot air balloon and going for a ride exposes Amelia to a whole new challenge: getting home from the gold fields. And if she can do that, she'll be ready to be a girl again.

> **Keywords:** Disguised as Boy; Family; Nineteenth Century; Women's Roles

Kirkpatrick, Katherine.

The Voyage of the Continental. Holiday House, 2002. 978-0-8234-1580-9 (hardcover). 297pp. **J** **S**

> Emeline works in a textile mill in Lowell, Massachusetts. Now that the Civil War is over, there's not a lot of cotton coming out of the South, and the foremen run the mills with an iron hand. When sixteen-year-old Emeline hears about an expedition to far-off Seattle, she is intrigued. Mr. Asa Mercer is outfitting a steamship to carry 500 women to the Pacific Northwest, where they can be teachers, nurses, or storekeepers. It seems too good to be true, especially when Mr. Mercer promises to pay her passage. But what does Emeline have to lose? She sets out on the journey, recording her experiences in her journal. There are misunderstandings, attacks on her friend Ruby, and even the takeover of the

steamship by Mercer's creditors. But her trip is a life-changing experience, and Emeline keeps looking forward to arriving in Seattle for a new life.

Keywords: Diary; Nineteenth Century

Larson, Kirby.

Hattie Big Sky. **Delacorte Books for Young Readers, 2006. 978-0-385-73313-7 (hardcover); 978-0-440-23941-3 (softcover). 304pp. Ⓜ Ⓙ**

There's no chance that a sixteen-year-old girl, all on her own, can handle a homestead: fence and cultivate 320 acres to own the land herself. Yet when Hattie inherits a homestead claim from her uncle, she leaves Iowa behind and moves to Montana, looking for a place where she can belong. After years of feeling unwanted, Hattie is welcomed by the locals, who make her feel at home. While war rages in Europe, her best friend Charlie in its midst, Hattie struggles to survive during a fierce winter. She needs the help of friends like the Muellers. But should she accept the help of Germans, the people who are fighting against her best friend?

Awards: Newbery Honor Book.

Keywords: 1910s; Coming-of-age; Friendship; World War I

McCaughrean, Geraldine.

Stop the Train! **HarperCollins, 2003. 978-0-06-050749-7 (hardcover); 978-0-06-050751-0 (softcover). 304pp. Ⓙ**

Settling in the middle of the prairie is tough, hard work. That's what the people in the town of Florence find out. They all arrived at the same time, when Oklahoma Territory's northwest was opened for settlement. When Cissy and her parents arrive, Florence is just bare land. But soon people are building stores and houses, turning Florence into a fact. Only one settler gives up, selling his claim for fifty dollars to an agent of the railroad. Then the citizens of Florence get awful news: Because they wouldn't sell out to the railroad, which wants the land for a rail yard, the railroad will punish them by not stopping in Florence. Without train service, Florence can't survive. It will take Cissy and the other settlers a lot of ingenuity to stop the train—but that's the one thing the settlers have plenty of.

Awards: Carnegie Medal Finalist

Keywords: Coming-of-age; Nineteenth Century

The Civil War: 1861–1865

The American Civil War was begun over the principle of State's Rights: the idea that the federal government had become too strong, to the detriment of individual states. Yet the perception from the beginning of the war was that the conflict was truly about slavery. As North and South fought to find their future course, a vast number of dramas played out over those four years.

Armstrong, Jennifer.

The Dreams of Mairhe Mehan. **Knopf Books, 1996. 978-0-679-88152-0 (hardcover); 978-0-679-88557-3 (softcover). 119pp. Ⓜ Ⓙ**

> The Irish are the North's laborers. Even as far south as Washington, D.C., there are plenty of jobs for the Irish. But with Italians swarming into America, and the slaves being freed, the Irish are feeling squeezed from two sides. So while Mairhe works in a bar and makes lace, her father falls on the charity of the parish and her brother enlists in the Union Army. Mairhe is caught between her two worlds. Should she dream of Ireland, like her father? Or should she put down roots in America? In the chaos of the capital during the Civil War, Mairhe will have to find her own place.
>
> **Keywords:** Family; Immigrants

Bartoletti, Susan Campbell.

No Man's Land: A Young Soldier's Story. **Blue Sky Press, 1999. 978-0-590-38371-4 (hardcover). 176pp. Ⓜ Ⓙ**

> It's hard work for Thrasher, trying to please his father. No matter what he does or how he does it, Thrasher's actions don't seem good enough. When Thrasher freezes in fear when his father is attacked by a gator, it's the last straw. Thrasher joins the Okefinokee Rifle regiment to fight Yankees, determined to show his father just how brave he really is. At first soldiering is boring, just drilling and walking picket duty. But then glorious news arrives: They will be joining General Stonewall Jackson's troops in Virginia. Thrasher, with old and new friends, will soon be deep in fighting, finding out just what bravery is.
>
> **Keywords:** Army; Confederate; Father and Child

Brenaman, Miriam.

Evvy's Civil War. **Putnam Juvenile, 2002. 978-0-399-23713-3 (hardcover); 978-0-14-240039-5 (softcover). 210pp. Ⓙ**

> Becoming a lady means that Evvy has to confront several distasteful tasks. First and foremost are wearing a corset, managing a hoop skirt, and putting her hair up. But the physical discomfort of growing up is eclipsed by the mental and moral quandaries. Is it wrong for women to be educated? Why does her mother keep having babies despite her frailty? How might a war between the states affect Evvy and her family? Evvy is full of questions, very unladylike ones. As war looms, she must decide whether secrets should be revealed even if they could break her family apart.
>
> **Keywords:** Family; Women's Roles

Bruchac, Joseph.

March Toward the Thunder. **Dial, 2008. 978-0-8037-3188-2 (hardcover); 978-0-14-241446-0 (softcover). 304pp.** 🔲

> "War is hell" is the statement attributed to William Tecumseh Sherman. In the last year of the Civil War, a boy named Louis learns firsthand the truth of this. Louis is a Canadian, but he is also an Abenaki Indian, with a gift for languages. Only fifteen, he does his best to support himself and his mother. When a Union recruiter comes his way, Louis enlists, thinking of money and patriotism. Now a member of the New York 69th—The Fighting Irish—Louis will see action in many bloody battles. There is companionship with some soldiers and prejudice from others. From the Wilderness to Cold Harbor to Reams Station, Louis meets people like Walt Whitman and Clara Barton. Wounded, he is sent home to recover. Once he has healed he faces a choice: stay safe at home, or rejoin his brigade?

> **Keywords:** Army; Native American Issues; Union

Clapp, Patricia.

The Tamarack Tree. **HarperTeen, 1986. 978-0-688-02852-7 (hardcover); 978-0-14-032406-8 (softcover). 224pp.** 🔲

> After the death of their mother, Rosemary is brought from England to America by her older brother Derry. Settling in Vicksburg, Mississippi, Rosemary slowly learns about not just America but the South as well. She likes the people she meets, and she can't understand how such nice people could own slaves. Her brother cautions her to hold her tongue because they are outsiders, but Rosemary can't always stay quiet. With the secession of Southern states and the beginning of the Civil War, Rosemary will have to find her own place over the next two years. But when the Union begins shelling Vickburg, will she be able to preserve the life she has created for herself?

> **Keywords:** Confederate; Immigrants; Women's Roles

Collier, James Lincoln, and Christopher Collier.

With Every Drop of Blood. **Delacorte, 1994. 978-0-385-32028-3 (hardcover); 978-0-440-21983-5 (softcover). 235pp.** 🔲

> In the mountains overlooking the Shenandoah Valley, life has gotten tough. It's 1864, and Union and Confederate forces have been fighting and looting in the valley and surrounding mountains since the start of the war. Johnny is now the man of the house, helping his mother with chores and plowing. He has done that since his father enlisted, but he's become the actual man in the family since his father died from a bullet wound. Johnny's father had enough time to tell Johnny some of the things a man needs to know—and to get a promise from Johnny to stay at home and protect the family. But for

a fourteen-year-old boy, that's a tall order. When the chance comes to earn a lot of money, on what's promised as an easy hauling job to Richmond, Johnny takes it. But the wagon train is attacked by Union troops, and Johnny is captured by a Federal soldier, an escaped slave called Cush. For the first time in his life Johnny will take orders from a black. This is just the first of many things Johnny will have to face, especially if he wants to get home.

Keywords: African American Issues; Family

Durrant, Lynda.

My Last Skirt: The Story of Jennie Hodgers, Union Soldier. **Clarion Books, 2006. 978-0-618-57490-2 (hardcover). 192pp.** 🄜 🄙

The first time Jennie puts on a pair of trousers, it changes her life. Wearing pants and acting as a boy gives her freedom to move and to earn more money. Whether being a shepherd for the bishop's sheep or working in a store, Jennie finds being a boy is much better. But not everyone agrees—like her brother Tom, who's jealous of what she has achieved as a boy. When he spills the beans to her employer, Jennie takes her share of their savings and heads west, taking the name of Albert Cashier. For two years she works on an Illinois farm. Then Albert Cashier joins the Union Army in the fight against the Confederacy.

Keywords: Army; Disguised as Boy; Union; Women Soldiers; Women's Roles

Elliott, L. M.

Annie, Between the States. **Katherine Tegen, 2004. 978-0-06-001211-3 (hardcover); 978-0-06-001213-7 (softcover). 496pp.** 🄙 🄢

The Civil War did more than split apart the Union and the families in it. It could also create new families. Annie is a true Southern lady, but is also a tomboy and a bookworm. The coming of war to her home state of Virginia means she has to nurse wounded soldiers and go without her former comforts. It would be one thing if they were Southern soldiers—but to nurse Federal troops, as well! Especially a man like Thomas Walker, a Massachusetts man who likes poetry as Annie does, but also strips the romance from Southern attitudes. Annie is loyal to the South, to her brothers who fight, and to dashing Jeb Stuart. She'll even ride to the Confederate lines to pass information about Northern movements. But when she is captured and accused of treason, an unlikely person risks everything to save her.

Keywords: Coming-of-age; Confederate; Romance

Ernst, Kathleen.

Hearts of Stone. **Dutton Juvenile, 2006. 978-0525-47686-3 (hardcover). 240pp.** 🄙

The two years since the start of the Civil War have been difficult for Hannah and her family. Her father joined the Union Army but was killed after four months.

Her best friend Ben is from a family of Confederate sympathizers, so Hannah turns her back on him. When their mother dies, Hannah is left responsible for the care of her three younger siblings. The neighbors want to split them up, but none of the children wants that. So Hannah decides to set off for Nashville, for the home of their Aunt Ellen. It's a journey of more than 200 miles, difficult for anyone. Add in three children, a worn-out mule, and a war, and it seems impossible. But if there's one thing Hannah has in her favor, it's her stubbornness.

Keywords: Brothers and Sisters; Coming-of-age

Forrester, Sandra.

Sound the Jubilee. **Dutton Juvenile, 1995. 978-0-525-67486-3 (hardcover); 978-0-14-037930-3 (softcover). 192pp. Ⓜ**

At age eleven, Maddie is expected to do the work of a full-grown slave. But she's smart and restless, so she gets distracted easily. That doesn't mean she doesn't notice things, like the tension between her parents. Her father loathes the bonds of slavery and hopes that Federal troops fighting the Confederacy might come to the plantation and set them free. Maddie's mother, though, can only think about the advantages of being a slave. When Maddie and her family accompany the mistress to the summer house at Nags Head, they don't know what chance they'll have of gaining freedom. Nags Head is on one of the islands of North Carolina's Outer Banks, and a nearby island is the home to a colony of self-freed slaves. Will Maddie and her family find freedom and happiness on Roanoke Island?

Keywords: Coming-of-age; Family; Slavery

Hahn, Mary Downing.

Hear the Wind Blow: A Novel of the Civil War. **Clarion Books, 2003. 978-0-618-18190-2 (hardcover). 224pp. Ⓜ Ⓙ**

An act of kindness brings disaster down upon Haskell Magruder. At age thirteen, he's the man of the house, with his father dead and his older brother fighting in Petersburg. When a wounded Confederate soldier rides up to their farm looking for shelter, Haskell's mother wants to turn him away. But Haskell persuades her to care for the soldier. When the Yankees arrive on the soldier's trail, it all ends badly. Haskell is left alone with his younger sister Rachel, their mother dies, and their farm is burned. The only thing Haskell can think to do is leave Rachel with relatives and journey deep into Virginia, searching for his brother. Finding his brother will also help Haskell journey to adulthood.

Keywords: Coming-of-age; Family

Promises to the Dead. **Clarion Books, 2000. 978-0-395-96394-4 (hardcover); 978-0-547-25838-6 (softcover). 208pp.** Ⓜ Ⓙ

It all started when Jesse's uncle sent him into the marsh for a turtle. On Maryland's Eastern Shore, in the days just before the Civil War, people were waiting to see what would happen. In the marsh that day, Jesse doesn't find a turtle, but a runaway slave with her son. As she dies, the slave makes Jesse promise to take Perry, her son, to a relative in Baltimore. Jesse knows that it's against the law to help a runaway slave, but he promised. So the twelve-year-old sets off with little Perry, making their way to a city full of Secessionists. With a successful slave-catcher, General Abednego Botfield, on their heels, Jesse and Perry will have to work together to reach Baltimore.

Keywords: Coming-of-age; Slavery

Hill, Pamela Smith.

📖 *A Voice from the Border*. **Holiday House, 1998. 978-0-8234-1356-0 (hardcover); 978-0-380-73231-9 (softcover). 244pp.** Ⓜ Ⓙ

In 1861 Missouri is split between two warring sides. The governor has been run out of the capital for his secessionist tendencies, and Federal troops are trying to root out any Southern sympathizers. For Margaret O'Neill, known as Reeves, it's a troubling time. Her father, who is loyal to Missouri and his friends, has joined the Confederate cause. Reeves's mother, who refuses to swear a loyalty oath, must try to preserve the family's home. By staying neutral, the O'Neill family could be victimized by both sides. Reeves misses her father greatly, pouring out her feelings in her diary and her writer's notebook. Soon the only person she can confide in is Percival Wilder, a young Yankee soldier. Torn between her father and her friend, between South and North, Reeves will have to find her own course in this difficult ethical battle.

Keywords: Coming-of-age; Family

Hunt, Irene.

Across Five Aprils. Berkley, 2002. 978-0-425-18278-9 (softcover). 224pp. Ⓜ Ⓙ

Jethro is nine years old in April1861, the youngest in his large family. Though he lives in southern Illinois, they have plenty of family in Kentucky. When news of the firing on Fort Sumter reaches them, all the questions and debates about politics become more than dinner table arguments. Jethro watches as his respected schoolteacher, his father, and his brothers leave to join the Union Army—all except his favorite brother, Bill, who chooses to fight for the South. Left on the farm with his mother and other femsale relations, Jethro will have to figure out how to grow up and become a man on his own. It'll be tough work, maybe as tough as what all those soldiers are facing.

Awards: Newbery Honor Book

Keywords: Confederate; Family; Union

Keehn, Sally.

Anna Sunday. Philomel, 2002. 978-0-399-23875-8 (hardcover); 978-0-14-240026-5 (softcover). 266pp. ◻

Ever since their father joined the Union Army, Anna and her brother Jed have lived with their cousin Ezekiel on their farm. But the news that their father is injured makes Anna and Jed take action. From their home near Gettysburg to where Pa is in Winchester, Virginia, is 108 miles. Of course they can make it—Pa needs them! Anna cuts off her curls and masquerades as a boy. Together, armed with a few supplies and Samson, the horse that responds only to Bible verses, Anna and Jed cross enemy lines. Will they find their father—and will he still be alive?

Keywords: Disguised as Boy; Family

Keith, Harold.

Rifles for Watie. HarperCollins, 1991. 978-0-690-70181-4 (hardcover); 978-0-06-447030-8 (softcover). 332pp. ◻

Living in Kansas, just over the line from Missouri, was difficult in the mid-1800s. At age sixteen Jeff joins the Union Army, wanting to fight back against the bushwhackers—Rebel sympathizers from Missouri who raid Kansas farms. Soon Jeff is fighting in the Civil War, marching across Kansas, Missouri, and Arkansas. The most dangerous fight, though, is against Stand Watie, leader of the Cherokee Indian Nation. From Indian Territory, in what is now Oklahoma, Watie leads his men on raids against the Union. Jeff fights Watie's men as part of a unit of Kansas Volunteers and sees the destruction of war and how it hurts civilians. Surrounded by friends and enemies, Jeff will keep fighting so that at war's end, he can return to his family's farm.

Awards: Newbery Medal

Keywords: Army; Native American Issues; Union

Kilgore, James.

The Passage. Peachtree, 2006. 978-1-56145-384-9 (hardcover). 249pp. ◻ ◻

Ostracized by most of the town due to his grandfather's pacifist views, Sam can't help feeling that he should join up. He wants to defend the South against the invaders, because it's the honorable thing to do. Although his grandfather disagrees, Sam is determined to enlist even though he is only fifteen. He forges a letter from his grandfather and joins the Confederate Navy. Along with his best friend Albert, Sam is assigned to the CSS *Arkansas*, a newly constructed ironclad. At first navy life is difficult: long hours, hard labor, and tense relationships with other sailors. But when the

Arkansas is ordered to proceed to Vicksburg, fighting its way past Federal ships, Sam and Albert face great danger.

Read-alike: To learn more about naval warfare during the Civil War, read *Secrets of a Civil War Submarine: Solving the Mysteries of the* H.L. Hunley by Sally M. Walker.

Keywords: Coming-of-age; Confederate; Navy

Matas, Carol.

The War Within: A Novel of the Civil War. **Scholastic, 2001. 978-0-439-98810-0 (hardcover); 978-0-689-84358-7 (softcover). 154pp.** Ⓜ Ⓙ

Hannah is a proper Southern lady. The Civil War rages on, and Federal troops have occupied her hometown of Holly Springs, Mississippi. For Hannah, the sides are drawn, and she dislikes the Union soldiers who are invited to her home by her older sister Joanna. True, Captain Mazer is Jewish, like Hannah and her family, but he's still a Yankee. Then two disasters strike Hannah's family. Their home is destroyed when the Confederates blow up ammunition rather than let the Union have the supplies. Then there is General Order No. 11, which orders all Jews to leave Mississippi and other Southern states. As Hannah and her family head toward Memphis, Hannah will face religious discrimination for the first time. In the months to come, Hannah reconsiders her faith and her patriotism.

Keywords: Confederate; Family; Religious Conflicts

McMullan, Margaret.

📖 *How I Found the Strong.* **Houghton Mifflin Books, 2004. 978-0-618-35008-7 (hardcover); 978-0-553-49492-1 (softcover). 144pp.** Ⓜ Ⓙ

A skinny ten-year-old can't be called up to fight for the South in 1861. This fact makes Frank, also called Shanks, unhappy. Maybe if he could go and fight with his father and his brother Henry, his father might love him. But instead, Frank will have to stay home, helping keep the farm going. On the farm are his pregnant mother, his blind grandmother, his crotchety grandfather—and Buck, the family slave. As 1861 reaches its end, and everyone begins to see the war won't be over by Christmas, Frank and his family struggle to survive. There's never enough food, never enough time for all the chores that need to be done. As Frank begins to question the war that has taken so much, he becomes friends with Buck. And that leaves Frank with the biggest question of all: Is the war right?

Keywords: Coming-of-age; Slavery

Myers, Anna.

Assassin. **Walker Books for Young Readers, 2005. 978-0-8027-8989-1 (hardcover); 978-0-8027-9643-1 (softcover). 192pp.** Ⓙ

A story in two voices unfolds around a climactic event. Bella first sees John Wilkes Booth at the age of eight, marveling at his charm and looks. Bella's mother dreams of seeing her daughter on the stage, but when she dies, Bella is sent to live with her grandmother. Living in Washington, D.C., Bella is taught to sew by her grandmother, displaying a great talent for it. Bella wants to fulfill her mother's wish, but her grandmother disapproves, so the closest she gets to the theater is moonlighting in the Ford Theater costume shop. There she meets John Wilkes Booth again and becomes enchanted with his energy and passion. Booth has a plan to strike a blow against the Union, and he enlists Bella to help. Fourteen-year-old Bella agrees, even though it means doing evil and going against her antislavery beliefs.

Keywords: Multiple Voices; Performing

Paulsen, Gary.

Soldier's Heart. **Scholastic, 1999. 978-0-439-10991-8 (hardcover); 978-0-440-22838-7 (softcover). 107pp.** Ⓜ

Charley isn't the only boy to lie about his age and enlist in the Union Army. Everyone says that the war is going to be a big show, and it'll be over soon. Fifteen-year-old Charley isn't about to miss that. But once he joins, seeing action from Bull Run to Gettysburg, Charley changes his mind. War isn't a show—it's a bloody, deadly hell. He sees comrades mowed down by bullets and cannonballs, lives on coffee and beans, and becomes old beyond his years. It will take all his courage to go on and keep fighting, especially when an injury ends his service.

Keywords: Army; Coming-of-age; Union

Rinaldi, Ann.

An Acquaintance with Darkness. **Harcourt Children's Books, 1997. 978-0-15-201294-6 (hardcover); 978-0-15-205387-1 (softcover). 304pp.** Ⓜ Ⓙ

The death of her mother, on the day that Lee surrenders to Grant, leaves fourteen-year-old Emily an orphan. Her Uncle Valentine, a prominent surgeon in Washington, wants her to live with him. But that was the last thing that Emily's mother wanted, for reasons Emily doesn't know. And Emily would rather live with the Surratts, old friends from Maryland. After all, Annie Surratt is her best friend, and Annie's older brother Johnny is Emily's secret crush. Nevertheless, Emily soon finds herself living with her uncle. She soon discovers that her uncle has terrifying secrets. Yet she cannot flee to her friend's house, because Annie's family is implicated in the assassination of President Lincoln. Emily needs to find a way to travel out of darkness and find the light.

Keywords: Coming-of-age; Family

Amelia's War. **Scholastic, 1999. 978-0-590-11744-9 (hardcover); 978-0-439-32666-7 (softcover). 272pp.** Ⓜ Ⓙ

Living in Hagerstown, Maryland, during the Civil War is an uncomfortable proposition. Both Union and Confederate supporters live side-by-side, leading to frayed friendships and divided families. Amelia tries to take a moral stand early in the war, inspired by her abolitionist grandmother. But it backfires, and she decides to be on nobody's side. That's easier said than done when you're from a Union family and your best friend is the son of a Southern sympathizer. Amelia finds out where her sympathies truly lie when Hagerstown is held for ransom by the Confederate Army. Together with her friend Josh, Amelia uses the power of the pen to save her town.

Keywords: Family; Friendship; Writing

Girl in Blue. Scholastic, 2001. 978-0-439-07336-3 (hardcover); 978-0-439-67646-5 (softcover). 310pp. ◼

Sarah Wheelock knows she's worth more than her father thinks! She can use a gun, works hard, and wants to stand on her own two feet. At age fifteen she escapes marriage to the disagreeable Ezekiel Kunkle and runs off to Flint. Sarah disguises herself as a man and enlists in the 2nd Michigan Infantry. Now Neddy Compton, Sarah fits in well with the other soldiers, serving as nurse and entertaining the wounded with her impersonations. She even catches the attention of General McClellan, commander of all the Union troops! But when her true identity is discovered, the general can't allow her to keep serving. Instead of punishing her, McClellan introduces Sarah to Alan Pinkerton, head of a famous detective agency and Union spymaster. Sarah becomes an agent, spying on the Confederate spy Rose Greenhow.

Keywords: Army; Disguised as Boy; Spies; Union; Women Soldiers; Women's Roles

In My Father's House. Scholastic, 1994. 978-0-590-44731-7 (softcover). 336pp. ◼

Being stubborn can be a blessing or a curse. Ever since her mother married Will McLean, Oscie has done her best to match him in arguments. Even though she's only seven when they meet, Oscie is smart and full of opinions. And she's not happy about this stepfather who holds her to a higher standard. But slowly Oscie begins to learn how and when to held her tongue, thanks to the lessons of her Yankee governess. As Oscie grows up, the tensions between North and South grow even more strained. In their home near Manassas, Oscie's family entertains all sorts of Southerners, even Confederate soldiers. The first battle of the Civil War starts on their land. After the Battle of Manassas, the McLean family moves around, eventually ending up in the tiny village of Appomattox Court House. There, Oscie and Will finally end their war, just as the Civil War ends in their house.

Keywords: Coming-of-age; Family

Juliet's Moon. Harcourt Children's Books, 2008. 978-0-15-206170-8 (hardcover); 978-0-547-25874-4 (softcover). 256pp. ◼

Not many girls have to grow up at the age of twelve. But that's what happens to Juliet when Yankee soldiers burn her home and kill her father for resisting arrest. Rescued by her brother Seth, who serves the Confederacy as a member of Quantrill's Raiders, Juliet is taken to a neighbor's house. It's the home of the

Anderson sisters, whose older brother Bill serves with Seth, and Martha Anderson is sweet on Seth. Juliet watches as Seth ignores Martha to flirt with Sue Mundy, a woman who serves in Quantrill's Raiders. Finding out that Sue is really a man is a shock, and a secret Juliet will keep when she, Sue, and the Anderson sisters are arrested by Yankees. Juliet finds her own way, struggling to survive as the Confederacy descends into lawlessness.

Keywords: Confederate; Women's Roles

The Last Silk Dress. **Holiday House, 1988. 978-0-8234-0690-6 (hardcover); 978-0-440-22861-5 (softcover). 368pp. Ⓜ Ⓙ**

At age fourteen, Susan thinks she understands all the changes that are happening. The start of the Civil War has inflamed her hometown of Richmond. Susan is eager to show her support for the Cause, but her mother refuses to let her join sewing circles or visit with her friends. Her mother, who is abusive and cruel, wants to prevent Susan from knowing anything about her older brother Lucien. Lucien was disowned by the family years ago, for reasons that Susan doesn't really know. But Susan is determined, no matter what, to help the South. She starts collecting silk dresses from the women of Richmond, which will be turned into a spy balloon. As Susan learns the real reason for Lucien's banishment, she struggles with how to do the right thing, even if it hurts the ones she loves.

Keywords: Confederate; Family

Leigh Ann's Civil War. **Harcourt Children's Books, 2009. 978-0-15-206513-3 (hardcover). 320pp. Ⓜ Ⓙ**

When the Civil War breaks out, Leigh Ann Connors is bothered more by the war within her family. After all, the war with the North will be over by Christmas—but Leigh Ann doesn't know when her family problems will be done. Her parents are estranged because her mother is a Yankee sympathizer and her father is going crazy. Neither of her parents has done much to help Leigh Ann; in her opinion, her beloved older brothers Teddy and Lou have brought her up. It's that love that leads to great trouble. When the Yankees arrive in their town, Leigh Ann flies a French flag over the family's mill. She thinks it will protect the mill, but instead it gets her arrested, along with the other mill workers. Hiding as a boy, Leigh Ann tries to protect herself and what's left of her family until they can all be reunited.

Keywords: Confederate; Disguised as Boy; Family

Mine Eyes Have Seen. **Scholastic, 1998. 978-0-590-54318-7 (hardcover); 978-0-590-54319-4 (softcover). 288pp. Ⓜ Ⓙ**

Having John Brown as a father is a cross to bear. Annie has carried the guilt of the death of a child on her shoulders, even though it wasn't her fault. But she knows her father blames her for the death. So Annie is excited when her father asks her to come to Maryland, as he prepares for his latest attack against slavery. Arriving at a small farm in Maryland in the summer of 1859, Annie is tasked by her father with maintaining constant vigilance. As the summer passes, Annie watches, observing any behavior that could ruin her father's plan. In addition, she does her best, as a fifteen-year-old girl, to keep the peace in a house full of men. When John Brown tells his followers about his plan—a raid on Harper's Ferry to free blacks from bondage—Annie watches their reactions. And Annie, in the end, is a witness to a cataclysmic moment in American history.

Keywords: Coming-of-age; Father and Child; Slavery

My Vicksburg. Harcourt Children's Books, 2009. 978-0-15-206624-6 (hardcover). 160pp. Ⓜ Ⓙ

Thirteen-year-old Claire Louise is confused by her family. Why is her father sometimes distant and cold but then at others loving and affectionate? Why has her older brother Landon joined the Yankee army? Living in Vicksburg with her mother and younger brother, Claire Louise will have to live with her questions. Vicksburg is under siege by the Union Army, subjected to hours of shelling every day. For protection, the residents of Vicksburg live in caves dug into the hillsides surrounding the city. In those close quarters, Claire Louise often steals outside when the shelling stops. On one of these trips, Claire Louise meets her brother Landon while he treats a Confederate soldier named Robert. Claire Louise senses that Robert has a secret, and that Landon knows it. When she learns what this secret is, Claire Louise confronts questions about family and loyalty.

Keywords: Confederate; Family

Numbering All the Bones. Hyperion, 2002. 978-0-7868-0533-4 (hardcover); 978-0-7868-1378-0 (softcover). 170pp. Ⓜ Ⓙ

As the Civil War came closer to its inevitable end, people focused on themselves, on surviving as long as they could and preserving their way of life. That's how it is on the plantation where Eulinda lives near Andersonville, Georgia. Eulinda is a lovely thirteen-year-old, caught between worlds. She's the daughter of a slave woman and the white master, and she alternates between being a slave and being a member of the family. All Eulinda wants is to gain her freedom and be with her older brother Neddy, who ran away to join the Union Army. But when Eulinda hears rumors that her brother might be in the nearby prison camp, she realizes that she will have to pick one world to live in. Soldiers die by the hundred inside Andersonville Prison. Only with the help of others, like Miss Clara Barton, may Eulinda find her brother.

Keywords: Brothers and Sisters; Slavery

Sarah's Ground. Simon & Schuster Children's Publishing, 2004. 978-0-689-85924-3 (hardcover); 978-0-689-85925-0 (softcover). 192pp. Ⓜ Ⓙ

Being the youngest is a difficult position for Sarah. She's nearly nineteen, yet she's almost never been given credit for her abilities. Instead she's been watched and chaperoned within an inch of her life, all in hopes of finding her a husband. But that's the last thing Sarah wants, so she applies for a job. The position is serving as a secretary for the association that has just purchased Mount Vernon. The home of General Washington is in disrepair, and the Association wants to restore it. This task is made more difficult by the outbreak of hostilities between North and South. Aided by Miss Cunningham, the head of the Association, and the superintendent of Mount Vernon, Mr. Herbert, Sarah attempts to keep the plantation as neutral ground. She may be able to convince generals, even the president, to maintain the peace, but Sarah finds more than peace at Mount Vernon—she finds love.

Keywords: Coming-of-age; Romance

Sappey, Maureen Stack.

Letters from Vinnie. **Front Street, 1995. 978-1-886910-31-7 (hardcover); 978-1-59078-538-6 (softcover). 248pp. ◼**

When war begins between the Union and the Confederacy, Vinnie's father moves the family from Arkansas to Washington, D.C. Vinnie is excited about the possibilities of living in a city, but saddened at being so much farther away from her friend Regina. So Vinnie writes letters to her friend, explaining her new life in Washington. Once there, Vinnie's father is often sick, her mother worries about money, and her brother runs off to join the Confederate Army. Through it all, Vinnie grows from a talented thirteen-year-old into a young woman of great musical and artistic skill. When Vinnie develops a knack for sculpture, she uses it in order to memorialize one of our greatest presidents.

Keywords: Art; Friendship; Letters

Wells, Rosemary.

Red Moon at Sharpsburg. **Viking Juvenile, 2007. 978-0-670-03638-7 (hardcover); 978-0-14-241205-3 (softcover). 256pp. ◼ ◼**

In the Shenandoah Valley of Virginia, families help each other in good times and bad. No one realizes that the war between North and South, which started so well for the South, will quickly lead to very dark days. For India Moody, life is full of chores and work because her father has enlisted. The only bright spot are her lessons with Emory Trimble, son of a prominent local family. India's curiosity is welcome to Emory, who begins teaching her science in addition to writing and other female studies. These studies just might help India in an unexpected way. As the war continues, one of the worst battles happens in the nearby town of Sharpsburg. It will take all of India's courage and strength to face the utter destruction of war. But for her father, her family, and her friends, India meets the challenge.

Read-alike: *A Savage Thunder: Antietam and the Bloody Road to Freedom* by Jim Murphy discusses the nearby battle that changes India's life.

Keywords: Coming-of-age; Family

Modern Times: 1900–1980

A great wave of immigration increased America's population, but also created new tensions at the beginning of the twentieth century. Yet these new Americans helped the United States as it faced two world wars, a depression, and a struggle for civil rights.

Banks, Steven.

King of the Creeps. **Knopf Books for Young Readers, 2006. 978-0-375-83291-8 (hardcover). 176pp. M ⓜ ⒥**

In 1963 every boy wanted to look like President Kennedy. After all, girls liked boys who were like JFK. Tom Johnson knows that he couldn't look more different from the president. He's short, with fuzzy hair and glasses. He knows he's a creep. So how can he get a girl to notice him? When he sees a picture of Bob Dylan, Tom has the answer. Becoming a folk singer is bound to get him a girl! Tom goes into New York and buys a guitar. But as soon as he gets it, the guitar is stolen.While he's trying to figure out what to do, a girl finds him.

Keywords: 1960s; Coming-of-age; Music

Blundell, Judy.

What I Saw and How I Lied. **Scholastic, 2008. 978-0-439-90346-2 (hardcover); 978-0-439-90348-6 (softcover). 288pp. ⒥ ⓢ**

Now that the war is over, life in Queens in 1947 is looking up. At least that's what everyone thinks. But Evie just wants to be older: old enough to wear lipstick, to smoke, to date. The more that Evie's mother tells her to enjoy being a girl, the more Evie wants to be a woman—a woman like her beautiful, fascinating mother. When Evie's stepfather Joe announces they're taking an extended vacation to Florida, Evie sees it as her chance to start growing up. She even finds an older man to pin her hopes on: Peter Coleridge, a member of her stepfather's army company. As Evie begins to spread her wings, she realizes that maybe she doesn't want to be like her mother. And when Peter disappears, questions swirl around Evie's parents. She has to figure out how to answer these questions and how to create a believable lie.

Awards: National Book Award

Keywords: 1940s; Family; Women's Roles

Bryant, Jen.

Kaleidoscope Eyes. **Knopf Books for Young Readers, 2009. 978-0-375-84048-7 (hardcover); 978-0-440-42190-0 (softcover). 272pp. ⓜ ⒥**

It's 1968, and thirteen-year-old Lizza has been dealing with many losses. First her mom left, then some young men from her hometown died in Vietnam. Worse of all is the death of her grandfather. The two of them always had a lot of fun pouring over maps, and Lizza didn't get a chance to say good-bye to him. But to her surprise, she finds his good-bye to her: a mysterious letter and three maps, meant for her only. With the help of her friends Malcolm and Carolann, Lizza sets off on a treasure hunt that began back in the late seventeenth century. That's when the famous Captain Kidd visited her hometown and may have left behind a great treasure. This novel in verse brings alive the turbulent summer of 1968.

Keywords: 1960s; Family; Novel in Verse; Pirates

Ringside, 1925: Views from the Scopes Trial. **Knopf Books for Young Readers, 2008. 978-0-375-84047-0 (hardcover); 978-0-440-42189-4 (softcover). 240pp. Ⓜ Ⓙ**

The small town of Dayton, Tennessee, is quiet, growing smaller as people leave for big cities. But in the summer of 1925, people all over the country—even the world—will be reading and hearing about Dayton. There is a trial going on, about a teacher who taught the theory of evolution contrary to Tennessee's law prohibiting such lessons. Is teaching evolution the latest evidence of the sins that are destroying the American way of life? Or is this about science and the freedom to teach new ideas? Although Mr. Scopes is not in any real danger, because this trial is more about changing the law than any criminal act, the trial changes things in Dayton. Its citizens start questioning not just science, but also the lives they lead. These questions end up meaning more than the trial itself.

Keywords: 1920s; Multiple Voices; Novel in Verse; Religious Conflicts

Carney, Jeff.

The Adventures of Michael MacInnes. **Farrar, Straus & Giroux, 2006. 978-0-374-30146-0 (hardcover). 244pp. Ⓢ**

Bootleg whiskey, Ford flivvers, and prep school hijinks in a novel set in 1924. Stoney Batter Prep School welcomes two new students, who will turn the school on its ear. Both Roger Legrande and Michael MacInnes are juniors, and from the moment they meet, they're chums. Roger is a skilled scientist, intrigued by physics. He's been dismissed from two other schools and certainly doesn't want to leave another. Michael, on the other hand, is determined to shake things up. An orphan with a gift for poetry, Michael brings Roger along on a series of adventures and escapades. Whether starting an unauthorized literary magazine or taking down the school's bootlegger, Michael and Roger are two rebels.

Keywords: 1920s; Friendship

Collier, James Lincoln.

The Empty Mirror. **Bloomsbury, 2004. 978-1-58234-949-7 (hardcover); 978-1-58234-904-6 (softcover). 192pp. Ⓙ**

Growing up in a small town means there are always people watching you, trying to keep you in line. Nick talks back to his teacher and cuts school with his friend Gypsy. But really, he's not that different from other thirteen-year-olds. He lives with his Uncle Jack and helps in his store. One day strange things start to happen. A neighbor sees Nick by the pond when he was actually up in the woods. Nick realizes that he has no reflection. Then people see him all over town, acting up, committing acts of vandalism, even setting loose boats. What is the explanation for these sightings? It could have something to do with the 1918 flu epidemic—the epidemic that left Nick an orphan. But in a town that won't talk about the flu epidemic, how will Nick figure out what's happening to him?

Keywords: 1920s; Identity; Illness

Collier, Kristi.

Throwing Stones. **Henry Holt, 2006. 978-0-8050-7614-1 (hardcover). 208pp.** ▪

Ever since his dynamic older brother Pete died, Andy's family has been drifting apart. His father doesn't laugh, and his mother focuses more on her charity work. Andy just wants to play basketball and lead the team to the state championship, as Pete did. Maybe if he does that his family will be healed. Andy is determined to be a winner. But then his pride—and his interest in his best friend's sister—leads to an accident that changes his life. Without basketball, Andy will have to find a new way to fit into his family. This story of life in 1920s Indiana shows the contrast between old ways and new.

Keywords: 1920s; Family; Illness; Sports

Crew, Linda.

Brides of Eden: A True Story Imagined. **HarperTeen, 2001. 978-0-06-028750-4 (hardcover); 978-0-06-447217-3 (softcover). 240pp.** ▪ Ⓢ

Eva Mae isn't that different from other sixteen-year-olds. She likes clothes and wants to be thought well of by the other girls. She is religious and dedicated to her faith, but she's not a zealot—not like her older sister Maud. Maud doesn't bend when it comes to religion. When a charismatic young man comes to town, preaching a passionate form of Christianity, Maud and Eva Mae are swept up in it. Soon the new congregation is almost all female, and their preacher has taken the name Joshua. Some of his teachings are welcome to his flock: What woman would prefer a corset over loose dresses? But others, like his antimarriage sermons, are harder to accept. When Joshua announces that one special woman will be the mother of the Second Christ, it's the beginning of the end. The town, already suspicious of Joshua's motives, now works to undermine his group. As husbands, fathers, and sweethearts try to rescue their women, Eva Mae must try to find the right path for herself, both socially and spiritually.

Keywords: 1900s; Religious Conflicts; Women's Roles

Crocker, Nancy.

Billie Standish Was Here. Simon & Schuster Children's Publishing, 2007. 978-1-4169-2423-4 (hardcover). 288pp. **J** **S**

In the summer of 1968, the town of Cumberland, Missouri, empties out. Everyone thinks the levees are going to break and flood the town. Only two houses still have people in them. In one house is Billie Standish and her parents. But Billie feels alone, because her hard-working, small-minded parents spend all their time working their farm. She starts spending time with Miss Lydia, a neighbor. Thanks to the affection and caring shown her by Miss Lydia, Billie begins to blossom. Suddenly life is full of possibilities. But then tragedy strikes Billie when she is attacked by Miss Lydia's adult son. The attack makes Miss Lydia recall a painful event in her own past, which makes her take action against her son. Soon all alone, Billie must discover if Miss Lydia's love has done enough to help her carry on.

Keywords: 1960s; Coming-of-age; Women's Roles

Cushman, Karen.

The Loud Silence of Francine Green. Clarion Books, 2006. 978-0-618-50455-8 (hardcover); 978-0-375-84117-0 (softcover). 225pp. **J**

She's not popular, because she never wants to do anything fun. But in her head, Francine Green is daring, witty, and funny. It's 1949, and she's lucky enough to live down the street from a movie studio. For the most part she's happy to dream about Montgomery Clift and suffer through Catholic school. But that's before she becomes friends with Sophie Bowman, an activist in the making. Sophie is serious and questioning, earning punishment from nuns and other authority figures for all her questions. Together, Francine and Sophie are best friends and good influences on each other. Thanks to Sophie, Francine starts asking her own questions. In a world full of communists, atomic bombs, and censorship, Francine starts to understand why Sophie is so worried. And like Sophie, Francine begins to break her silence.

Keywords: 1940s; Cold War

Day, Karen.

No Cream Puffs. Wendy Lamb Books, 2008. 978-0-375-83775-3 (hardcover); 978-0-375-83776-0 (softcover). 224pp. **M** **J**

Madison has a great arm and is a good hitter, too. Being a girl didn't matter that much before. But now that she's twelve, it seems the boys want her to stay with the girls, whereas the girls think she's not really a girl. Joining the town's baseball league lets her show off her skills, but Madison is the only girl. That means the media want to write stories and hold interviews with her. Madison just wants to play—and to get her teammate Tommy to notice her as a girl. As the summer goes on, Madison struggles to find a balance. Can she wear lip gloss and learn to throw a curve ball? In the summer of 1980, one girl learns how to win, and not just at baseball.

Keywords: 1980s; Sports

Edwardson, Debby Dahl.

Blessing's Bead. **Farrar, Straus & Giroux, 2009. 978-0-374-30805-6 (hardcover). 192pp. ⓜ ⓙ**

Nutaaq is a young girl, interested in running after the reindeer herds. But she also looks forward to getting a new parka, for she is nearly a woman. Her older sister Aaluk is a woman, complete with ceremonial tattoos. When they travel from their small island to the Alaskan mainland, Aaluk attracts the attention of a Siberian with a string of blue beads. They are married, and Aaluk gives her sister two beads before she leaves. Nutaaq and her village are victims of the 1918 flu epidemic, an event that changes Nutaaq's life. Seventy years later, Nutaaq's great-granddaughter runs away from Anchorage to the village, where learning about her ancestors' history changes her life.

Keywords: 1910s; Family; Illness; Sisters

Fletcher, Ralph.

The One O'Clock Chop. **Henry Holt, 2007. 978-0-8050-8143-5 (hardcover). 192pp. ⓙ**

Matt wants to buy a boat for himself, but with jobs scarce, he's not sure how he's going to get the money. Then he gets a job digging clams with Dan, a waterman and Vietnam War veteran. Clamming is hard and dirty, but it's good money and gives Matt time to think. He is still dealing with his parents' divorce, even though it happened four years before. He also thinks about baseball and Watergate. But most of all, Matt thinks about his cousin Jazzy, an exotic, lively girl. Visiting from Hawaii for the summer, she enchants Matt. He's ready to tell her how he feels, when Jazzy changes everything between them. Matt learns much about the world and the people in it over the course of the summer of 1973.

Keywords: 1970s; Family

Frost, Helen.

Crossing Stones. **Farrar, Straus & Giroux , 2009. 978-0-374-31653-2 (hardcover). 192pp. ⓙ**

A novel in verse reveals the complexity of a nation going to war. The Jorgensen and Norman families have lived near each other for years, their lands separated by Crabapple Creek. The mothers have it all planned out: Muriel will marry Frank, and Muriel's brother Ollie will marry Frank's sister Emma. Emma and Ollie are fine with this plan, but Muriel isn't so sure. She chafes at the restrictions placed on her just because she's a girl. She's expected to bite her tongue, she's not allowed to be valedictorian of her graduating class, and she doesn't get a voice or a vote. What's fair about a world that wants women to raise good children but doesn't give the women a voice in the wars those children will fight? Everyone tells Muriel to watch herself; they would rather she behave like other young women. How can Muriel balance being true to herself with fitting in?

Keywords: 1910s; Multiple Voices; Novel in Verse; World War I

Gordon, Amy.

When JFK Was My Father. **Houghton Mifflin Books for Children, 1999. 978-0-395-91364-2 (hardcover); 978-0-14-131279-8 (softcover). 202pp.** 🇯

Georgia's father isn't really President Kennedy. But it's easier to think that, because Georgia's father is in Brazil, living with the Brazilian woman he's in love with. Georgia and her mother move back to the United States, but she's soon sent to a boarding school in Connecticut. All Georgia takes with her is a picture of JFK, her stamp collection, and a white pebble given to her by her friend Tim. At her new school she tries to fit in, make friends, and do well in her classes. But Georgia can't overcome her feelings of being an outsider. Lonely and failing her classes; not even JFK can change that. Will Georgia find somewhere that she belongs? Or will it take learning about the people in her life to find the place for her?

Keywords: 1960s; Coming-of-age; Family

Hale, Marian.

Dark Water Rising. **Henry Holt, 2006. 978-0-8050-7585-4 (hardcover); 978-0-312-62908-3 (softcover). 240pp.** 🇯 🇸

The last thing Seth wants to do is move to Galveston. It might be the New York City of Texas, but Galveston has a medical college that Seth's father wants him to attend. Seth doesn't want to be a doctor—he wants to be a carpenter like his father. But a seventeen-year-old in 1900 still has to listen to his parents. So Seth accepts his fate, and he starts cheering up when his family arrives in the city. They have a nice house with the beach nearby, with lots of new people to meet, like the girl with blonde hair who lives across from them. Best of all, Seth gets a job as a carpenter's helper. His parents want him to save most of his wages for college, but Seth looks on this job as a way to prove himself to his father. Seth doesn't know that he'll find another way to show that he's a man. A few days after he starts working, a storm warning is posted. This is no ordinary storm, but rather a huge, destructive hurricane. And no one in Galveston, a city on a low-lying island, realizes the danger.

Keywords: 1900s; Disasters; Family

The Goodbye Season. **Henry Holt, 2009. 978-0-8050-8855-7 (hardcover). 288pp. Ⓘ Ⓢ**

For the daughter of a Texas sharecropper, Mercy has big dreams. She has worked hard her whole life, and the last thing she wants is to end up like her mother, wasting her brain and talents with a bunch of kids and too much work. With food short in the aftermath of World War I, Mercy has to go live on another farm, helping out there. There's word of a flu epidemic that's killing a lot of people. This flu works fast; soon Mercy is left all alone, with no family or friends. Suddenly Mercy realizes that her family wasn't just a burden. Grief-stricken, she makes her way to town, finding some help from kind strangers. She gets a job watching a widow's two children. Cora Wilder, the widow, has a mystery that swirls around her, not to mention a handsome stepson Mercy's age. Mercy has gone through a lot for a seventeen-year-old girl; can she move beyond her grief and live her life to the fullest?

Keywords: 1910s; Illness

Hijuelos, Oscar.

📖 *Dark Dude.* **Atheneum, 2008. 978-1-4169-4804-9 (hardcover); 978-1-4169-4945-9 (softcover). 448pp. Ⓢ**

Rico gets called "dark dude" a lot—and it's not a compliment. Thanks to his light skin and hair, everyone thinks he's white, not Cuban. Because he spent nearly two years in hospitals when he was little, he can't speak Spanish very well, and his mother holds the still-unpaid medical bills against him. Rico works after-school jobs, dreams of creating comic books with his friend Jimmy, and misses his brother figure Gilberto. Gilberto took his lottery winnings and left Harlem for college in Wisconsin. When the violence at his school, Jimmy's problems with drugs, and his parents get to be too much, Rico runs away. With Jimmy he hitchhikes to Wisconsin to live on Gilberto's farm. There, Rico figures out whether he's just a dark dude.

Keywords: 1960s; Coming-of-age

Ingold, Jeanette.

The Big Burn. **Harcourt Children's Books, 2002. 978-0-15-216470-6 (hardcover); 978-0-15-204924-9 (softcover). 304pp. Ⓘ**

The summer of 1910 is dry, following a dry spring. In the woods of Idaho and Montana, the smallest spark could start a fire. Most people want to stamp out fire, not even allowing controlled burning. The Forest Service, newly formed, is trying to protect the land and forests as best it can. But in late August many small fires combine, and the woods as far as the eye can see are on fire. In the midst of the fire are three teenagers. Jarrett works with his ranger brother, looking for fires and trying to keep them in check. Lizabeth lives with her aunt on a homestead claim, on land she loves like it's her own. And Seth, who lied about his age to get in, is a member of the black-only 25th Infantry. These three teens join hundreds of people who fight back the Big Burn.

Keywords: 1910s; Disasters; Multiple Voices

Pictures, 1918. Harcourt Children's Books, 1998. 978-0-15-201809-2 (hardcover); 978-0-14-130695-7 (softcover). 160pp. **J**

> Several plot threads entwine to tell the story of a girl growing up. An arson fire burns down her family chicken coop and takes the life of Asia's pet jackrabbit. Asia can't help wishing things weren't changing, like how her friend Nick is looking at her like a girl, her grandmother is slipping into dementia, and Nick's cousin Boy is also interested in her. Then she sees a Kodak camera in the window of the drugstore, and she has to have it. After weeks of working to make the money, the camera is hers. She starts taking pictures, trying to ignore the people who tell her that it's not ladylike to be a photographer. Asia focuses on being able to preserve her memories, the people and places she loves. Eventually Asia will realize that pictures can't freeze life, and she can't live life through a camera.

> **Keywords:** 1910s; Art; Romance; World War I

Kanell, Beth.

The Darkness Under the Water. Candlewick , 2008. 978-0-7636-3719-4 (hardcover). 320pp. **J**

For as long as she can remember, April has been a sad month for Molly. It's not just the constant rain that pours down, melting the last of the snow and flooding Vermont's rivers. April is when Gratia, the sister she never knew, drowned. Even now, sixteen years later, her mother still grieves for this loss. Molly feels haunted by Gratia—and there's a new threat ahead. The governor of Vermont is leading a charge against foreigners, wanting only real Yankees to live in the state. For Molly, whose family is Abenaki, and for her Irish best friend Katy, there are questions about identity. Molly is torn between being faithful to her Abenaki roots and wanting to stay in her home. Her family will have to find a way to survive, before the state interferes in the very basics of life.

Keywords: 1920s; Mother and Child; Native American Issues; Sisters

Kerley, Barbara.

Greetings from Planet Earth. Scholastic, 2007. 978-0-439-80203-1 (hardcover); 978-0-439-80204-8. 256pp. **M** **J**

Theo's favorite teacher is Mr. Meyer, his science teacher. Lately they've had a lot of lessons about space because NASA is getting ready to launch the Voyager missions, probes that will travel to Jupiter and beyond. Mr. Meyer gives his class an assignment: If you could pick what went on each probe's golden record, what message would you send to explain Earth to aliens? Theo, who is a space nut, finds himself considering lots of different ideas. Should it be something simple, like French fries or the Redskins? Or could he talk about his family: his sad mom, his nice grandmother, his annoying sister, and his missing father? As Theo tries to answer the question of who we are, he seeks to answer some questions of his own.

Read-alike: For more about the space program, read *Moonshot: The Flight of Apollo 11* by Brian Floca.

Keywords: 1970s; Family

Kidd, Ronald.

The Year of the Bomb. **Simon & Schuster Children's Publishing, 2009. 978-1-4169-5892-5 (hardcover); 978-1-4169-9625-5 (softcover). 208pp.** Ⓜ

For Paul, horror movies feel more real than his life. His family and home are normal and plain and boring—just like him. But in horror movies, there's danger and excitement. With his three friends, Paul sees all the horror movies that are shown either in his hometown or in nearby Hollywood. All four boys can't believe their luck when they find out a movie will be shooting in their sleepy town! At first, just getting to watch the filming and meeting the movie people is plenty of excitement. But then the boys discover that some of the actors are more than they appear. With worries about the communists and the A-bomb always hanging over their heads, how will Paul and his friends react to finding communists in their own hometown?

Keywords: 1950s; Cold War; Performing; Politics

Krisher, Trudy.

Fallout. **Holiday House, 2006. 978-0-8234-2035-3 (hardcover). 364pp.** Ⓢ

Since her best friend moved away, Genevieve has felt very alone. Starting high school without anyone to pass notes to or share lunch with is a daunting prospect, especially in the small town of Easton, North Carolina. But then Brenda Wompers moves to town. It's 1954, and even for a girl used to hurricanes, the new "Cold War" between the USSR and United States, with its threats of nuclear destruction, is very scary. Genevieve's father fully supports Senator McCarthy's anticommunist crusade. Brenda, though, newly arrived from California, has liberal ideas and speaks out against the bomb. As Genevieve is exposed to more of Brenda's beliefs, she starts to question everything she's been told about the world.

Keywords: 1950s; Cold War

LaFaye, A.

The Keening. **Milkweed Editions, 2010. 978-1-57131-692-9 (hardcover); 978-1-57131-694-3 (softcover). 224pp.** Ⓙ

For years, Lyza and her parents have been outcasts. Her father is seen as crazy by everyone else, and her mother is the only one who helps him hold onto reality.

Lyza looks at her parents, each gifted with artistic ability, and wonders why her only talent is carving letters into wood. Her mother thinks Lyza will find her gift by leaving their small Maine town and attending college. But Lyza hates the thought of leaving and going to the city. When her mother dies in the flu epidemic of 1918, Lyza knows she will stay with her father, protecting him from those who would send him to the work farm. In staying, Lyza will also find her talent.

Keywords: 1910s; Family; Illness

Milford, Kate.

The Boneshaker. **Clarion Books, 2010. 978-0-547-24187-6 (hardcover); 978-0-547-55004-6 (softcover). 384pp. ◑**

Thirteen-year-old Natalie has a talent for mechanical things. Bicycles, newfangled automobiles, or clockworks—she likes them all. That skill will come in handy when a strange threat comes to her hometown. Arcane, Missouri, is located near the crossroads of two major roads. But for some reason, travelers don't like to spend a lot of time in Arcane. That makes even more noteworthy the arrival of Dr. Jake Limberleg's Nostrum Fair and Technological Medicine Show. The people of Arcane are captivated by the show, with its unusual medicines and strange machines. But when Natalie explores the inner workings of the fair's wagon train, it's clear that something very wrong is going on. Arcane is in danger, and it's up to Natalie to save her hometown.

Keywords: 1910s

Moranville, Sharelle Byars.

A Higher Geometry. **Henry Holt, 2006. 978-0-8050-7470-3 (hardcover). 224pp. ◑ ⑤**

For Anna, mathematics is simple and logical and easy. It's a shame that life isn't like math. Ever since the death of her beloved grandmother, Anna has felt lost and alone. She's not like other girls; she can't figure out a sewing pattern at all, and she wants to go to college and study math. Her parents, not to mention everyone else in town, expects girls to get married and have babies, in that order. Until Anna meets Mike, that sounds dreadful. But Mike really likes her, and Anna finds herself falling for him. That just makes things even more complicated. How can Anna choose between the boy she loves and her natural talent for math? And what will people say if she makes the "wrong" choice?

Keywords: 1950s; Romance; Women's Roles

Naylor, Phyllis Reynolds.

Blizzard's Wake. Atheneum, 2002. 978-0-689-85220-6 (hardcover); 978-0-689-85221-3 (softcover). 224pp. **M** **J**

> The death of her mother in an accident with a drunk driver changed Kate. Even though it was four years ago, Kate is still angry at Zeke Dexter, the driver who was charged in her mother's death. Fifteen-year-old Kate is forced to face Zeke, and her feelings, as the blizzard of 1941 sweeps through North Dakota and catches everyone by surprise. Kate's father and brother, stranded in their old car, find Zeke out in the storm, on the verge of freezing to death. They bring him into the car until Kate rescues them, for the car was stuck in their own driveway. After the storm comes the real struggle, as bitter Kate and the recovering Zeke live in the same house. Kate must learn to let go of her anger if she wants to make peace and move on.
>
> **Keywords:** 1940s; Disasters; Family; Mother and Child; Multiple Voices

O'Dell, Kathleen.

Bad Tickets. Knopf Books for Young Readers, 2007. 978-0-375-83801-9 (hardcover); 978-0-440-23967-3 (softcover). 240pp. **J** **S**

> All her life Mary Margaret has done the right thing. She goes to Mass like a good Catholic girl, always does what her parents tell her to, and respects her teachers. Then she meets the irreverent, rebellious Jane. Jane says that Mary Margaret should say yes to life—that she shouldn't risk being like her mother and getting a bad ticket. At first Mary Margaret just leaves school at lunch and smokes cigarettes. But when Jane seeks more fun, and Mary Margaret's instincts make her hang back, she will have to make a choice. Mary Margaret begins plotting a course between her mother's life of babies and laundry and Jane's life of bad boys and drugs. A good girl in 1967 Oregon learns how to create her own ticket to life.
>
> **Keywords:** 1960s; Family; Friendship; Women's Roles

Paterson, Katherine.

Jacob Have I Loved. HarperTeen, 1980. 978-0-690-04078-4 (hardcover); 978-0-06-440368-9 (softcover). 224pp. **M** **J**

> Like the biblical Esau and Jacob, Jean Louise lives in the shadow of her sister Caroline. Caroline is golden and ladylike and blessed with a beautiful voice, but Jean Louise is dark and tomboyish and works with her father on his fishing boat. In the 1940s, on a small Chesapeake Bay island, there aren't many ways for a girl to be special. Jean Louise struggles to find a place for herself, looking toward her father, her best friend Call, and the mysterious Captain to help her break away from Caroline. Yet it is only when Jean Louise leaves the island and listens to herself that she is able to make peace with her sister.
>
> **Awards:** Newbery Medal
>
> **Keywords:** 1940s; Coming-of-age; Family; Sisters

Peck, Richard.

Here Lies the Librarian. Dial, 2006. 978-0-8037-3080-9 (hardcover); 978-0-545-04661-9 (softcover). 160pp. ⓜ

> Peewee has it good. She likes helping her brother in his garage, seeing different kinds of autos come along for repair or gas. In her small town, most people would rather go back to the horse-drawn buggy, but not Peewee and her brother Jake. So when a woman comes along in a nice little runabout, Peewee and Jake both take notice, but for different reasons. The woman is Irene Ridpath, and she and her friends are all library science students. When the town decides to reopen its library, the four young librarians share the duties and the salary. These sophisticated, feminine women make Peewee start rethinking how she feels about being a girl. After all, it's 1914—maybe being a girl isn't so bad now.
>
> **Keywords:** 1910s; Humor; Women's Roles

The Teacher's Funeral. Dial, 2004. 978-0-8037-2736-6 (hardcover); 978-0-439-90035-5 (softcover). 208pp. ⓜ

> No one is really going to miss the schoolteacher, Miss Myrt. Russell is especially excited, and not just because Miss Myrt dropped dead in August. He's fifteen, after all, and he's eager to head off to the Dakotas. He'll be a farmer, using the newest, most up-to-date threshers and farm machines. To be a farmer, he doesn't have to pass the eighth-grade examination. But then horrible news comes out. The school board has hired a new teacher—and it's Russell's older sister Tansy. It's the end of Russell's dream, but perhaps this school year might give him a new one.
>
> **Keywords:** Brothers and Sisters; Coming-of-age; Humor

Peck, Robert Newton.

A Day No Pigs Would Die. Knopf, 1972. 978-0-394-48235-4 (hardcover). 160pp. ⓜ

> In the mountains of Vermont, the traditions of the Shakers have lived on: no frills, a lot of hard work, and not being beholden are what Bob knows. The world may be changing, with a Vermonter elected president and baseball every boy's favorite game, but Bob continues on with the old ways. He helps deliver the calf of his neighbor's cow, all alone. When he is injured in the process, the neighbor repays him with a piglet. Bob loves the pig, which he names Pinky, raising her up and helping her grow. Whenever he has a question, he asks his father. Illiterate but a strong worker, Bob's father seems to be as strong and eternal as the Vermont mountains. But Bob will discover that nothing last forever: not a person, and not a way of life.
>
> **Keywords:** 1920s; Coming-of-age; Father and Child; Shakers; Sports

Platt, Randall.

Hellie Jondoe. **Texas Tech University Press, 2009. 978-0-89672-663-5 (softcover). 216pp.** 🅜 🅙

In the tough streets of New York, Hellie Jondoe knows what to do. She can pick pockets, run cons, and take care of any problems with her slingshot. She and her brother Harry have been on their own for years, occasionally joining up with other gangs. But now that Hellie is thirteen, Harry knows they can't go on like this much longer. So Harry arranges for Hellie to go west on an orphan train, tricking her into thinking he's dead so that she'll go. Hellie hates this, but she doesn't have anywhere else to go. In Oregon Hellie gets taken in by a tough ranch woman. Three years of work lie ahead of her, as well as taking care of half-blind Lizzie and crippled Joey. After years of looking out for just herself, Hellie learns how to look out for others.

Keywords: 1910s; Disguised as Boy; Family; Orphans

Rinaldi, Ann.

Brooklyn Rose. **Harcourt Children's Books, 2005. 978-0-15-205117-4 (hardcover); 978-0-15-205538-7 (softcover). 240pp.** 🅜 🅙

Fifteen-year-old Rose has had a wonderful life on St. Helena's Island, located near Beaufort, South Carolina. 1899 will soon be 1900, and Rose is happy to ride her horse Tom Jones, play with her little brother Benjamin, and write in her diary. Then, as her older sister Heppi prepares to get married, Rose learns that her father is having financial difficulties. If Rose could be married, her father's burdens would be eased. Meeting Rene Dumarest seems like just the opportunity Rose needs. Soon she's living in the North, learning how to be a wife and run her own home. It's tough work, but as she falls more in love with her husband. Rose finds her happiness in a way she never expected.

Keywords: 1900s; Romance

Schmidt, Gary D.

Lizzie Bright and the Buckminster Boy. **Clarion, 2004. 978-0-618-43929-4 (hardcover); 978-0-375-84169-9 (softcover). 224pp.** 🅙

Turner Buckminster spends only six hours in Phippsburg, Maine, before he's ready to run away to the Wild West. Everyone talks differently than the people in Boston, Maine baseball is very strange, and everyone knows that he's the new minister's son. Turner's about ready to drown in all the expectations when he meets Lizzie Bright. She's smart, good at baseball, and the daughter of a preacher. She's a perfect friend, except in the eyes of Turner's father. There are two things working against Lizzie: She's black, and she lives on Malaga Island, in a settlement full of outsiders and undesirables. Turner doesn't care about that, because there's so much that Lizzie can teach him. Phippsburg starts looking like a good place to live, until the town fathers finally succeed in clearing Malaga Island, wanting to improve Phippsburg's standing as a tourist attraction. That action destroys Turner's friendship with Lizzie.

Awards: Printz Honor Book; Newbery Honor Book

Keywords: 1910s; African American Issues; Father and Child; Friendship; Multiple Voices

The Wednesday Wars. **Clarion, 2007. 978-0-618-72483-3 (hardcover); 978-0-547-23760-2 (softcover). 272pp. Ⓜ Ⓙ**

Wednesdays are not exactly Holling's favorite day. Though his Catholic and Jewish classmates leave school early for religious instruction, he's a Presbyterian and has to stay at school. Making things even worse, his teacher, Mrs. Baker, expects way too much from him. She wants him to read Shakespeare, of all things! Meanwhile, his father demands a certain standard of behavior, which doesn't really jive with life in late 1960s America. Holling tries to live up to that standard, but his sister isn't interested. Thanks to Mrs. Baker, the teacher he thought hated him, Holling finds some answers.

Awards: Newbery Honor Book

Keywords: 1960s; Father and Child

Smelcer, John.

The Great Death. **Henry Holt, 2009. 978-0-8050-8100-8 (hardcover). 176pp. Ⓙ**

Since she's the oldest, Millie is responsible for her younger sister Maura. Even though they're only thirteen and ten, Millie and Maura have several chores and know how to do many things. In their Alaskan village, everyone is relied on in order to survive. Then the white men come, with their diseases that are unknown to the villagers. Soon almost everyone in the village is sick, covered with red spots. For some unknown reason, Millie and Maura do not get sick. They take care of their parents, watching as the dead attract dogs, seagulls, and even bears to feast upon the flesh. When their parents die, Millie and Maura cannot stay alone in their village. They load a canoe with supplies and sail away. It's sure to be scary and dangerous, but as long as they have each other, Millie and Maura can face the challenge.

Keywords: 1910s; Illness; Sisters

Thesman, Jean.

Kate Keely Series. Ⓜ Ⓙ

After surviving the San Francisco earthquake, Kate has even more challenges to face. Can she find a way to stay strong without giving in to cynicism?

Keywords: 1900s; Family; Illness; Multiple Voices

A Sea So Far. Viking Juvenile, 2001. 978-0-670-89278-5 (hardcover); 978-0-14-230059-6 (softcover). 195pp.

> The San Francisco earthquake of 1906 is just the beginning of the story for two young women. Kate, an orphan who lives with her aunt, dreams of being a schoolteacher and maybe seeing Ireland someday. Jolie longs to be strong again after her bout of scarlet fever. But with the earthquake, Kate loses her future and Jolie loses her mother. Through a chance encounter a year later, Kate becomes Jolie's companion. The two girls slowly start building a friendship, in stops and starts. When Kate learns a secret about Jolie's family—told to her by Jolie's father—will a trip to Ireland for the two girls change them?

Rising Tide. Viking Juvenile, 2003. 978-0-670-03656-1 (hardcover). 240pp.

> After Jolie Logan, her friend and employer, dies from consumption in Ireland, Kate Keely makes her way home to San Francisco. Once she's back home, Kate must find a way to support herself and her Aunt Grace. Although she's always dreamed of being a teacher, Kate knows the salary isn't enough. So she and her friend Ellen plan to open a unique shop selling Irish linen and lace. But there are plenty of pitfalls. Ellen has spent much of the money she was supposed to save in pursuit of the rich young man whose family owns a department store—the store that Ellen works at. And that's even before they get the shop open—what problems await them once they're in business? This novel in two voices explores two young women seeking independence.

Weaver, Will.

Full Service. Farrar, Straus & Giroux, 2005. 978-0-374-32485-8 (hardcover); 978-0-374-40022-4 (softcover). 240pp. **M** **J**

In Paul's small town, everyone knows the rules. Town kids work in the grocery store and farm kids work at the mill. At age sixteen Paul is quiet, an outsider due to belonging to a nondenominational Christian church. At the start of the summer Paul's mother suggests that he get a job in town, in order to meet people. Paul goes along with her and falls into a job at the local service station. Working at the station, Paul begins to learn about people. There are tourists passing by, the local golden boy and his beautiful girlfriend, the ex-gangster. There are also Paul's coworkers, like Kirk, who cheats on his wife, and quiet, simple Bud. In the summer of 1965, Paul takes his questions and observations and learns how to become his own man.

Keywords: 1960s; Coming-of-age

Wolff, Virginia Euwer.

Bat 6. Scholastic, 2000. 978-0-590-89800-3 (softcover). 240pp. **M**

For the past forty-nine years, the sixth-grade girls of the Bear Creek Ridge and Barlow Road schools have played a baseball game. The fiftieth anniversary of the game promises to be a good one, a way to keep moving on after the events of World War II. But for two players, the events of the war are still very present. Shazam lost her father in the Japanese attack on Pearl Harbor; Aki spent the war years in an internment camp with the rest of her Japanese family. When an assault brings these two girls together, they and their teammates are forced to ask themselves many hard questions.

Keywords: 1940s; Japanese Internment; Multiple Voices; Sports

A Wave of Immigrants: 1900–1925

The turn of the twentieth century saw a new group of immigrants arriving, from Southern and Eastern Europe. Though America had taken in many immigrants, these new arrivals were affected by their lack of English literacy and resentment from older immigrants such as the Irish.

Auch, Mary Jane.

Ashes of Roses. **Henry Holt, 2002. 978-0-8050-6686-9 (hardcover); 978-0-440-23851-5 (softcover). 256pp. 🄼 🄳**

Arriving in America from Ireland was supposed to be the start of something good for Rose and her family. But her little brother is sent back to Ireland for an eye infection, and her father goes with him. Her Uncle Patrick didn't know the family was coming—and his wife and stepdaughters aren't thrilled to have four guests staying with them. But Rose isn't giving up just yet. She knows that America has more opportunities than Ireland, and she wants a chance to stand out. She gets it, but in an unexpected way, when she starts working at the Triangle Shirtwaist Factory with her sister Maureen. The two of them are surrounded by Polish, Italian, and Russian girls, but in spite of the lack of a common language, Rose makes friends and enjoys making money. Then on one horrible day, a fire breaks out and threatens the lives of Rose, Maureen, and all their friends.

Keywords: 1910s; Disasters; Family

Davies, Jacqueline.

📖 *Lost.* **Marshall Cavendish, 2009. 978-0-7614-5535-6 (hardcover). 242pp. 🄳 🄢**

When Essie meets Harriett, she can see immediately that Harriett is lost. After all, a rich girl like Harriett working in a factory? There's a story there, one that Essie wants to figure out. Learning about Harriett will help distract Essie from her problems: worrying about her siblings, wondering if the neighbor boy likes her, fighting with her mother, and trying to stretch her money. When Essie learns Harriett's secret, it doesn't change the fact that Essie has a secret of her own, one that she's kept even from herself. And she won't find herself until disaster strikes. Because the factory that Essie and Harriett work in is the Triangle Shirtwaist Factory, and one day a fire changes the factory workers' lives.

Keywords: 1910s; Disasters; Friendship; Sisters

Franklin, Kristine L.

Grape Thief. **Candlewick, 2003. 978-0-7636-1325-9 (hardcover). 304pp.** **J**

Slava is usually called Cuss by his friends and family, because he can curse in fourteen languages. In his Washington State mining town there are many immigrants. Even though America is supposed to be a melting pot, the older people like Cuss's mother are Old Country—which means you stick to your own kind. Younger people can cross the lines, though: One of Cuss's friends is black. Cuss doesn't care so much about that, though. He's busy planning raids on the grape train and trying to stay out of the mines long enough to finish the seventh grade. But then the yellow-haired man who was making eyes at Mary, Cuss's sister, accidentally dies while Cuss's two brothers are fighting him. The death of a man sends the town of Roslyn into a tailspin and changes the lives of Cuss and his family.

Keywords: 1920s; Family; Murder

Haddix, Margaret Peterson.

Uprising. **Simon & Schuster Children's Publishing, 2007. 978-1-4169-1171-5 (hardcover); 978-1-4169-1172-2 (softcover). 352pp.** **J** **S**

Many changes awaited immigrants to America: finding a job, learning English, paying back the money loaned for their passage. Bella arrives from her Italian village and finds work at the Triangle Shirtwaist Factory. She meets Yetta at the factory, a Russian Jew who's determined to improve working conditions. Yetta is inspired by her revolutionary sister to try to start a union. But Yetta's union has few members, and calls for a strike don't change anything at first. But Yetta persuades many of the girls who have been kept in a cage by their wealth, girls like Jane, who begins to become part of the turbulent events at the Triangle Factory. On March 25, 1911, when fire tears through the factory, all three girls are there, and only one of them survives.

Keywords: 1910s; Disasters; Friendship

Hesse, Karen.

Brooklyn Bridge. **Feiwel & Friends, 2008. 978-0-312-37886-8 (hardcover). 240pp.** **M** **J**

It is 1903, and all Joseph wants is to see the bright electric lights of Coney Island. Unfortunately Joseph's father keeps saying, "Next month, Joseph." Joseph's whole family is kept busy all day, making a new toy known as the teddy bear. Ever since the family's candy shop became a toy factory, Joseph can almost never play stick ball. With the money to be made, his parents can't stop working. Soon they might even leave Brooklyn, moving someplace with more space for the bears. Leaving Brooklyn is the last thing Joseph wants—even though with his family's financial position, he doesn't really fit in with the other boys. In the shadow of the Brooklyn Bridge, Joseph, his family, and his friends live and work, dream and die. Joseph and his family might seem lucky to other immigrants, but Joseph takes a long time to figure out whether they are.

Keywords: 1900s; Family

Civil Rights: 1920–1970

Although legally African Americans had the same rights as Caucasians in the first half of the twentieth century, in actual practice they were kept segregated from the better facilities that whites enjoyed. For decades, strong and determined people campaigned and pressed for true equality for blacks. To learn more about this period, read *Claudette Colvin: Twice Toward Justice* by Phillip Hoose or *Marching for Freedom: Walk Together Children and Don't You Grow Weary* by Elizabeth Partridge.

Davis, Tanita S.

Mare's War. **Knopf Books for Young Readers, 2009. 978-0-375-85714-0 (hardcover); 978-0-375-85077-6 (softcover). 352pp. J S**

The last thing Octavia wants to do on her summer vacation is spend it with her sister Talitha and their grandmother Mare. Mare's not your typical grandmother, and Talitha is grumpy about not being able to make the money for a car. The girls are going to have to spend most of the summer with Mare, driving from California to Alabama. But Mare has a lot of stories to tell, about how she ran away from home, lied about her age, and joined the Women's Army Corps. Part of the 6888th African American battalion, Mare got to have experiences that other young black girls didn't—experiences that helped her become who she is now. Through these stories, Octavia and Tali gain a new understanding of their grandmother and see just how far African Americans have come.

Keywords: 1940s; Family; World War II

Draper, Sharon.

Fire from the Rock. **Dutton Juvenile, 2007. 978-0-525-47720-4 (hardcover); 978-0-14-241199-5 (softcover). 240pp. M J**

It's been three years since *Brown vs. Board of Education*, but Little Rock's schools are still segregated. The start of the 1957 school year is when integration will finally happen, starting with Central High School. Sylvia Patterson is surprised when her teacher asks her to think about being one of Central's first black students. Of course she's eager to go to high school, learning more and joining clubs. And Central has the best resources, the best teachers. But if Sylvia goes to Central, she will leave behind her friends, even her new boyfriend. Worst of all, she will be an outcast at Central. Sylvia's older brother Gary encourages her to go to Central. Before she decides, though, the tensions in Little Rock explode, showing Sylvia that whether she goes or not, change is coming.

Keywords: 1950s; Coming-of-age; Friendship

Hesse, Karen.

Witness. **Scholastic Press, 2001. 978-0-439-27199-8 (hardcover); 978-0-439-27200-1 (softcover) 161pp. Ⓜ Ⓙ**

In a town in Vermont, people live and work and hope. They hope for better lives, or for happiness, or for peace. It is 1924, and the world is changing fast. It's changing too fast for those who don't want blacks or Catholics or Jews around. The Ku Klux Klan is in town, trying to preserve its version of America. So Leonora Sutter, a colored girl, and Esther Hirsch, a young Jewish girl, shouldn't fit in. But they're part of their town, bringing hope and pride. The citizens of this small Vermont town, in their own voices, tell the story of what happened when the Klan came and how they sent the Klan away.

Keywords: 1920s; Multiple Voices; Novel in Verse

Houston, Julian.

New Boy. **Houghton Mifflin, 2005. 978-0-618-43253-0 (hardcover); 978-0-618-88405-6 (softcover). 288pp. Ⓢ**

Being an outsider is tough. Rob knew it would be difficult to be the only African American at his new school. It's a boarding school in Connecticut, and Rob can't help feeling he's in a whole new world. It's hard to fit in and figure out how to interact with these boys. But even harder is feeling torn between going to school to get an education and staying at home in Virginia to help with the developing civil rights movement. What will be the right choice for Rob?

Keywords: 1960s; Coming-of-age

Johnston, Tony.

Bone by Bone by Bone. **Roaring Brook Press, 2007. 978-1-59643-113-3 (hardcover). 192pp. Ⓙ**

David and his best friend, Malcolm, are always playing together. They act out the story of Brer Rabbit and have a pissing contest. They also talk about things like religion, like how they don't understand what it means to be a Methodist or a Baptist. But Malcolm has never come over to David's house. That's because Malcolm is black, and David's father says that if he ever catches Malcolm in the house, he'll get shot. David thinks his father was just joking. Sure, his father has a temper, sometimes being very cruel. And he's got a lot of guns, but most Southerners do. So when David finally works up his courage to have Malcolm over, he doesn't realize what will happen.

Keywords: 1950s; Friendship; Murder

Lee, Harper.

📖 *To Kill a Mockingbird.* **Lippincott Williams & Wilkins, 1960. 978-0-397-00151-4 (hardcover); 978-0-06-093546-7 (softcover). 296pp. 🕮 🖲**

A quiet old town: that's where Scout lives. Her days are full of playing with her brother Jem and her friend Dill, reading with her father Atticus, and trying to make Boo Radley come out of his house. Yet when a black man is accused of raping a white woman, the sleepy town of Maycomb, Alabama, is woken up. Scout is in the middle of it, because her father is defending Tom Robinson, the accused. And what's more, Atticus is defending Tom with all his energy, breaking all the rules in the Deep South of the 1930s.

Keywords: 1930s; Brothers and Sisters; Family; Great Depression

Levine, Kristin.

The Best Bad Luck I Ever Had. **Putnam Juvenile, 2009. 978-0-399-25090-3 (hardcover); 978-0-14-241648-8 (softcover). 272pp. 🕮**

Dit sure didn't expect to become friends with a girl, and a black girl to boot. But when Emma and her family move to town, Dit has to follow his mother's rule: be nice to everyone. So Dit and Emma start spending time together, learning from each other. Dit teaches Emma how to fish and throw a baseball. Emma shows Dit how to think, how to puzzle out why things are the way they are. Why don't white kids and black kids go to the same school? Dit doesn't know the answer, but if Emma is asking that, it's a good question to ask. And when the local barber, a hard-working African American, is accused of a crime, Dit and Emma will be asking a lot of questions to figure it out.

Keywords: 1910s; Friendship

Magoon, Kekla.

The Rock and the River. **Aladdin, 2009. 978-1-4169-7582-3 (hardcover); 978-1-4169-7803-9 (softcover). 304pp. 🕮 🖲**

As the struggle for civil rights grows more intense, a boy must decide how to play his role in the drama. Thirteen-year-old Sam is the son of Roland Childs, a well-known figure in civil rights circles. Like his mentor Dr. Martin Luther King Jr., Sam's father supports nonviolence. He expects Sam and Sam's older brother Stick to turn the other cheek. Sam finds this very hard, especially because he can't talk over his doubts with his father.

But he's surprised to find literature from the Black Panthers under Stick's bed. This group argues for armed violence to gain rights for African Americans. Sam doesn't want to turn his back on his father, but maybe Stick and the Black Panthers have the answers. As 1968 progresses, Sam finds his own path between the two great forces in his life: his father and his brother.

Keywords: 1960s; Brothers; Father and Child

McDonald, Joyce.

Devil on My Heels. **Delacorte Books for Young Readers, 2004. 978-0-385-73107-2 (hardcover); 978-0-440-23829-4 (softcover). 262pp.** ◨

Dove's life is about as sweet as the oranges her father grows. She has friends to see movies and drink Cokes with. The family housekeeper, Delia, cooks and cleans and serves as a mother to fifteen-year-old Dove, whose mother died when she was four. And Chase Tully, with his blue T-bird, is paying attention to her. But there's some bitterness in all this sweetness. Local orange groves have caught fire, and suspicion falls on the pickers. Gator, Dove's childhood friend, is drawing the wrong kind of attention. He's African American, but he has a white girlfriend and is speaking out against the pickers' working conditions. Dove discovers that there's more than meets the eye about her hometown as she sees racial tension and prejudice lead to violence.

Keywords: 1950s; Coming-of-age

McMullan, Margaret.

Sources of Light. **Houghton Mifflin Books for Children, 2010. 978-0-547-07659-1 (hardcover). 240pp.** ◨

Moving to Mississippi in 1962 means upheaval for fourteen-year-old Samantha. Called Sam, she has a hard time adjusting to life in the South. She's an army brat who's moved around a lot, and it's hard to make friends. The fact that Sam and her mother moved from Pittsburgh after the death of her father in Vietnam makes life even harder. She escapes through the camera she is given by her mother's new friend, Perry. Through the lens, Sam starts looking at her world, trying to figure it out. People are talking about civil rights, keeping their women safe—things that Sam doesn't really understand. The camera lets her hide—but perhaps it will also let her discover herself.

Keywords: 1960s; Art; Coming-of-age

Moses, Sheila P.

Buddy Bush. Ⓜ ◨

Patti Mae idolizes her uncle Buddy. His mistreatment due to the color of his skin will inspire her to set her own course, to somewhere that she can be equal.

Keywords: 1940s; Coming-of-age; Family

The Legend of Buddy Bush. **Margaret K. McElderry, 2003. 978-0-689-85839-0 (hardcover); 978-1-4169-0716-9 (softcover). 224pp.**

1

All Patti Mae wants is to go North like her sister BarJean. To live in Harlem just like her uncle Buddy did sounds like heaven—way better than living on Rehobeth Road in Rich Square, North Carolina. The only person who livens things up is Uncle Buddy. He's one of Patti Mae's three favorite men, and he's full of Northern ideas. He doesn't believe in ghosts, he's the only black who works at the mill, and he doesn't move off the sidewalk when a white person is walking toward him. When Buddy and Patti Mae go into town to take in their regular Friday night movie, Buddy speaks to a white woman and doesn't move off the sidewalk for her. The woman goes to the police and accuses Buddy of attempted rape. In a case like this, even a witness like Patti Mae doesn't matter. Buddy is put on trial and found guilty, but he manages to escape from jail. Through it all, Patti Mae wonders at the unfairness, the inequality of it all. Will she ever find somewhere where people like her get a fair shake?

2

3

Awards: National Book Award Finalist

The Return of Buddy Bush. Margaret K. McElderry, 2005. 978-0-689-87431-4 (hardcover); 978-1-4169-3925-2 (softcover). 160pp.

4

Patti Mae has lost some people: first her uncle Buddy and now her grandfather. At least Uncle Buddy is still alive, though hiding somewhere; her grandfather is dead. But she has something to take her mind off things when her sister BarJean takes her north to Harlem. For Patti Mae, Harlem is a whole new world, an equal world. Colored people are just like whites, even owning their own businesses. She wants to take it all in, remembering everything and holding on to the idea that she can make something out of her future. Patti Mae thinks there's nothing she can't do—including finding her uncle Buddy. Once she finds him, he can go back to North Carolina to get his name cleared. Patti Mae doesn't realize that even though she feels invincible, it doesn't mean she is. Will blind faith be enough to help Patti find Buddy?

5

6

Myers, Walter Dean.

7

Harlem Summer. **Scholastic, 2007. 978-0-439-36843-8 (hardcover). 165pp.** ❶

It's the summer of 1925 in Harlem, and Mark has been roped into a job. The pay's not bad, but the job is way downtown. And working at *The Crisis*, a magazine for African Americans, is pretty boring even with all the talk about the New Negro. Mark would rather be playing his sax or seeing Fats Waller, a local kid who made good, play at Harlem's clubs. To get in good with Fats, Mark agrees to help with a delivery job. But when the job goes wrong, Fats, Mark, and Mark's friend Henry are all in trouble with Dutch

8

Schultz. If the bootlegger and gangster doesn't get his money, he'll start chopping off body parts. It'll be a hot time in Harlem unless Mark can clear the debt.

Keywords: 1920s; Friendship

Nolan, Han.

A Summer of Kings. **Harcourt Children's Books, 2006. 978-0-15-205108-2 (hardcover). 352pp.** ▣ ▣

In her family of performers and stars, Esther is the oddball. She's a fourteen-year-old tomboy, wishing she could wear pants to school. In the summer of 1964, her parents agree to take in the son of her mother's best friend, a young black man who is accused of killing a white man. Before he arrives, Esther thinks of the excitement of his visit and the shock value of starting a romance with this young man. But when King-Roy arrives, Esther becomes friends with him. He is disillusioned with the ideas of Martin Luther King Jr. and supports the revolutionary violence of Malcolm X. Esther doesn't fully understand King-Roy's anger, but she's sympathetic. Together, each will learn how to understand people in a troubled time.

Keywords: 1960s; Coming-of-age; Friendship

Rodman, Mary Ann.

Yankee Girl. **Farrar, Straus & Giroux, 2004. 978-0-374-38661-0 (hardcover); 978-0-312-53576-6 (softcover). 224pp.** ▣

Moving to Mississippi from Chicago in 1964 is a culture shock. Alice Ann's father, a FBI agent, has been transferred to the South to help protect blacks during the civil rights movement. Eleven-year-old Alice has a hard time understanding why things are so different. Why can't boys be friends with girls? Why do you call blacks by their first name? Although Alice makes a friend in Jeb, her next door neighbor, they can't talk at school. And since the popular girls in the sixth grade don't like her, Alice is in the market for a friend. She thinks she might have one in Valerie, one of the black students who have been integrated into the school. But Valerie isn't looking for a friend. Can Alice change Valerie's mind, or will Alice stop thinking like a Yankee girl and become like everyone else?

Keywords: 1960s; Friendship

Sharenow, Robert.

My Mother the Cheerleader. **HarperTeen, 2007. 978-0-06-114896-5 (hardcover); 978-0-06-114898-9 (softcover). 304pp.** ▣

Louise's mother isn't cheering at a football game. When schools in New Orleans's Ninth Ward are integrated, including Louise's school, her mother pulls her out of school and joins the group of women who taunt Ruby Bridges, the black first-grader who attends the local elementary school. To outsiders, this looks wrong. For Louise, it's just how life is: Blacks and whites should live separate lives. Then Mr. Morgan Miller arrives and rents a room from Louise's mother. Mr. Miller is from New York, he's Jewish, and his politics are suspect. He's the last person Louise should listen to about anything. But his anger about segregation is so powerful, Louise can't help questioning all those beliefs she's never examined. As 1960 fades into 1961, Louise realizes that she can't go on thinking the same way. And it won't just be Louise who changes.

Keywords: 1960s; Coming-of-age; Family

Smith, Sherri L.

Flygirl. **Putnam Juvenile, 2009. 978-0-399-24709-5 (hardcover); 978-0-14-241725-6 (softcover). 256pp.** 🇯 🇸

Ida Mae was born with wings, it feels like. Her father was a pilot, and he taught her to fly. But as an African American woman, she faces twice the discrimination. Even though she has light skin and "good" hair, Ida Mae is still black. When she learns about the WASPs, Ida Mae takes a huge risk. The Women's Airforce Service Pilots were formed in 1943 to train women pilots to ferry planes and do other noncombat flying. But African American women were not accepted into the WASPs, so Ida Mae decides to pass for white. If she's found out, she'll be kicked out and lose her dreams of flying. But she makes it through training and begins serving, keeping her secret. Ida Mae is tempted by all the opportunities in her new life. Will she keep passing or will she be true to her heritage and her family?

Read-alike: *Almost Astronauts: 13 Women Who Dared to Dream* by Tanya Lee Stone tells more about women's struggle to be treated equally in the air.

Keywords: 1940s; Romance; World War II

Taylor, Mildred D.

Roll of Thunder, Hear My Cry. **Dial, 1976. 978-0-8037-7473-5 (hardcover); 978-0-14-038451-2 (softcover). 276pp.** 🇲 🇯

Growing up African American in the South during the 1930s, Cassie is both lucky and unlucky. Her family owns the land they live and work on; she didn't suffer the indignities of slavery or Reconstruction. She's been sheltered and loved by her parents and extended family members. But when Cassie begins to realize that many people hold the color of her skin against her, she doesn't know how to react. As she slowly learns to face prejudice and racism, she learns to appreciate her advantages.

Awards: Newbery Medal

Keywords: 1930s; Family; Great Depression

Vaught, Susan.

Stormwitch. Bloomsbury, 2004. 978-1-58234-952-7 (hardcover). 200pp. **J** **S**

Ruba is suffering from an extreme case of culture clash. She grew up in Haiti, being trained by her grandmother in her African heritage. But Ba, her grandmother, is too old to take care of Ruba, so she is sent to the United States to live with her other grandmother. Grandmother Jones is full of rules; she wants Ruba to fit in. A colored girl in 1969 Mississippi has to know her place, respect white folks, and content herself with slow, steady progress toward true equality, even though the gains of the Freedom Summer, five years before, brought quick, violent change. What Grandmother Jones doesn't know—and Ruba does—is that something is coming. Ruba, thanks to the gods, fears that a great storm is coming, caused by the spirit Zashar. It will be up to Ruba to confront Zashar and her monster storm, Hurricane Camille.

Keywords: 1960s; Disasters; Family; Religious Conflicts

Voigt, Cynthia.

The Runner. Simon & Schuster, 2005. 978-1-4169-0341-3 (softcover). 320pp. **J** **S**

He's called Bullet because of how fast he runs. He's not just running for running's sake; going as fast as he can, all by himself, lets him ignore his problems: the way his father is domineering and unable to see any point of view but his own; the way his mother won't stand up to his father; the way his town is changing. When Bullet is asked to help coach a new teammate on the track team—an African American—he doesn't want to at first. But slowly, Bullet learns to run with someone else.

Keywords: 1960s; Coming-of-age

The Great Depression: 1930s

With the crash of the stock market in 1929, and the unsuccessful economic policies of the early 1930s, America—and the rest of the world—was plunged into a deep financial depression. During this decade many families experienced hardship and deprivation, yet it often drew them closer together.

Choldenko, Gennifer.

Al Capone Series. **M** **J**

These slice-of-life novels imagine the life of a boy on Alcatraz Island. Featuring humor mixed with family drama, Choldenko offers up two winning stories.

Keywords: Coming-of-age; Family; Humor; Mental Disability

Al Capone Does My Shirts. **Putnam, 2004. 978-0-399-23861-1 (hardcover); 978-0-14-240370-9 (softcover). 240pp.**

Not everyone who lives on Alcatraz Island is a convict. Nevertheless, Moose Flanagan, the son of a new electrician, feels like a prisoner. He misses his friends and his life back in Santa Monica, and now that they're on Alcatraz, his dad is too busy with his job to spend time with twelve-year-old Moose. But Moose knows he has to bear it, because now his sister Natalie can attend a special school, which might help her unusual condition. Slowly, Moose starts to fit in. He makes friends on the island and finds kids to play baseball with. And then there's the business that the warden's daughter Piper ropes him in for. The business? Selling the laundry services of Alcatraz's most notorious prisoners, like the mobster Al Capone.

Awards: Newbery Honor Book; Carnegie Medal Finalist

Al Capone Shines My Shoes. **Dial, 2009. 978-0-8037-3460-9 (hardcover); 978-0-14-241718-8 (softcover). 288pp.**

The downside to someone doing you a favor is that they usually want you to repay it. For Moose Flanagan, the twelve-year-old son of an Alcatraz worker, this concept is trickier than it is for other people. Moose asked Al Capone for help getting his sister back into her special school. Natalie got thrown out, and it was with Capone's help that Natalie went back. But if Moose repays the favor, he'll be in big trouble. Kids aren't supposed to have any contact with the prisoners, and helping one would be grounds for his dad losing his job and the whole family getting kicked off the island. What's more, Natalie could be kicked out of her school again. Caught between a rock and a hard place, Moose will have to figure out who are the good guys and who are the bad guys.

Hesse, Karen.

Out of the Dust. **Scholastic Press, 1997. 978-0-590-36080-7 (hardcover); 978-0-590-37125-4 (softcover). 240pp. 🅜 🅙**

It's been years since it rained enough to grow wheat. With no rain and the sod all torn up and plowed under, the soil has become dust. Billie Jo and her family are trying to keep the dust out and protect their food, their piano, and their crops. But there's no escaping the dust. As tragedy splits apart Billie Jo's family and takes away the music she loved to create, she can only think about getting out of the dust. Slowly Billie Jo begins to heal, just as the Dust Bowl begins to recede. In free verse, Billie Jo shows how to put back together a life that became scattered.

Read-alike: To learn more about the Dust Bowl, you might like *The Dust Bowl Through the Lens: How Photography Revealed and Helped Remedy a National Disaster* by Martin W. Sandler.

Awards: Newbery Medal; Scott O'Dell Award for Historical Fiction

Keywords: Disasters; Music; Novel in Verse

Ingold, Jeanette.

Airfield. **Harcourt Children's Books, 1999. 978-0-15-202053-8 (hardcover); 978-0-14-131216-3 (softcover). 160pp. ⬛ ⬛**

For as long as she can remember, Beatty has lived like a tumbleweed, moving from one aunt to another. She'd spend four months in Dallas, four months in San Antonio, four months in Waco, and on and on. Now, though, she has landed with her youngest aunt. She's newly married in the small town of Muddy Springs. Beatty finds herself spending a lot of time at the local airfield where her Uncle Grif works. Beatty's father is a pilot who occasionally flies through the Muddy Springs airport, and Beatty is eager to take advantage of that opportunity. That's not the only reason to go to the airstrip, though: there's Moss, the poor boy who's trying to make enough money to survive. There are also the planes themselves, which Beatty dreams of flying or at least getting a ride in one. Slowly Beatty learns a lot about airplanes and airfields, knowledge she'll need when on a stormy night her father is trying to land at the field. With no lights for the airstrip, how will Beatty and Moss help him land?

Keywords: Family; Father and Child

Laskas, Gretchen Moran.

The Miner's Daughter. **Simon & Schuster Children's Publishing, 2007. 978-1-4169-1262-0 (hardcover). 256pp. ⬛**

For Willa, life is a never-ending round of housework. Keeping everything clean with the coal dust settling on it is a tough task. With her mother sick after having a baby, it's up to sixteen-year-old Willa to keep the house going. The winter of 1932–1933 has been long and hard, made even worse by the coal mine being shut down after Roosevelt was elected president. But then Willa's older brother hears about good work on a crew building a tunnel through the mountains. Leaving the family behind, her older brother and their father head off to Hawk's Nest. Willa knows this means more work for her, but she doesn't mind, because Miss Grace McCartney has come to town and opened a library. It's just the start of good times for the community known as Arthurdale—a community that will help Willa when disaster strikes.

Keywords: Coming-of-age; Family; Women's Roles

Meltzer, Milton.

Tough Times. **Clarion Books, 2007. 978-0-618-87445-3 (hardcover). 176pp. ⬛ ⬛**

The Great Depression is making life even more difficult for Joey and his family. His father has fewer windows to wash, and his mother tries to make extra money selling stockings door-to-door. Joey's job on the milk run doesn't bring in much money, either. It's like that all through New England, in towns that have only one industry. The only hope for Joey's family is the long-promised but never-delivered bonuses for World War I veterans. With nothing to lose, Joey's father, a veteran of the great conflict, decides to join a march to Washington, to pressure President Hoover to pay the bonuses. Joey goes with him, camping out in a Hooverville outside Washington. But when federal soldiers break up the march, and Joey gets separated from his father, he will start on a journey that will keep him away from home.

Keywords: Coming-of-age; Family

Peck, Richard.

📖 <u>Grandma Dowdel Stories.</u> **Ⓜ** **Ⓙ**

Peck's humorous and heart-warming novels in stories present one of the most vivid characters ever seen in young people's literature: the irrepressible and indefatigable Grandma Dowdel. She faces the Great Depression with a lifetime of knowledge in how to survive—knowledge that she passes along to her grandchildren.

Keywords: Family; Humor; Short Stories

A Long Way from Chicago. Dial, 1998. 978-0-8037-2290-3 (hardcover); 978-0-14-240110-1 (softcover). 192pp.

Grandma Dowdel isn't like other grandmothers. She keeps to herself, which is an accomplishment when you live in a small town in southern Illinois. What's more, she's a crack shot with her Winchester shotgun and can tell the biggest whoppers you've ever heard. That's what Joey and Mary Alice discover on their annual visits to Grandma Dowdel. Each August holds a new, unbelievable adventure. She may be sitting up with the corpse of Shotgun Cheatham, stealing the sheriff's boat for some fishing, or arranging an elopement, but Grandma Dowdel can handle anything.

Awards: Newbery Honor Book

A Year Down Yonder. Dial, 2000. 978-0-8037-2518-8 (hardcover); 978-0-14-230070-1 (softcover). 130pp.

After years of visits to Grandma Dowdel, Mary Alice isn't really looking forward to this next one. Instead of a week in August with her older brother Joey, she'll be spending a whole year with Grandma, alone. Times are hard in 1937, and Mary Alice needs to spend the year "down yonder" until her parents get back on their feet. Grandma is just as Mary Alice remembers, but now that she's fifteen, she starts seeing new sides to Grandma. Whether she's baking pies for the whole town to enjoy—with stolen ingredients from those very townspeople—or browbeating everyone to pay up for burgoo to help a veteran, Grandma reveals the soft side under her crusty exterior. By the end of the year, Mary Alice will have a different attitude about a lot of things.

Awards: Newbery Medal

World War II: 1941–1945

For many people, World War II was America's finest hour. The United States devoted itself to the war effort, doing whatever was necessary to help win the war. Whether sacrificing gas or silk, getting a job, or sending loved ones off to war, America stepped up. Yet there were unknown stories and unhappy secrets during this period, too.

Bruchac, Joseph.

Code Talker: A Novel About the Navajo Marines of World War II. **Dial, 2005. 978-0-8037-2921-6 (hardcover); 978-0-14-240596-3 (softcover). 240pp. ◨**

Navajos at the start of the twentieth century slowly realized that they must acquire some of the white man's skills. First and foremost was learning English. Unfortunately, this often came at the expense of their mother tongue. But some Navajo, like narrator Ned Begay, manage to learn English while remembering Navajo. After America enters World War II, it soon becomes clear that an unbreakable code is needed for military communications. Native American languages were very difficult for America's enemies to translate. Beginning in 1942, Navajos were recruited for a special project. Their language would be a code that the Japanese would not be able to break. After lying about his age, Ned joins the Marines. Easily getting through boot camp, Ned finds out that he will be one of the code talkers, a top secret project. This means great danger for him and his fellow Navajos. But the Navajos are not just Indians, they are Americans, too. They will fight for the United States—and some will die for it.

Keywords: Marines; Native American Issues

Chapman, Fern Schumer.

Is It Night or Day? **Farrar, Straus & Giroux, 2010. 978-0-374-17744-7 (hardcover). 224pp. ◨**

Edith is twelve and very confused. She's being sent to America to live with an uncle she's never met. Life in Germany is too dangerous for Jews, so Edith's parents send her away. Knowing little about it, Edith struggles to adjust to this new country. Her uncle's wife is cruel to her, and there's anti-Semitism in America, too. Because she doesn't know English, she has to start school as a first grader. The only bright spot is following the achievements of Hank Greenberg, a Jewish baseball player. But when Edith receives horrible news from Europe, nothing can soften the blow.

Keywords: Family; Holocaust; Immigrants

Fletcher, Christine.

Ten Cents a Dance. **Bloomsbury, 2008. 978-1-59990-164-0 (hardcover); 978-1-59990-462-7 (softcover). 368pp.**

The illness of Ruby's mother means she has to find a job. She tries working at the meat-packing plant, just like everyone else in her Chicago neighborhood. But Ruby doesn't suffer in silence, and the backbreaking, smelly work won't help her catch the eye of Paulie, the local bad boy. There is a job that is much better than the meat-packing factory: being a taxi dancer. For ten cents a dance, Ruby will charm and flatter the men who flock to the dance hall. With the war on, Chicago is full of men, many willing to spend their money on a girl and a night on the town. Ruby thinks dancing is her way out of the tenements . . . but it turns out that taxi dancing introduces her to some very dangerous characters. Add in Paulie, and Ruby has her hands full. Can she find a way to save herself from trouble?

Keywords: Coming-of-age; Romance

Hesse, Karen.

Aleutian Sparrow. **Margaret K. McElderry, 2003. 978-0-689-86189-5 (hardcover); 978-1-4169-0327-7 (softcover). 156pp.**

This novel in verse tells an unknown story. The Aleut Islands, stretching from Alaska out into the northern Pacific, were windswept and treeless. But for the Aleuts who lived there, it was their home. In 1942, however, the Japanese invade and the Aleuts are evacuated to a camp in southeast Alaska. In the damp forests the Aleuts can't see the sea and almost never see the sun. Vera sees the changes happening to her people and feels a great sorrow in her heart. She will do all she can to preserve the old ways for the day when the Aleuts can return to their homes.

Keywords: Family; Native American Issues; Novel in Verse

Hughes, Dean.

Missing in Action. **Atheneum, 2010. 978-1-4169-1502-7 (hardcover); 978-1-4424-1248-4 (softcover). 240pp.**

Twelve-year-old Jay knows what it's like to be called names. His father is half Navajo, so Jay has heard Indians be called dirty and lazy. At least in Delta there's not a lot of name calling, because Jay's grandfather is important in the community. Jay and his mom have moved to Delta because his dad's ship was torpedoed, and now Jay's dad is missing in action. Jay hopes his dad is safe and not being tortured by the Japanese. Everyone knows what the Japs are like. But then Jay meets Ken, an older boy who lives at the nearby internment camp. Ken's a nice guy: He helps Jay with his baseball skills and shows Jay how to dance. But Ken is Japanese. Does that make him Jay's enemy?

Keywords: Father and Child; Japanese Internment; Native American Issues; Navy

Kadohata, Cynthia.

Weedflower. Atheneum, 2006. 978-0-689-86574-9 (hardcover); 978-1-4169-7566-3 (softcover). 272pp. **M** **J**

> Sumiko often feels lonely. Even though she lives with her large extended family, she doesn't have any friends at school. Being one of the few Japanese in the district, she's the only one in her class—and parents don't want their children to be friends with a Japanese girl. At least Sumiko has her family and the work she does on their flower farm. But then the Japanese bomb Pearl Harbor, and America is at war. It's not enough for Japanese Americans to show their loyalty by burning anything Japanese. Sumiko and her family are forced to leave, along with all the other local Japanese. Sent to an internment camp in Arizona, Sumiko and her family must live without color in a world of dust storms. Worst of all, the internment camp is sharing the land of a Native American reservation—and some Indians don't want the Japanese there. But Sumiko just might find a friend at last.

> **Keywords:** Japanese Internment; Native American Issues

Kerr, M. E.

Slap Your Sides. HarperCollins, 2001. 978-0-06-029481-6 (hardcover); 978-0-06-447274-6 (softcover). 208pp. **M** **J**

> When war is declared and a draft is instituted, some young men refuse to serve. They are called conscientious objectors; because of their religions or moral beliefs, they will not serve in the military. During World War II, many conscientious objectors were belittled, accused of being cowards. That's what happens to Jubal's older brother, Bud. Bud has the leadership of the Boy Scout troop taken away, and then he's sent to a camp in Colorado. That doesn't end things, though. Jubal's whole family is looked at differently. People soap the windows of the family's department store. Even within the Shoemaker family, some members don't admire Bud's stance. Jubal doesn't know what to believe. He has to reconcile all his feelings to figure out what's right.

> **Keywords:** Coming-of-age; Family; Religious Conflicts

Klages, Ellen.

The Green Glass Sea. Viking Juvenile, 2006. 978-0-670-06134-1 (hardcover); 978-0-14-241149-0 (softcover). 336pp. **M** **J**

> It's 1943, and nearly eleven-year-old Dewey is arriving in New Mexico to live with her dad. He's involved in some secret project—so secret that no one knows what anyone does, or even what the name of the town is. Dewey doesn't like all the secrets, but she knows that during wartime, loose lips sink ships. Anyway, there are lots of scientists to talk to, people to ask about math and radios. Over the next year Dewey sees adults who are working on the "gadget" that is part of the war effort. As she makes a friend and loses her father, she meets men

like Richard Feynmann and J. Robert Oppenheimer. Only after the war can Dewey tell people that she lived in Los Alamos, where the United States built an atomic bomb.

Awards: Scott O'Dell Award for Historical Fiction

Keywords: Coming-of-age; Friendship

Kluger, Steve.

The Last Days of Summer. William Morrow, 1998. 978-0-380-97645-4 (hardcover); 978-0-380-79763-9 (softcover). 368pp. **S**

For a Jewish kid living in an Italian American neighborhood in Brooklyn during World War II, it's difficult to know who to look up to. So Joey Margolis settles on Charlie Banks, the New York Giants superstar. Joey writes letters to Charlie, full of bluff and swagger, and eventually Charlie becomes intrigued by this kid's letters and starts replying. Their friendship develops through their letters, and Joey keeps them, as well as newspaper stories, notes from school, and other clippings. He'll need something to help him remember, once Charlie is sent off to fight in the war.

Keywords: Coming-of-age; Friendship; Sports

Patneaude, David.

Thin Wood Walls. **Houghton Mifflin Books for Children, 2004. 978-0-618-34290-7 (hardcover); 978-0-618-80915-8 (softcover). 240pp. M J**

Joe is American. He dreams of being a writer, listens to the radio, and plays basketball with his friend Ray. But when the Japanese bomb Pearl Harbor, Joe becomes the enemy because he is Japanese, too. His father is taken away by the FBI, and former friends turn their backs on Joe's family. One of Joe's few comforts is writing in his journal and composing haiku. It's a comfort he'll need when he has to leave his home. All people of Japanese ancestry are ordered to leave the West Coast, moving inland to a group of internment centers. Arriving at the Tule Lake War Relocation Camp, Joe and his family have to endure the boredom of their confinement. They are also worried about his father and about his older brother Mike when he joins the army. Through it all, Joe learns new skills and improves old ones, as he waits for the day when Japanese Americans are trusted again.

Read-alike: Find out more about the Japanese internment camps in the classic memoir *Farewell to Manzanar* by Jeanne Wakatsuki Houston and James D. Houston.

Keywords: Family; Japanese Internment

Vietnam War: 1960–1975

Unlike previous wars, the Vietnam War prompted extensive public protests and draft-dodging. For some Americans, getting involved in the Southeast Asian conflict was meddling, while others saw it as a way to halt communism's spread. Whichever side teens in this period were on, Vietnam had an impact on their lives.

Crist Evans, Craig.

Amaryllis. Candlewick, 2006. 978-0-7636-1863-6 (hardcover); 978-0-7636-2990-8 (softcover). 192pp. **J** **S**

In 1967 the war in Vietnam is raging on. For Jimmy, it's difficult to worry about Nam with the war in his own house. His father, an alcoholic, is never satisfied with Jimmy or Jimmy's older brother Frank. Frank has a rough relationship with their dad—it's so bad that Frank enlists and gets shipped to Vietnam. Without his brother, Jimmy feels lost. Now there's no one to help with chores and deal with their dad. Worst of all, Jimmy doesn't have his surfing buddy anymore. The waves in Florida aren't that great, but on nearby Singer Island, the wreck of the ship *Amaryllis* creates some waves. It's up to Jimmy to figure out how to live with his dad and to find out what he really wants.

Keywords: 1960s; Brothers; Father and Child; Sports

Hobbs, Valerie.

Sonny's War. Farrar, Straus & Giroux, 2002. 978-0-374-37136-4 (hardcover); 978-0-374-46970-2 (softcover). 224pp. **M** **J**

The recent, unexpected death of her father makes fourteen-year-old Dory cling to her older brother Sonny. He's a quiet guy, happiest working on his old Ford and cruising in their small, sleepy town. But then he's drafted and sent to Vietnam. Cory feels lost with Sonny gone. She helps her mother run their café and starts high school. There she becomes entranced by Lawrence, her substitute history teacher. Lawrence is against the war and encourages the students in his classes to debate the issues. Cory can't help agreeing with him, seeing things from Lawrence's perspective. But when Lawrence's actions make Cory question him, and Sonny returns home injured, Cory learns that there are many different ways to promote peace.

Keywords: Coming-of-age; Family

Kadohata, Cynthia.

Cracker! The Best Dog in Vietnam. Atheneum, 2007. 978-1-4169-0637-7 (hardcover); 978-1-4169-0638-4 (softcover). 320pp. **M** **J**

Military equipment isn't just guns or tanks—it also includes dogs. Dogs were used to sniff out the enemy or even bombs. Before that happens, a dog is paired with a handler and they both get training. Cracker, short for Firecracker, has excellent breeding and is very smart. But she's also stubborn, and she misses her old owner. Rick, her handler, didn't have a dog growing up, but he likes dogs. Cracker has a bad reputation—one that matches Rick's. They're both stubborn and aggressive. They will have to learn to trust each other before they can become a team. Otherwise, there's no chance they will survive in Vietnam.

Keywords: Animals; Friendship; Multiple Voices

Myers, Walter Dean.

Fallen Angels. **Scholastic, 1988. 978-0-590-40942-1 (hardcover); 978-0-545-05576-5 (softcover). 320pp. J S**

After graduating from high school, Richie wants to go someplace without questions. Joining the army seems like the best choice, especially since everyone's saying the war in Vietnam is pretty much over. But that doesn't mean that Richie won't get shipped out. Soon he's in country, learning to stay alert and being the only kind of good soldier—an alive one. Richie makes friends with the guys in his unit, like Peewee, who talks all the time. Lobel imagines life as a movie, Johnson is tall and strong, and most of the other guys are okay. But Richie and the rest of his squad don't just play volleyball and sit in their barracks. As they do guard duty and go out on patrol, the young soldiers see all the horrible sights of wartime. They leave Richie with a whole bunch of questions, for which he can't find the answers.

Keywords: 1960s; African American Issues; Army; Friendship

Qualey, Marsha.

Too Big a Storm. **Dial, 2004. 978-0-8037-2839-4 (hardcover). 256pp. S**

Brady is a born worrier. She can't seem to help it, and it's just gotten worse since her brother went missing in Vietnam. Then Brady meets Sally, a rich girl who follows her every whim. Thanks to Sally, Brady starts to leap before she looks, exploring the world with new eyes. But Sally is a radical, supporting left-wing causes and protesting against the Vietnam War. She urges Brady to join her in revolutionary action, but Brady finds she's more interested in being with Will, a quiet, steady young man she meets at the local community center. As men walk on the moon, Brady starts to figure out just how she wants to make her mark on Earth.

Keywords: 1960s; Brother and Sisters; Coming-of-age

The Americas

The titles in this section reflect the history of the Americas: North, South, and Central America, as well as nations like Cuba and the Dominican Republic. Ranging from peaceful times to turmoil and strain, we see the full range of human experiences in these works.

Canada: Nineteenth and Twentieth Centuries

America's neighbor to the north has much in common with the United States in terms of history. Yet for decades Canada was a refuge for Americans without rights; many slaves escaped to freedom by crossing into Canada. The novels in this section explore stories of Canadians of various backgrounds.

Bates, Judy Fong.

Midnight at the Dragon Café. McClelland Stewart, 2003. 978-0-7710-1098-9 (hardcover); 978-1-58243-189-5 (softcover). 328pp. **S**

Life as an immigrant involves many changes. Su-Jen and her mother move to Canada when she is six, joining Su-Jen's father and his brother. In their family restaurant, the Dragon Cafe, they serve meals to their white customers, making both Chinese and *are fen* or white food. As Su-Jen learns English and plays with her best friend Jonette, she sees that her parents remain the same, wearing the same clothes, listening to the same music, and even speaking the same few words or phrases in English. There is prejudice against the Chinese, but Su-Jen, known as Annie, is able to adapt and thrive.Then a greater change occurs: the arrival of her half-brother, Lee-Kung, which will cause Su-Jen's life to become about secrets and grudges. Su-Jen watches as her brother and her mother share their bitterness about life in a foreign country and her father works and tries to maintain face. Su-Jen grows up over one summer as her family struggles to stay together.

Keywords: 1950s; Family; Immigrants

Curtis, Christopher Paul.

Elijah of Buxton. Scholastic, 2007. 978-0-439-02344-3 (hardcover); 978-0-439-02345-0 (softcover). 352pp. **J**

Elijah Freeman was the first child born in the settlement of Buxton, Canada. Settled by slaves who had escaped from the Southern United States, Buxton is a place where blacks can be free. Now age eleven, Elijah is known as the boy who spit up on Frederick Douglass as a baby. His mother wants Elijah to wise up, to not be so gullible. But a boy who has been protected from the uglier aspects of life has a hard time learning how to be cautious. When a dishonest preacher steals money from Elijah's friend—money he had been saving to buy his family's freedom—Elijah knows he has to do something. So he heads off after Preacher, journeying into America and seeing for himself what the residents of Buxton had escaped.

Awards: Newbery Honor Book; Geoffrey Bilson Award for Historical Fiction for Young People

Keywords: African American Issues; Nineteenth Century

Hunter, Bernice Thurman.

The Girls They Left Behind. Fitzhenry and Whiteside, 2005. 978-1-55041-927-6 (softcover). 192pp. 🔲 🔲

The first way Beryl asserted herself was to rename herself. Now known as Natalie, the seventeen-year-old sets out to help in the Canadian war effort during the 1940s. At first she works in a Toronto department store and uses some of her earnings to buy war stamps. Then she decides to make more money and become an actual war worker in a munitions factory. Even though the work is hard and dirty, Natalie knows she's helping all the boys overseas—her friends and relatives. But her life isn't just all work and no play. Natalie spends time with her friends and goes to dances. She has dates with men in uniform and wonders if she'll find love. Natalie is doing much for the war effort, but she can't help wondering if she could do more.

Keywords: 1940s; Diary; World War II

Jocelyn, Marthe.

Mable Riley: A Reliable Record of Humdrum, Peril and Romance. Candlewick, 2004. 978-0-7636-2120-9 (hardcover); 978-0-7636-3287-8 (softcover). 288pp. 🔲 🔲

Most of the time having an imagination is an asset. Mable Riley has traveled with her older sister Viola to the town of Sellerton, Ontario. Viola is the new schoolteacher, and Mable will be both scholar and assistant. It's difficult to have any fun with a prim sister and watchful neighbors. At first she can only confide in her diary and her letters to her friend back home. But then Mable meets Mrs. Rattle, an eccentric woman who wears bloomers. Thanks to Mrs. Rattle and the Ladies Reading Society, Mable will get an opportunity to give her imagination free rein.

Keywords: Nineteenth Century; Sisters

Mexico; Central and South America: Medieval to Nineteenth Century

Life in the countries south of the United States is often, like the weather, hot and oppressive. Yet from their earliest existence there has been a sense of opportunity and possibility in these nations. Whether explorers looking for gold or individuals looking for freedom, dreams have seemed more possible in Central and South America.

Durango, Julia.

The Walls of Cartagena. Simon & Schuster Children's Publishing, 2008. 978-1-4169-4102-6 (hardcover). 160pp. 🔲 🔲

The New World city of Cartagena is full of riches: gold, jewels, slaves. Within its high walls lives the slave Calepino. Born on a slave ship to a mother who died, Calepino was brought up by a rich woman, treated more like a member of the family than a slave. At age thirteen it is time for him to begin preparing for his future. Father Pedro, his priest, asks to train Calepino as an interpreter. Blessed with a gift for languages, Calepino can speak four European tongues and seven African dialects. But going into the holds of slave ships, helping the newly arrived Africans, is a disturbing challenge for Calepino. When he meets a woman named Mara and her son Torri, they remind Calepino of his own history. There's no way Calepino can help them, no way for them to escape . . . or is there?

Keywords: Colombia; Seventeenth Century; Slavery

Eboch, Chris.

The Well of Sacrifice. **Clarion, 1999. 978-0-395-90374-2 (hardcover). 240pp. Ⓜ Ⓙ**

Eveningstar Macaw is not a typical Mayan girl. It's not just her intelligence and courage; she seems destined to follow in her mother's footsteps and become a healer. Even after her brother gains glory in battle and is rewarded with noble status for the whole family, Eveningstar is set on her path. But the death of the king causes great tragedy in the city. The high priest, Great Skull Zero, has taken control—and he doesn't like Smoke Shell, Eveningstar's brother. To appease the gods, Great Skull Zero orders several young males to be sacrificed, including Smoke Shell. Eveningstar refuses to accept that her beloved brother must die. She speaks out against the High Priest, bringing on herself a horrible punishment. She is to become the latest offering to the Well of Sacrifice. How will Eveningstar save herself and her brother? Life in a ninth-century Mayan village is vividly portrayed.

Keywords: Brothers and Sisters; Medieval; Religious Conflicts

Garland, Sherry.

In the Shadow of the Alamo. **Harcourt Children's Books, 2001. 978-0-15-201744-6 (hardcover). 282pp. Ⓙ**

Getting drafted into the Mexican army isn't what Lorenzo wanted. If it wasn't for Catalina the goat herder and Esteban the rich man's son, he'd still be a farmer like everyone else in his village. But now he's a fifteen-year-old soldier, part of the army under the command of General Santa Anna. The army marches north, heading for Texas and a battle against the *noreteamericanos* who are rebelling against Mexico. As they march, Lorenzo finds himself becoming friends with Esteban. When they arrive in San Antonio de Bexar, surrounding the old mission known as the Alamo, both young men prepare for battle. Little do they know that this conflict will be a turning point in history—and their lives.

Keywords: Mexico; Nineteenth Century; Political Rebellions

Van de Grier, Susan.

A Gift for Ampato. Groundwood Books, 1999. 978-0-88899-358-8 (hardcover). 112pp. **M**

> High in the mountains, in the country now known as Peru, there is a great mountain that sometimes lets out fire and ash. When that happens, the people know that the mountain gods are displeased. If they are not satisfied, the gods will block the sun, damaging crops and weakening llamas. So the priests make sacrifices, and the *acllas*—girls who serve in the temple— make prayers. Timta has only been in the temple a short time. She admires her friend Karwa for her goodness and serenity. Timta is often restless, uncertain. But she has always done as she was told, until she is chosen for the greatest honor: to live with the gods. Suddenly Timta realizes that she would not have chosen this. When Karwa discovers Timta's feelings, she offers Timta another choice. If she takes it, she will dishonor her family and possibly anger the gods . . . but she will be alive.
>
> **Keywords:** Medieval; Parallel Narratives; Peru; Religious Conflicts

Caribbean: Seventeenth to Twentieth Centuries

The island nations in the Caribbean offer a study in contrasts. The natural beauty of the lands, rich in plant and animal life, has been the garden where adversity and political repression have grown and flourished. But there are still stories of happiness and family to be found.

Alvarez, Julia.

Before We Were Free. **Knopf Books for Young Readers, 2002. 978-0-375-81544-7 (hardcover); 978-0-440-23784-6 (softcover). 166pp. M J**

> It has become very lonely in the compound where Anita lives. It used to be overflowing with her family: grandparents, aunts and uncles, and lots of cousins. But now there's just Anita, her parents, and her brother and sister. As she slowly learns, it is growing more dangerous in the Dominican Republic, and the only way to be safe, to be free, is to leave. Until then Anita will have to figure out why the secret police keep searching her house, why her father gets phone calls about butterflies, and why she can't write in her diary. For talkative, impulsive Anita, it's difficult to live with so many unanswered questions. Will she ever get answers? And will her family ever be safe?
>
> **Keywords:** 1960s; Dominican Republic; Family; Political Rebellions

📖 *In the Time of the Butterflies*. **Alonquin Books, 1994. 978-1-56512-038-9 (hardcover); 978-0-452-27442-6 (softcover). 344pp. S**

> The Mirabel sisters are called Las Mariposas: the Butterflies. Strong-willed Minerva, devout Patria, and the baby Maria Theresa are amongst those

who stand against the regime of the dictator Rafael Trujillo. But they started off as typical girls in the Dominican Republic, concerned with school, family, and church. How did they come to be a revolutionary force, so feared by the government that they are murdered in 1960? And where does that leave Dede, the sister who did not become involved in revolutionary activities?

Keywords: 1960s; Dominican Republic; Political Rebellions; Sisters

Engle, Margarita.

The Firefly Letters: A Suffragette's Journey to Cuba. **Henry Holt, 2010. 978-0-8050-9082-6 (hardcover). 160pp.** Ⓜ

In many countries, being a woman was only a few steps up from being a slave. Fredrika Bremer, a rich young Swedish woman, believes in equality between women and men. She decides to travel to the New World, seeing these lands often called Eden. When she arrives in Cuba in 1851, the lush beauty of the island makes it appear a paradise. But then Fredrika sees the cruelties faced by females and slaves. Women have practically no freedom—and slaves have none. Fredrika draws out two young girls to explore with her. Through Fredrika, rich Elena and slave Cecilia experience a new world of liberty.

Keywords: Cuba; Female Equality; Multiple Voices; Nineteenth Century; Novel in Verse; Slavery; Women's Roles

Tropical Secrets: Holocaust Refugees in Cuba. **Henry Holt, 2009. 978-0-8050-8936-3 (hardcover). 208pp.** Ⓜ Ⓙ

This novel in verse tells about a little-known chapter in World War II. Thousands of Jewish refugees, turned away by the United States and Canada, managed to find safety in Cuba—after paying off corrupt officials. Against this backdrop, the story of three people is told: Daniel, a Jewish refugee, Paloma, the daughter of one of those corrupt officials, and David, a Russian Jew who came to Cuba years before. Daniel slowly becomes used to his new home, learning Spanish and hearing the music of the island. But he always wonders about the fate of his parents. Paloma, whose father changed after her mother ran off with another man, at first hides in her dovecote. But slowly, thanks to her friendship with David and Daniel, she begins helping the Jewish refugees. As the war continues, will the refugees find safety in Cuba? For Daniel and Paloma, it's not just about safety—it's about freedom.

Keywords: 1940s; Cuba; Holocaust; Multiple Voices; Novel in Verse

Gonzalez, Christina.

The Red Umbrella. **Knopf Books for Young Readers, 2010. 978-0-375-86190-1 (hardcover). 288pp.** 🅜 🅙

1

Lucia can't understand why her parents are so worried and paranoid. Everyone knows that since the revolution, Fidel Castro is working to make life better in Cuba, to remove corruption and improve the government. But slowly Lucia begins to see that the revolution is about restrictions, not improvement. To protect Lucia and her little brother Frankie, their parents make a heartbreaking decision: to send Lucia and Frankie to America, alone. Lonely and unsure, Lucia arrives in Nebraska and has to adapt. Without her language, her culture, and her parents, Lucia discovers that she must fight to remember who she is. And she must hold on to the hope that she will see her parents again.

Keywords: 1960s; Cuba; Family

2

3

O'Dell, Scott.

My Name Is Not Angelica. **Houghton Mifflin Books for Children, 1989. 978-0-395-51061-2 (hardcover); 978-0-440-40379-1 (softcover). 144pp.** 🅜

4

Raisha lives in a village in Senegal, the daughter of a subchief and the promised wife of their king, Konje. But then a neighboring king betrays them by handing them over to a slave ship. After a long voyage, they arrive at the Danish Virgin Islands in the Caribbean. Luckily, Raisha and Konje are bought by the same owner. Unluckily, they are renamed and set to hard, even back-breaking work. Raisha, now Angelica, is a house slave but worries about the way Konje is treated. When he runs away, Raisha eventually follows him. Together, in a settlement of runaway slaves, they manage to hold off an attack by the planters. The slave revolt cannot be allowed to continue and spread, though, so a troop of French soldiers marches on their camp, set on quashing the rebellion. As the soldiers approach, the slaves make a terrible decision.

Keywords: Romance; Seventeenth Century; Slavery

5

6

7

8

Chapter 4

Historical Mysteries

Mysteries hold appeal for readers of all ages. Whether featuring a grisly murder, political intrigue, or a missing person, there is something about solving the mystery—spotting the clues and putting them together—that appeals to many readers. Often we follow in the footsteps of the detective on the case, but readers are still trying to solve the mystery on their own, hoping to get ahead of the characters and solve it first. Even if we spot the solution quickly, we read along to see how the detective will discover the same answer.

Historical mysteries set the action in the past, creating a different kind of tension within the story. The focus is still on determining who is the murderer or where the missing person is. But the historical setting adds another dimension. For example, in the historical mystery, a female detective not only has to do everything a male detective does, but she has to work within the strictures of her society, as seen in Y. S. Lee's <u>Mary Quinn Mysteries</u>. For the historical mystery to be authentic to the period, the author must find a way to allow the heroine to investigate without upsetting social norms.

In addition, these detectives do not benefit from the modern tools of crime fighting. For historical sleuths, tools like computers, DNA, even fingerprints, are often unavailable. Therefore, the protagonists must rely on other tools and techniques, such as their powers of observation and knowledge of human nature.

The mysteries in this chapter are set in the past; these are not modern-day examinations of historical questions like Shakespeare's identity. However, mysteries set in the past that explore those kinds of questions are included. A variety of mystery types, from cozy to gruesome, are explored. Many of these mysteries feature amateur sleuths—teenagers or young adults who discover a mystery and set out to solve it. Of particular interest are the novels or series that reimagine classic mystery characters, such as Sherlock Holmes. Nancy Springer's <u>Enola Holmes Mysteries</u> creates a younger sister for the great detective, who is just as observant as he is, whereas Shane Peacock's <u>The Boy Sherlock Holmes</u> imagines the great detective's first investigations.

Traditional Historical Mysteries

This section presents whodunits that are neither too sweet nor too gritty. Yet there are still unfortunate victims, unusual behavior, and strange clues for the detectives in these stories. And whether detectives are amateurs or a professionals, they have to rely on their powers of observation to solve the case.

Avi.

Murder at Midnight. Scholastic, 2009. 978-0-545-08090-3 (hardcover). 272pp. **M** **J**

Fabrizio thinks he's very lucky to have become a servant to Magnus the Magician. After all, his master is the greatest magician in the Kingdom of Pergamontio. But Italy in the late fifteenth century is being swept by change—something the King does not want to happen in Pergamontio. When hints of a coup are discovered, Magnus is accused of treason. The only way to save himself is to find whoever has created hundreds of treasonous posters. Fabrizio can't believe his master might suffer the fate of a traitor. He sets out to help Magnus find the real traitor. But will they find the identity of the traitor in time?

Keywords: Fifteenth Century; Italy; Treason

The Traitor's Gate. Atheneum/Richard Jackson Books, 2007. 978-0-689-85335-7 (hardcover); 978-0-689-85336-4 (softcover). 368pp. **M** **J**

John's father might act high and mighty, playing at being the gentleman. But his position as a clerk in the Naval Ordinance Office doesn't pay enough to keep the Huffman family in the lap of luxury. Still, when his father is arrested for debt and thrown into prison, John can't help sensing that there's a mystery afoot. For one thing, the man who claims the debt isn't owed any money by Mr. Huffman. For another thing, there seem to be many people who want to keep Mr. Huffman in prison. John sets out to discover just who the traitor is and rescue his family. It's a lot for one fourteen-year-old boy to accomplish . . . but just maybe his age will work to his advantage.

Keywords: England; Father and Child; Nineteenth Century; Treason

Bajoria, Paul.

Mog Winter Mysteries. **J**

Questions about identity create two mysteries for Mog Winter. There's the ship with an unknown cargo, which is a victim of thieves. And then there are the questions about Mog's past. The answers to both of these mysteries are surprising.

Keywords: Brother and Sister; Disguised as Boy; England; Identity; Murder; Nineteenth Century

The Printer's Devil. Little, Brown, 2004. 978-0-316-01090-0 (hardcover); 978-0-689-87285-3 (softcover). 384pp.

> Young Mog Winter has made out better than most orphans. He works as a printer's devil, assisting Cramplock, his master, with all kinds of tasks. Whether it's running errands, working the press, or dirtier jobs, twelve-year-old Mog does it. One of Mog's favorite tasks is printing wanted posters, glorying in the meanness of the pictured criminals. But meeting a real convict will have a big impact on Mog. This meeting will begin a dark, dangerous adventure. A mystery swirls around a theft, mistaken identities, and a ship recently arrived from India. How do all these things connect to Mog's unknown past? In the streets of London, Mog will have to use a lot of brains to avoid ending up in the place that devils go.

The God of Mischief. Little, Brown, 2007. 978-0-316-01091-7 (hardcover); 978-1-4169-0113-6 (softcover). 400pp.

> Mog Winter, revealed to be a girl, has been reunited with her twin brother Nick. After growing up separated, they are now living together in the home of a distant relative. But life at Kniveacres Hall with Sir Septimus Clay is not a family reunion. Kniveacres Hall might look impressive, but it's cold and drafty. The twins barely see Sir Septimus; instead, they're kept in line by their fear of his manservant. Bonefinger is creepy and mean, with a sharp tongue and the ability to know all that goes on at the hall. When the twins see him burying a corpse, they're unable to ignore it. Mog and Nick set out to unravel the family secrets that are present—and they have to work quickly. A series of mysterious deaths shows that anyone who gets too curious is eliminated. Does the same fate await Mog and Nick?

Cheaney, J. B.

The True Prince. **Knopf Books, 2002. 978-0-375-81433-4 (hardcover); 978-0-440-41940-2 (softcover). 352pp.** ▣

> Except for one person, Richard Malory is quite content with his life as a stage boy. He has food and a roof over his head, the company of other boys and men, and growing success in the roles he performs. The one fly in the ointment is Kit Glover, a fellow apprentice who is haughty, proud, and cold. Even though Richard and Kit perform well together onstage, this doesn't lead to friendship. Since Kit seems quite happy with the drunks and low-born as his companions, though, Richard can't help wondering. Why would a boy who acts like a prince want to associate with thieves and scoundrels? As Richard slowly enters Kit's world, seeking an answer to this question, he finds that appearances can be as deceiving in real life as on the stage.

Keywords: England; Identity; Performing; Sixteenth Century

Crowley, Bridget.

Feast of Fools. **Margaret K. McElderry, 2003. 978-0-689-86512-1 (hardcover); 978-0-340-85082-4 (softcover). 272pp. 🄜 🄙**

> An accident totally changed John's life. One moment he was whole and training to learn his father's trade of stone carving. In the next moment, his father is dead and John's foot is crushed. Now lame, John is taken in by the church and becomes a member of the boys' choir. It's a difficult transition, with cruel boys bullying him and harsh treatment by some of the canons who run the school and the church. John's new friend Hugh helps him adjust, though, and there's the excitement of St. Nicholas's Day and a feast for the boys. But the holiday is ruined when one of the canons is killed and Hugh vanishes. Only John, the newest boy and an outsider, can find the solution to this mystery.
>
> **Keywords:** England; Medieval; Missing Person; Murder; Music; Physical Disability

Dunlap, Susanne.

The Musician's Daughter. **Bloomsbury USA, 2008. 978-1-59990-332-3 (hardcover); 978-1-59990-452-8 (softcover). 336pp. 🄙 🅂**

> The sparkle of eighteenth-century Vienna hides darkness. Theresa's family depends on her father's income from playing the violin in Prince Esterhazy's orchestra. But his death on Christmas Eve throws the family into turmoil. Theresa's mother is stricken with grief, and only a job from her godfather, Franz Joseph Haydn, enables Theresa to make money. Although Theresa is a talented violinist, her job is as a copyist to Herr Haydn, the concertmaster of the prince's orchestra, who is slowly losing his sight. Theresa has many questions. How did her father die? What happened to his Christmas bonus and his violin? And what is the gold pendant found around his neck? Theresa is determined to learn the truth, even as it leads her down an unexpected path.
>
> **Keywords:** Austria; Eighteenth Century; Family; Female Detective; Murder; Music

Grove, Vicki.

Rhiannon. **Putnam Juvenile, 2007. 978-0-399-23633-4 (hardcover). 352pp. 🄙 🅂**

> Along the coast of Wales, giant, dangerous cliffs look out over the waves. Rhiannon loves her home, perched on a high hill overlooking the water. Even though England and Wales are still racked by the loss of the White Ship and the heir to the throne, Rhiannon's life has not changed too much. But then a stranger is found murdered at the base of the cliffs. When one of the village's residents, one-legged Jim, is declared the murderer, Rhiannon can't believe it. With the aid of a monk, a pirate, and a little girl, Rhiannon discovers the real solution to this mystery.
>
> **Keywords:** Female Detective; Medieval; Murder; Wales

Hoffman, Mary.

The Falconer's Knot: A Story of Friars, Flirtation and Foul Play. **Bloomsbury USA Children's Books, 2007. 978-1-59990-056-8 (hardcover); 978-1-59990-229-6 (softcover). 288pp. 🗓 Ⓢ**

> As Italy enters the final days before the Renaissance, a group of previously unrelated people are caught up in a mystery. Silvano is a young nobleman, the only heir to his father's riches and title. Infatuated with a married woman, he falls under suspicion when her husband is stabbed—with Silvano's knife. Spirited away to a nearby friary, Silvano's only amusements are his weekly early-morning hunts and watching for the bold-eyed girl in the adjoining convent. Soon they meet and become friends: the young nobleman and the young commoner named Chiara. When another murder occurs, threatening their friendship, Silvano and Chiara join together to find the true murderer.
>
> **Keywords:** Italy; Murder; Renaissance; Romance

Lee, Y. S.

Mary Quinn Mysteries. 🗓 Ⓢ

> Based on extensive research into Victorian England, these mysteries feature Mary Quinn. Acting as part spy, part detective, Mary moves hin various circles of society, relying on the invisibility of women to gather facts and clues.
>
> **Keywords:** Disguised as Boy; England; Female Detective; Murder; Nineteenth Century; Spies

A Spy in the House. Candlewick, 2010. 978-0-7636-4067-5 (hardcover); 978-0-7636-5289-0 (softcover). 352pp.

> Mary Lang was sentenced to hang at the age of twelve. This sentence wasn't the end of her life, but the beginning. Mary was rescued from the gallows and became a student at Miss Scrimshaw's Academy for Girls. After five years, the young woman known as Mary Quinn has learned much—but she longs for something more than being a teacher or nurse. It's then that Mary learns about the Agency: a secret organization hidden by the Academy. As an operative in training, Mary takes a position as a companion to a merchant's daughter. She spies on the merchant, who is suspected of selling stolen Indian artifacts. Mary must remember her role as she tries to learn the truth, because forgetting her cover could be disastrous.

The Body at the Tower. Candlewick, 2010. 978-0-7636-4968-5 (hardcover). 352pp.

> It's been a year since Mary Quinn's first assignment, and she is almost a full member of the Agency. The group of female detectives work for

clients who require observant, trained women to report, investigate, and spy. But Mary's next assignment is very different. She will have to masquerade as a boy and work on a construction site at the Houses of Parliament. The recent death of a worker has prompted rumors of suicide, but the Agency's client thinks it was murder. Mary mingles with the other workers, trying to learn the truth. But she must maintain her disguise or risk losing the case. What's more, James Easton, her friend who might be more, has returned to London. Can Mary return to the world she grew up in and still be able to get back to the new life that she wants?

Levin, Betty.

Shadow-Catcher. **Greenwillow Books, 2000. 978-0-688-17862-8 (hardcover). 160pp.** Ⓜ Ⓙ

When Jonathan is told he'll be going with his grandfather for the summer, he's not sure what to think. His parents want him to help his grandfather, but his grandfather doesn't seem to need the help. Jonathan, who wants to be a big-city detective, can't seem to pick up the clues that will let him figure out this puzzle. As they travel, it takes a long time for his grandfather to unthaw. Their horse-drawn cart carries them along muddy roads, to stops like a logging camp and a large town. Through it all, Grandfather is taking photographs, for that's his profession and what he's supposed to be teaching Jonathan. Even though Jonathan doesn't understand his methods and approach, it seems like his grandfather might have stumbled on something. The negatives of a series of pictures, showing what looks like a logger at work, might be much more than they appear. Just what has his grandfather's camera captured? Will Jonathan get his chance to be a detective?

Keywords: America; Family; Nineteenth Century

Peck, Richard.

The River Between Us. **Dial, 2003. 978-0-8037-2735-9 (hardcover); 978-0-14-240310-5 (softcover). 164pp.** Ⓜ Ⓙ

In the spring of 1861, southern Illinois was divided between Southern sympathizers and Union followers. Fifteen-year-old Tilly Pruit's biggest concerns are her psychic sister and her twin brother, who's hungry for war. Then two strange women come to town on a riverboat from New Orleans. Just who is Delphine Duval, the beautiful, violet-eyed young woman? And is Calinda, the dark-skinned servant with her, actually Delphine's slave? It's a great mystery, one that will involve suffering and hardship before the truth can be revealed.

Awards: National Book Award Finalist; Scott O'Dell Award for Historical Fiction

Keywords: African American Issues; America; Civil War; Family; Identity; Nineteenth Century

Stead, Rebecca.

When You Reach Me. Wendy Lamb Books, 2009. 978-0-385-73742-5 (hardcover); 978-0-375-85086-8 (softcover). 199pp. **M** **J**

Ever since her best friend Sal got punched in the stomach by a kid they didn't know, Miranda has been at loose ends. Sal is avoiding her, so she's on her own when she walks home from school and lets herself into the apartment she shares with her mom. Her mom is busy preparing to appear on the *$200,000 Pyramid*; if she wins it'll be the end to all their problems. So Miranda is just floating along, until two things happens. The spare key to her apartment vanishes from its hiding place. Even stranger is the first of a series of notes—notes that make Miranda think she can stop someone's death. But whose death? When will it happen, and why is she being asked to stop it? Miranda is going to do her best to find the answers. It's a good thing a latchkey kid in 1979 has some freedom.

Awards: Newbery Medal

Keywords: 1970s; America; Friendship

Sternberg, Libby.

The Case Against My Brother. Bancroft Press, 2007. 978-1-890862-51-0 (hardcover). 205pp. **J**

Leaving Baltimore was the last thing that Carl wanted. But his older brother Adam convinces him to move to Portland to live with their uncle. Carl tries to adapt to Portland, but he can't help feeling homesick for Baltimore. There's a lot of anti-Catholic sentiment in Portland, and Carl and Adam are Polish Catholics. Things get even worse when Adam is accused of stealing jewelry from his rich girlfriend's house. He has to lie low, and it's up to Carl to help protect him. But that means Carl is on his own for the first time in his life. As he tries to figure out who the real thief is, Carl begins to learn how to stand on his own two feet.

Keywords: 1920s; America; Brothers; Theft

Voigt, Cynthia.

The Callender Papers. Simon & Schuster, 1983. 978-0-689-30971-7 (hardcover); 978-0-689-83283-3 (softcover). 224pp. **M**

Working for Mr. Thiel has pluses and minuses for thirteen-year-old Jean. Spending the summer cataloging the papers of his dead wife's family would gain Jean forty dollars. For a girl in 1894, such a sum was good money. It would be the start of savings that could pay for her education. But Mr. Thiel is cold and distant, irritable and unfriendly. It's bound to be a lonely summer, even with the strange kindness of Mrs. Bywall, the housekeeper, and her new friend Mac. As Jean begins cataloging the Callender family papers, she asks questions. Why does Mr. Thiel have nothing to do with his wife's family? How did his wife, Irene Callender Thiel, die? And just what happened to their child after Mrs. Thiel's death? Living in a small village, Jean sees that everyone has suspicions. Reading the Callender papers might answer all these questions—and the answers could be unexpected.

Keywords: America; Family; Nineteenth Century

Wells, Rosemary.

Leave Well Enough Alone. **Dial, 1977. 978-0-8037-4754-8 (hardcover); 978-0-14-230149-4 (softcover). 218pp.** ◼

Dorothy's family is Irish, Catholic, and lower middle class. She's a good girl, but it's difficult to feel that way with mothers and older sisters and men drumming rules into her head. Dorothy welcomes the chance to get away for the summer, working as a mother's helper. But life on Philadelphia's Main Line is like another world. Her employers, the Hoardes, live in a grant house, spend nearly $200 on a party alone, and have very different standards than Dorothy. Mrs. Hoarde is scatter-brained, charming, and eccentric, and Dorothy is both intrigued and repelled by her. As Dorothy cares for the Hoardes's daughters, she slowly realizes that someone is being hidden on the estate. Dorothy fights her curiosity, but soon she has to pursue this secret. Dorothy will learn just what "leave well enough alone" means in 1950s Pennsylvania.

Keywords: 1950s; America

Cozy Historical Mysteries

The term "cozy mystery" was created to distinguish these stories from hardboiled mysteries. Instead of a grizzled detective neck-deep in murder and violence, cozy mysteries feature little violence and almost no bad language or adult content. In young adult fiction, the same holds true for cozy mysteries. Though murder might be the mystery to unravel, the death usually happens off-screen, and the solution is based just as much on characters as on clues.

Blackwood, Gary.

Shakespeare Series. ◼ ◼

This mystery series explores the world of late sixteenth-century England. In this cutthroat world, no one thought much of stealing sermons or plays, but perhaps protagonist Widge will discover his morality, thanks in part to his friendship with William Shakespeare.

Keywords: England; Identity; Shakespeare, William; Sixteenth Century; Theft; Writing

📖 *The Shakespeare Stealer.* **Dutton Juvenile, 1998. 978-0-525-45863-0 (hardcover); 978-0-329-22043-3 (softcover). 208pp.**

Life can be very difficult for orphans even if they've been taken in by someone. Widge spent seven years with a minister, learning to read and write Latin and English. He got this education to assist his master. Widge also learned a secret method of code writing that allowed him to copy speech as quickly as it was spoken. At first Widge uses this skill to help his master steal sermons. Then his service is transferred to a new master, with something bigger to steal. Simon Bass, Widge's master, wants him to copy *Hamlet* by William Shakespeare as it's performed. He wants his own company of players to perform Hamlet accurately, to earn large amounts of money. Widge, who's never been taught right from wrong, at first has no problem with this assignment. But once he starts to spend time with Shakespeare and his players, Widge questions what he's supposed to do.

Shakespeare's Scribe. Dutton Juvenile, 2000. 978-0-525-46444-0 (hardcover); 978-0-14-230066-4 (softcover). 224pp. 🅼 🅹

The spread of the plague means changes for Widge and his fellow players. The playhouses are ordered to close, and in order to make a living the players will go on tour. Widge is excited about touring the countryside and hopes that he'll start getting some better parts. Thanks to his special writing ability, Widge is valuable as a scribe— but he worries that he's not thought of as a player by his superiors. This feeling is made even worse when a new, talented apprentice is taken on. At his lowest, Widge gets a chance. Master Shakespeare breaks his arm and needs Widge to help him complete his new play. But will that be enough for Widge? Or will the chance to learn more about his real family give Widge a place to belong?

Shakespeare's Spy. Dutton Juvenile, 2003. 978-0-525-47145-5 (hardcover); 978-0-14-240311-2 (softcover). 288pp. 🅼 🅹

It can be hard to leave your past behind. That's what Widge discovers when thefts begin to occur among the Lord Chamberlain's Men. Since everyone knows about Widge's past thefts, he's a major suspect when things like costumes start disappearing. To prove his innocence, Widge decides to act as a spy. He will prevent further thefts, in particular of Master Shakespeare's plays. But even more, he will find the thief who's robbing the players. At the same time, Widge is trying to craft his own play. He hopes that his time spent as Shakespeare's scribe has made him a better writer. If Widge sells his play, he might earn the fortune that he's been foretold to win. With two different goals— finding the thief and selling his play—Widge has his hands full.

Collard, Sneed B., III.

Double Eagle. Peachtree Publishers, 2009. 978-1-56145-480-8 (hardcover). 256pp. **M** **J**

The summer of 1973 starts the same way for Mike as past ones: flying from California to Florida to be with his dad. But this summer his father is working at a marine lab on Mobile Bay. Fourteen-year-old Mike is happy to have college girls to look at, and he finds a new friend, Kyle, a local boy. There's also an interesting ship out in the bay, which is exploring a sunken Civil War vessel. Rumors swirl that the wreck actually holds a cache of gold coins. Mike, a coin collector, and Kyle start investigating. Soon they discover a mystery that's over a hundred years old.

Keywords: 1970s; America; Civil War; Father and Child; Navy

Erikson, John R.

Texas Mysteries. **M** **J**

Even in the 1920s, parts of America still felt like they were on the frontier. Texas was one of those places, and for a boy like Riley McDaniels, there were lots of chances to stumble upon a mystery.

Keywords: 1920s; America; Family; Native American Issues; Theft

Moonshiner's Gold. Viking Juvenile, 2001. 978-0-670-03502-1 (hardcover); 978-0-14-250023-1 (softcover). 199pp.

Even though it's 1927, life in the Texas Panhandle is still rough. People have cars, but there's still a lot of land for cattle to roam—and a lot of places for outlaws to hide. Prohibition is in effect, and moonshiners use canyons as hideouts in which to make their whiskey. When fourteen-year-old Riley discovers some moonshiners on his family's ranch, it's just the beginning of a vast conspiracy. Why would his great-aunt evict them from the ranch? Who hid a sack of gold in the schoolhouse stove? And is all this connected with the recent death of Riley's father? Riley sets out to save his family home, helped by his grandfather. They're on their own, because the local sheriff won't stop the moonshiners. But Riley's determined, and his grandfather's got quite a few tricks up his sleeve.

Discovery at Flint Springs. Viking Juvenile, 2004. 978-0-670-05946-1 (hardcover). 192pp.

Now that the moonshiners and other criminals have been run off, life at the McDaniels' ranch is easier. With Grampy Dawson around, Riley and his brother Coy have enough time to argue and bicker. Luckily, before their mother gives them enough chores to wear them out, they are given an interesting project. They meet an archeologist who's studying the history of their part of Texas. Dr. Montrose has come all the way from Massachusetts to study the items left behind by the Indians a thousand years before. As

Riley starts learning more, and his family helps Dr. Montrose, they all get swept up in history—and they might even learn something new about Texas's ancient past.

Karr, Kathleen.

📖 *The 7th Knot.* **Marshall Cavendish, 2007. 978-0-7614-5368-0 (softcover). 149pp. Ⓜ Ⓙ**

Miles and Wick are disappointments to their parents. Miles is a chemical tinkerer, creating various concoctions and explosions. Wick is a playboy, smoking cigars and gambling at cards and horses. After their latest scrape, they're sent to Europe with their Uncle Eustace. They're supposed to help him locate art to purchase, helped by knowledgeable valet José Gregorio. The brothers make secret plans to escape their uncle, but those plans change when José vanishes. Miles and Wick set out to find José, as well as six woodcuts made by Albrecht Dürer, a Renaissance artist. Traveling across Italy and Germany at the turn of the twentieth century, Miles and Wick face off against dungeons, zeppelins, and a secret society. Will they rescue José—and the artwork?

Keywords: Art; Brothers; Europe; Missing Person; Nineteenth Century; Theft

MacDonald, Bailey.

Wicked Will. **Aladdin, 2009. 978-1-4169-8660-7 (hardcover); 978-1-4169-8661-4 (softcover). 208pp. Ⓜ Ⓙ**

Tom is hiding a secret. From outside appearances, he's just an apprentice for his uncles' collection of players, since his parents died from the plague. In reality, his parents are in hiding because they helped a priest escape from England—and Tom is really a girl named Viola. "Tom" has managed to keep these things secret, until the players arrive in the small village of Stratford. There they meet a boy named Will Shakespeare, a boy full of questions and with a great amount of wit. When Will guesses Viola's true identity, they become unlikely allies. This partnership leads them into a mystery: the murder of a rich, mean man. As Will chases after a solution, Viola follows him, becoming equally curious about just who killed the most hated man in Stratford.

Keywords: Disguised as Boy; England; Murder; Performing; Shakespeare, William; Sixteenth Century

MacLean, Sarah.

The Season. **Orchard Books, 2009. 978-0-545-04886-6 (hardcover); 978-0-545-04887-3. 352pp. Ⓙ Ⓢ**

The time has come for Lady Alexandra Stafford to make her debut in society by participating in her first Season. Although this is what Alex's mother has been waiting for, Alex is dreading it. She loathes the thought of being married off to some dull, old man—a dislike shared by her best friends, Ella and Vivi. But to preserve their families' reputations and make their mothers happy, the three girls start making the rounds, attending balls and parties and dinners. There's even something to distract Alex from her eventual fate: a mystery. A friend of her family, Gavin Sewall, has just become the Earl of Blackmoor after the death of his father. But the death was a strange one, and even though it was ruled an accident, Gavin is suspicious. Alex joins Gavin to discover the truth. In the process, she just might discover true love.

Keywords: England; Murder; Nineteenth Century; Romance

Newbery, Linda.

Set in Stone. **David Fickling Books, 2006. 978-0-385-75102-5 (hardcover); 978-0-440-24051-8 (softcover). 368pp.** 🅹 🆂

When he arrives at the isolated country mansion known as Fourwinds, Samuel Godwin considers himself very fortunate. The house is truly inspiring to the young artist, and Samuel looks forward to capturing its appeal in the paintings commissioned by his employer. Also a pleasure are the lessons Samuel will give to Mr. Farrow's two daughters. Julianna is quiet and pale, and only slightly talented. Her younger sister Marianne—vibrant, gifted Marianne—captivates Samuel. But questions swirl around Marianne and Fourwinds. What causes Marianne's strange moods? What happened to the carving of the West Wind that once was part of a series of sculptures mounted on the mansion? With the help of Charlotte Agnew, the governess to the Farrow sisters, Samuel seeks answers to these questions and more.

Keywords: America; Art; Nineteenth Century; Sisters

Platt, Kin.

A Mystery for Thoreau. **Farrar, Straus & Giroux, 2008. 978-0-374-35337-7 (hardcover). 176pp.** 🅹 🆂

In the village of Concord, Massachusetts, there is no love lost for Henry David Thoreau. A nature lover and all-around oddity, his latest act is refusing to pay his poll tax, leading to his being jailed. Yet his imprisonment means he might be the only townsperson who's not a suspect in a grisly murder. The local mad woman is found by Walden Pond, her head bashed in. The only clue is a parasol near the body—a parasol that belonged to a newcomer to Concord, Miss Margaret Roberts. Now Miss Roberts is missing, and no one knows what to do. Oliver Pickle, nephew of the newspaper owner and a reporter, sets out to investigate both of these cases. He met Margaret briefly and was taken in by her beauty. But Oliver's skills, for words and for observation, are not enough; he'll need help. Who better than the only nonsuspect, Henry David Thoreau? The village of Concord, with all its famous residents, is brought to life as Oliver and Thoreau attempt to solve this mystery.

Keywords: America; Missing Person; Murder; Nineteenth Century

Scott, Regina.

La Petite Four. Razorbill, 2008. 978-1-59514-208-5 (softcover). 231pp. **M** **J**

Lady Emily and her three best friends are looking forward to planning and presenting the ball of the Season. Priscilla hopes the ball will land her a rich husband; sisters Daphne and Ariadne want to enjoy polite society. Lady Emily hopes to win the favor of Lady St. Gregory, the president of the Royal Society for the Beaux Arts. But then the horrid Lord Robert arrives and announces that he and Lady Emily will be married during the ball. The ball will be ruined if Emily is not there, and the four friends aren't ready to be separated. There must be a reason for Lord Robert's haste in arranging the wedding. And if there's anyone who can find out that answer, it's La Petite Four—with a little help.

Keywords: England; Nineteenth Century

Slade, Arthur.

Dust. Wendy Lamb, 2003. 978-0-385-73004-4 (hardcover); 978-0-440-22976-6 (softcover). 192pp. **J** **S**

The day that he walks to town for the first time, Matthew vanishes. Everyone in this part of Saskatchewan searches for him, but after a few weeks the search goes cold. But for Robert, Matthew's older brother, the disappearance stays with him. Even with the troubles of no rain and bad crops, Robert keeps thinking about Matthew. Then a man named Abram Harsick comes to town, casting a spell over everyone—except Robert and his Uncle Alden. Abram Harsick claims he can make it rain, ending the troubles. The townspeople even build a rain mill so Harsick can perform this miracle. But as he keeps everyone in a spell, other children are disappearing. To save the children, Robert will have to find out just who— or what—Harsick is.

Keywords: 1930s; Canada; Family; Great Depression; Missing Person

Springer, Nancy.

Enola Holmes Mysteries. **M**

The younger sister of Sherlock Holmes shares more than his blood; she has his talent for investigation. Rather than submit to being sent to a boarding school by her brothers, Enola hides in the East End of London, helping its residents.

Keywords: Brothers and Sisters; England; Female Detective; Missing Person; Nineteenth Century

The Case of the Missing Marquess. Philomel, 2006. 978-0-399-24304-2 (hardcover); 978-0-14-240933-6 (softcover). 208pp.

> Her fourteenth birthday is life-changing for Enola Holmes. The disappearance of her mother leaves Enola alone, forcing her to contact the two older brothers whom she barely knows. When they arrive, Mycroft and Sherlock Holmes reveal that Enola's mother has been hoarding money—and they suspect her of running away with these funds. Enola is shocked and disbelieving. She decides to start looking for her mother herself, and she will start in London. With her trusty bicycle and disguised as a widow, Enola navigates Victorian London, trying to pursue her investigation without attracting the attention of her famous detective brother. As she gets caught up in an investigation of the Marquess of Basilweather's kidnapping, Enola wonders if she will ever find her mother.

The Case of the Left Handed Lady. Philomel, 2007. 978-0-399-24517-6 (hardcover); 978-0-14-241190-2 (softcover). 192pp.

> Enola Holmes is in London, determined to stay free of her brothers and the confined, genteel life they wish to force upon her. Disguising herself, she has set up shop as the assistant to Dr. Ragostin, an aspiring detective. But there is no Dr. Ragostin—just Enola. And although she's distressed to learn how upset her brother Sherlock is over her disappearance, Enola has a case to keep her busy. The Lady Cecily, a talented artist, has vanished. Although at first there were suspicions that she had run off with a young man, there are now no clues to her whereabouts. Enola is determined to find Cecily. But as she deciphers the clues, Enola finds that this rescue might reveal all of her own secrets.

The Case of the Bizarre Bouquets. Philomel, 2008. 978-0-399-24518-3 (hardcover); 978-0-14-241390-6 (softcover). 176pp.

> Hiding from her brothers is practically a full-time job for Enola Holmes. It requires much thinking to make sure her brother Sherlock, the genius detective, does not uncover her identity and location. And Enola's newest case is bound to bring her into contact with her brother, for Dr. Watson is missing. Enola respects and admires Sherlock's companion and wants to find him, but she knows her brother does as well. So putting on her most elaborate disguise yet, Enola makes friends with Mrs. Watson, discovers a disturbing flower arrangement, and seeks the truth about Dr. Watson, all under the nose of Sherlock. Will she succeed, or is this the end of Enola's freedom?

The Case of the Peculiar Pink Fan. Philomel, 2008. 978-0-399-24780-4 (hardcover); 978-0-14-241517-7 (softcover). 192pp.

> The latest case for Enola Holmes involves the reappearance of an old friend. Enola is surprised to see Lady Cecily again, dressed in the latest fashion but wielding a cheap pink fan. Enola doesn't get a chance to talk to Lady Cecily, but she knows something is wrong. Enola's suspicion is confirmed when Cecily slips the pink fan to Enola, and Enola sees the coded message hidden

on it. After decoding the message, Enola realizes how much danger Cecily is in. She's being held captive in preparation for a marriage she doesn't want! It's up to Enola to rescue Lady Cecily—and she might not be able to do it on her own. But if she seeks the help of her brothers, Mycroft and Sherlock Holmes, she can kiss her freedom good-bye. Will Enola value friendship more than staying independent?

The Case of the Cryptic Crinoline. Philomel, 2009. 978-0-399-24781-1 (hardcover). 176pp.

London is full of little old ladies—respectable, upstanding women. So what makes Mrs. Tupper, Enola Holmes's landlady, so unique? When she receives a threatening, anonymous note, Mrs. Tupper asks Enola for help. But before Enola can do much, Mrs. Tupper is kidnapped. Enola's not about to let anything happen to her kind, deaf landlady. This case will take Enola out of the stew of London's East End and into the finest homes. Mrs. Tupper's disappearance seems to have something to do with the Crimean War's Lady with the Lamp, the nurse Florence Nightingale. It will take all of Enola's talent for disguise to investigate the connection between Mrs. Tupper and Florence Nightingale, and to bring Mrs. Tupper home.

Thomson, Sarah L.

The Secret of the Rose. Greenwillow Books, 2006. 978-0-06-087250-2 (hardcover). 304pp. **M** **J**

When their father is arrested for being a Catholic, Rosalind and her brother Robin flee to London. Once they arrive, they learn that they have nowhere to go for protection, and they are robbed. Needing to hide, Rosalind disguises herself as a boy, and the two of them look into positions as apprentices. Rosalind becomes a servant to Christopher Marlowe, the well-known playwright. With the protection of her master, Rosalind thinks she and Robin and will be safe. But it turns out that Marlowe has a secret of his own—which might hurt Rosalind as well. What is his secret—and will Rosalind remain safe?

Keywords: Brothers and Sisters; Disguised as Boy; England; Religious Conflicts; Sixteenth Century

Noir Historical Mysteries

A contrast to the cozy mystery is the dark or hardboiled mystery, featuring a detective who has seen too much. The mysteries in this section involve gritty crimes and/or a dark, foreboding setting. The characters in these novels often don't want to just catch the killer—they want revenge, reward, or recognition.

Arnold, Ted.

Rat Life. Dial, 2007. 978-0-8037-3020-5 (hardcover); 978-0-14-241431-6 (softcover). 208pp. **J** **S**

When a body is pulled out of the local river, Todd doesn't think much of it. He's thinking more about finishing school, writing stories, maybe making some money. He gets a chance to raise some funds when he gets a job at the local drive-in. There, he works with Rat, who is only a few years older than Todd but already a Vietnam War veteran. Spending time with Rat, Todd starts asking questions about what he's taken for granted. Even more, he wonders if Rat had something to do with that murder. In the early 1970s, a boy tries to untangle a mystery in his small town.

Keywords: 1970s; America; Murder; Vietnam War

Avi.

The Man Who Was Poe. Orchard Books, 1989. 978-0-531-05833-6 (hardcover); 978-0-380-73022-3 (softcover). 208pp. **M** **J**

It's a true mystery: a girl, locked up in a room in a boarding house, disappears. Her twin brother is left behind, searching for her. That's what has happened to Edmund, recently arrived with his sister and aunt in Providence, Rhode Island. Edmund is in even worse straits when his aunt's body is pulled from the bay. Alone, cold, and hungry, Edmund's only hope is Mr. Auguste Dupin, a sad, melancholic man. He's bossy and occasionally cruel, and too fond of drink. But he insists he's the only one who can find Edmund's sister. Edmund doesn't know it, but Mr. Dupin is actually Edgar Allan Poe, the well-known mystery writer. Distracted by his own problems, Poe is still affected by Edmund's sadness. And he will search with Edmund for his sister.

Read-alike: Learn more about the haunted author in *Nevermore: A Photobiography of Edgar Allan Poe* by Karen Lange.

Keywords: America; Family; Missing Person; Nineteenth Century

Blackwood, Gary.

Second Sight. Dutton Juvenile, 2005. 978-0-525-47481-4 (hardcover); 978-0-14-240747-9 (softcover). 288pp. **M** **J**

The formerly quiet town of Washington, capital of the United States, is busy during the Civil War. In the boarding houses scattered around the town, entertainers practice their acts. Joseph and his father have created a mind-reading routine; it's all fake, but it looks good. Soon, people throughout Washington are attending their performances, utterly deceived. Joseph doesn't mind this deception, because he's too busy enjoying his fame. All that enjoyment ends when he meets a girl named Cassandra. She has a true gift for prophecy, which makes her nervous and scared. She has seen terrible things, like a plot against President Lincoln. Together,

Joseph and Cassandra join forces to find just who wants to assassinate the president. As the war draws to an end, the plot comes closer to its goal—unless Joseph and Cassandra can stop it.

Read-alike: To find out how John Wilkes Booth was captured after he succeeded in assassinating President Lincoln, read *Chasing Lincoln's Killer* by James L. Swanson.

Keywords: America; Civil War; Murder; Nineteenth Century; Treason

Donnelly, Jennifer.

A Northern Light. **Harcourt Children's Books, 2003. 978-0-15-216705-9 (hardcover); 978-0-15-205310-9 (softcover). 400pp. ⑤**

At the beginning of the twentieth century, the Adirondacks in upstate New York were a summer vacation destination. Thanks to the large hotels and resorts in the area, Mattie is able to get a paying position as a servant. She promised her mother that she would go to college and fulfill her potential as a great writer. Yet there's so much to keep her at home: her family and her responsibilities to them, plus the handsome boy who's courting her. But then Mattie has a chance encounter with a hotel guest named Grace Brown—a woman who disappears and is presumed drowned after a trip on the lake with her gentleman suitor. When Mattie reads the love letters that Grace asked her to burn, she begins to discover all the reasons she should leave.

Read-alike: Older teens might enjoy Theodore Dreiser's *An American Tragedy*, based on the same real-life events as *A Northern Light.*

Awards: Printz Honor Book; Carnegie Medal

Keywords: 1900s; America; Murder; Women's Roles

Hoobler, Dorothy, and Thomas Hoobler.

The Samurai Mysteries. ❶

These mysteries explore Japanese culture. Young Seikei gets the unusual opportunity to move from one station in life to another, becoming a samurai thanks to his innate intelligence and courage. With his adopted father, he assists the shogun and the Emperor in keeping eighteenth-century Japan peaceful and safe.

Keywords: Eighteenth Century; Family; Japan; Murder

The Ghost in the Tokaido Inn. **Philomel, 1999. 978-0-399-23330-2 (hardcover); 978-0-698-11879-9 (softcover). 214pp.**

Seikei wishes that he could be a samurai, facing death without fear and writing beautiful haiku. But as the fourteen-year-old son of a merchant, he's expected to become a merchant. On a trip with his father, they stay in an inn with a daimyo, a samurai lord. The lord has a precious jewel, a ruby that will go to the shogun. But then the ruby is stolen—and Seikei is the only one to see the thief. Even worse, the thief is a ghost. The samurai barricades the inn, looking for the thief while a judge is sent for. The judge who arrives, Lord Ooka, is a samurai—but a true samurai, unlike the daimyo. Lord Ooka needs help in his investigation, and he chooses Seikei. Can a merchant's son be as worthy as a samurai? Seikei is determined to prove that he is.

The Demon in the Teahouse. Philomel, 2001. 978-0-399-23499-6 (hardcover); 978-0-698-11971-0 (softcover). 182pp.

Seikei has been blessed since he met Judge Ooka. The samurai lord has adopted Seikei and started his samurai training. Seikei is determined to honor Ooka's trust and belief in him, but he is slow to learn. Yet his training will have to wait, for there is unease in Edo. Fires have been breaking out, and geisha are being killed. Judge Ooka, as a judge and the shogun's representative on fires, is caught up in both these cases. Seikei is tasked to work as a teahouse attendant, to see what information he can gather. But if someone—or something—is out to kill geishas and set fires, Seikei has a dangerous job. Will he solve this mystery and live to continue his training?

In Darkness, Death. Philomel, 2004. 978-0-399-23767-6 (hardcover); 978-0-14-240366-2 (softcover). 208pp.

The death of a samurai lord is the newest mystery for Seikei and his adopted father, Judge Ooka. Lord Inaba has just arrived in Edo and was under the protection of the shogun. Lord Inaba's murder is thus an embarrassment for the shogun, and the killer must be found. The only clue is a bloodstained origami butterfly. As rumors and suspicions spread, fingering a ninja as the killer, Seikei follows Ooka's lead in investigating the murder. They will have to travel far and face much danger to discover who is responsible.

The Sword That Cut the Burning Grass. Philomel, 2005. 978-0-399-24272-4 (hardcover); 978-0-14-240689-2 (softcover). 212pp.

Seikei's first mission without Ooka is a challenging one. The Emperor, who is a fourteen-year-old boy like Seikei, is refusing to perform his ceremonial duties. Instead, he has retreated to a monastery. The shogun thinks that Seikei might be able to convince the Emperor to return to the Imperial Palace. Traveling to Kyoto, Seikei meets the Emperor and begins to get to know him. But before Seikei can fulfill his mission, the Emperor is kidnapped. Following every available clue, Seikei must find the Emperor or risk the downfall of the shogun. If that happens, chaos will tear apart Japan. With help from another warrior, Seikei will find the Emperor and save the sacred sword.

A Samurai Never Fears Death. Philomel, 2007. 978-0-399-24609-8 (hardcover); 978-0-14-241208-4 (softcover). 176pp.

A visit to his former home opens up disturbing feelings in Seikei. He hasn't returned to Osaka since he was adopted by Judge Ooka, and he's unsure if he wants to see his old family. When he arrives at his family's tea shop, his older sister Asako doesn't seem happy to see him—and their brother Denzaburo seems to be involved in some suspicious business activities. Worst of all, though, is the case Seikei stumbles into: two murders that have occurred at the local puppet theater. These crimes are complex, far beyond the simple apprentice who is accused of committing them. The fact that his sister loves the apprentice motivates Seikei to find the true killer. Using all his skills, Seikei attempts to discover who really killed the puppet theater performers.

Seven Paths to Death. Philomel, 2008. 978-0-399-24610-4 (hardcover); 978-0-14-241466-8 (softcover). 192pp.

An attack on a tattooed man begins the most complex case faced by Seikei and Judge Ooka. The tattoo on the man is extensive, covering his whole back—and it seems to be part of a series. Seikei and Ooka begin investigating, finding other men with similar tattoos on their backs. The men, all criminals or yakuza, have no connection between them, other than the tattoos and that they're starting to turn up dead. The tattoos are actually an extensive treasure map, and someone is killing the men in order to copy the map portion and keep the treasure for themselves. It's up to Seikei and Judge Ooka to stop the murderer from succeeding.

Lawrence, Iain.

The Séance. Delacorte Books, 2008. 978-0-385-73375-5 (hardcover); 978-0-440-23970-3 (softcover). 272pp.

Scooter knows his mother isn't really a medium. After all, he's her assistant, helping her convince people that she receives messages from the Beyond. It's all just an illusion—not like Harry Houdini, the world's greatest magician. Scooter knows that Houdini is coming to town to perform in his Burmese Torture Tank, and Scooter can't wait. But then Scooter discovers a dead man in Houdini's tank. No one really seems to care who killed the man, one-half of a vaudeville team. So Scooter decides to solve the mystery himself and find the killer. The first question is, did the murderer mean to kill someone else, and the dead man was in the wrong place at the wrong time? Scooter has to consider this and more to find the answer. If he's not careful, he might be the next victim.

Keywords: America; Magic; Murder; Nineteenth Century; Psychics

Lisle, Janet Taylor.

Black Duck. Philomel, 2006. 978-0-399-23963-2 (hardcover); 978-0-14-240902-2 (softcover). 240pp.

David is on the trail of a story. He knows that in the 1920s the coast of Rhode Island was a hotbed of smugglers and rum runners. Rumor has it that Ruben Hart knows what happened back then. When David finds Mr. Hart, and he begins telling about the mystery, David knows he has something. Young Ruben, with his best friend Jeddy, discover a body on the beach in 1929. It's obviously a rich man; he has a gold wristwatch and is wearing an evening suit. When the local police, led by Jeddy's dad the police chief, seem to downplay their discovery—and the body has disappeared—Ruben, Jeddy, and Jeddy's older sister Marina start to investigate. But when they are drawn into the conflict between rival gangsters, Ruben, Jeddy, and Marina fing themselves in danger. Between the police and Coast Guard, the rum runners and the crew of the shore runner known as the *Black Duck*, the three teens attempt to learn just who the dead man was.

Keywords: 1920s; America; Murder

Masson, Sophie.

The Madman of Venice. **Delacorte Books for Young Readers, 2010. 978-0-385-73843-9 (hardcover). 288pp.** 🇯 🇸

Eighteen-year-old Ned finds himself juggling all sorts of mysteries during a visit to Venice in 1602. Ned is the clerk to Master Ashby, a London merchant. Pirates have been attacking merchant ships after leaving Venice, and Master Ashby has been asked to find these pirates in an undercover mission. Ned will accompany Ashby and his daughter Celia—the girl that Ned loves. Even before they leave for Venice, they're asked for help on another mystery: the disappearance of a beautiful Jewish girl, who was accused of witchcraft by the powerful Countess of Montemoro. Once they arrive in Venice, the two investigations and Ned's plan to woo Celia are complicated by the disappearance of Master Ashby. Can Ned and Celia work together to find the missing and punish the guilty? Only with Ned's imagination and Celia's practicality may they succeed.

Keywords: Italy; Missing Person; Romance; Seventeenth Century

Myracle, Lauren.

Bliss. **Amulet Books, 2008. 978-0-8109-7071-7 (hardcover); 978-0-8109-4072-7 (softcover). 464pp.** 🇯 🇸

The murders committed by the Manson family are front-page news, but Bliss is just as focused on the strange events at her new school. The daughter of hippies, Bliss has been dumped on her very proper grandmother. Instead of living in the commune, Bliss is now a resident of Atlanta. She doesn't know much about the way things are done beyond the commune, but Bliss will slowly find her way. Eager to make friends, she finds herself drawn to a girl who is eager to relive the school's darkest days. Bliss doesn't realize that the secrets of the past can impact the present. As Bliss tries to stop the girl, she starts to gain a better understanding of the darkness that created the Manson family.

Keywords: 1960s; America; Magic; Murder

Peacock, Shane.

The Boy Sherlock Holmes. ❚❙

The first adventures of Sherlock Holmes, the world's greatest detective, are told in a series of dark, gritty tales.

Keywords: England; Kidnapping; Missing Person; Murder; Nineteenth Century

Eye of the Crow. Tundra Books, 2007. 978-0-88776-850-7 (hardcover); 978-0-88776-919-1 (softcover). 264pp.

> A woman is cruelly murdered. A man is arrested for the crime, tried, and punished. It's all very open and shut, but not to the young Sherlock Holmes. The son of a Jewish father and a highborn mother, he has remarkable powers of observation and a brilliant mind. But with his mixed background and poverty, he can never rise much higher than clerk or teacher. So what's the use of going to school? He'd rather go to Trafalgar Square. But then the murder happens, and Sherlock finds himself puzzling over it, wondering who killed the woman. When he sees the suspect, a young Arab, he can't help himself. He must find the killer, because he doesn't believe this poor foreigner is the murderer. Through the dark streets of 1867 London, he puts together the pieces using the only witnesses to the crime: the crows.

Death in the Air. Tundra Books, 2008. 978-0-88776-851-4 (hardcover). 264pp.

> Seeing a trapeze artist fall to his death presents Sherlock Holmes with his next case. It seems clear that Monsieur Mercure's death is no accident; he had several enemies and the trapeze had been sabotaged. But just who acted on their dislike for the aerialist? Thirteen-year-old Sherlock is determined to find out, putting into practice his scientific method of detection. He's also determined to make some money and impress the police detectives. But even though he witnessed the crime, solving it won't be an easy task for the young detective. It will take some help from the Irregulars, a London street gang, and Sigerson Bell, Sherlock's new master and a master alchemist. And then there's Irene Doyle, a young lady Sherlock is trying to avoid, even though he cares for her. With all these distractions and demands, it will take all of Sherlock's talents to solve this mystery.

Vanishing Girl. Tundra Books, 2009. 978-0-88776-852-1 (hardcover). 320pp.

> The disappearance of a young woman of quality draws the attention of Sherlock Holmes, the teenage detective. Belittled by the detectives of Scotland Yard, Sherlock is on his own if he wants to solve this case. As a poor man, he'll need help—from Irene Doyle, the wealthy young woman Sherlock finds so dangerously attractive. Irene has her own

reason for working with Sherlock: to gain the assistance of the missing girl's father to heal a young orphan. Together, Sherlock and Irene pursue the abductors of the young woman. Their only clue is the watermark on the ransom note. These two young people have to find a way to work past their attraction if they are to save the orphan and the socialite.

Pullman, Philip.

The Sally Lockhart Mysteries. 🄢

Featuring a boundary-defying heroine, Pullman's mysteries plunge the reader into the politics of the Victorian world. Labyrinthine plots and vivid characters show what middle and lower class life was like.

Keywords: England; Nineteenth Century; Murder; Theft; Family; Female Detective

The Ruby in the Smoke. Knopf Books for Young Readers, 1987. 978-0-394-98826-9 (hardcover); 978-0-394-89589-5 (softcover). 230pp.

Not many girls have men die of fright at their feet. But then, Sally Lockhart isn't like most young girls. Sixteen and pretty, her most noticeable quality is her mind. Gifted with a talent for numbers and a cool logic, Sally will need these qualities to unravel the mystery she is facing. Her father died recently on his way back from the East. He was investigating problems with his business, but his knowledge has died with him. Now a woman named Mrs. Holland is after Sally, and it's thanks to Sally's new friends Jim and Fred that she stays one step ahead. The opium trade, a maharajah's stolen ruby, and her father's death are all entwined in a mystery that only Sally can solve. If she doesn't, she might lose her life.

The Shadow in the North. Knopf Books for Young Readers, 1988. 978-0-394-89453-9 (hardcover); 978-0-394-82599-1 (softcover). 320pp.

Six years after her first case, Sally Lockhart finds herself drawn into a new mystery. Detective work isn't her main job: She runs a financial consulting business, advising people how to manage and invest their money. When a former client comes to see Sally, having lost all her money from Sally's recommended investment in a shipping line, Sally grows suspicious. It seems like fraud might be the reason for the failure—and Sally wants to find the truth. Meanwhile, Fred Garland, a detective and Sally's love interest, has his own case, involving spiritualism and an aspiring medium. As Fred and Sally research, discovering the connections between their cases, they try to resolve the impasse between them. But this mystery concerns a rich industrialist and powerful forces. Just when Fred and Sally have truly gained their happiness, those forces will strike. And Sally will be left alone to solve the final puzzle.

The Tiger in the Well. Knopf Books for Young Readers, 1990. 978-0-679-80214-3 (hardcover); 978-0-679-82671-2 (softcover). 320pp.

> After the death of her love Fred, it would have been easy for Sally Lockhart to give in to despair. But she is too stubborn—and so is the baby created during Sally and Fred's one night together. Now Sally's world is about her daughter Harriet, her friends Webster and Jim, and her financial business. But everything comes crashing down when she is served with divorce papers—from a complete stranger. In the face of paperwork and witnesses, Sally doesn't know how to prove that this is all a lie. She will have to find a way, though, as her "husband" wants custody of Harriet. For her daughter's sake, Sally will have to find out who has set this plan in motion: Who has gone to such lengths to destroy her?

The Tin Princess. Knopf Books for Young Readers, 1994. 978-0-679-84757-1 (hardcover); 978-0-679-87615-1 (softcover). 290pp.

> A mysterious adventure is in the works for the friends of Sally Lockhart. Becky has a talent for languages, which she plans to make money with. She is hired to teach a young lady German. Imagine Becky's surprise when she finds out that the young lady is a princess! Adelaide is married to Prince Rudolf of Razkavia, a small country located between Germany and Austro-Hungary. Coincidentally, that's the country that Becky is originally from. Before Becky can teach Adelaide much German, a series of attacks, on both Prince Rudolf and members of the Razkavian royal family, requires the prince to return home. Going with the prince are Adelaide, Becky, and Jim, an old friend of Adelaide's who hasn't seen her for years. As political intrigue swirls in Razkavia, Adelaide and Jim fight their feelings for each other, and Becky seeks an adventure of her own. But all three will have to work together to discover who wishes to control Razkavia.

Sedgwick, Marcus.

Revolver. Roaring Book Press, 2010. 978-1-59643-592-6 (hardcover). 224pp.

> Fourteen-year-old Sig has been left alone with his father's body, while his sister and stepmother go for help. Sig's father Einar fell through the ice and froze to death—something that can happen when you live north of the Arctic Circle. Sig is numb from grief when a stranger arrives at the family's cabin. The stranger, who is named Wolff, claims that Einar owes him a horde of gold, acquired during the Yukon Gold Rush of 1897–1899. But Sig knows nothing about this. Wolff isn't going to accept this answer and threatens both Sig and his sister Anna. Can the siblings save themselves with the revolver hidden in the cabin?

Keywords: 1910s; America; Brothers and Sisters; Gold Rush; Nineteenth Century

Wulffson, Don.

The Golden Rat. **Bloomsbury USA Children's Books, 2007. 978-1-59990-000-1 (hardcover). 176pp.** Ⓜ Ⓙ

The death of his mother changes Baoliu's life. His father is bitter and downhearted, and his brother is wrapped up in his studies. When his father marries a beautiful yet shallow woman, Baoliu can't stand to see this woman wearing his mother's jewelry. Though his father is happy, Baoliu feels hate and anger growing in his heart. Yet this doesn't mean that he killed his stepmother. Although Baoliu is sentenced to death, his father manages to save him, but he disinherits him. Baoliu is now left on his own, an object of scorn. Yet he's determined to find out who really killed his stepmother—and thus clear his name.

Keywords: China; Family; Medieval; Murder

Chapter 5

Historical Adventures

Action, suspense, fast pacing, and daring escapes define historical adventure. Many periods of history lend themselves to novels that are full of excitement and derring-do. Whether pirate yarns, spy stories, or battle tales, historical fiction offers many examples of action-packed stories. The characters in these stories are often on a quest—searching for something. Sometimes the adventure itself is what the character is after. Other times, to find what they want the characters have to face great trials along the way.

This search gives historical action novels the plot-starter, a way for the action to be put into motion. It also allows the action to show us more about the characters we are reading about. An exciting story, full of battles and attacks, would be boring without interesting, engaging characters to cheer for. Authors of this type of historical fiction balance the fast-moving plot with the quieter character moments.

Seafarers and Pirates

Naval adventures have a certain flair and panache. Whether the law-and-order of naval ships sailing the high seas or engaging in warfare or the lawlessness of pirates engaging in pillage and plunder, these novels feature a hint of sea air.

Avi.

The True Confessions of Charlotte Doyle. HarperCollins, 2004. 978-0380-72885-5 (softcover). 240pp. **M** **J**

Miss Charlotte Doyle is the image of a proper young lady when she boards the *Seahawk*. Due to a miscommunication, she is the only passenger, which she knows is not at all proper. But thanks to the dashing, fatherly Captain Jaggery, she sets aside her misgivings. At first she is charmed by the flattery of the Captain, who treats her like an adult. Meanwhile, she steers clear of the crew, who she has been warned are a group of ruffians. But slowly she comes to realize that all is not as it seems. The captain is not the gentleman he appears to be, and the crew is not dishonorable and disobedient. When Charlotte realizes that, she has to make a choice . . . one that leads her to becoming part of the crew.

Awards: Newbery Honor Book

Keywords: Atlantic Ocean; Nineteenth Century; Women's Roles

Cadnum, Michael.

Peril on the Sea. **Farrar, Straus & Giroux, 2009. 978-0-374-35823-5 (hardcover). 256pp.** ◼ ◼

It is the summer of 1588, and tensions between England and Spain are rising. Pirates and privateers sail the Atlantic waters, raiding villages and other ships. One of these pirates is Captain Brandon Fletcher, on the ship *Vixen*. On his ship are two unusual passengers, a writer and a noblewoman. The writer, Sherwin Morris, was rescued from a shipwreck and has stayed aboard to write Captain Fletcher's story. The young woman, Katherine Westing, is from minor nobility and is trying to escape a marriage to a cruel earl. Together these three will be swept up in the adventure of the Spanish Armada. For though Fletcher is sailing toward a great treasure, the Spanish ships sailing toward England require the service of all Englishmen to defeat this great fleet. In the midst of the battle, the fates of many people will be decided.

Keywords: Atlantic Ocean; Pirates; Sixteenth Century

Dowswell, Paul.

Adventures of a Young Sailor. ◼ ◼

The world of naval ships during the Napoleonic Wars are brought to life in Dowswell's thrilling series. The sea is all Sam wants, but he'll discover that life on the open waters is full of adventure and danger.

Keywords: Atlantic Ocean; Australia; England; Napoleonic Wars; Nineteenth Century

Powder Monkey. Bloomsbury, 2005. 978-1-58234-675-5 (hardcover); 978-1-58234-748-6 (softcover). 200pp.

All his life, Sam has dreamt of being a sailor. His father finally gives in and lets him join the crew of a merchant ship. But then Sam is impressed: forced to join the British Navy and work on one of their ships. Now he's a powder monkey, responsible for providing one of the gun crews with their powder. It's a dangerous job, because one spark could send him to Kingdom Come. All Sam wants is to escape his commission—is he strong enough to survive the harsh conditions on board the HMS *Miranda* and get his wish?

Prison Ship. Bloomsbury, 2006. 978-1-58234-676-2 (hardcover); 978-1-59990-156-5 (softcover). 313pp.

After the shipwreck of the *Miranda*, Sam is happy to be alive. Soon he's back on the open sea, now serving on the HMS *Elephant*. The fleet is sailing toward

Scandinavia, commanded by Admiral Nelson himself. Sam is excited by the conditions on this ship: the pleasant captain, the company of his fellow sailors, and the chance to show his bravery. Things seem to be looking up, even with disagreeable men like Midshipman Pritchard. But when Sam overhears something he shouldn't have, he finds himself framed and condemned to execution. In the nick of time, his sentence is commuted to transportation to New South Wales in the far-off land of Australia. It will be a struggle for Sam to survive. Yet he's determined to do more than live—he wants revenge, to have his name cleared and to return to service in the Royal Navy.

Battle Fleet. Bloomsbury, 2008. 978-1-59990-080-3 (hardcover). 304pp.

Having cleared his name and been pardoned, Sam is sailing for England. On the long trip from Australia, the older teen survives pirates and a disastrous storm. Sam is convinced that he's done with the sea, but he finds that life on land doesn't agree with him. It seems clear that he's only fulfilled when he's under sail. So Sam decides to reenlist and take his chances in the Royal Navy. In 1805 Napoleon's armies are threatening England and Europe. On the sea, England has the advantage, but Napoleon is determined to conquer all of Europe. Assigned to the HMS *Victory*, Sam will once again be in the thick of battle, because the *Victory* is part of Admiral Nelson's fleet, and they are sailing toward the confrontation known as the Battle of Trafalgar.

Lawlor, Laurie.

Dead Reckoning. **Simon & Schuster Children's Publishing, 2005. 978-0-689-86577-0 (hardcover); 978-0-689-86578-7 (softcover). 272pp. Ⓜ Ⓙ**

Emmet thinks he's all alone when his mentor, Father Parfoothe, dies. He's small for his fifteen years and wishes to keep studying and learning. To his surprise, a cousin he doesn't remember shows up on his doorstep. And his cousin is no ordinary man; he's Sir Francis Drake. He wants Emmet to come with him on his next voyage. Emmet agrees but quickly feels like a fish out of water. How can good people suffer and die while the wicked prosper and flourish? As Drake leads his ships on an amazing journey, Emmet learns how to steer his own course.

Keywords: Atlantic Ocean; Family; Identity; Sixteenth Century

Lee, Tanith.

Piratica. Ⓙ Ⓢ

These two novels offer an unusual take on pirate adventures. Not just about determining reality from fiction, they involve exploration of women's roles in an alternate universe.

Keywords: Alternate Universe; Atlantic Ocean; England; Nineteenth Century; Pirates; Women's Roles

Piratica. Dutton Juvenile, 2004. 978-0-525-47324-4 (hardcover); 978-0-14-240644-1 (softcover). 304pp.

> Hitting her head on the banister at her school does more than give Artemesia a headache. It brings back her memories of childhood, when she was the daughter of the most daring pirate queen ever. Renaming herself Art, she sets off to find her mother's crew. She's bound and determined to return to the sea. But when Art is reunited with the pirates, she's confused by the way they can walk around the city in freedom, why these former pirates are serving as adventuring spokesmen. That's when they reveal the truth: Art's memories are of the pirate play they all appeared in, not reality. Art is left reeling, but she is still set on a life at sea. She commandeers a ship and brings on board the actors. In spite of the risks and dangers, Art leads her ship to riches and fame. An alternate universe reveals similar joys in a life at sea.

Piratica II. Dutton Juvenile, 2006. 978-0-525-47769-3 (hardcover); 978-0-14-241094-3 (softcover). 360pp.

> How does a pirate queen adapt to land? After Art's adventures lead to the gallows, she is rescued by Felix, her true love. They marry, gain new riches, and settle into a mansion. But Art can't help longing for the sea. When war is declared on England, Art gets a chance to be a pirate again. This time, though, she'd be a legal pirate, a privateer, harassing England's enemies on the high seas. But adventure doesn't come easily. Art's foe Little Goldie Girl is still sailing, and out to sink Art and her ship. But maybe the fierce storms pounding the Atlantic will do the job for Goldie. There is also the widow who's out to destroy all pirates, in revenge for the death of her husband. Even if Art makes it through all this, will Felix still be waiting for her when she returns to shore?

McCaughrean, Geraldine.

The Pirate's Son. Scholastic, 1999. 978-0-590-20348-7 (softcover). 294pp. **J** **S**

> When his father dies, Nathan and his sister Maud are left penniless. Nathan is expelled from school, since his father has not paid his school fees for the last two terms. Without any other relations and no options, life looks bleak for Nathan and Maud. Then a notorious schoolmate of Nathan's comes up with a plan. Tamo White is the son of a pirate, who wanted his son to be an educated, normal Englishman. But that's not what Tamo wants—he wants to go back to Madagascar and live his own life. And he invites Nathan and Maud along. Arriving in Madagascar, Nathan's eyes are opened to an exotic new world. But the peace Tamo sought is elusive, especially when their home is attacked by pirates. Will Tamo rely on his heritage to beat back the marauders? And how will Nathan face up to dangerous buccaneers?

Keywords: Africa; Brothers and Sisters; Nineteenth Century; Pirates

Meyer, L. A.

The Bloody Jack Adventures. 🅜 🅙

Like a female Horatio Alger, Mary "Jacky" Faber rises from the streets of London to become an accomplished lady, a ship's captain, and more. Using her wits and pluck, Jacky hopscotches from Britain to America to France to the Caribbean, striving to stay one step ahead of the authorities.

Keywords: America; Atlantic Ocean; Disguised as Boy; England; France; Napoleonic Wars; Nineteenth Century; Women Soldiers

Bloody Jack: Being an Account of the Curious Adventures of Mary "Jacky" Faber, Ship's Boy. Harcourt Children's Books, 2002. 978-0-15-216731-8 (hardcover); 978-0-15-205085-6 (softcover). 336pp.

> Becoming an orphan at the age of eight changes Mary Faber's life. She only survives thanks to being taken in by one of London's roaming street gangs. As part of Rooster Charlie's group, she learns how to beg and steal. Her ace in the hole is her ability to read. But when Charlie is killed, Mary has had enough of life on the streets. She takes Charlie's clothes and reinvents herself as Jacky, finding that being a boy is better than being a girl. Because she is literate, Jacky gets taken on as a ship's boy on the HMS *Dolphin*. She gets regular food and the ship is spic-and-span clean—even more, there are adventures on the high seas, learning about the nautical life, and even a shipboard romance. Jacky is determined to maintain the deception and keep her real sex hidden. It remains to be seen if she can manage that.

Curse of the Blue Tattoo: Being an Account of the Misadventures of Jacky Faber, Midshipman and Fine Lady. Harcourt Children's Books, 2004. 978-0-15-205115-0 (hardcover); 978-0-15-205459-5 (softcover). 496pp.

> After her secret is discovered, Jacky Faber can no longer serve on the HMS *Dolphin*. What's more, they can't even take her back to England. Instead, the Captain puts her ashore in Boston, enrolling her in a boarding school that will turn her into a lady. But that might be impossible, because Jacky isn't good at female accomplishments like embroidery and etiquette. She would rather go home, to be reunited with her love Jaimy. Jacky Faber isn't about to be beaten by a bunch of pampered princesses, and there might be adventure even at a school like this—if there is, Jacky will find it.

Under the Jolly Roger: Being an Account of the Further Nautical Adventures of Jacky Faber. Harcourt Children's Books, 2005. 978-0-15-205345-1 (hardcover); 978-0-15-205873-9 (softcover). 528pp.

> The return to England is a homecoming for Jacky Faber. She's looking for Jaimy, from whom she hasn't heard anything since they parted in Boston. But she also has time to catch up with the kids from her

old gang and even rescue a friend from drudgery. Then Jacky drops her lady act and puts on the silks of a jockey, to sneak into Epsom Downs to see Jaimy. But at the racetrack Jacky sees Jaimy holding hands with another girl. Rushing away, Jacky makes a wrong turn and runs into a press gang. Once again, she's back on a Royal Navy ship—but this time isn't like the first time she served. With a cruel captain, it's not long before Jacky is out to take control. But taking over will have unexpected consequences . . . .

In the Belly of the Bloodhound: Being an Account of a Particularly Peculiar Adventure in the Life of Jacky Faber. Harcourt Children's Books, 2006. 978-0-15-205557-8 (hardcover); 978-0-15-206166-1 (softcover). 528pp.

If you take a Royal Navy ship as your own, the navy is bound to be vexed. That's what Jacky is discovering. After the horror of Trafalgar, she escaped to America, only to find that she's been declared a pirate. There's a price on her head, but Jacky is determined not to be caught. She decides to hide in the most unlikely of places: the Lawson Peabody School for Young Girls, her former school. Now accorded a measure of respect by Mistress Pimm and the other students, Jacky finds school more to her liking. But because she's Jacky Faber, life cannot stay peaceful for long. In Boston for a field trip, the girls of Lawson Peabody are kidnapped—destined for service in Arabian harems. Jacky wants to rescue all the girls, but it's a tough assignment for one girl surrounded by such milk-and-water misses. Only if Jacky can convince the girls to help themselves will they succeed.

Mississippi Jack: Being an Account of the Further Waterborne Adventures of Jacky Faber, Midshipman, Fine Lady, and Lily of the West. Harcourt Children's Books, 2007. 978-0-15-206003-9 (hardcover); 978-0-15-206632-1 (softcover). 624pp.

Returning to Boston with the girls of the Lawson Peabody School, Jacky has eyes only for her Jaimy. She thinks they are reunited at last—but the captain of the rescue ship throws her into the brig, arresting her for her piratical crimes. Jacky has another few escapes in her, thanks to her friends. Accompanied by John Higgins and Jim Tanner, she heads for the untamed West, trying to stay ahead of the British. She manages to acquire a riverboat when they reach the Mississippi. Jacky sails her new ship down to New Orleans, playing her fiddle and pennywhistle when the mood strikes her. She encounters bandits and scoundrels, soldiers and escaping slaves. Jacky doesn't know that Jaimy is following along, only a few days behind her. Soon, she's tired of the West. Will she ever get back her two loves, the sea and Jaimy?

My Bonny Light Horseman: Being an Account of the Further Adventures of Jacky Faber, in Love and War. Harcourt Children's Books, 2008. 978-0-15-206187-6 (hardcover). 448pp.

Being captured by British Intelligence is somewhat different than Jacky's past adventures. For one thing, she is treated well . . . until she's ordered to be a spy. Jacky has never wanted to perform such work, but she's left with little choice in this case, especially when her execution is faked to throw her friends off the scent. Jacky is set up as a dancer, working to get military secrets out of a French general. It is 1806, and war between Britain and France has led the English to take advantage of any opportunity. But Jacky's not about to keep dancing when so much is on the line: her friends, her life, and her virtue. Instead, she will once again don boy's clothes. This time she will talk her way into the French army, following Napoleon on his march through Europe. Jacky will find herself smack dab in the middle of a war, and it will take all her wits to survive this adventure.

Rapture of the Deep: Being an Account of the Further Adventures of Jacky Faber, Soldier, Sailor, Mermaid, Spy. Harcourt Children's Books, 2009. 978-0-15-206501-0 (hardcover). 464pp.

The day Jacky has been waiting for has arrived: her wedding to her beloved Jaimy. She's in her wedding dress, ready to head to the church, when disaster strikes—she is captured by British Intelligence, pressed into service again. This time she sails for Havana, joining an expedition to recover treasure sunk in the Caribbean. But there are several treasure-seekers after the same prize. And though Jaimy is posted on a nearby naval ship, he and Jacky are kept apart. All Jacky wants is to marry Jaimy and run her shipping business. Will this be her last adventure before she gets the life she wants, or only the latest one?

Rees, Celia.

Pirates! Bloomsbury, 2003. 978-1-58234-816-2 (hardcover); 978-1-58234-665-6 (softcover). 340pp. **J S**

Nancy Kington knows that as a girl, she has little say over the direction of her life. But when her brothers take advantage of her father's death to arrange her marriage to an evil, controlling man, Nancy rebels. Running away with her new friend Minerva, a slave, Nancy joins a pirate ship. Together, the two girls set out on a merry adventure, casting aside all the rules for females and tasting real freedom. Nancy hopes to find her love William, a sailor in the Royal Navy, while Minerva is content with being free of slavery's bonds. These two women have the chance of a lifetime . . . but what happens when they have to face Nancy's past, in the form of her intended husband?

Keywords: Atlantic Ocean; England; Nineteenth Century; Pirates; Slavery; Women's Roles

Torrey, Michele.

Voyage of Plunder. Knopf Books for Young Readers, 2005. 978-0-375-82383-1 (hardcover); 978-0-440-41887-0 (softcover). 208pp. **Ⓜ** **Ⓙ**

> When he was young, pirates often visited Daniel's house. They came to visit his father, but Daniel loved the pirates and the gifts they brought. However, when his father remarries, much to Daniel's displeasure, the visits stop. Daniel doesn't like Faith, his father's new wife, especially when her health makes Daniel's father move them to Jamaica. On the journey the ship is taken by pirates and Daniel's father is killed. Daniel is shocked to find out his father has double-crossed the pirates. And they're not content with killing his father to finish their revenge. Taken aboard the pirate's vessel, Daniel burns to take vengeance for his father's death. But how does a boy of fourteen do that? Daniel finds a way to fit in as he learns pirate ways, all the while remembering his goal to avenge his father's death.
>
> **Keywords:** America; Atlantic Ocean; Coming-of-age; Pirates; Seventeenth Century

Spies

Throughout history, espionage has played a role in conflicts between countries. Spies have relied on gadgets, knowledge, or cunning to gain information that gives their country the upper hand.

Bradley, Kimberly Brubaker.

For Freedom: The Story of a French Spy. Delacorte, 2003. 978-0-385-72961-1 (hardcover); 978-0-440-41831-3 (softcover). 192pp. **Ⓙ**

> At first the invasion of France by Germany doesn't affect Suzanne. Her life of school, weekends at home, and singing lessons continues uninterrupted. But then, when the town square is bombed while she is in it, Suzanne suddenly realizes that France is at war. As a result of the bombing, her best friend is now catatonic. Suzanne's family is forced to give up their house and live in a dingy apartment. Worst of all, the German soldiers and their spies strike fear into everyone. But in the midst of it all, Suzanne still has singing. As she travels through towns for lessons and performances, she attracts the attention of the Resistance. Soon she is passing information, working to save France.
>
> **Keywords:** 1940s; France; Music; Spies; World War II

Cadnum, Michael.

Ship of Fire. Viking Juvenile, 2003. 978-0-670-89907-4 (hardcover). 208pp. **Ⓙ**

> Life in Elizabethan London is full of adventure. Bear-baiting pits, brothels, and taverns are side-by-side with businesses and homes. Young Thomas Spyre works with his master, the surgeon William Perrivale, learning how to heal men

of all manner of injuries. Thomas's master has but one flaw, a weakness for gambling. When William loses all his money at bear-baiting, Thomas worries what is to become of them. Through chance, Surgeon Perrivale and Thomas are then given a great opportunity. They are appointed as ship's surgeons on the *Golden Hind*. This is no ordinary assignment, for the *Golden Hind* is the flagship of Sir Francis Drake. Drake is infamous as an explorer and privateer. His superiors wonder if all the gold he captures goes to the queen. William and Thomas have adventures that make London's pale in comparison, as they attempt to be loyal to both their admiral and their country.

Keywords: England; Sixteenth Century

Molloy, Michael.

Peter Raven Under Fire. **The Chicken House, 2005. 978-0-439-72454-8 (hardcover); 978-0-439-72457-9 (softcover). 512pp. ◻ ◻**

In 1800 the war between England and France has been dragging on for years. Although the French are led by the military genius Napoleon, British naval skill has kept England even with France. But now Napoleon has a plan to pull the young nation of the United States into the battle. To defeat such a plan, the British intelligence network springs into action. The man known as Commodore Beaumont needs help to defeat the French plot, so he calls upon thirteen-year-old Peter Raven, Royal Navy midshipman. Peter speaks French like a native and is well-educated, making him the perfect assistant for Beaumont. Together they travel from Paris to the Caribbean, trying to protect England from a French attack.

Keywords: Napoleonic Wars; Nineteenth Century; Spies

Rees, Celia.

◻ *Sovay*. **Bloomsbury, 2008. 978-1-59990-203-6 (hardcover); 978-0-7475-9808-4 (softcover). 416pp. ◻**

Sovay meant to play highwayman only once. She wanted to prove that the man she thought she loved was more interested in her dowry than her. Once she had gained that proof, though, she found she liked being Robin Hood. And she needs something to keep her mind off the rumors swirling around her father. He has unconventional ideas, which are called treason by other landowners. One day her real life and her secret life intersect. In a stolen wallet, she discovers that her missing father is officially accused of treason. Now Sovay is determined to clear her family's name and rescue her father. In a world of spies and intrigues, Sovay shows that her most valuable feature is her brains.

Keywords: England; Father and Child; Seventeenth Century; Spies

Travelers and Adventurers

At different times, the world has been much smaller, yet this does not lessen the danger in striking out for new lands. For these explorers, voyaging to exotic locations took great courage.

Avi.

Crispin. Ⓜ Ⓙ

The tale of a young orphan who doesn't even know his name, this series combines chases with self-reflection. The medieval setting creates a shadowy world, full of unknowns for the characters.

Keywords: England; Fourteenth Century; Identity

Crispin: The Cross of Lead. Hyperion, 2002. 978-0-7868-0828-1 (hardcover); 978-0-7868-1658-3 (softcover); 272pp.

Life as a poor peasant is difficult, especially when you lose the only family you know. Known only as Asta's son, the narrator faces starvation even before the manor steward accuses him of theft. No one in the village believes this allegation, especially not Father Quinel. He reveals that Asta's son was named Crispin at his baptism. Before the priest can tell Crispin more, he is murdered—and Crispin is blamed for this crime as well. Declared a wolf's head, Crispin can be killed on sight. So he runs, searching for someplace where he can hide, prove his innocence, and gain his freedom. All he has is his new name and the small lead cross that belonged to his mother. Can one peasant boy manage to elude the high and mighty in fourteenth-century England?

Awards: Newbery Medal

Crispin: At the Edge of the World. Hyperion, 2006. 978-0-7868-5152-2 (hardcover); 978-1-4231-0305-9 (softcover); 240pp.

During his previous adventures, Crispin was helped by Bear, a huge man who makes his living as a juggler. After Crispin manages to rescue Bear from a dungeon, the two must get away from their enemies. Weakened by his stint in prison, Bear requires healing. He receives it from an old crone who is training a girl named Troth. Run out of the village by those who killed the crone, Crispin and Bear take Troth with them and set out on a new journey. They move through the villages along England's coast, performing a juggling act to earn enough pennies to feed them. Yet it seems they will have to travel even farther to escape those who chase them.

Crispin: The End of Time. Balzer + Bray, 2010. 978-0-06-174080-0 (hardcover). 240pp.

The death of their father figure, Bear, leaves Crispin and Troth alone. The two youngsters are stranded in France, unable to speak French and with no food. Their only hope is to reach Iceland, a land that Bear told them about. In Iceland there are no lords or kings, and everyone is free. Crispin is set on making their way to Iceland, to honor Bear's memory. Troth, however, is less certain of this path. She chooses to stay in a French convent, healing the sick and injured. Crispin, now truly alone, wanders through the French countryside, looking for a way to Iceland. To find his freedom, Crispin will suffer much hardship.

Curry, Jane Louise.

A Stolen Life. **Margaret K. McElderry, 1999. 978-0-689-82932-1 (hardcover); 978-0-439-40908-7 (softcover). 208pp. 🅜 🅙**

Twelve-year-old Jamesina Mackenzie is a spirited Scottish girl. Her father is in exile in France with one of her brothers; the rest are in King George's army. When news arrives that her father has been killed, Jamesina's family attempts to protect her from harm by disguising her as a boy. The plan backfires, but Jamesina isn't caught by the English. In fact, Jamesina is captured by spiriters, men who kidnap children and sell them into servitude in the New World. She survives the harsh journey, arriving in Virginia and continuing to act like a boy. From the Scottish highlands to the Cherokee settlements in eighteenth-century Carolina, Jamesina discovers new worlds.

Keywords: America; Disguised as Boy; Eighteenth Century; Scotland

Golding, Julia.

Cat Royal Quartet. 🅙

Featuring a plucky, irresistible heroine named Cat, Golding's series is a wonderful look at late eighteenth-century England. Cat, thanks to her job in the theater and being a young girl, is able to cross social lines, going from theater life to taking tea with the nobility.

Keywords: Coming-of-age; Eighteenth Century; England; France; Performing

The Diamond of Drury Lane. Roaring Brook Press, 2008. 978-1-59643-351-9 (hardcover); 978-0-312-56123-9 (softcover). 432pp.

Amid the hustle and bustle of late eighteenth-century London, Cat Royal sees it all. Abandoned as a baby on the steps of the Theatre Royal in Drury Lane, Cat was taken in by the theater's owner, Mr. Sheridan. Now at the age of ten, there's nothing that she doesn't know about theatrical life—or about how to get by in rough-and-tumble London. Bare-knuckled boxers and street gangs, nobles and an African violinist named Pedro who becomes her friend: that's what Cat knows. And when she learns that Mr. Sheridan has hidden a diamond somewhere in the theater, Cat is the perfect person to discover where it is and what its purpose is.

Cat Among the Pigeons. Roaring Brook Press, 2008. 978-1-59643-352-6 (hardcover); 978-0-312-60215-4 (softcover). 384pp.

> Danger and mystery, drama and fun are all part of Cat Royal's life. She and her friend Pedro live in the Drury Lane Theatre, where Pedro is beginning to gain fame for his acting talent. But just as he is preparing for a great role, Pedro's past comes back to haunt him. Pedro's cruel master has found him, and Mr. Hawkins wants his property back. Cat mobilizes all their friends to help Pedro, from actors and Covent Garden toughs to nobles and abolitionists. To keep Pedro free, Cat will have to go undercover and face her enemy, Billy "Boil" Shepherd. Will Cat be able to save Pedro and herself?

Den of Thieves. Roaring Brook Press, 2009. 978-1-59643-444-8 (hardcover); 978-0-312-62910-6 (softtcover). 432pp.

> Change is coming, for the Drury Lane Theatre and for Cat Royal. When the theater owners decide to renovate, Cat is left without a job or a home—the only home she's known. With her friends scattered, Cat is left alone and has to rely on herself. She tries to make a living by writing, but her works are stolen by an unscrupulous publisher. At her lowest, Cat gets an offer from Mr. Sheridan to go to France as a spy. He wants to know more about the revolution in France, and Cat's just the person to find out what's what. Disguised as a ballerina, Cat serves as a reporter, saves her friends from prison, and nearly gets hung as an antirevolutionary traitor. But all this danger doesn't compare to one that Cat can't combat: growing into a young woman.

Cat O' Nine Tails. Roaring Brook Press, 2009. 978-1-59643-445-5 (hardcover). 400pp.

> Life in high society is very boring for a girl like Cat Royal. Well-bred girls embroider or read love stories, not go hunting or use strong language. Fortunately, Cat won't have to struggle with those standards very long. While investigating her friend Syd's disappearance, Cat leads a group to a Bristol pub. There the adventure begins as Cat and her friends are impressed into the British Navy. Kidnapped and forced to sail to the New World, Cat has her hands full. When she discovers there's also a plot to do away with Lord Frank, her friend, its all she can do to keep everyone alive. But there's little that Cat Royal can't do.

Haas, Jessie.

Chase. **Greenwillow Books, 2007. 978-0-06-112850-9 (hardcover). 256pp.** ⬛

In Pennsylvania's coal country, the owners were just one group of men to fear. But the owners are distant and lofty. The Sleepers, though—they're among you. Phin isn't a miner, doesn't have a problem with anyone. He just happens to be in the wrong place at the wrong time, when the Sleepers come to kill Engelbreit, one of the mine foremen. The Sleepers are the Irish version of the mob, working in the coalmines to protect the Irish. When Phin witnesses the murder, he has to run. With a man on a fast horse chasing him, Phin does his best to keep running and stay free.

Keywords: America; Coming-of-age; Murder; Nineteenth Century

Hart, Lenore.

The Treasure of Savage Island. **Dutton, 2005. 978-0525-47092-2 (hardcover). 275pp.** 🅼 🅹

Life on the barrier islands of Virginia is very tough. The land isn't good for farming, storms lash the island all the time, and worst of all, pirates sail the nearby waters. The American colonies have been free and independent for several years, but several Loyalists, who refuse to swear allegiance to America, prey on the ships and islands along the coast. Molly Savage lives on Savage Island, settled by her ancestor. Ever since her father gambled away the tavern they owned, they've worked for a cruel widow and scraped by. Then Molly discovers a shipwrecked boy named Rafe—a runaway slave. She hides Rafe, giving him food and keeping him safe from the slave-catchers. But if she turns him in, the reward will help her gain her own freedom. Rafe and Molly begin to trust each other when a bloodthirsty pirate attacks Savage Island, looking for a rumored great treasure. Perhaps this treasure will be salvation for both Molly and Rafe, if they can find it first.

Keywords: America; Nineteenth Century; Slavery

Hemphill, Helen.

The Adventurous Deeds of Deadwood Jones. **Front Street, 2008. 978-1-59078-637-6 (hardcover). 228pp.** 🅼 🅹

Ever since the day he was born, Prometheus Jones has been a free black. But in 1876 Tennessee, some folks don't want to remember that. When trouble happens after he wins a horse in a raffle, Prometheus doesn't waste time hightailing it out of town. He and his cousin Omer head for Texas. Prometheus is looking for his father, who was sold off to Texas at the beginning of the war. But first they need money, and they find work on a cattle drive. Heading toward Deadwood in the Dakota Territory, Prometheus and Omer both learn a lot on the trail. Already a great horseman and a good shot, Prometheus becomes educated about people. Between Indians, a gold rush, and a trail, Prometheus has a series of adventures.

Keywords: African American Issues; America; Family; Nineteenth Century

Karr, Kathleen.

Born for Adventure. **Marshall Cavendish, 2007. 978-0-7614-5348-2 (hardcover). 200pp.** 🅜 🅙

Tom is a devoted reader of penny dreadfuls, novels full of brave, adventurous boys exploring unknown lands. He longs to be like those characters—and when he gets a chance, he takes it. Henry Morton Stanley, the rescuer of Livingston and a great explorer, is putting together an expedition to rescue a captured pasha. Thanks to his pluck, Tom is picked by Stanley to join the group. As they set sail for Africa, Tom is full of excitement at his chance to be a dashing hero. But it doesn't take long for Tom to become disillusioned with such ideas. Seeing the cruelty and savagery, it's difficult to remain idealistic. Amid slaves and cannibals, whites and blacks, Tom journeys deep into Africa and finds himself as well as adventure.

Keywords: Africa; Coming-of-age; England; Nineteenth Century

Mowll, Joshua.

The Guild of Specialists. 🅜 🅙

In novels designed like scrapbooks, the story of Doug and Becca McKenzie is brought to life with clippings, drawings, and more. A strong basis in historical and scientific fact underlies these thrill-a-minute adventures.

Keywords: 1930s; Brothers and Sisters; China; Family; Pacific Ocean

Operation Red Jericho. Candlewick, 2005. 978-0-7636-2634-1 (hardcover). 288pp.

The disappearance of their parents has greatly affected Doug and Becca McKenzie. Doug has grown idle, and Becca has become rebellious. Now, after being expelled from their boarding schools and passed from relative to relative, they're staying with their uncle, Captain Fitzsy McKenzie. Joining him on the ship he commands, Doug and Becca see strange sights, experience new adventures, and even try to help solve a scientific mystery. But this mystery just creates new questions and introduces Doug and Becca to a very unusual secret society. The reader is part of the action with the maps, photos, and illustrations.

Operation Typhoon Shore. Candlewick, 2006. 978-0-7636-3122-2 (hardcover); 978-0-7636-3808-5 (softcover). 277pp.

After their last adventure, it should be smooth sailing for the McKenzies. But they're not so lucky; their ship gets caught in a vicious typhoon. Tossed about by the ocean, Captain McKenzie makes the decision to shelter in a cove on a nearby island. Once they're safe, Becca and Doug expect to just wait out the storm and then return to a project close to their hearts—the search for their missing parents. But their uncle is more focused on a missing piece of equipment, a gyrolabe that seems connected with a group of strange warriors. It's up to Doug and Becca to find a way to defeat these warriors so they can carry on with the search for their parents.

Operation Storm City. Candlewick, 2009. 978-0-7636-4224-2 (hardcover). 288pp.

> Becca and Doug are back in action and back in Lucknow, their former home. They need to gather more information on their parents' last assignment for the Guild of Specialists—an exploration of the Sunkiang Desert of China. Did their parents find Ur-Cam, the legendary Storm City? And is that why they disappeared, or was there foul play from the Guild's enemy, the Coterie? It's up to Becca and Doug, helped by their friends, to journey to China and find their parents. They will have to risk their lives and more to save not just their parents, but the whole world.

Warriors

Adventure and war are synonymous. In conflicts both great and small, the action creates tales of derring-do and bravery. And though such tales can end sadly, with death and defeat, the warriors live on.

Black, Kat.

The Book of Tormod: A Templar's Apprentice. **Scholastic, 2009. 978-0-545-05654-0 (hardcover); 978-0-545-23411-5 (softcover). 288pp. Ⓜ Ⓙ**

> Life in fourteenth-century Scotland is harsh. Few can read, bread is rare, and those who are different are treated poorly. For Tormod, who suffers abuse from his father, his gift of prophecy does not seem to ease his burdens. His only hope is to grow old enough to leave the village and make his way in the world. Suddenly Tormod has his chance. Sent on a mission by a passing Knight Templar, Tormod stumbles on a plot by King Philippe of France. After he saves the Knight's life, Tormod is taken on as an apprentice, joining the small band of Templars as they try to stay out of reach of Philippe's men. Tormod's ability to see the future might just save them, if he can learn how to use it.

Keywords: Coming-of-age; Fourteenth Century; Scotland

Ford, John.

Spartan's Quest. Ⓜ Ⓙ

> The adjective "spartan" lives on to this day, evoking a lifestyle of few comforts and much strength. Originally used to describe the people of Sparta, a Greek city-state, in this series the term describes the efforts of one young teen to go beyond his status to become who he truly is: a warrior.

Keywords: Before Common Era; Coming-of-age; Greece; Slavery

The Fire of Ares. Walker Books for Young Readers, 2008. 978-0-8027-9744-5 (hardcover); 978-0-8027-9827-5 (softcover). 256pp.

> Lysander may be only twelve, but he can do the work of two men. He is a helot, a slave, and toils in the fields, trying to make enough to feed his mother and himself as well as pay for his mother's medicines. But helots have no rights and no recourse, so Lysander is often cheated and abused. Lysander wishes he could train as a Spartan warrior, but it's not permitted. At least he has the amulet his father passed down to him, known as the Fire of Ares. He has kept it secret his whole life, but when it's discovered, Lysander is shocked to learn that he can begin warrior training. Although he learns fighting strategy and how to use weapons, Lysander has to learn for himself whether to stand with the Spartans or the helots.

Birth of a Warrior. Walker Books for Young Readers, 2008. 978-0-8027-9794-0 (hardcover); 978-0-7475-9387-4 (softcover). 272pp.

> Lysander must push aside the tensions between Spartans and helots, because a new, dangerous challenge looms before him: the Ordeal. As part of his training, Lysander is sent into the mountains with two other boys. For five days they must survive without weapons or shelter. As if that weren't tough enough, one of the boys is Demaratos, Lysander's enemy. The conditions are brutal: Autumn nights are chilly and none of the boys have cloaks. Prodded by Agesilous, the third boy who is actually nearly a man, Lysander and Demaratos must learn to work together if they are to survive. But Lysander realizes one of the boys is trying to sabotage him. Will he discover the traitor and return home in time to face a war with Persia?

Legacy of Blood. Walker Books for Young Readers, 2009. 978-0-8027-9844-2 (hardcover). 304pp.

> Although Sparta celebrates its victory over the Persians, Lysander has nothing to cheer about. Close friends, comrades, and his grandfather died during the battle. Pushed aside from his rightful inheritance, Lysander is too miserable to regret this latest loss. He finds an outlet for his feelings in war. The Spartan army must rebuild after the war with the Persians, but a distant outpost needs protection. Lysander and the rest of his barracks are sent to defend the village and the honor of the Spartan Empire. The men of the settlement have revolted, and it's up to Lysander and his fellow boy-soldiers to keep this trading center from breaking away from the Empire. But when Lysander sees a great statue in the village, a man who wears the Fire of Ares, his thoughts become muddled. What connection does he have with these people, and what does the Fire of Ares represent?

Malone, Patricia.

Lady Ilena. ⓜ ⓙ

In medieval England, a woman needed strength and protection. Ilena can protect herself, but will that be enough to achieve what she wants—to rule over her people?

Keywords: England; Medieval; Women Soldiers

The Legend of Lady Ilena. Delacorte, 2002. 978-0-385-72915-4 (hardcover); 978-0-440-22909-4 (softcover). 232pp.

Being raised as a warrior has helped Ilena survive in the rugged Vale of Enfert. Life in the far north of England in the sixth century is only for the strong. Ilena has to draw on her strength as she finds herself an orphan, left with her father's last words: "Go to Dun Alyn. Find Ryamen." Ilena sets off on her journey, trying to beat the winter snows and avoid anyone who would delay her. When a knight from the southern court of King Arthur comes upon her, Ilena is loath to wait for him. But Durant insists on accompanying her to Dun Alyn, protecting her on the way. As Ilena arrives, after fighting off several different tribes with Durant's help, she finds her greatest challenge is taking her place in Dun Alyn.

Lady Ilena: Way of the Warrior. Delacorte, 2005. 978-0-385-73225-3 (hardcover); 978-0-440-23901-7 (softcover). 208pp.

Finding a home for herself in Dun Alyn, Ilena is trying to settle into her role as its hereditary chief. She knows that once Durant, her betrothed, returns from his time in the south, they will marry and rule over Dun Alyn together. Trouble is brewing, though. The Saxons have invaded in the south and allied themselves with northern chiefs, some near to Ilena's lands. As the Saxons move on Dun Alyn, Ilena finds herself faltering, not living up to her warrior heritage. Now she will have to prove herself to her people by fighting off the invaders. Will Ilena be able to save her home?

Roberts, Judson.

The Strongbow Saga. ⓜ ⓙ

Medieval Scandinavia is the setting for a young man's discovery of his true nature. First as a slave and then as a warrior, Halfdan's journey lets him experience many aspects of Viking life.

Keywords: Family; France; Ninth Century; Scandinavia

Viking Warrior. HarperTeen, 2006. 978-0-06-079996-0 (hardcover); 978-0-06-079999-1 (softcover). 368pp.

> Born a slave in ninth-century Denmark, Halfdan lives in the household of the great chieftain Hrorik. Yet Hrorik is also Halfdan's father. When Hrorik is mortally wounded in battle with the Saxons of England, he is brought home to die. Thanks to the demands of Halfdan's mother, Hrorik frees Halfdan and acknowledges him as his son. With his change in status, Halfdan must begin learning the ways of a warrior. Taught by his brother Harald, Halfdan quickly shows he is a natural—especially with a longbow. With his new skills, Halfdan attempts to create a new life for himself, yet the peace he seeks eludes him.

Dragons from the Sea. HarperTeen, 2007. 978-0-06-081300-0 (hardcover); 978-0-06-081303-1 (softcover). 352pp.

> Continuing the adventure from *Viking Warrior*, Halfdan sets off on a quest for vengeance. He is determined to avenge the death of his brother Harald. Finding a place on an unusual longship, Halfdan crosses the sea, hunting for Toke, the foster brother of Harald and his murderer. At the same time, Halfdan's fellow Vikings seek treasure and glory in a war with the Franks. Even amid battles, Halfdan is still searching for Toke. But as a warrior, he cannot let his thirst for revenge interfere with the fight against the Franks. Separated from his comrades, Halfdan moves among the Franks, harassing them at every turn—he even takes captive the daughter of a powerful Frankish count. The book ends on a cliffhanger, with Halfdan's fate and that of his captive unknown.

The Road to Vengeance. HarperTeen, 2008. 978-0-06-081304-8 (hardcover). 352pp.

> Halfdan and the Vikings have captured a Frankish town and are preparing for battle. They know the Frankish army is gathering, and the Vikings are reviewing strategy. Halfdan, though, has other goals. He wants to gain strength and skills so he can exact revenge on his brother's killer. Slowly, Halfdan becomes a better archer and shows his cunning. He gains praise for capturing a young Frankish noblewoman as a prisoner to ransom. But Halfdan is focused on revenge, not praise. Is he strong enough to take on a murderer?

Spradlin, Michael P.

The Youngest Templar. Ⓜ Ⓙ

Known as Christ's warriors, the Knights Templar played a large role in the Crusades. By joining this order, Tristan is expected to meet their high standards of holiness and warfare.

Keywords: Crusades; Europe; Identity; Medieval; Religious Conflicts

Keeper of the Grail. Putnam Juvenile, 2008. 978-0-399-24763-7 (hardcover); 272pp.

> As a newborn, Tristan was left on the steps of a monastery. Brought up by monks, he has some education but believes he'll stay a servant for the rest of his life. But when a group of Knights Templars stop at the monastery, Tristan finds himself drawn to the idea of travel and adventure. One of the knights takes him on as a squire, and Tristan is swept away into a journey to the Holy Land. Dangers do not lie just in Jerusalem, but along Tristan's path as well. Another knight is very hostile to him, he must learn fighting skills, and he still wonders who his parents are and what are his roots. Yet Tristan is determined to serve his master well and find salvation in the Holy Land.

Trail of Fate. Putnam Juvenile, 2009. 978-0-399-24764-4 (hardcover). 240pp.

> Tristan the squire might have helped to locate the Holy Grail, but there are still plenty of challenges ahead of him. The ship he is sailing on with his friends gets caught in a storm and sinks. Waking up on the shore of southern France, Tristan is helped by a young noblewoman named Celia and a small group of her followers. Celia and her companions are Cathars, a religious sect recently outlawed by the pope. Reunited with his friends Robard the archer and Maryann the Saracen assassin, Tristan plans to return to England, only to find himself drawn into the conflict between the Cathars and the establishment. Tristan will have to find out if the Holy Grail can protect his heart as well as his life.

Tingle, Rebecca.

Women of Wessex. Ⓜ Ⓙ

Two unusual roles for medieval women are seen in a mother and daughter: warrior and scholar. Both Æthelfæd and Ælfwyn l find that their skills are not enough; they have to grow beyond their stubbornness to find happiness.

Keywords: Disguised as Boy; England; Identity; Ninth Century; Women Soldiers

The Edge on the Sword. Putnam Juvenile, 2001. 978-0-399-23580-1 (hardcover); 978-0-439-41796-9 (softcover). 277pp.

> In the late ninth century, England was divided into small kingdoms, with squabbles and alliances causing relations to shift. When Æthelfæd, the daughter of Alfred of Wessex, is betrothed to Ethelred of Mercia, it has the potential to bring two kingdoms together. But Æthelfæd is not happy. Not only does she not know her betrothed at all, but she now has to be guarded at all times. Used to the freedom to go where she wants, Æthelfæd does her best to escape her protector, named Red. Yet when her escape nearly leads to her abduction, Æthelfæd finds that she must trust Red. And Red will repay that trust

by training her in the skills of battle, skills that are normally only taught to boys. These skills give Æthelfæd a new kind of freedom.

Far Traveler. Putnam Juvenile, 2005. 978-0-399-23890-1 (hardcover); 978-0-14-240630-4 (softcover). 240pp.

The daughter of Æthelfæd is quite different from her warrior mother. Ælfwyn loves reading and books, hiding whenever a horseback ride is suggested. The death of her mother leaves Ælfwyn unprotected and at the mercy of her uncle, King Edward of Wessex. Edward gives her an ultimatum: marry one of his allies or become a nun. Faced with these choices, Ælfwyn makes her own choice: to disguise herself as a boy and become a wandering bard, telling the stories she has learned from her beloved books. Traveling across the country, she is able to do as she likes. But then she is asked by a rival king to join in a plot against her uncle. Ælfwyn must decide if she will follow her heart and turn her back on her royal heritage.

Chapter 6

Historical Fantasy

We often hear that truth is stranger than fiction. Yet it is possible for fiction to surpass reality. That happens when worlds are imagined that combine history with fantasy. When a vampire enters a story set in modern society, it creates tension between what we know is scientifically true and the magic of old ways and forgotten fears. But what does it mean when a vampire exists in a less scientific time? What does this supernatural creature tell us about the past?

Fantastic creatures take leading roles in some of the world's earliest stories. From Greek myths to the King Arthur legends, these stories take place in times when magic was the only answer for how the world worked. These stories are more than fantasy—they also represent the history of the times. By reading novels featuring mythological or fantastical characters that were often perceived as real during those times, readers can imagine what it was like to live in ancient Greece or England during the Dark Ages. For that reason, this chapter includes sections that explore historical fiction based on myths and legends.

Other examples of the merger of historical fiction and fantasy can be found in alternate universes or alternate histories. Although such novels are sometimes classified as science fiction, there are cases in which the history has been altered not by a scientific method but by a magical one. A past that imagines the existence of magic is thus classified as a blend of fantasy and historical fiction. These books let us see that normal is all in one's perspective; for the characters in such works, a world without magic would be abnormal.

Fantastic Creatures and Abilities

A hallmark of fantasy is unusual animals and special talents. Whether they involve dragons or vampires, magicians or psychics, the novels in this section seem to define this fantasy element. At the same time, they use fantastical concepts to explore the historical setting or comment on the past.

Carey, Janet Lee.

Dragon's Keep. Harcourt Children's Books, 2007. 978-0-15-205926-2 (hardcover); 978-0-15-206401-3 (softcover). 320pp. 🅜 🅙

When Rosalind was born, she had a dazzling destiny ahead of her. She is the daughter of the Queen of Wilde Island, a small island off the coast of England. Rosalind is the twenty-first queen in the Pendragon line, prophesied by the great Merlin to end war and bring peace. But that destiny is cast into doubt, because Rosalind is born with a dragon's claw as the fourth finger on her left hand. To hide it, she spends her life with gloved hands, enduring the cures prescribed by many healers. Rosalind's mother keeps trying to find a cure, but Rosalind is beginning to despair. Then the local dragon snatches her away, taking her to Dragon's Keep. There Rosalind will learn the secret of her birth and bloodline, and she will have to decide whom to believe: her mother or the dragon.

Keywords: Dragons; England; Medieval; Mother and Child; Royalty

Dunkle, Claire.

The Hollow Kingdom. Henry Holt, 2003. 978-0-8050-7390-4 (hardcover); 978-0-8050-8108-4 (softcover). 240pp. 🅜 🅙

It's the nineteenth century, a time of reason and logic. The old superstitions are beginning to die out . . . or are they? After the death of their father, Kate and Emily are sent to their distant relatives, who live on the estate that Kate owns but has never seen. It is called Hallow Hill, and it's thought that it was once a great holy place for the Druids. Ever since she arrived, Kate has felt uneasy. She has a strange feeling about this place—which grows stronger after she and Emily are lost in the darkness. An unusual man named Marak helps them get home, but he hasn't done this out of the kindness of his heart. Marak is a goblin, the king of a magical race. His first wife has died without giving him a son and heir, and Marak is looking for a new wife. And he thinks he has found her in Kate.

Read-alike: For a continuation of the story of Kate and Emily, with more fantasy and less history, read *Close Kin* and *In the Coils of the Snake*.

Keywords: England; Goblins; Nineteenth Century

Farmer, Nancy.

The Jack Trilogy. 🅜 🅙

Farmer creates a world where magic and religion have more sway than science. In a Saxon village during the time of the Viking invasions, Jack relies just as much on his humor as his magical abilities.

Keywords: England; Magic; Medieval; Scandinavia; Trolls

The Sea of Trolls. Atheneum/Richard Jackson, 2004. 978-0-689-86744-6 (hardcover); 978-0-689-86746-0 (softcover). 459pp.

1

> Becoming an apprentice to the Bard seems like it will be the making of Jack. He begins to look at the world in a new way, appreciating the hardships faced by his father. As the Bard teaches him songs and magic, Jack begins to feel the life force that binds all creatures together. But then raiders from across the sea begin to pillage the area near Jack's home. The Northmen destroy the abbey on the Holy Isle, then come to Jack's village. Jack and his little sister, Lucy, are captured and become slaves. Their owner is Olaf One-Brow, the leader of the invading Vikings. Taken away from their home, brother and sister are thrown into a strange new world. And Jack will discover a quest that is his destiny. Not just humans live in this northern land; there are trolls.

2

3

The Land of the Silver Apples. Atheneum/Richard Jackson Books, 2007. 978-1-4169-0735-0 (hardcover); 978-1-4169-0736-7 (softcover). 496pp.

> Jack's younger sister Lucy has always been a little spoiled. But ever since the Yule ceremonies at the end of the year, Lucy has acted mad, claiming she's a princess and talking to creatures that aren't there. Jack saw Lucy acting strangely when they were slaves in the Northland, but this behavior is beyond that. So Jack, along with the Bard, Father Aidan, and his father, set out on a journey to discover what is wrong with Lucy. Old friends like Thorgil and new ones like the servant girl Pega join the quest to save Lucy. But when Jack discovers Lucy's jailer is the Lady of the Lake, will anyone be able to save her? It's now up to Jack and his skills to see if a rescue is possible.

4

5

The Islands of the Blessed. Atheneum/Richard Jackson Books, 2009. 978-1-4169-0737-4 (hardcover). 496pp.

6

> Jack, back in his village, learns more from the Bard and dealing with Thorgil. A former slave who wants to be a berserker, Thorgil refuses to accept that her damaged hand will never let her be a warrior. Her stubbornness and rudeness drive Jack crazy, but he can't help caring about her. The bond between Jack and Thorgil is tested as calamity falls upon the village. A tornado tears through the fields, destroying grain and dooming the villagers to a hard winter and possible starvation. Even worse, various monsters are being drawn to the village. Some, like the hogboon, are easy for Jack and Thorgil to tackle. But facing the deadly draugr is going to take all their skill, as well as the Bard's. There's a death to avenge and a journey to take to Notland, which is Not Always There. The thrilling conclusion to a trilogy of novels set in a fantastic, dangerous, exciting time.

7

8

Furlong, Monica.

Cornish Magic Trilogy. Ⓜ Ⓙ

Set in Cornwall in the early medieval period, Furlong explores how Christianity came to England and the time when the Christian God existed in tandem with ancient religious practices.

Keywords: England; Magic; Medieval; Political Rebellions

Juniper. Random House Books for Young Readers, 2004. 978-0-394-83220-3 (hardcover); 978-0-679-83369-7(softcover). 208pp.

> From childhood Ninnoc seemed to have a strange power. She could find water by dowsing and could heal cuts and bruises with her touch. Perhaps these skills are hinted at by her true name, Juniper—not that Ninnoc understands how. As the daughter of a Cornish high chief, Ninnoc is also a princess, coddled and haughty. It's common for such children to be sent to live with other noble families, to gain knowledge and social skills. So Ninnoc is surprised when her parents send her off to her godmother Euny. A doran—a woman of power and magic—Euny will teach Ninnoc how to use her own power. It's a long, difficult process for Ninnoc, unused to the hard work and conditions that she faces with Euny. But slowly she gains skill and power. And it's just in time, for her aunt is determined to usurp Ninnoc's father and raise her own son to the position of high chief. Can Ninnoc use her skills and the power of her true name to defeat her aunt?

Wise Child. Random House Books for Young Readers, 2004. 978-0-394-89105-7 (hardcover); 978-0-394-82598-4 (softcover). 240pp.

> When her grandmother dies and her remaining family can't take her, the girl known as Wise Child is left defenseless. Her mother left years ago, and her father is a sailor, traveling the seas. Following tradition, the villagers gather to "auction" Wise Child, to find someplace for her to live. Everyone is surprised when Juniper, the wise woman, offers to care for Wise Child. Although Juniper is skilled in healing and herbal arts, she is also an outsider—some in the village even think she is a witch. But Wise Child finds she has nothing to fear from Juniper. Juniper teaches her about herbs, reading, even magic. Wise Child's life seems to be looking up, but then her mother, the mysterious Maeve, returns. It soon becomes clear that she has come for Wise Child, for dark reasons. Wise Child must now find a way to save herself and Juniper from her mother and superstition.

Colman. Random House, 2004. 978-0-375-81514-0 (hardcover); 978-0-375-81515-7 (softcover). 288pp.

> When accusations against Juniper and Wise Child force them to flee their village, Wise Child's cousin Colman joins them. Eager to escape his father's abuse and to have an adventure, Colman is content to go with the women to Cornwall. In the land where Juniper grew up, the refugees hope to find

peace. Instead, they discover anything but, for Meroot, Juniper's aunt who tried and failed to gain the throne, has finally succeeded. Juniper's father is dead, and her brother, the true King, is held prisoner by Meroot. Juniper defeated Meroot once before, but she will not be able to do it on her own again. She needs the help of Wise Child and Colman. As his magical powers slowly start to appear, Colman plays a critical role in saving Cornwall from the evils of the black witch.

Gardner, Sally.

I, Coriander. **Dial, 2005. 978-0-8037-3099-1 (hardcover); 978-1-84255-290-2 (softcover). 288pp.**

One day a pair of silver shoes are delivered to Coriander's house on the banks of the Thames. Her mother doesn't want her to have them and even tries to distract her with a pair of shoes that are a pale copy. But the silver shoes whisper to Coriander, and she must have them. Putting on the shoes sets in motion a chain of events that Coriander didn't anticipate. The shoes don't just *seem* magical—they are magical. Coriander travels to the fairy realm of her mother, but she will return to a world of fear as Cromwell changes England. Will Coriander be able to have both of these worlds—or will she have to choose one?

Keywords: England; Magic; Religious Conflicts; Seventeenth Century

Hightman, J. P.

Spirit. **HarperTeen, 2008. 978-0-06-085063-0 (hardcover); 978-0-06-085065-4 (softcover). 224pp.**

The mistakes of the past don't always stay in the past. Two hundred years after the Salem witch trials, a pair of ghost hunters learn that some of the accused had fled Salem and settled in the village of Blackthorne. Now stories about a witch, the successor to those Salem witches, swirl around Blackthorne. It's a challenge for any spiritualist, but Tobias and Tess Goodraven are experts. Both only seventeen, the young married couple were drawn together when they survived a theater fire. This event awakened in Tess and Tobias their spiritual sensitivity and laid the groundwork for their love. They need all their advantages when they face Old Mother Malgore, a witch who is hungry for destruction.

Keywords: America; Ghosts; Nineteenth Century; Witch Trials

Jennings, Patrick.

The Wolving Time. **Scholastic Press, 2003. 978-0-439-39555-7 (hardcover); 978-0-439-39556-4 (softcover). 208pp.**

Laszlo's family keeps to themselves, because they are Magyars, from a region they call Erdely; but the French they live among call Laszlo's homeland Transylvania. Laszlo and his parents live far from the village because they are a family that transform into wolves. Laszlo's parents already have the skill, and he expects to complete his first transformation soon. But there is a strange feeling brewing in France, and it has come to the village near their home. The young orphan girl who is shown charity by Laszlo's parents is no different from the people in the village, and she goes to the local priest to tell him about the family's secret. The discovery of his family's gift forces Laszlo to make a choice. Should he become a wolf and fully give in to his animal nature, or will he be able to live as both man and wolf?

Keywords: France; Medieval; Werewolves

Lake, Nick.

Blood Ninja. **Simon & Schuster's Children's Publishing, 2009. 978-1-4169-8627-0 (hardcover); 978-1-4169-8628-7 (softcover). 369pp.** Ⓜ Ⓙ

For years, Taro and his best friend Hiro have talked about being samurais. While Hiro just dreams about it, Taro is determined to be one. But in his small fishing village, with a dying father and overworked mother, becoming a samurai is impossible. On a dark night, Taro's dreams change when a group of ninjas—silent, strong, and fast—kill his father and try to kill Taro and his mother. It's only with the help of another ninja that they survive. In the battle with the ninjas, Hiro helps defeat them, but Taro is injured gravely. To save his life, the good ninja turns Taro into a kyuuketsuki: a vampire. The powers of a vampire are what give a ninja its abilities, and now Taro is such a creature. Accompanied by Hiro and the good ninja Shusaku, Taro begins ninja training. He is determined to protect his mother and get his revenge on his father's killers. The legends of seventeenth-century Japan are blended into a stirring tale.

Keywords: Japan; Medieval; Vampires

Mah, Adeline Yen.

Chinese Cinderella and the Secret Dragon Society. **HarperCollins, 2004. 978-0-06-056734-7 (hardcover); 978-0-06-056736-1 (softcover). 256pp.** Ⓜ Ⓙ

Life at home is difficult for Ye Xian. Not unlike Cinderella, she has a cruel stepmother and a father who doesn't notice her. The only bright spot is her Big Aunt, who teaches her English and gives her treats. When her aunt has to leave, Ye Xian realizes she's a Chinese version of her namesake, Cinderella. Taking an English name of Chinese Cinderella or C.C., she tries to defend herself from her stepmother—but is thrown out. Running away, she is taken in by the Dragon Society. To outsiders, they are a martial arts school. But in reality, the Dragon Society is working to free China from Japanese oppression. Chinese Cinderella, and her new friends David, Marat, and Sam, are eager to help. How will four children play a part in freeing China?

Keywords: 1940s; China; Magic

Mosley, Walter.

47. Little, Brown Books for Young Readers, 2005. 978-0-316-11035-8 (hardcover); 978-0-316-01635-3 (softcover). 240pp. **S**

Life for a slave is one long, hard, back-breaking day after another, lasting until you die. The slave only known as 47 has been spared from this life so far. But now that he's fourteen, he has to start working in the fields. But then 47 meets Tall John, a mysterious copper-colored man. He has a yellow carpet bag full of magic potions, and he says he has crossed galaxies to arrive in the American South of 1832. Tall John is engaged in a battle with the evil Calash—aliens who have traveled to Earth as well and are now within the bodies of the white master and overseer. Tall John knows this battle will go on for many years, and 47 will be the one to keep up the fight after Tall John falls. But that will only happen after Tall John has given 47 some special skills.

Keywords: America; Magic; Nineteenth Century

Noyes, Deborah.

The Ghosts of Kerfol. Candlewick, 2008. 978-0-7636-3000-3 (hardcover); 978-0-7636-4825-1 (softcover). 176pp. **S**

For centuries, the grand estate of Kerfol has been haunted. There's the sound of barking dogs, although no dogs live there. And there are the strange deaths and disappearances that blight the estate's history. All who visit can't help but notice the mysterious, unsettling feel of this place. It all goes back to 1613, when a cruel, elderly nobleman takes a young, beautiful wife. The wife is very unhappy, for her husband allows her no freedom and no pleasure. He won't even let her have a pet dog—and when she tries, he kills the dog. So one day, when the nobleman is found dead, everyone suspects his wife. The signs that he died from a dog attack, even though no dogs were on the estate, don't matter. So through the years, the people who come to Kerfol—an artist after the French Revolution, a 1920s flapper with a secret, or a young couple backpacking through France—are all disturbed by their visit. Only in the modern day are the ghosts at Kerfol, human and animal, put to rest.

Keywords: 1920s; Eighteenth Century; France; Ghosts; Multiple Voices; Seventeenth Century; Short Stories

Owen, James.

Here, There Be Dragons. Simon & Schuster Children's Publishing, 2006. 978-1-4169-1227-9 (hardcover); 978-1-4169-1228-6 (softcover). 336pp. **J S**

On a rainy night in 1917, three young men are bound together in an important quest. All three, from Oxford University, meet when a professor each man had an appointment with is found dead. The three men—Jack,

John, and Charles—are pondering the professor's death when a small, strange man approaches them, explaining that they have been brought together for a special reason. The professor was the caretaker for a very special book, the *Imaginarium Geographica*, or the *Imaginary Geographies*. This book is an atlas to a vast array of imaginary lands that make up the Archipelago of Dreams. Forces of evil wants this book—and it is now up to John, as the new primary caretaker, and his assistants Jack and Charles, to protect it. This task will lead them on the journey of a lifetime.

Read-alike: Continue the story of Jack, John, and Charles in *The Search for the Red Dragon* and *The Shadow Dragons*.

Keywords: 1910s; Dragons; England; Magic

Sedgwick, Marcus.

The Foreshadowing. **Wendy Lamb Books, 2006. 978-0-385-74646-5 (hardcover); 978-1-84255-219-3 (softcover). 304pp. ⏺ ⓢ**

Even before the war began, Sasha was not an ordinary girl. She had strange visions, little flickers of premonition. Now that she's seventeen, the flickers are coming more often; and during the destruction of the world war, there's more for her to see. No one believes her, so Sasha tries to cope as best she can and hopes she can persuade her father to let her serve as a nurse. Then Sasha has a terrifying vision: She sees the death of her beloved older brother, Tom. He dies in the fields of France with his unit . . . but Sasha can't let that happen. She will save her brother, even if it means journeying to France and crossing the trenches. Sasha will do anything to prevent this foreshadowing from coming true.

Keywords: 1910s; Brothers and Sisters; England; France; Psychics; World War I

My Swordhand Is Singing. **Wendy Lamb Books, 2007. 978-0-375-84689-2 (hardcover); 978-0-375-84690-8 (softcover). 224pp. ⏺ ⓢ**

Deep in Eastern Europe, there is a land covered in trees. It is called the Land Beyond the Forests: Transylvania. In this land, small villages are scattered across the landscape, the houses and huts close together for protection—not just from the harsh winters and the wolves, but from other creatures, too. In the village of Chust, Peter lives with his father Tomas. They are woodcutters, although Tomas drinks more than he cuts. But Tomas has a secret that he's kept from everyone, even Peter, a secret that has something to do with a wooden box. Now, with rumors of strange visitors—villagers who have died but are now returning to their wives or killing people—Tomas will have to reveal his secret. It will be up to Tomas and Peter to defeat the creatures of the night.

Read-alike: For another take on how vampire myths were developed, read *Sweetblood* by Pete Hautman.

Awards: Carnegie Medal Finalist

Keywords: Seventeenth Century; Vampires

Tarr, Judith.

His Majesty's Elephant. **Harcourt Children's Books, 1993. 978-0-15-200737-9 (hardcover). 224pp. ◫**

> When monarchs wish to honor each other, they give gifts. Thus, when the caliph of a Middle Eastern empire sends gifts to Charlemagne, the Emperor of the West, they are elaborate. Jewels and gold, fine fabrics, and more are the norm. Even more amazing are the caliph's last two gifts: an elephant and a jewel with an embedded sliver of the True Cross. Rowan, a daughter of Charlemagne, is awed by the elephant. Perhaps it's because her now-dead mother was a witch, but Rowan senses something strange about the True Cross talisman. It seems to hold trouble, and the only one she can tell is Kerrec, the elephant's new keeper. In one of the greatest empires ever known, are there forces working against the Emperor? Rowan and Kerrec might be able to save Charlemagne, if they are willing to use magic.
>
> **Keywords:** Germany; Magic; Medieval; Royalty

Taylor, G. P.

Mariah Mundi: The Midas Box. **Putnam Juvenile, 2008. 978-0-399-24347-9 (hardcover). 292pp. ◫ ◫**

> After his parents disappeared and died in the Sudan, Mariah Mundi is left to make a living for himself. He leaves his school in London and heads north, for a job at the Prince Regent Hotel. Yet from the beginning, mysterious questions keep arising. Who is the stranger who gives Mariah a pack of playing cards to keep safe? What happened to the four boys who had Mariah's job and all disappeared? Why does Mister Lugor, the hotel's eccentric owner, never sleep? With the help of his new friend Sacha, Mariah tries to learn the answers, as well as settle in to his job as magician's assistant.
>
> **Keywords:** England; Magic; Nineteenth Century

Wormwood. **Putnam, 2004. 978-0-399-24257-1 (hardcover); 978-0-14-240469-0 (softcover). 259pp. ◫ ◫**

> A comet streaking across the skies of mid-eighteenth-century England sets the stage for a fantastical tale. The comet causes Earth to fall into darkness, making animals mad and people disturbed. For Dr. Sabian Blake, the comet and the upheaval were prophesied in the *Nemorensis*, a book of dark and ancient power. It seems this book is a beacon for evil spirits, and Dr. Blake is not sure he will be able to resist their pull. The fate of the world may rest in the hands of Agetta, Dr. Blake's housemaid. She's been working for Dr. Blake to make money, supplementing her salary by picking the pockets of his guests and Dr. Blake himself. What decision will Agetta make—and what does that mean for the world?
>
> **Keywords:** Eighteenth Century; England; Magic

Weyn, Suzanne.

Distant Waves: A Novel of the Titanic. Scholastic Press, 2009. 978-0-545-08572-4 (hardcover). 336pp. **J**

Five sisters grow up in an unusual setting. The Taylor sisters, living at the turn of the twentieth century, are the daughters of a famous medium. Living in Spirit Vale, New York, amid other spiritualists, the girls have a childhood of freedom. As they grow up, however, things begin to change. Mimi, the oldest, discovers a secret about herself. The twins, Emma and Amelie, have a gift for contacting the spirit world. Blythe focuses on appearances and wants to be famous. And then there's Jane, the narrator, who lives by science and logic, following the exploits of Nikola Tesla and Sherlock Holmes. The fate of the Taylor sisters depends on what happens when they sail on the *Titanic*. On a cold night in April 1912, the sisters discover whether their bond can eclipse anything—even death.

Keywords: 1910s; America; Disasters; Ghosts; Sisters

Romantic Historical Fantasy

The combination of romance, history, and fantasy is a potent one. Whether old romantic legends such as Tam Lin and the fairies or romance between witches and mortals, these novels sweep readers into a world where romance is just as magical as spells.

Bray, Libba.
The Gemma Doyle Trilogy. **J** **S**

These three novels by Bray are set in turn-of-the-century England, featuring elements of Gothic mystery and fantasy. Gemma, the main character, seems to have an unusual destiny; not for her is the life of a late-Victorian wife.

Keywords: England; Fairies; Nineteenth Century

A Great and Terrible Beauty. Delacorte, 2003. 978-0-385-73028-0 (hardcover); 978-0-385-73231-4 (softcover). 403pp.

After the mysterious suicide of her mother, sixteen-year-old Gemma is sent from India, where she has lived her whole life, to gray, rainy England. At the Spence Academy, she is ostracized and kept on the outside of the school's social life, until she is able to work her way into the ruling clique. Once that happens, the strange happenings at Spence—the burned-down East Wing, lights in the forest, and the strange boy who has followed her from India— cause Gemma to question her odd abilities. When she discovers the Realm, a shadowy place that she is able to visit along with her friends, she finds that her mother's death had more meaning than she thought.

Rebel Angels. Delacorte, 2005. 978-0-385-73029-7 (hardcover); 978-0-385-73341-0 (softcover). 548pp.

> Gemma and her friends continue their trips to the exotic Realm, a place very different from Victorian England. They struggle to balance both parts of their lives and find that it's just as easy to be tempted by a London Season and young men as by the unearthly delights in the Realm. Gemma herself is attracted to two young men, her father is suffering from an opium addiction, and one of her friends seems interested in her misbehaving brother. Meanwhile, dark shadows are falling over the Realms. How will Gemma be able to restore peace and order to the lands that are her birthright?

The Sweet Far Thing. Delacorte, 2007. 978-0-385-73030-3 (hardcover); 978-0-440-23777-8 (softcover). 832pp.

> As the time for Gemma's debut in society looms, she also faces the challenges of a final confrontation with the forces that would destroy the Realms. She doesn't fit in Victorian circles and is seen as a misfit, yet should she take her place in the Order, the group that her mother belonged to?

Bunce, Elizabeth C.

📖 *A Curse Dark as Gold.* **Arthur A. Levine Books, 2008. 978-0-439-89576-7 (hardcover); 978-0-439-89577-4 (softcover). 400pp. S**

> When her father dies, everyone expects Charlotte to sell the family's mill and leave town with her younger sister Rosie. But Charlotte is a stubborn, independent seventeen-year-old, and she's not about to hurt her hometown by closing the mill. Her Uncle Wheeler comes from town to stay with Charlotte and Rosie, and Charlotte takes over as the miller. No matter how hard she works, though, it seems misfortune has a home in the mill. Desperate, and unwilling to ask for help, Charlotte makes a deal with a strange creature called Jack Spinner. He provides her with gold thread that saves the mill. For a while, Charlotte breathes easier, even falling in love and marrying a fine young man named Randall. But when Jack Spinner returns and demands payment for his service, Charlotte realizes the mill is cursed. If she can't defeat this curse, those she loves most will be hurt. This retelling of Rumplestiltskin is set in the pre–Industrial Revolution period.

> **Keywords:** England; Magic; Nineteenth Century

Doyle, Marissa.

Leland Sisters. 🞔 S

> A little-known period—England after the Regency and before the reign of Queen Victoria—is explored in this enchanting series. The Leland sisters,

identical twins named Penelope and Persephone, attempt to improve their magical talents while navigating society.

Keywords: England; Ireland; Magic; Nineteenth Century; Sisters

Bewitching Season. Henry Holt, 2008. 978-0-8050-8251-7 (hardcover); 978-0-312-59695-8 (softcover). 352pp.

> Persephone Leland and her twin sister Penelope are the very image of proper ladies. They are well-mannered and educated, looking forward to their first Season and catching a glimpse of Princess Victoria. Well, Pen is looking forward to the Season. Persy would rather study magic with their governess, Miss Allardyce. The Leland twins are both gifted with magical ability, and Persy longs for a career, not marriage. But then Lochinvar Seton, from the neighboring estate, returns from university and casts a spell over Persy. She wants to make an impression on Lochinvar, amid the ballrooms of London, yet she always seems to be tongue-tied and awkward. To make things even worse, Miss Allardyce vanishes, and it's up to Persy and Pen to rescue her. They might just rescue Princess Victoria from an evil plot, too.

Betraying Season. Henry Holt, 2009. 978-0-8050-8252-4 (hardcover); 978-0-312-62916-8 (softcover). 336pp.

> Coming to Ireland to further her magical studies is just what Penelope Leland needs. Not only will it improve her weak skills, but it gives her relief from her twin sister. Pen is truly happy for Persy's happiness with her new husband . . . but it's hard not to feel envious. At least in Ireland, she's able to become a stronger witch and to spend time with Ally, the twins' former governess. But Ally is also happily married, and pregnant to boot. Pen, at loose ends, makes the acquaintance of Niall Keating, a charming, intelligent young man. It's not long before Pen is in love, and Niall seems to be equally attracted to her. But how will she handle her pain when she discovers that Niall courts her on the orders of his mother, a powerful witch? Lady Keating has plans for Pen, and it will take all her courage—and all of Niall's true love—for her to defeat Lady Keating.

Kolosov, Jacqueline.

The Red Queen's Daughter. Hyperion, 2007. 978-1-4231-0797-2 (hardcover); 978-1-4231-0798-9 (softcover). 416pp. **J S**

> The death of both her parents before she was a year old left Mary Seymour an orphan. Penniless, she was taken in and raised by her mother's best friend, a kind-hearted duchess. The only thing Mary has to recommend herself is her lineage, but it is a somewhat stained one. For though her mother is Katherine Parr, last queen of Henry VIII, Mary's father was executed for treason. When the duchess dies when Mary is nine, she is unsure what will happen next. Then Lady Strange arrives to adopt Mary. The aristocratic and kind lady will be more than

just a mother to Mary; she will be a teacher as well. Mary's destiny is to be a white magician, using her abilities for good. What's more, she will be the one to protect the virgin queen, Elizabeth I, from evil. Mary begins to learn, growing her powers. When she arrives at Elizabeth's court to serve as a lady-in-waiting, Mary discovers that there are many temptations. She must work hard to not only protect Elizabeth, but also resolve the struggle between her heart and her powers.

Keywords: England; Magic; Royalty; Sixteenth Century

McNaughton, Janet.

An Earthly Knight. HarperTeen, 2004. 978-0-06-008992-4 (hardcover); 978-0-06-008994-8 (softcover). 272pp. **J** **S**

Due to her older sister's scandalous behavior, Jenny has been thrust into the role of hostess for her widowed father. Although she can perform her duties adequately, she is still considered too willful, prone to slipping out to ride over the fields and through the forests. To keep her in line, an engagement is arranged with the brother of the King. It's an excellent match—but Jenny finds herself becoming drawn to Tam Lin, a young, mysterious nobleman with a claim to the land in Jenny's dowry. It is rumored that Tam Lin was kidnapped by the fairies once, and some of that otherworldly nature seems to cling to him. As Jenny begins to learn his story, she discovers the rumors are true . . . and the full story is even stranger and scarier. Jenny needs stoutness of heart to fight for her love, and she has that in spades.

Read-alike: For a darker look at the world of fairies, set in modern-day New Jersey, try *Tithe: A Modern Fairy Tale* by Holly Black.

Keywords: Fairies; Medieval; Scotland

Pope, Elizabeth Marie.

The Perilous Gard. Houghton Mifflin, 1974. 978-0-395-18512-4 (hardcover); 978-0-618-15073-1 (softcover). 280pp. **M** **J**

Kate Sutton may be plain and forthright, but she's also smart and has a good head on her shoulders. After her dimwitted sister makes a mistake, Kate has to suffer the consequences: exile from Queen Mary's court and house arrest at the Perilous Gard. The remote northern castle is set in an area that has a history of fairies and magic. Soon she becomes drawn in by the mysterious Christopher Heron, who is rumored to have killed his niece. When Christopher is taken by the Queen of the Faeries, Kate follows him and becomes trapped under the hill. After Christopher is set as a sacrifice, Kate does everything in her power to save him, and herself.

Awards: Newbery Honor Book

Keywords: England; Fairies; Sixteenth Century

Whitcomb, Laura.

The Fetch. **Houghton Mifflin, 2009. 978-0-618-89131-3 (hardcover); 978-0-547-41163-7 (softcover). 384pp. $\mathbf{S}$**

> When you die, a Fetch escorts your spirit to its final destination. Calder has been a Fetch for over 300 years, and he's never thought about telling anyone about himself. Not until he meets Glory, a beautiful, caring woman—a woman he's sure is supposed to be his squire, someone who will be trained to be a Fetch. Glory is the governess to the son of the Russian tsar, a boy named Alexis who suffers from hemophilia. Calder is so determined to have Glory that he will do the near-impossible: He will take the body of a man about to die, a man who had a connection to the Russian royal family. But Calder doesn't know three things: 1) The man is Rasputin, the "mad monk" who helped heal Alexis; 2) Glory is not Alexis's governess but his mother, the Tsarina Alexandra; and 3) the year is 1916, and the earthly revolution that is coming is no match for the spirit revolution that Calder has caused.
>
> **Keywords:** 1910s; Ghosts; Russia

Greek Mythology

It used to be thought that the Greek myths were complete fiction, created from the minds of artists like Homer. Yet ever since the archeological expeditions performed by men like Heinrich Schliemann, these ancient stories have been understood to have a kernel of truth. The discovery that Troy was an actual city, and that there is evidence that the city was once the site of great destruction, makes stories of the Trojan War seem more realistic. Just because the people believed the gods controlled everything does not negate the history within those myths. By reading these novels, teens can observe a very different world than their own, where religion is the source of actions both good and bad.

> **Read-alike:** Consider how stories of the Greek gods can work in modern times by reading the <u>Olympian</u> series by Rick Riordan or the <u>Oh My Gods</u> books by Tera Lynn Childs.

Cooney, Caroline B.

Goddess of Yesterday. **Delacorte Books for Young Readers, 2002. 978-0-385-72945-1 (hardcover); 978-0-385-73865-1 (softcover). 264pp. $\mathbf{M}$ $\mathbf{J}$**

> At age six, Anaxandra was taken as a hostage by Nicander, king of the island of Siphnos. When she was twelve, the island was attacked, leaving Anaxandra the only survivor. As a hostage, she has no value and will likely be killed. So when Menelaus, the king of Sparta, stops at Siphnos to examine the damage, Anaxandra makes a decision. Although it's tempting the gods to destroy her, Anaxandra claims to be Nicander's daughter, the princess Callisto. Menelaus believes her, bringing Anaxandra to his palace near Sparta. There Anaxandra must keep living her lie, hoping the gods won't punish her. Just as dangerous

as the gods is Queen Helen, Menelaus's wife. Half-god herself, Helen does not believe the red-haired Anaxandra is the princess. As turmoil sweeps through the land thanks to the Trojan prince Paris, Anaxandra must find a way to protect herself—without angering the gods even more.

Keywords: Before Common Era; Coming-of-age; Greece; Royalty

Friesner, Esther.

Helen of Troy Series. ◼▮

A feminist take on an unlikely heroine. Helen of Troy is usually seen as the reason for the Trojan War, by leaving her husband for another man. In Friesner's series, a teenage Helen, full of feistiness and determination, is portrayed.

Keywords: Before Common Era; Disguised as Boy; Greece; Women Soldiers

Nobody's Princess. Random House Books for Young Readers, 2007. 978-0-375-87528-1 (hardcover); 978-0-375-87529-8 (softcover). 320pp.

> Does beauty give you power? Growing up, Helen is very pretty—everyone notices it. While her twin sister Clytemnesta works at being good, Helen is charming and impulsive. And Helen doesn't seem to get into the same kind of trouble as her sister or her twin brothers, Castor and Polydeuces. So perhaps being pretty is enough. But slowly Helen begins to realize that beauty isn't enough for her. She wants people to listen to what she says. Taking advantage of her resemblance to Polydeuces, she begins physical training in secret. Then she starts learning how to use weapons with Glaucus, her brothers' tutor. Helen is determined to succeed. She is destined to be Queen of Sparta; she will be strong enough to hold her throne and protect her people. Not even the son of a god will stop her.

Nobody's Prize. Random House Books for Young Readers, 2008. 978-0-375-87531-1 (hardcover); 978-0-375-87532-8 (softcover). 320pp.

> The young Spartan princess Helen is set on joining the greatest quest ever: the quest for the Golden Fleece. Prince Jason has brought together some of Greece's greatest heroes, setting off on the ship *Argo* to capture the golden wool of a ram, guarded by a fierce, never-sleeping serpent. It promises to be a great adventure, and Helen is going to be part of it. With her friend Milo, Helen disguises herself as a boy and joins the crew of the *Argo*. But there are several problems with this. Helen's older brothers are also on the *Argo*, and she must avoid them. Helen also has an unexpected crush on Hylas, the weapons bearer of Herakles. Finally, Helen is growing older, her beauty developing—and her body is becoming that of a woman. She isn't going to waste her last chance for adventures and freedom, but when her future is at risk, she will have to decide what's more important, freedom or duty.

Geras, Adèle.

Ithaka. Harcourt Children's Books, 2006. 978-0-15-205603-2 (hardcover); 978-0-15-206104-3 (softcover). 368pp. **S**

> After a war is over, families wait to be reunited, for the men to come home, for life to start again. It is ten years after the Trojan war, but on the island of Ithaka, they are still waiting for Odysseus, their king, to return. His wife Penelope grows pale and thin, and his son Telemachus grows into a headstrong, moody boy. Klymene and her twin brother Ikarios grow up with Telemachus. They are all waiting, looking for Odysseus to return even though there's no reason to hope. But Penelope will not give up, even when all sorts of men come to the palace seeking her hand in marriage. Penelope will not accept these offers and uses a cunning trick to maintain her freedom—a trick that will also preserve Odysseus's life. Klymene, who is in love with Telemachus, is a spectator of this great love story. It remains to be seen if the gods will give her such a love as Penelope has.
>
> **Keywords:** Before Common Era; Greece; Romance

Troy. Harcourt Children's Books, 2001. 978-0-15-216492-8 (hardcover); 978-0-15-204570-8 (softcover). 352pp. **S**

> The war between the Greeks and the Trojans has dragged on for ten years. Everyone is weary of war—even the gods. As the women take care of the children, the old, and the injured, the gods decide to have some entertainment. Aphrodite, tired of watching Paris and Helen's romance, sends her son Eros to create a new one. His arrow finds Xanthe, a poor girl who works in the Blood Room tending to wounded soldiers. She takes a look at the rich young soldier Alastor and falls in love. The only person Xanthe can talk to about her new love is Marpessa, her sister, a handmaiden to Helen of Troy. As the final week of the Trojan War unfolds, romance manages to flower amid death.
>
> **Awards:** Carnegie Medal Finalist
>
> **Keywords:** Before Common Era; Romance; Sisters; Trojan War

Halam, Ann.

Snakehead. Wendy Lamb Books, 2008. 978-0-375-84108-8 (hardcover); 978-0-375-84109-5 (softcover). 304pp. **J S**

> Serifos, like many of the islands in the sea now called the Aegean, is caught between the Archaens to the north and the Trojans in the east. On this small island, Perseus lives with his mother and works in a tavern. It's an unusual life for a young man who is the son of a princess and a god, but Perseus is satisfied with it. Or at least he is until a mysterious girl arrives on the island. A refugee, the girl named Kore doesn't talk about herself but carries herself like a queen. Perseus finds himself caring about Kore, even with no encouragement from her. When he discovers the truth about her, it will change his life. For Kore is actually Andromeda, a princess—and she is escaping her fate as a sacrifice to a horrible

monster. The only way Perseus can save her is by killing the dreaded Medusa, the woman with snakes for hair, who turns men to stone with one look. Perseus will have to discover what kind of hero he is, if he wants a life with Andromeda.

Keywords: Before Common Era; Greece; Romance

Kindl, Patrice.

Lost in the Labyrinth. **Houghton Mifflin Books for Children, 2002. 978-0-618-16684-8 (hardcover); 978-0-618-39402-9 (softcover). 208pp.**

Xenodice is a princess, living in the lap of luxury. She has fine foods, lush quarters, even elaborate bathing facilities! Yet there is darkness amid the light. Her brother Asterius is a strange creature, kept shut up in a complex maze under the palace. Her sister Ariadne, who will be queen someday, is insufferable. And Icarus, Xenodice's crush, doesn't seem to notice her as a girl. Soon Xenodice will have even greater concerns, because it seems the gods are displeased with the people of Kefti. All sorts of betrayals and disasters keep occurring. Could this be linked to the Athenian slaves the kingdom receives each year? There is one special young man among this year's slaves—a man who has captured the eye of Ariadne—and Xenodice will have to do all she can to protect her brother Asterius.

Keywords: Before Common Era; Family; Greece

McLaren, Clemence.

Inside the Walls of Troy: A Novel of the Women Who Lived the Trojan War. **Atheneum, 1996. 978-0-689-31820-7 (hardcover); 978-0-689-87397-3 (softcover). 208pp.**

For years, rumors of Helen's beauty have spread through Greece. With blonde hair and blue eyes, she stands out. At age twelve she is kidnapped by Theseus. When she is returned to her home, suitors swarm over her father's lands. Helen would rather play games or ride a horse, but she doesn't have any choice. Married to King Menelaus, Helen grows older and even more beautiful. When she meets Paris, prince of Troy, Helen falls in love and begins an affair. Touching off a war, Helen and Paris head to Troy, where Helen meets Cassandra, one of Paris's sisters. Cassandra has the gift of prophecy, seeing events in her dreams that come true. She dreamed of Helen a year before the affair began, and Cassandra realizes that Helen is to blame for the war between Troy and Greece. But Cassandra can't help liking Helen. Within the walls of a city under siege, two different young women will become friends.

Keywords: Before Common Era; Friendship; Trojan War

Napoli, Donna Jo.

Sirena. Scholastic, 1998. 978-0-590-38388-2 (hardcover); 978-0-590-38389-9 (softcover). 256pp. Ⓜ Ⓙ

The beginning of the Trojan War is a great opportunity for Sirena and her sisters. They are mermaids, gifted with beautiful voices that enchant men beyond all reason. Until now, ships passed their island rarely. But Greek ships, full of Greek men, are sailing past their island constantly. This gives the mermaids hope. They are mortal due to a curse, and can only become immortal if a human man loves a mermaid despite her tail. So Sirena and the other mermaids lure the men to their island with their voices. Yet when Sirena realizes this leads the men to their deaths, she can't stand it. She swims away, finding a new home on another island. She is content with being alone, but then she finds a single Greek soldier, a man cast off on the island. This man sees Sirena and wants to be her friend. And Sirena is torn between her desire to save him and the love that will lift her curse of mortality.

Keywords: Before Common Era; Greece; Mermaids; Trojan War

Shipton, Paul.

The Pig Scrolls. Ⓜ Ⓙ

With humor and wit, the tale of a man turned into a pig is placed within the Greek world after the Trojan War.

Keywords: Animals; Before Common Era; Greece; Humor

The Pig Scrolls by Gryllus the Pig. Candlewick, 2005. 978-0-7636-2702-7 (hardcover); 978-0-7636-3302-8 (softcover). 288pp.

Gryllus has been a bit down on his luck. True, he survived the Trojan War (thanks to his position as a potato peeler) and the long journey with Odysseus. When the ships arrive at the island home of Circe, the last thing Gryllus expects is to be turned into a pig. All that's left of his humanity is his talent for limericks and wisecracks. But strangely enough, Gryllus finds it's easier to be a pig, so he's quite happy to remain in porcine form. Life is good for Gryllus, who passes his time eating and sleeping. Then catastrophe happens: A young priestess named Sibyl captures him. Sibyl has been sent on a mission by Apollo himself. The gods have suddenly withdrawn into hiding, leaving the world overrun with monsters. And the world's only hope . . . is a talking pig.

The Pig Who Saved the World by Gryllus the Pig. Candlewick, 2007. 978-0-7636-3446-9 (hardcover). 272pp.

After saving the Cosmos, Gryllus the Pig decides that it's time to return to his human form. With Sibyl the ex-priestess and Homer the epic poet/pimply teenager, Gryllus heads to the island home of Circe. She's the one who turned him into a pig, and she's the only one who can turn him back into a man. But Circe's not to be found—she's far away on Crete. Soon the three travelers find out that Gryllus's transformation will have to wait. The gods are being held captive by Sisyphus, who is seeking revenge for his years of unending torture in Hades. Once again, it looks like it'll be up to Gryllus to rescue the gods and save the Cosmos. It would seem that a pig's work is never done.

Spinner, Stephanie.

Quicksilver. Knopf Books for Young Readers, 2005. 978-0-375-82638-2 (hardcover); 978-0-440-23845-4 (softcover). 240pp. **J** **S**

Gods can be just like mortals. Just like humans, gods deal with family squabbles, take pride in their skills, and have fun. Hermes, son of Zeus, does all of these things and more. He is the messenger of the gods, the guide of the dead on their journey to the underworld. He protects animals and invents musical instruments. But first and foremost, Hermes is the Prince of Thieves. He's been stealing things since he was one day old, and no one does it better than he does. Whether it's stealing Persephone from Hades or rustling Apollo's cattle, Hermes has done it all with his wits. But when his wits fail him at a crucial moment, this lighthearted god learns how guilt feels.

Keywords: Before Common Era; Family; Greece

Quiver. Knopf Books for Young Readers, 2002. 978-0-375-81489-1 (hardcover); 978-0-440-23819-5 (softcover). 192pp. **J** **S**

Among the legions of Greek heroes, there is a young woman named Atalanta. She is a huntress, gifted with a bow and the fastest runner among all mortals. Dedicated to the goddess Artemis, Atalanta has taken a vow of chastity, living the way the virgin goddess lives. What could be more natural for the girl who was abandoned as a baby, nursed by a she-bear, and then raised by hunters? But when she is at her lowest, Atalanta gets shocking news: The father who abandoned her is returning to claim her, and he is a king. He only has one reason for claiming her—to arrange her marriage so she can produce an heir. Unwilling to break her vow to Artemis, Atalanta comes up with a contest to win her hand. The man who can beat her in a foot race will be her husband . . . the men who lose will be put to death. Will Atalanta's contest help her stay true to Artemis, or will the goddess send her a sign that will save her?

Keywords: Before Common Era; Greece; Sports; Women's Roles

Tomlinson, Theresa.

Woman Warriors series. **J**

These novels put a spin is put on the legends of the Amazons. Women are seen as perfectly capable of riding horses, serving their deity, and defending their people.

Keywords: Before Common Era; Greece; Trojan War; Women Soldiers

The Moon Riders. HarperTeen, 2006. 978-0-06-084736-4 (hardcover). 400pp.

> Myrina has finally arrived at the day she's been waiting for: She is ready to join the Moon Riders as a priestess to the Great Mother Maa. She will dance and ride, joining with the other Moon Maidens to help those in need. But on the day Myrina rides away with her new family, a surprise is found. A young woman has stowed away on one of the baggage horses—and it's not just any young woman. Cassandra, daughter of King Priam, has no desire to be a princess of Troy. She does not want to be given in marriage to a man, like a possession no different than a horse or a bolt of cloth, especially since her gift of prophecy has made her fearful of the future. She wants to be a Moon Rider. Myrina doesn't know what to think, especially when she learns that Cassandra has prophesied the fall of Troy. As Cassandra's prophecies come true, the Moon Riders, Cassandra, and Myrina must join together to ease the destruction.

Voyage of the Snake Lady. HarperTeen, 2007. 978-0-06-084739-5(hardcover). 400pp.

> After the turmoil of the Trojan War, the Moon Riders hope to rebuild and return to their traditions. But it is not to be; the fishing village that they have settled in falls under attack, and all the women and small children are loaded onto ships that will carry them into slavery. Myrina, the leader of the Moon Riders, is determined that they will be free. After the women defeat their male captors, the ships will split up. One will sail back to the village, while the other will press on across the sea. Myrina, with the help of her friends Cassandra and Iphigenia, will have to be strong and find a home for the Moon Riders. As they search for peace, they face their greatest challenges and struggles.

Arthurian Legend

Like many legends, the story of King Arthur has some basis in fact. There is evidence, although it is contradictory, that there was a high chief or leader who did much to preserve the people of Britain. This occurred in the fourth or fifth century, as Roman power was fading and the Vikings were beginning to launch raids on Britain. Through the centuries, this minor leader has been made greater, the stories expanded and embroidered. Not unlike historical fiction itself, those additions tell much about the period of the authors. For example, the tragic love stories in Arthurian legends are a product of the twelfth century, during the courtly love period. The novels included here allow teens to explore medieval Britain through a different lens, one that adds a romantic touch to history.

Crossley-Holland, Kevin.

Arthur Trilogy. 🟦 🅢

Crossley-Holland explores the importance of historical figures and how that influence can change one's life. Pairing Arthurian times with the Crusades provides an interesting commentary on the medieval wars of religion.

Keywords: Crusades; England; Magic; Medieval; Middle East; Religious Conflicts

📖 *The Seeing Stone.* Orion Children's Books, 2000. 978-1-85881-397-4 (hardcover); 978-0-439-43524-6 (softcover). 336pp.

On his family's estate, lying on the border between Wales and England, Arthur de Caldicot wants nothing more than to become a squire and eventually a knight. For now, he lives on the estate, studying and trying to stay out of trouble. Then one day he receives an unusual present from Merlin, his father's friend. The gift is a black stone—but Arthur can see in it stories about his namesake, the legendary King Arthur. As daily life on the de Caldicot estate continues, the stories of King Arthur start becoming part of life. And the stories of these two Arthurs come together in an unexpected way.

At the Crossing Places. Orion Children's Books, 2001. 978-1-85881-398-1 (hardcover); 978-1-84255-200-1 (softcover). 384pp.

The day Arthur has been waiting for has arrived: He is leaving Caldicot and preparing to serve as a squire to a knight. As he leaves, he makes sure to take with him the seeing stone, which guides him with its stories of King Arthur. Arthur will need its wisdom as he seeks more information about his true nature and journeys to his knight's home. Lord Stephen, Arthur's master, plans to join the Crusade and travel to the Holy Land. Yet before he can leave, the troubles on his estate must be settled. For there has been murder and blackmail among Lord Stephen's people, and this is what Arthur finds himself in the middle of. Can King Arthur guide him to safety and knowledge, and will Arthur get to serve Lord Stephen in battle?

King of the Middle March. Orion Children's Books, 2003. 978-1-84255-060-1 (hardcover); 978-1-84255-155-4 (softcover). 416pp.

Excitement is in the air for Arthur de Caldicot: He has become a knight and is starting on the journey to the Holy Lands. It's bound to be dangerous, but Arthur has his seeing stone to advise him. It turns out the Crusade will be much worse than Arthur imagined, because the fight is not just Christian against Saracen, but Christian against Christian. It throws Arthur's beliefs and dreams into disarray. Even worse, Arthur sees that the court at Camelot was equally disordered. Arthur must struggle to find his way. With his present and his future on the line, Arthur will not be able to rely on the past he views in his seeing stone—only on himself.

McCaffrey, Anne.

Black Horses for the King. **Harcourt Children's Books, 1996. 978-0-15-227322-4 (hardcover); 978-0-15-206378-8 (softcover). 240pp. S**

For a leader hoping to develop a cavalry, horses are an obvious requirement. So Lord Artos, Count of Briton, is journeying far from home to the horse fair in Septimania. Assisting Artos is a young man named Galwyn. Talented with languages and horses, Galwyn was unhappily working on his uncle's sailing ship, so meeting Lord Artos is a great opportunity for him. Soon he is helping Artos acquire the horses he needs. But Galwyn's service also extends to breeding the horses and developing horseshoes. With his help, Artos could succeed in his quest to drive the Saxons from the British lands. Will Galwyn be able to serve this great cause?

Keywords: Animals; England; Medieval

McKenzie, Nancy.
The Chrysalis Queen Quartet. Ⓜ Ⓙ

A sassy, brave heroine is created in this reimagining of the young Guinevere. She's more interested in horses than marriage, but learning of a prophecy that concerns her makes Guinevere start to grow up.

Keywords: Family; Medieval; Wales

Guinevere's Gift. Knopf Books for Young Readers, 2008. 978-0-375-84345-7 (hardcover); 978-0-440-24020-4 (softcover). 336pp.

Just looking at her, you wouldn't think Guinevere is the subject of a prophecy. She's a gangly bookworm, who likes spying on the adults with her cousin Elaine. Yet it has been foretold that one day she will be the wife of a great king and the highest lady in the land. It's doubtful, despite her intelligence and her potential for beauty, that this will happen. For Guinevere's aunt and guardian is determined to gain a powerful husband for her own daughter. As she discovers trouble afoot in her uncle's castle, Guinevere must struggle to make a choice. She can either stay the quiet girl she's always been or become the great woman she's destined to be.

Guinevere's Gamble. Knopf Books for Young Readers, 2009. 978-0-375-84346-4 (hardcover). 368pp.

Being the subject of a prophecy has complicated Guinevere's life. She has been protected by a group of pagans since her birth, because it has been foretold that Guinevere and her future husband—a great king—will save the Old Ones from being destroyed. Now protected by Llyr, a member of the Old Ones, Guinevere would rather ride her horse than think about the prophecy. It's certainly more fun to ride than put up with her cousin Elaine's tantrums and sulks. Elaine is angry over missing her chance to marry the High King Arthur; never mind that she's only twelve and much too young for marriage. Fortunately, there's something to distract both girls from their troubles: The High King has called a meeting of the Welsh kings, which will include Elaine's father, King Pellinore. Guinevere finds that this trip holds much danger, and not just for her. Will she live to see her destiny fulfilled?

Morris, Gerald.
The Squire's Tales. 🅜 🅙

With rollicking humor, Morris explores several Arthurian myths. From squires and knights to ladies and hermits, not to mention well-known figures like Gawain, Lancelot, and Guinevere, all kinds of characters join in the fun.

Keywords: England; Humor; Medieval; Wales

The Squire's Tale. Houghton Mifflin, 1998. 978-0-395-86959-8 (hardcover); 978-0-618-73743-7 (softcover). 224pp.

> An orphan who never knew his parents, Terence was lucky enough to be brought up by Trevisant the Hermit. His life is quiet until one day a young man passes through the forest. The stranger is Gawain, who is on his way to the court of King Arthur. When he defends Terence and Trevisant against a rampaging knight, armed only with a stew pot, Gawain proves his worth. As a result, Terence finds himself serving Gawain as his squire. Together they set off for Camelot, a journey that will become a larger quest for Terence. As Gawain's fame as a knight grows, Terence seeks to discover who his parents were—and whether it matters.

The Squire, His Knight, and His Lady. Houghton Mifflin, 1999. 978-0-395-91211-9 (hardcover); 978-0-440-22885-1 (softcover) 240pp.

> Camelot is racked by scandal as Arthur's Queen Guinevere betrays him with the dashing Sir Lancelot, a French knight. Gawain and Terence are among the few to see how this wounds Arthur. Yet there are still battles to fight and quests to undertake. During the feasting between Christmas and New Year's, an unknown knight comes forward with a challenge. Any knight will be given one swing at his neck—but in exchange the knight must come back in a year and accept a blow in return. The Round Table should be suspicious of this deal, for the strange knight is green: green hair, green skin, even a green horse. But Gawain takes the challenge, and when the green knight is unaffected by his blow, Gawain and Terence have a hard year ahead of them.

The Savage Damsel and the Dwarf. Houghton Mifflin, 2000. 978-0-395-97126-0 (hardcover); 978-0-547-01437-1 (softcover). 224pp.

> There are many castles in the land, posing a great temptation for evil knights to besiege them. Each of those castles has a beautiful, rich maiden inside, eager to marry the good, brave, true knight who will deliver her. When Lynet sneaks out of her castle to King Arthur's court, trying to find a knight who will take on the Knight of the Red Lands, she's greeted with skepticism. The only one who's willing to take the risk is Beaumains, the kitchen knave. Lynet isn't sure if he'll be able to succeed, but what can she do? When Lynet and Beaumains, accompanied by the dwarf Roger, return to her castle, Lynet discovers that appearances can be very deceiving.

Parsifal's Page. Houghton Mifflin, 2001. 978-0-618-05509-8 (hardcover); 978-0-618-43237-0 (softcover). 240pp.

> It's difficult when you feel stuck in the wrong place. Piers, who works in his father's forge, would rather be Pierre and a page to a noble knight. When a strange knight comes to his father's shop, saying he is on a great quest, Piers is eager to go with him. Yet his service doesn't last long before his knight is killed by an uneducated yet gifted yokel named Parsifal. Piers is now at loose ends and chooses to stay on with Parsifal. It's a good decision, because Parsifal knows nothing about being a knight. It's be up to Piers to train him, not just in combat skills but in knightly manners. Will Piers have Parsifal ready in time to set off on the greatest journey of all, the quest for the Holy Grail?

The Ballad of Sir Dinadan. Houghton Mifflin, 2003. 978-0-618-19099-7 (hardcover); 978-0-618-54894-1 (softcover). 256pp.

> Second sons are not highly valued. In the case of Dinadan, it's like he barely exists. He has no talent for knightly pursuits like jousting or romancing fair ladies. He'd much rather be a minstrel, traveling to noble households, telling stories, and playing music. Yet his father doesn't value these talents at all, so Dinadan becomes a knight. With his knighthood thrust upon him, Dinadan wanders the countryside, heading toward King Arthur's Court. He falls in with a young Welsh boy named Culloch. Dinadan doesn't realize that Culloch will pull him, as well as two other knights from the Round Table, into a foolish quest. But through it all, Dinadan will keep his rebec close and maintain his sense of humor.

The Princess, the Crone, and the Dung-Cart Knight. Houghton Mifflin, 2004. 978-0-618-37823-4 (hardcover); 978-0-618-73748-2 (softcover). 320pp.

> Ever since the murders of her mother and her guardian, Sarah has been searching for the knight responsible. She intends to exact vengeance upon him, but for that she needs a weapon. When she sees a chance to steal a sword from a nobleman, she tries to take it but fails. The nobleman, however, takes an interest in her and gifts her with a sword and a few quick lessons. The lady with him treats Sarah just as kindly, giving Sarah a day of respite. But

the day quickly takes a turn for the worse, when a knight captures the nobleman and the lady. Sarah didn't realize that she had been with Queen Guinevere and Sir Kai. The only one who knows they have been captured, Sarah must set out for Camelot and King Arthur's Court. And the search for Sir Kai and Queen Guinevere will also lead Sarah to answers to her own questions.

The Lioness and Her Knight. Houghton Mifflin, 2005. 978-0-618-50772-6 (hardcover); 978-0-547-01485-2 (softcover). 352pp.

At age sixteen, Luneta is desperate to get away from her parents' castle. She wants to see more of the world, and her family's lands in Orkney are anything but exciting. It's a great opportunity for excitement when Luneta is permitted to visit the castle of Lady Laudine, a friend of her mother's. When her parents are unable to take her immediately, though, Luneta starts scheming for a way to go. The arrival of her cousin Ywain, a young knight, is just the opening Luneta needs. Together they set off on a journey, planning a stop in Camelot along the way. They also meet a knight turned jester called Rhience, who accompanies them on their trip. Magic and adventure lie in their path: How will each of these three people meet their challenges?

The Quest of the Fair Unknown. Houghton Mifflin, 2006. 978-0-618-63152-0 (hardcover); 978-0-547-01484-5 (softcover). 264pp.

For his entire life, Beaufils has lived with his mother, deep in the forest. Before she dies, she tells Beaufils to journey to Camelot. His father is there, a knight serving King Arthur. But since Beaufils does not know the names of his mother or his father, this is certainly a difficult quest. Add in Beaufils's lack of knowledge about the outside world, and it's even more difficult. He manages to make it to Camelot, assisted by those who recognize his naïve nature. Once Beaufils is at Camelot, his search is overtaken by a greater one: the quest for the Holy Grail. Helping Sir Gawain and Sir Galahad on their journeys, Beaufils learns about friends and foes. And his own quest just might connect with the Holy Grail, the young Lady Ellyn, and Camelot.

Reeve, Philip.

Here Lies Arthur. **Scholastic, 2008. 978-0-545-09334-7 (hardcover); 978-1-4071-0358-7 (softcover). 352pp. J/S**

The Roman legions left Britain a long time ago, and ever since, small clans have been fighting nonstop. None of the war chiefs has been strong enough to become a leader—until now. A man named Arthur is sweeping through the land, waging war and gathering supporters. One of the most important supporters is the bard Merlin, teller of tales and maker of magic. He creates the stories that give Arthur a magical touch, making Arthur seem as if he's favored by both old and new gods. Merlin is helped by Gwyna, a slip of a girl. But she can't stay a girl. Masquerading as a boy, Gwyna sees Arthur growing more and more powerful, yet his power is based on Merlin's tricks. And if the tricks are discovered, not only Arthur will be harmed.

Awards: Carnegie Medal

Keywords: Disguised as Boy; England; Magic; Medieval

Sandell, Lisa Ann.

Song of the Sparrow. **Scholastic Press, 2007. 978-0-439-91848-0 (hardcover); 978-0-439-91849-7 (softcover). 416pp. ◑**

This novel in verse expands the story of Elaine, the Lady of Shalott. Elaine is the only girl in the middle of an army. Her mother died when she was eight, and Elaine's father brought her along with him as he performed his military service. Now age seventeen, Elaine sews and mends, surrounded by men like Arthur, Lancelot, Gawain, and Tristan. But she only has eyes for Lancelot—and it seems that he is finally seeing her as a girl, not a child. But then a girl named Gwynivere arrives, who will marry Arthur. Not only is she distant and even cruel, but Lancelot has fallen in love with her. How will Elaine bear this? Will she be able to heal her broken heart when her home is wracked by warfare?

Keywords: England; Medieval; Novel in Verse; Romance

Spinner, Stephanie.

Damosel: In Which the Lady of the Lake Renders a Frank and Often Startling Account of Her Wondrous Life and Times. **Knopf Books for Young Readers, 2008. 978-0-375-83634-3 (hardcover); 978-0-553-49511-9 (softcover). 208pp. ◑ Ⓢ**

Living a life by the rules can be easy. You know what's permitted and what's not. For Damosel, the creature known as the Lady of the Lake, the rules are all she knows and she obeys them all—rules like *The Rule of Thorough Preparation for a Difficult Task* and the *Rule of Service to Future Kings*. So when Merlin, the great wizard, comes to request a sword for the future King Arthur, she agrees. Through nine years' hard work, she produces an enchanted sword and gives it to Arthur, asking only for a favor from him at some point in the future. Arthur agrees and takes the sword, achieving great things and becoming the king of all the legends. But Damosel makes a mistake—one that will lead to the downfall of Arthur. What will happen to this magical world without its king?

Keywords: England; Magic; Medieval

Wein, Elizabeth E.
The Arthur and Aksum Trilogy. ◑ Ⓢ

A folklorist by training, Wein combines myth and fact in this unusual series. The kingdom of Arthur in what is now England is linked with the African empire of Aksum, present-day Ethiopia.

Keywords: Africa; England; Family; Medieval; Political Rebellions

The Winter Prince. Baen, 1994. 978-0-671-87621-0 (softcover). 202pp.

> If life was fair, Medraut would be his father's heir. Medraut is intelligent, forceful, possessing all the skills that a king needs. But even though he is his father's oldest son, he is not legitimate. So it is Medraut's younger half-brother Lleu, weak and sickly, who is destined to take the throne. Everyone recognizes that Medraut should be the king, from his father Artos to the lowliest servant. Medraut knows he should accept Lleu as his future king, but he cannot. So he chooses to hatch a plot with his Aunt Morgause to kidnap Lleu and force Artos to name Medraut his heir. Medraut subjects Lleu to great dangers, trying to destroy him. But as Lleu meets these challenges, Medraut begins to question the plot and everything he had thought about his half-brother.

A Coalition of Lions. Viking Juvenile, 2003. 978-0-670-03618-9 (hardcover); 978-0-14-240129-3 (softcover). 204pp.

> The battle between Medraut and Lleu, although ended, did not prevent disaster from striking the kingdom of Britain. At the end of the tragedy, the only one left is Goewin, twin sister of Lleu and a valuable prize for any power-hungry man. She chooses to flee to the African empire of Aksum to find Constantine, the British ambassador to Aksum and her betrothed. Arriving in Aksum, Goewin discovers that Constantine is now heir to the Aksumite throne. Goewin finds herself torn between two countries and two men: Constantine and Preamos, Aksum's former ambassador to Britain. Will she return to Britain and be queen, or will she take on a different role in Aksum?

The Sunbird. Viking Juvenile, 2004. 978-0-670-03691-2 (hardcover); 978-0-14-240171-2 (softcover). 184pp.

> Telemakos was born of two worlds. The son of an Aksumite woman and a British noble, he has a degree of status but is mistrusted by most. He is practically invisible and likes to eavesdrop on and observe others while hiding in plain sight. These abilities, and his skill as a tracker, could save his country. There are rumors of plague spreading across the world, stretching from the Red Sea to Britain. Goewin, the British ambassador to Aksum, has learned that this rumored plague was caused by salt traders to increase demand for salt. She calls upon her nephew, Telemakos, to discover the truth. If Telemakos fails, he will lose his life and endanger the empire. So he cannot fail.

The Mark of Solomon. ⬛ ⬛

Continuing where the <u>Arthur and Aksum</u> trilogy leaves off, Wein explores the connections between Africa and the Middle East while focusing on the character of Telemakos.

Keywords: Africa; Brothers and Sisters; Medieval; Middle East; Physical Disability

The Lion Hunter. Viking Juvenile, 2007. 978-0-670-06163-1 (hardcover). 208pp.

> Telemakos is still recovering from his experiences with the salt dealers when he suffers a grave injury. Fighting to recover, he relies on his family and friends to pull him through. Most of all he's trying to live for his new sister Athena, a stubborn, needy baby. Brother and sister are very close—so close that when threats are made against Telemakos, both will flee. Threatened with death, Telemakos is sent to live with Abreha, ruler of Himyar and a historical enemy of Aksum. And Athena goes with him. Telemakos is warned to be cautious, but these warnings put him in even more danger. It takes all his skill to protect himself and his sister.

The Empty Kingdom. Viking Juvenile, 2008. 978-0-670-06273-7 (hardcover). 208pp.

> When Telemakos was sent with his little sister, Athena, to the Kingdom of Himyar, it was for their protection. But after eavesdropping on conversations, Telemakos is harshly punished: imprisoned inside the palace and separated from his sister. He's even forced to wear bells on his ankles to alert people to his presence. Telemakos must endure these punishments, because any further betrayal and Abreha, the King of Himyar, will have him executed. With his death warrant already written, Telemakos feels trapped. He knows that Abreha is plotting against Aksum, the home of Telemarkos. Abreha wants to capture the Hanish Islands of Aksum, freeing the criminals lodged there and capturing the obsidian and pearls held there. But how can Telemakos warn his mother and his aunt of this treachery? The odds against a one-armed boy are great, but Telemakos is determined to gain his freedom and save his people.

Yolen, Jane.

Sword of the Rightful King: A Novel of King Arthur. Harcourt Children's Books, 2003. 978-0-15-202527-4 (hardcover); 978-0-15-202533-5 (softcover). 368pp. **Ⓜ Ⓙ**

> The familiar story of Arthur pulling the sword from the stone is retold in a new way. Young and newly installed as High King of Britain, Arthur is well aware that there are those who would usurp him. Most dangerous is Morgause, stepdaughter of the last High King and Queen of the Orkney Islands. Morgause is also a powerful witch, enchanting and spellbinding men to be under her control. Four of her sons are heading to Arthur's court, and one is suspected of being a spy. Arthur and his loyal court want to protect against these threats, so Merlinnus, the mage who guides Arthur, devises a plan to consolidate Arthur's power. He creates a sword and places it in a stone, spreading word that anyone who can draw out the sword is the rightful High King. But before Arthur can do so, someone else pulls the sword.

Keywords: England; Magic; Medieval

Alternate Worlds

It may seem like splitting hairs, but this section exists due to books like *Sorcery and Cecelia* and the <u>Bartimaeus</u> trilogy, in which magic is not a secret. In both of these works, in fact, there are government offices to regulate and control the use of magic. This means that their worlds are quite different from ours, yet they still include historical figures like the Duke of Wellington or historical events like wars and scientific advances. Some authors that have created fantasies that are strongly based on a country's history. These novels are listed in this section; books set in the past but relying on science or technology for altering the world are listed in chapter 5. For readers of the following novels, different thoughts are provoked. How would our past be different if magic or fantastical creatures truly existed back then?

Hearn, Lian.

Tales of the Otori. ⓢ

Hearn, the pseudonym of Australian author Gillian Rubenstein, has crafted a thrilling saga, set in a world that is closely related to feudal Japan. The novels revolve around the Clan of the Otori and the mystical world that the main character, Takeo, finds himself thrust into.

Read-alike: <u>Inu-Yasha</u> by Rumiko Takahasi, a long-running manga series, sends a modern girl to medieval Japan, where she has experiences similar to those in the Tales of the Otori.

Keywords: Alternate Universe; Japan; Magic; Medieval; Romance

> *Across the Nightingale Floor.* Riverhead Trade, 2003. 978-1-57322-332-4 (softcover). 305pp.
>
> A member of a persecuted religious sect, Takeo returns to his village to find it burning and his whole family killed. When he is rescued by Lord Otori Shigeru, his life changes dramatically, with a rise in status and an awareness of the mystical powers that lie untapped within him. He also meets Lady Kaede, the beautiful noblewoman whom fate decrees will never be his.
>
> **Awards:** Carnegie Medal Finalist

> *Grass for His Pillow.* Riverhead Trade, 2004. 978-1-59448-003-4 (softcover). 368pp.
>
> Takeo continues to develop his abilities, but his temper might sabotage his progress. He is also torn between his allegiance to the Otori and the mysterious Tribe. They both have saved his life, yet both have secrets. Meanwhile, Kaede is struggling to defend her lands, moving beyond the traditional role for women.

Brilliance of the Moon. Riverhead Trade, 2005. 978-1-59448-086-7 (softcover). 368pp.

> Now secretly married, both Takeo and Kaede must fight to protect their realms, together and apart. Takeo strives to find a way to fulfill the prophecy that his lands will stretch from sea to sea, but only at the cost of great bloodshed.

The Harsh Cry of the Heron. Riverhead Trade, 2007. 978-1-59448-257-1 (softcover). 592pp.

> Set fifteen years after the end of the previous book, Takeo has ruled wisely and his lands are at peace. Yet a conflict looms between his legitimate daughter and heir and his illegitimate son, who has been raised by a member of the Tribe. Takeo must use all his mystical powers to protect his daughter and the future of his realm.

Heaven's Net Is Wide. Riverhead Trade, 2008. 978-1-59448-332-5 (softcover). 576pp.

> This prequel to the series concerns the adolescence of Otori Shigeru, Takeo's future foster father. Once a strong family, dedicated to loyalty and tradition, the family is destroyed in an epic battle that leads to Shigeru becoming an outcast.

Stroud, Jonathan.

The Bartimaeus Trilogy. Ⓜ Ⓙ

This action-packed trilogy mixes magical training with a Victorian-esque British Empire, rivaled by a Czech Empire that rules most of Europe. Featuring pitch-perfect characterization and humorous footnotes, Stroud creates a world that draws in the reader.

Keywords: Alternate Universe; Djinn; England; Humor; Magic; Nineteenth Century

📖 *The Amulet of Samarkand.* Disney-Hyperion, 2003. 978-0-7868-1859-4 (hardcover); 978-0-7868-5255-0 (softcover). 464pp.

> Nathaniel is a sensitive, ambitious boy, in training to become a magician with a shiftless master. After he is insulted by another magician, he vows to get his revenge. He tries to act as usual, while studying and learning as much as he can. He slowly gains power—enough to summon an ancient djinni named Bartimaeus. Yet while Nathaniel was able to summon him, Bartimaeus is much too powerful for the young magician to control. And Bartimaeus isn't about to let that fact go unnoticed.

The Golem's Eye. Disney-Hyperion, 2004. 978-0-7868-1860-0 (hardcover); 978-0-7868-3654-3 (softcover). 576pp.

> After two years, Nathaniel has risen in the ranks of the Ministry, gaining more power and influence. He now leads a department that is seeking to

stop a minor rebellion of commoners against magical people. When he crosses paths with Kitty, a girl who is resistant to magic, he thinks he'll be able to break the Resistance. At the same time, a strange creature is terrorizing London. When Nathaniel realizes it's a golem, a man of clay brought to life with magic, the only way to fight it is to call upon Bartimaeus again.

Ptolemy's Gate. Disney-Hyperion, 2005. 978-0-7868-1861-7 (hardcover); 978-0-7868-3868-4 (softcover). 512pp.

Thanks to his work destroying the golem, Nathaniel is now among the greatest magicians in the British Empire. Yet the Empire is beginning to crumble around him, as the government starts to fail. Nathaniel has grown strong and has kept Bartimaeus under his control. While the djinni longs to be released from service and return to the spirit world to regain his strength, Nathaniel will not let him free. There are too many things that Nathaniel needs Bartimaeus for. When he discovers that Kitty, the magic-resilient girl that he met and grudgingly befriended, has begun studying magic herself, Nathaniel has his work cut out for him. Forces are at work that will draw these three individuals together, in a climactic battle.

Thal, Lilli.

Mimus. Annick Press, 2005. 978-1-55037-925-9 (hardcover); 978-1-55037-924-2 (softcover). 398pp. **J S**

A world much like our Germany is presented during a dark period in its history. Florin's days are full of studying, weapons training, and being with his friends. There is hope in his father's kingdom of Moltavia because the long war with Vinland will soon be over. Now that the peace treaty has been signed, King Phillip has traveled to Vinland for a series of celebrations— and he has sent back a messenger to bring Florin to Vinland. Some of the court officials wonder at King Phillip's choice of messenger, a noble who is not well-trusted. But Florin is so excited about visiting the Vinlandian court and seeing his father that he doesn't see any reason to worry. When Florin arrives at the court of Theodo of Vinland, he discovers treachery and tragedy. Theodo has tricked Phillip, slaughtering his men and imprisoning his nobles. Florin, instead of joining his father in the dungeon, is instead made an apprentice to Mimus, the court jester. Wily and deceitful, Mimus belittles Florin . . . but perhaps if Florin plays the fool, he can save his father and Moltavia.

Keywords: Alternate Universe; Germany; Medieval

Wooding, Chris.

The Haunting of Alaizabel Cray. Orchard, 2004. 978-0-439-54656-0 (hardcover); 978-0-439-59851-4 (softcover). 304pp. **J** **S**

> A fantasy version of Victorian London is the setting for this Gothic horror story. Thaniel is a wych-hunter, a life that is all he has known. Son of a famous wych-hunter, Thaniel works with his friend Cathaline, an accomplished wych-hunter herself, to rid London's Old Quarter of supernatural creatures. Then one evening Thanial discovers a young girl. She seems crazy, delusional. It is slowly revealed that there is something much more wrong with Alaizabel Cray. But by that time, it is too late. Thaniel has fallen under her spell, and now he will race to rescue her from the evil that she is a victim of. The only question is whether he will save her in time.
>
> **Keywords:** Alternate Universe; England; Magic; Nineteenth Century; Romance

Wrede, Patricia C., and Caroline Stevermer.

The Sorcery and Cecelia Trilogy. **M** **J** **S**

> Originally begun as a writing exercise, this trilogy imagines the world of early nineteenth-century England with magical practices. Drawing comparisons to Jane Austen, Wrede and Stevermer write their novels as correspondence and testimony, with each author taking a different character.
>
> **Keywords:** Alternate Universe; England; Family; Letters; Magic; Multiple Voices; Nineteenth Century; Romance

> *Sorcery and Cecelia or The Enchanted Chocolate Pot: Being the Correspondence of Two Young Ladies of Quality Regarding Various Magical Scandals in London and the Country.* Harcourt, 2003. 978-0-15-204615-6 (hardcover); 978-0-15-205300-0 (softcover). 336pp.
>
>> This Season, Kate is in London while Cecelia is in the country. The two cousins are very close, and to stay in contact, they write each other long letters. In their correspondence, they share news about everything that is happening to them, such as a strange man following Cecelia's every move and someone trying to poison Kate at an affair at the Royal College of Wizards. In an England where magic is commonplace, it's going to take all their wit and courage to get to the bottom of these strange goings-on.

> *The Grand Tour: Being a Revelation of Matters of High Confidentiality and Greatest Importance, Including Extracts from the Intimate Diary of a Noblewoman and the Sworn Testimony of a Lady of Quality.* Harcourt Children's Books, 2004. 978-0-15-204616-3 (hardcover); 978-0-15-205556-1 (softcover). 480pp.
>
>> After defeating magical plots that threatened not just their lives, Kate and Cecelia are trying to focus on married life. For the new Lady Schofield and Mrs. Tarleton, a rushed wedding is followed by a marvelous wedding

trip. The four of them are off for Europe on the Grand Tour, visiting places like Paris and Venice, traveling through the Alps and enjoying sightseeing and shopping. But soon the two couples find themselves in the middle of a mystery. It starts with a small flask, full of unknown oil, and leads to an exciting chase across the Continent. Along the way, Cecelia tries to improve her magical abilities, Kate gets used to being part of the nobility, and both attempt to unravel this puzzle.

The Mislaid Magician or Ten Years After: Being the Private Correspondence Between Two Prominent Families Regarding a Scandal Touching the Highest Levels of Government and the Security of the Realm. Harcourt Children's Books, 2006. 978-0-15-205548-6 (hardcover); 978-0-15-206209-5 (softcover). 336pp.

For cousins Kate and Cecelia, the ten years since their weddings have been busy, happy ones. They care for their children, run their estates, and spend time with their husbands. Cecelia is even able to continue her magical endeavors. However, the ascendancy of the Duke of Wellington, their husbands' former commander, to the office of prime minister creates work for Thomas and James. James has been asked to investigate the disappearance of a German surveyor-magician, a man who was investigating the best way to build a railway. Meanwhile, Thomas supplies gossip and magical research to James, while Kate cares for both couples' children. As James and Cecelia keep investigating, Kate and Thomas deal with Kate's sister, who has left her husband, and a mysterious mute girl. Are all these events connected? It's up to Kate and Cecelia to put all the pieces together as the letters fly fast and furious between them.

1

2

3

4

5

6

7

8

Chapter 7

Time Travel

For decades, the idea of time travel has intrigued readers and authors. The thought of being able to go back in time, to observe an event or make changes, has crossed many people's minds. Until, and if, a time machine is invented, we have to content ourselves with novels that explore time travel. Though there are novels that show characters traveling from the present into the future, many more look toward the past. Going into the future, characters can only see how the future is different from their time; any changes they make will not have an impact on their lives. But by traveling to the past, characters can do more than observe. They can change history, for good or bad. That moral dilemma is often seen in time travel stories and helps create the drama and tension in these works.

As far as we know, time travel has not been achieved. The novels that feature a trip to the past by a modern character therefore are a type of speculative fiction. Like fantasy or science fiction, time travel novels create a what-if scenario. Instead of imagining what the future might be like or if elves were real, though, time travel has a factual basis. The facts are about the historical period, not the science of time travel. This grounding in dates means that time travel novels are more realistic than other examples of science fiction. For this reason, novels that feature a trip to the past might appeal to readers who dislike futuristic sci-fi.

This chapter explores historical fiction that relies on characters traveling into the past. How the time travel is achieved is less important than what the character experiences in the past. This travel is typically through a strange, mysterious time portal, although there are instances of time machines. In addition, there are alternate universe works, in which science or technology has created worlds that are similar to our own but with histories that vastly differ. For alternate universe stories that feature magic, refer to chapter 6.

Coming-of-Age

Being sent into a different time often helps shake up a character, leading to growth and change. No matter how immature the character, going through such an event inspires the coming-of-age process.

Curry, Jane Louise.

The Black Canary. **Margaret K. McElderry, 2005. 978-0-689-86478-0 (hardcover). 288pp. ❿**

Having a family tradition is great, but only if one wants to be part of that tradition. James's parents and grandparents are all musicians, and they expect James to follow in their footsteps. But that's the last thing James wants—he just wants normal parents. On a trip to London with his parents, twelve-year-old James discovers a strange portal. When he goes through it, he's shocked to discover he has traveled back in time to 1600. Worse, he can't get home. To survive, he joins a children's chorus that performs for the queen. Thanks to his musical ability and his biracial background, James is quickly advanced to a high position in the chorus. And maybe his skills will be the way he gets back to his own time.

Keywords: African American Issues; England; Music; Seventeenth Century

Dark Shade. **Margaret K. McElderry, 1998. 978-0-689-81812-7 (hardcover). 176pp. ❿**

Sometimes the past isn't as far away as we think. Maggie is worried about her friend and neighbor, Kip. He's been acting strange lately, and it's not just because of the death of his parents several months earlier. When Maggie follows him into the woods, she discovers his secret. Kip has found a doorway to the past, which leads to 1758 Pennsylvania, when dense forest covered the land. It's a dangerous world for a modern girl like Maggie—and not just because she found a wounded British soldier. When Kip tells her he's going to stay in the past and become an adopted member of the Lenape Indian tribe, Maggie's worry turns to fear. She can't let Kip stay in the past; not only would she lose her oldest friend, but Kip would probably change history. Maggie must find a way to convince Kip to stay in the present.

Keywords: America; Eighteenth Century; Native American Issues

De Alcontara, Pedro.

Backtracked. **Delacorte Books for Young Readers, 2009. 978-0-385-73419-6 (hardcover); 978-0-440-23990-1 (softcover). 272pp. Ⓜ ❿**

Tommy Latulla is a slacker. He knows he'll never live up to his brother's example, so why bother trying? After all, Jimmy was a fireman who was killed on September 11, 2001: a heroic death for a guy Tommy knew wasn't really a hero. So Tommy spends his time cutting school and riding subway trains all over the five boroughs, tagging graffiti as he goes. When a prank in the Times Square station goes very wrong, Tommy finds himself thrown back in time to 1918. Italian immigrants are helping dig tunnels for new subway lines, and Tommy gets a job working with them. He travels to two other times in New York's past, seeing how the subways shaped the city. He also learns a lot about himself—but will he be able to return to his own time and use that knowledge?

Read-alike: Find out more about the original New York City subway system in *Secret Subway: The Fascinating Tale of an Amazing Feat of Engineering* by Martin W. Sandler.

Keywords: America; Immigrants; Nineteenth Century

Griffin, Peni R.

Switching Well. **Margaret K. McElderry, 1993. 978-0-689-50581-2 (hardcover); 978-0-14-036910-6 (softcover). 224pp. Ⓜ Ⓙ**

Two girls, a hundred years apart, get to experience each other's lives. Ada is part of a big family in San Antonio. She has very progressive ideas, which aren't very accepted in 1891. Amber is an only child, worried about her parents' separation. She thinks the past, with no drug addicts or dirtiness or broken families, is better than today. On the same day, each girl makes a wish at the well in the vacant lot. Ada finds herself in 1991, when women could vote and work. Amber arrives in 1891 and is swept away by the beauty of early San Antonio. But soon each girl realizes that her own time is the right place for her. How can they return to their right times?

Keywords: America; Nineteenth Century; Parallel Narratives

Haddix, Margaret Peterson.

📖 *Running Out of Time.* **Simon & Schuster Children's Publishing, 1995. 978-0-689-80084-9 (hardcover); 978-0-689-81236-1 (softcover). 184pp. Ⓜ Ⓙ**

Jessie's always been curious. She asks a lot of questions and helps her mother pick herbs and heal people. It's 1840 in Clifton, Indiana, and times are hard, between a financial depression and a strange illness that's attacking the children. But then Jessie's mother tells her a great secret: Even though in Clifton, it's 1840, in the rest of the world, it's 1996. Clifton is a tourist attraction like Colonial Williamsburg, but designed to be "real." The sick children have a disease called diphtheria, and they need medicine—which Matt Clifton, the millionaire who founded Clifton, won't let the villagers have. Someone has to escape and get medicine. The adult women can't fit into the modern clothes that Jessie's mother smuggled into Clifton. But thirteen-year-old Jessie can, and it's up to her to save the people of Clifton.

Keywords: America; Illness; Nineteenth Century

Rabin, Staton.

Black Powder. Margaret K. McElderry, 2005. 978-0-689-86876-4 (hardcover). 256pp. ◼

If you could change history, would you? Langston's best friend Neely has just died in a gang shooting. Langston is upset and wishes he could change what happened. Then he gets his chance, thanks to his science teacher. Mrs. Centauri has invented a time machine, which could send Langston to any time and leave behind a holographic double. Langston wants to do more than just save Neely, though—so he's going back to 1278. Sir Francis Bacon has created the first gunpowder in the West. If Langston can destroy the formula for gunpowder, he can save many people. But can Langston stop progress? And will he be able to get back to his own time?

Keywords: England; Thirteenth Century

Vanderwal, Andrew H.

The Battle for Duncragglin. Tundra Books, 2009. 978-0-88776-886-6 (hardcover). 320pp. ◼

Alex isn't happy about spending his summer in Scotland. He still misses his parents and wonders how they disappeared. While staying with a local family, Alex sets out to find the caves under the ruins of Duncragglin Castle. That's the area his parents were last seen in, and although the caves were supposedly blocked decades ago, Alex thinks they're the key to his parents' disappearance. But instead of just the caves, Alex and his new friends Annie, Willie, and Craig find something much more. The four are transported back in time, to thirteenth-century Scotland. It's a time of danger and bloodshed, as the English attempt to take control of Scotland. The only man who could stop England is William Wallace. And to Alex's surprise, Wallace needs his help to save Scotland.

Keywords: Political Rebellions; Scotland; Thirteenth Century

Westerfeld, Scott.

📖 *Leviathan.* Simon Pulse, 2009. 978-1-4169-7173-3 (hardcover); 978-1-4169-7174-0 (softcover). 448pp. ◼ Ⓢ

An alternate take on the destruction of World War I. Europe is split between two military mindsets. Germany and Austria-Hungary favor Clankers, great machines with guns and shielding. On the other side are the Darwinists of Britain and France, with their genetically fabricated animals. When the heir to the throne of Austria-Hungary is assassinated, a network of alliances plunges Europe into war. Prince Aleksandar, the son of the assassinated heir, is now in great danger. Even though he is legally not entitled to the throne, enemies on both sides wish to capture him. Fleeing from them with a small crew in a battered Stormwalker, Alex crosses paths with a very unusual girl. Deryn Sharp is a natural pilot, but since she's a girl, she could never serve in the British Air Service. So Deryn disguises herself as a boy and quickly gains respect for her skills. She's posted to the *Leviathan*, a vast whale warship. When the *Leviathan* crashes in Switzerland, she meets Prince Aleksandar, and these two young people have a life-changing adventure ahead of them.

Keywords: 1910s; Disguised as Boy; Europe; World War I

Yolen, Jane.

📖 *The Devil's Arithmetic.* **Viking Juvenile, 1988. 978-0-670-81027-7 (hardcover); 978-0-14-034535-3 (softcover). 176pp.** Ⓜ Ⓙ

Passover falling on the same day as Easter means that Hannah is tired by the time her extended family gathers for Seder. She ate a lot of Easter candy with her Catholic best friend and is stuffed, not to mention a bit bored and cranky. But when Hannah opens the door for Elijah, something strange happens. Hannah finds herself in a strange house, with strangers who call her Chaya. Slowly she realizes she has been sent back to a Polish shtetl. As Hannah begins to lose her memories of anything other than Chaya's life, the Jews in the village are rounded up and sent to a camp. They are tattooed, dressed in poor clothes, forced to work long hours, and barely fed. Hannah/Chaya tells stories, keeping up the spirits of her friends. She tells stories until the very end, and then finds herself back in her own time, with her family, and with a deep understanding of the devil's arithmetic.

Keywords: 1940s; Friendship; Holocaust; Poland

Family Issues

Often a trip to the past involves family. Whether it's to rescue an ancestor or to interact with a grandparent, the time travel in these novels lets characters gain a new perspective on their families.

Bell, Ted.

Nick McIver Adventures. Ⓜ Ⓙ

Part of a tradition of boys' reads, these novels read like modern-day yarns. With his wits and bravery, Nick is always ready to jump in and save his home.

Keywords: 1930s; 1940s; American Revolution; Atlantic Ocean; Brothers and Sisters; Eighteenth Century; England; France; Nineteenth Century

Nick of Time. St. Martin's Griffith, 2008. 978-0-312-38068-7 (hardcover); 978-0-312-58143-5 (softcover). 448pp.

In this ripping sea yarn that spans two centuries, Nick lives on Greybeard Island, one of the Channel Islands between England and France. It's 1939, and even though war seems to be looming, Nick's still able to keep sailing his small boat. There's also time to play with his little sister Kate. One day when they're out on the beach, they find an old sea chest. Curiously, it seems to be the one that belonged to their ancestor and Nick's namesake, who fought with Admiral Nelson. When Nick opens the chest, he discovers a plea for help from the first Nicholas McIver. Transported back to 1805, it's up to Nick to save the English Navy. Meanwhile, Kate does her part as German submarines are spotted off the island. Time will tell if these two siblings are able to save England in two different times.

The Time Pirate. St. Martin's Griffin, 2010. 978-0-312-57810-7 (hardcover); 978-0-312-66549-4 (softcover). 464pp.

Old enemies and new adventures await Nick McIver. It's 1940, and it appears the Germans will soon be invading the Channel Islands where Nick lives. Nick is determined to help beat the Nazis, so after a lot of hard work, he manages to repair his father's old plane. Flying over the island, Nick photographs the German ships, gathering information. But then a figure from his past strikes out against Nick and his family. Captain Billy Blood returns and kidnaps Nick's little sister Kate. The ransom? The marvelous Tempus Machina, a time machine invented by Leonardo da Vinci. Nick must travel back to 1781 Jamaica to make the trade. But once he arrives in the past, he learns of a plot that could crush the American Revolution. With two wars and his sister's life in the balance, it will take all of Nick's wits to defeat Captain Billy.

Hautman, Pete.

Mr. Was. Simon & Schuster Children's Publishing, 1996. 978-0-689-81068-8 (hardcover); 978-0-689-81914-8 (softcover). 256pp. **J** **S**

Moving to the big house in Memory is a new start for Jack and his mother. It's the start of a life without his drunken, abusive father. The house, left to his mother by her father, is full of secrets, like the strange door that sends people into the past. When Jack's father comes back and attacks his mother, Jack runs away, going through the door and ending up in the 1940s. There, he meets Scud and his girl Andie. Jack begins to fall for Andie, even as he and Scud are sent to fight in World War II. Jack just intends to wait fifty years and keep his father from hurting his mother. But there are two problems: Jack has already changed the future, and Scud and Andie are his grandparents.

Keywords: 1940s; America; World War II

Heneghan, James.

The Grave. Farrar, Straus & Giroux, 2000. 978-0-374-32765-1 (hardcover); 978-0-440-22948-3 (softcover). 256pp. **J**

Moving from one foster home to another, Tom has always been alone. But the thirteen-year-old is about to find out what it's like to be part of a family. While exploring a giant hole behind his school, he discovers bones and coffins. As if that's not disturbing enough, Tom falls into the twenty-foot pit. But he falls much farther than just a few feet. Tom travels from 1974 back to 1847 Ireland, during the potato famine. Arriving on a windswept beach, he joins a crowd of people and uses CPR to save the life of a boy a bit older than he is. Tom is surprised when he learns when and where he has ended up, but even more surprised to see that the boy he rescued is the spitting image of himself.

Keywords: Disasters; Family; Ireland; Nineteenth Century

Reeve, Philip.

Victorian Scientific Tales. ◼J

An imaginative blending of science and history, this series envisions a very different world, with Victorian morals and mindset coupled with outer-space travel and exploration.

Keywords: England; Family; Nineteenth Century

Larklight. Bloomsbury, 2006. 978-1-59990-020-9 (hardcover); 978-1-59990-145-9 (softcover). 250pp.

> Life in the floating house called Larklight is full of the unexpected. No one knows which way is up, the gravity generator often fails, and the servants are clockwork droids. But it's home for Art, his sister Myrtle, and their father. Art is happy to stay there, floating in space near the moon, although Myrtle wishes they could go to London. But everything changes when they get word that a visitor will be coming. The visitor turns out to be a strange space spider, with a gang of more of the creatures—and their web wraps up the house and their father. Managing to escape, Art and Myrtle crash on the moon—and that's only the first of their adventures. Falling in with a bunch of space pirates, Art and Myrtle are faced with several capers as they try to find out their father's fate.

Starcross. Bloomsbury, 2007. 978-1-59990-121-3 (hardcover); 978-1-59990-296-8 (softcover). 320pp.

> The return of their mother has made Art and Myrtle feel like a real family again. They're even taking a family holiday while Larklight, their home on an orbiting satellite, is renovated. With their mother, Art and Myrtle head to the luxurious Starcross resort at the invitation of its owner, Mr. Titfer. But soon Art realizes there are strange goings-on at this resort. Why does the sea vanish, leaving behind desert? What do the tall, shiny top hats have to do with this? With British initiative and the help of some old friends, Art and Myrtle set out to save the universe yet again.

Mothstorm. Bloomsbury Publishing, 2008. 978-1-59990-303-3 (hardcover). 400pp.

> The Mumby family is ready to celebrate the Christmas holidays when a Pudding Worm, unplanned visitors, and unexpected news combine to ruin the holiday. An unknown object, a kind of cloud, is moving into the solar system, threatening the planet Georgian Sidus, known to the lower class as Uranus. The only residents of the planet are the missionary Reverend Mr. Shipton and his daughter—and they are now missing. Mr. Shipton is an old friend of Mr. Mumby's, so he leads his whole family to the edge of the universe to rescue the Shiptons. Mrs. Mumby is trying to help the British figure out what danger is posed by the cloud, and Myrtle is lovesick over Jack Havock, sometime pirate and dashing adventurer. And Art wants to have as much excitement and adventure as possible.

Romance

Journeying into the past has a certain romantic element. Anyone who has felt out of place in his or her own time can read these novels and feel swept up in a great romance.

Cooney, Caroline B.

Time Quartet. ◼▮

Featuring time travel back to the past and into the future, Cooney shows the power of love and how it can cross the boundaries of time itself.

Keywords: America; Egypt; Family; Nineteenth Century

Both Sides of Time. Delacorte Books, 2001. 978-0-385-72948-2 (hardcover); 978-0-440-21932-3 (softcover). 224pp.

> Annie, like so many fifteen-year-olds, imagines that the past was much more romantic than the present. Living in beautiful mansions, wearing beautiful dresses, and attended to by handsome, courteous young men—a girl would feel like a princess. Annie is sure that she was born in the wrong time, but there isn't anything she can do except try to make her boyfriend Sean be more romantic. But during a thunderstorm on the last day of school, Annie falls through time. Arriving at the local railroad baron's mansion, no longer a decaying wreck, Annie marvels at the differences from what she knows. And the most different thing is the boy she meets: Hiram Stratton Jr. Known as Strat, he's fascinated by Annie's strange ways, just as she's enchanted by him. But she's there for unexplained reasons; will time let her stay?

Out of Time. Delacorte, 2001. 978-0-385-72951-2 (hardcover); 978-0-440-21933-0 (softcover). 240pp.

> In the three years that have passed since Annie Lockwood returned to her time, the people she left behind have suffered. Strat has been locked up in an insane asylum by his father, because only a crazy person would believe in time travel and visitors from the future. Strat's fiancée Harriet, stricken with consumption, is in a sanatorium in upstate New York. And Strat's sister Devonny is trying everything she can to rescue Strat—even calling to Time to send back Annie Lockwood to fix everything. Annie, who longs to come back to Strat, manages to fall through time again, arriving in New York City in 1898. Even though Annie's family is in equally dire straits, Annie just can't let Strat suffer. And perhaps she may learn why the Stratton family seemed to vanish from history at some point before 1900.

Prisoner of Time. Delacorte, 1998. 978-0-385-32244-7 (hardcover); 978-0-440-22019-0 (softcover). 208pp.

> Devonny Stratton is in a desperate situation. Her brother Strat is reputed to have died in a hunting accident—the facts that he was considered insane and that no trace of his remains were found are ignored. Now her father's sole heir, Devonny is completely controlled by him. His decree that she will marry a soulless British lord who only wants her money pushes Devonny to take action. Her only hope is asking Time to send Annie Lockwood to her. But instead of Annie, she gets Tod, Annie's brother. When he brings her into the twentieth century, Devonny is overwhelmed by all the choices for women. It's all she's ever wanted. Now she'll have to see whether she can truly escape the prison that is the past.

For All Time. Delacorte Books, 2001. 978-0-385-32773-2 (hardcover); 978-0-440-22931-5 (softcover). 263pp.

> Annie Lockwood is tired of being at the whim of Time. All she wants is to be with Strat, in any time. When she learns that Strat was part of an Egyptian expedition in 1899, she fights with everything she has to be sent to him. Unfortunately things go wrong: Annie is sent to the Egypt of the ancient past, a time of pharaohs and treachery. There is also danger for Strat. After he manages to escape the clutches of his father, Hiram Stratton Sr. has arrived in Egypt to gain control of Strat. Will the two lovers remain crossed by Time? Or perhaps they can finally find happiness together?

Garfinkle, D. L.

Stuck in the 70s. **Putnam Juvenile, 2007. 978-0-399-24663-0 (hardcover). 192pp. ◧ ⑤**

Finding a beautiful girl in his bathtub is the last thing Tyler expected. Even more unexpected is the girl's belief that she has traveled back in time. For Shay, it's 2006, and finding out she's in 1978 is a rude awakening. There's no Double Stuf Oreos or thongs, she has to eat huge slabs of meat, and women aren't equal to men. To get home, Shay needs help—and that's where science geek Tyler comes in. The two of them strike a deal: Shay will improve Tyler's popularity while Tyler works to get her back to 2006. It doesn't take long for Shay to turn Tyler's world upside down, from making over his sister to getting his mom a job. Even stranger, Shay finds that she's starting to like it in 1978. If she can't get home, maybe staying stuck in the seventies isn't so bad.

Keywords: 1970s; America; Women's Roles

Hubbard, Mandy.

Prada and Prejudice. **Razorbill, 2009. 978-1-59514-260-3 (softcover). 270pp. ◧ ⑤**

Callie is a complete klutz. She always seems to say the wrong thing or trips over her own feet. Her faux pas attract the wrong kind of attention from the A-list, but Callie can't help wanting to impress them—even to the point of impulsively coming on a school trip to England. She wants to put her best foot forward, so she buys a pair of real Prada heels. But disaster strikes as she leaves the store: Callie trips and hits her head. When she wakes up, she's in some strange world, one that seems like the past. Soon she discovers that she really is in the past—1815, to be exact. She is taken in by Emily, who thinks Callie is her childhood friend from America. Callie keeps making a muddle of things. It doesn't help that the house she's staying in is owned by the Duke of Marksbury, a very hot guy named Alex. Sparks fly between them, but Alex, like Callie, is not what he seems to be. Callie can find the answers—and maybe get a kiss—but will she find them before she returns to her own time?

Keywords: England; Nineteenth Century

Montes, Marisa.

A Circle of Time. **Harcourt Children's Books, 2002. 978-0-15-202626-4 (hardcover). 272pp. Ⓜ ◧**

Allison is riding her bike around the mountain known as Devil's Drop. When a car hits her, she's thrown off her bike and hits her head. Deep in a coma, a strange thing happens to Allison. She's transported back in time, into the body of Becky Lee Thompson. Becky lives in 1906, trying to avoid the abuse of her mother as she falls in love with Joshua, the boy she has known forever. But something happens to Becky—something that her spirit is determined to fix. And she has decided that Allison is the one to help her. Allison's willing to give Becky the help she needs—but when she learns that her body in her time is growing weaker, Allison has to hurry. Will she find out how to save Becky in time to save herself?

Keywords: 1900s; America

O'Brien, Judith.

Timeless Love. **Simon Pulse, 2002. 978-0-7434-1921-5 (softcover). 240pp.** ◗

When she wrecks her father's new BMW, Sam McKenna would do anything to be someplace else. But the last thing she expects is to find herself in the bedchamber of Edward VI, King of England. The young King, steadily growing weaker from illness, thinks Sam is an angel sent to take him to heaven. Instead, Sam realizes that the King suffers from allergies and helps cure him. As Edward grows stronger, Sam meets the handsome Sir Barnaby Fitzpatrick, and soon the two teens are in love. But their feelings lead them into trouble with the King. Sam once again wishes to be far, far away, and again her magical necklace complies. But returning to her time makes Sam realize that by changing the past, she has also altered her own present. To get history back the way it's supposed to be, Sam will have to make some difficult choices.

Keywords: England; Illness; Sixteenth Century; Royalty

Rallison, Janette.

My Fair Godmother. **Walker Books, 2009. 978-0-8027-9780-3 (hardcover); 978-0-8027-2073-3 (softcover). 320pp.** ◗

Savannah's life is perfect. She's perfectly beautiful, has the perfect boyfriend, and has just found a perfect prom dress. But then everything becomes horrible: Her boyfriend dumps her for her older sister. Miserable and unhappy, she's the picture of a damsel in distress. And that's how Chrissy comes into Savannah's life. In training as a fairy godmother, Chrissy can grant wishes; she's just not very good at it. She sends Savannah back to the Middle Ages three times, but none of the wishes is quite right. Will Savannah discover what she really wants? And will Chrissy ever become better than a fair godmother?

Keywords: England; Fairies; Medieval

Chapter 8

Other Resources

Few reference guides are comprehensive. All are based in some part on the works that came before. In this chapter, a range of resources are provided to promote further study and exploration of historical fiction.

Historical Fiction Resources

These works provide an understanding of historical fiction and often include an extensive number of titles that fit the author's definition of the genre.

Adamson, Lynda G.

Literature Links to American History, 7–12: Resources to Enhance and Entice. **Libraries Unlimited, 2010. 978-1-59158-469-8 (hardcover). 400pp.**

Literature Links to World History, K–12: Resources to Enhance and Entice. **Libraries Unlimited, 2010. 978-1-59158-470-4 (hardcover). 600pp.**

Both of these references, forthcoming at the time of this guide's publication, provide assistance for anyone wishing to use literature to explain history. Ranging from fiction and biographies to graphic novels and audiovisual materials, the works included help explore topics in world and American history.

Brown, Joanne, and Nancy St. Clair.

The Distant Mirror: Reflections on Young Adult Historical Fiction. **Scarecrow Press, 2005. 978-0-8108-5625-7 (hardcover). 224pp.**

In this critical work, the YA historical fiction genre is analyzed, highlighting the contradictions within this type of fiction. Authors Brown and St. Clair examine how historical fiction illuminates not just the morals and attitudes of the past but our current values as well, and how this clash of values plays out in different works. Although not a readers' advisory tool, it does provide a great deal of background on the development and status of YA historical fiction.

Gillespie, John T.

Historical Fiction for Young Readers (Grades 4–8): An Introduction. **Libraries Unlimited, 2008. 978-1-59158-621-0 (hardcover). 504pp.**

> A guide for teachers and librarians seeking historical fiction titles, this resource examines eighty titles for an age group that overlaps child and teen service areas. Each title is extensively annotated, with historical notes, a plot summary, booktalk suggestions, and more.

Hooper, Brad.

Read On . . . Historical Fiction: Reading Lists for Every Taste. **Libraries Unlimited, 2006. 978-1-59158-239-7 (softcover). 153pp.**

> A resource for both librarians and fans of historical fiction, Hooper provides a range of reading lists, grouping titles based on unusual themes such as humor, royalty, and strong women. Each reading list features bibliographic information and plot synopses for the included titles.

Johnson, Sarah L.

Historical Fiction: A Guide to the Genre. **Libraries Unlimited, 2005. 978-1-59158-129-1 (hardcover). 836pp.**

> For readers' advisors looking for historical fiction recommendations, this well-regarded work provides a dizzying number of choices. Focusing on historical fiction published between 1995 and 2004 and set prior to 1950, this genre guide gives a broad overview of adult historical fiction.

Historical Fiction II: A Guide to the Genre. **Libraries Unlimited, 2009. 978-1-59158-624-1 (hardcover). 738pp.**

> In this volume Johnson continues her first guide, annotating more than 2,000 titles published from 2004 to 2008. Keywords allow an at-a-glance discovery of a title's major themes.

Young Adult Literature Resources

If you are just beginning to learn about young adult literature, or wish to get a sense of those works of historical fiction that are widely popular, these guides will give you further information.

Barr, Catherine, and John T. Gillespie.

Best Books for High School Readers: Grades 9–12. **2nd ed. Libraries Unlimited, 2009. 978-1-59158-576-3 (hardcover). 1075pp.**

> Fifteen thousand YA literature titles are included in this extensive guide to older teens' reading interests. Featuring bibliographic information and brief

annotations, the titles listed in this work span multiple genres. This second edition features books from 2004 to 2008.

Best Books for Middle School and Junior High Readers: Grades 6–9. **2nd ed. Libraries Unlimited, 2009. 978-1-59158-573-2 (hardcover). 1242pp.**

> Similar to its complementary volume for high school readers. Barr and Gillespie provide a vast number of titles designed for younger teens.

Hahn, Daniel, Leonie Flynn, and Susan Reuben.

The Ultimate Teen Book Guide: Over 700 Great Books. **Walker Books for Young Readers, 2007. 978-0-8027-9730-8 (hardcover); 978-0-8027-9731-5 (softcover). 448pp.**

> Designed particularly for interested readers, this guide gathers the suggestions of librarians, publishers, and authors to discuss their favorite young adult works. Each review includes read-alike suggestions, and sidebars throughout the work highlight topics such as short books, top ten lists for different genres, and more.

Herald, Diana Tixier.

Teen Genreflecting. . **2nd ed. Libraries Unlimited, 2003. 978-1-56308-996-1 (hardcover). 272pp.**

> In this readers' advisory and collection development tool, Herald presents a large number of popular genres that are found in young adult literature. Genres are often subdivided to provide further depth. A third edition is forthcoming in late 2010.

Pearl, Nancy.

Book Crush: For Kids and Teens—Recommended Reading for Every Mood, Moment and Interest. **Sasquatch Books, 2007. 978-1-57061-500-9 (softcover). 304pp.**

> Popular librarian Pearl applies the Book Lust formula to children's and young adult literature. A vast number of booklists, varying in style and approach, allow readers to discover new titles and remember favorite books. Although not written exclusively for librarians, this work can be helpful to librarians and teachers.

Silvey, Anita.

500 Great Books for Teens. **Houghton Mifflin Harcourt, 2006. 978-0-618-61296-3 (hardcover). 416pp.**

> Silvey creates a diverse collection of titles in this guide for parents, teachers, and librarians. Thematic and genre booklists include adult titles

and nonfiction in addition to young adult fiction. Silvey selected titles that met her definition of quality writing and popular appeal.

Thomas, Rebecca L., and Catherine Barr.

Popular Series Fiction for Middle School and Teen Readers: A Reading and Selection Guide. 2nd ed. **Libraries Unlimited, 2008. 978-1-59158-660-9 (hardcover). 724pp.**

> A helpful guide for librarians and teachers faced with avid series readers. A wide range of series is included in this updated edition, with each series listing featuring bibliographic data, a general plot summary, and a title listing.

Resources for Teaching Young Adult Literature

For teachers who wish to integrate historical fiction or other types of literature into their classroom teaching, the following can provide useful information and suggestions.

Cole, Pam B.

Young Adult Literature in the 21st Century. **McGraw-Hill, 2008. 978-0-07-352593-8 (softcover). 720pp.**

> This accomplished work provides both a solid overview of young adult literature and a collection of approaches to integrating literature into classrooms. Each genre chapter provides an analysis of the genre, then moves on to exercises and assignments for teaching literature. Selections from young adult titles and essays from YA authors make this work useful not just for teachers.

Online Resources

These Web sites and blogs can supplement the print resources previously listed. By highlighting new and forthcoming titles and trends, online resources can help you stay current. Don't overlook any databases or online sites to which your system or school provides access.

Historical Fiction Resources

Historical-Fiction.com
http://historical-fiction.com/

> This book review site examines new and forthcoming releases, primarily of adult titles. Offers giveaways.

Historical Fiction Network

http://www.histfiction.net/

> An extensive database of historical fiction titles and authors is included on this site. Includes a selection of historical films and documentaries, as well as a lengthy list of young adult historical fiction links.

Historical Fiction Online

http://www.historicalfictiononline.com/

> A discussion board site that invites new members to join discussions. There is a young adult historical fiction subsection.

Historical Novel Society

http://www.historicalnovelsociety.org/

> This membership organization is designed for the true fan of historical fiction. Membership includes the quarterly publication *Historical Novels Review*, which reviews over 800 works of historical fiction a year, including some YA titles.

Nancy Keane's Booktalks—Quick and Simple: Historical Fiction

http://nancykeane.com/booktalks/shistfic.htm

> Provides short booktalks, designed to attract the attention of potential readers. These booktalks are all for young adult historical fiction.

Resources for Teaching Young Adult Literature

Lindquist, Tarry. Why and How I Teach with Historical Fiction

http://teacher.scholastic.com/lessonrepro/lessonplans/instructor/social1.htm

> A National Elementary Teacher of the Year, Lindquist explains how she uses historical fiction in her classroom, offering tips and recommended titles.

Rubrics and Self-Assessment Project: Rubric for the Historical Fiction Essay

http://pzweb.harvard.edu/research/RubricsSelfHF.htm

> For teachers looking for guidance in how to grade historical fiction essays, as well as providing their students with tools to evaluate their own work, this Web site offers a very complete rubric.

Award-Winning Historical Fiction

Historical fiction has often been identified as well-written and thus has been rewarded with the various awards given for young people's literature. Refer to this list when award-winning titles are needed. Only works of historical fiction published since 1975 are included in this appendix; for full award lists, please consult the Web sites for the individual awards. Titles in bold are included in this work; consult the annotations for those titles for further information.

The Michael L. Printz Award for Excellence in Young Adult Literature

http://www.ala.org/yalsa/printz

Administered by the Young Adult Library Services Association (YALSA), this award is given yearly to a work of young adult literature that has the greatest literary excellence.

2010 Honor Book: *Tales of the Madmen Underground: An Historical Romance, 1973* by John Barnes

2009 Honor Book: ***The Astonishing Life of Octavian Nothing, Traitor to the Nation, Volume II: The Kingdom on the Waves*** by M. T. Anderson

2007 Honor Books: ***The Astonishing Life of Octavian Nothing, Traitor to the Nation, Volume I: The Pox Party*** by M. T. Anderson; ***The Book Thief*** by Markus Zusak

2005 Honor Books: *Airborn* by Kenneth Oppel; ***Lizzie Bright and the Buckminster Boy*** by Gary D. Schmidt

2004 Honor Book: ***A Northern Light*** by Jennifer Donnelly

2003 Printz Medal: ***Postcards from No Man's Land*** by Aidan Chambers

National Book Award

http://www.nationalbook.org

The National Book Award, given in five categories by a panel of writers, honors the best of American literature each year. The National Book Award for Young People's Literature has been awarded since 1996.

2008 National Book Award: *What I Saw and How I Lied* by Judy Blundell

2008 Finalist: *Chains* by Laurie Halse Anderson

2006 National Book Award: *The Astonishing Life of Octavian Nothing, Traitor to the Nation, Volume I: The Pox Party* by M. T. Anderson

2004 Finalist: *The Legend of Buddy Bush* by Sheila P. Moses

2003 Finalist: *The River Between Us* by Richard Peck

2000 Finalists: *Forgotten Fire* by Adam Bagdasarian; *The Book of the Lion* by Michael Cadnum

The Carnegie Medal

http://www.carnegiegreenaway.org.uk

First awarded in 1936, the Carnegie recognizes the author of the best work for children published in Britain, as determined by CILIP, the Chartered Institute of Library and Information Professionals. It is similar to the American Library Association's Newbery Medal.

2008 Carnegie Medal: *I Am Arthur* by Philip Reeve

2008 Finalists: *Crossing to Paradise* by Kevin Crossley-Holland (published in Britain as *Gatty's Tale*); *I Am Apache* by Tanya Landman (published in Britain as *Apache: Girl Warrior*)

2007 Finalist: *My Swordhand Is Singing* by Marcus Sedgwick

2004 Finalists: *Al Capone Does My Shirts* by Gennifer Choldenko; *The Star of Kazan* by Eva Ibbotson

2003 Carnegie Medal: *A Northern Light* by Jennifer Donnelly (published in Britain as *A Gathering Light*)

2003 Finalists: *Private Peaceful* by Michael Morpurgo; *Sisterland* by Linda Newbery

2002 Finalists: *Across the Nightingale Floor* by Lian Hearn; *The Shell House* by Linda Newbery; *The Dark Horse* by Marcus Sedgwick

2001 Finalists: *Stop the Train!* by Geraldine McCaughrean; *The Kite Rider* by Geraldine McCaughrean

2000 Finalists: *Coram Boy* by Jarmila Gavin; *Troy* by Adele Geras

1999 Carnegie Medal: *Postcards from No Man's Land* by Aidan Chambers

1997 Finalist: *Fire, Bed and Bone* by Henrietta Branford

1996 Finalist: *Johnny and the Bomb* by Terry Pratchett

1975 Carnegie Medal: **The Machine Gunners** by Robert Westall

The John Newbery Medal

http://www.ala.org/ala/mgrps/divs/alsc/awardsgrants/bookmedia/newberymedal/newberymedal.cfm

One of the oldest awards for children's literature, the Newbery Medal was first awarded in 1922. Administered by the Association for Library Service to Children (ALSC), the Newbery recognizes books of the highest quality, written for children.

2010 Winner: **When You Reach Me** by Rebecca Stead

2010 Honor Books: **The Evolution of Calpurnia Tate** by Jacqueline Kelly; *The Mostly True Adventures of Homer P. Figg* by Rodman Philbrick

2008 Honor Books: **Elijah of Buxton** by Christopher Paul Curtis; **The Wednesday Wars** by Gary D. Schmidt

2007 Honor Books: *Penny from Heaven* by Jennifer L. Holm; **Hattie Big Sky** by Kirby Larson

2005 Honor Books: **Al Capone Does My Shirts** by Gennifer Choldenko; **Lizzie Bright and the Buckminster Boy** by Gary D. Schmidt

2003 Newbery Medal: **Crispin: The Cross of Lead** by Avi

2002 Newbery Medal: **A Single Shard** by Linda Sue Park

2001 Newbery Medal: **A Year Down Yonder** by Richard Peck

2000 Newbery Medal: *Bud, Not Buddy* by Christopher Paul Curtis

1999 Honor Book: **A Long Way from Chicago** by Richard Peck

1998 Newbery Medal: **Out of the Dust** by Karen Hesse

1996 Newbery Medal: **The Midwife's Apprentice** by Karen Cushman

1996 Honor Book: *The Watsons Go to Birmingham, 1963* by Christopher Paul Curtis

1995 Honor Book: **Catherine, Called Birdy** by Karen Cushman

1991 Honor Book: **The True Confessions of Charlotte Doyle** by Avi

1990 Newbery Medal: *Number the Stars* by Lois Lowry

1986 Newbery Medal: *Sarah, Plain and Tall* by Patricia MacLachlan

1983 Honor Book: **The Sign of the Beaver** by Elizabeth George Speare

1981 Newbery Medal: **Jacob Have I Loved** by Katherine Paterson

1980 Newbery Medal: *A Gathering of Days: A New England Girl's Journal, 1830–1832* by Joan W. Blos

1977 Newbery Medal: *Roll of Thunder, Hear My Cry* by Mildred D. Taylor

1975 Honor Book: *My Brother Sam Is Dead* by James Lincoln Collier & Christopher Collier

1975 Honor Book: *The Perilous Gard* by Elizabeth Marie Pope

The Scott O'Dell Award for Historical Fiction

http://www.scottodell.com/Pages/ScottO%27DellAwardforHistoricalFiction.aspx

Established by the well-known author of historical fiction, the Scott O'Dell Award recognizes an author for an outstanding work of historical fiction for children or young adults. The award was established in 1982 and has been awarded since 1984.

2010: *The Storm in the Barn* by Matt Phelan

2009: *Chains* by Laurie Halse Anderson

2008: *Elijah of Buxton* by Christopher Paul Curtis

2007: *The Green Glass Sea* by Ellen Klages

2006: *The Game of Silence* by Louise Erdrich

2005: *Worth* by A. LaFaye

2004: *The River Between Us* by Richard Peck

2003: *Trouble Don't Last* by Shelley Pearsall

2002: *The Land* by Mildred D. Taylor

2001: *The Art of Keeping Cool* by Janet Taylor Lisle

2000: *Two Suns in the Sky* by Miriam Bat-Ami

1999: *Forty Acres and Maybe a Mule* by Harriette Robinette

1998: *Out of the Dust* by Karen Hesse

1997: *Jip, His Story* by Katherine Paterson

1996: *The Bomb* by Theodore Taylor

1995: *Under the Blood Red Sun* by Graham Salisbury

1994: *Bull Run* by Paul Fleischmann

1993: *Morning Girl* by Michael Dorris

1992: *Stepping on Cracks* by Mary Downing Hahn

1991: *A Time of Troubles* by Pieter van Raven

1990: *Shades of Grey* by Carolyn Reeder

1989: *The Honorable Prison* by Lyll Becca de Jenkins

1988: *Charley Skedaddle* by Patricia Beatty

1987: *Streams to the River, River to the Sea* by Scott O'Dell

1986: *Sarah, Plain and Tall* by Patricia MacLachlan

1985: *The Fighting Ground* by Avi

1984: **The Sign of the Beaver** by Elizabeth George Speare

Geoffrey Bilson Award for Historical Fiction for Young People

http://www.bookcentre.ca/awards/geoffrey_bilson_award_historical_
fiction_young_people

Beginning in 1988, the Geoffrey Bilson Award honors a work of historical fiction written by a Canadian author. Administered by the Canadian Children's Book Center, this prize rewards excellence in historical fiction writing. Finalists are announced every year in addition to a winner; those finalists are listed at the award's Web site.

2009: *The Landing* by John Ibbitson

2008: **Elijah of Buxton** by Christopher Paul Curtis

2007: *Kanada* by Eva Wiseman

2006: *The Crazy Man* by Pamela Porter

2005: *Good for Nothing* by Michael Noel

2004: *Boy O'Boy* by Brian Doyle

2003: *The Word for Home* by Joan Clark

2002: *If I Just Had Two Wings* by Virginia Frances Schwartz

2001: *Charlie Wilcox* by Sharon E. McKay

2000: No award given

1999: *The Wreckers* by Iain Lawrence

1998: *Good-bye Marianne* by Irene N. Watts

1997: *To Dance at the Palais Royale* by Janet McNaughton

1996: *Rebellion: A Novel of Upper Canada* by Marianne Brandis

1995: *The Dream Carvers* by Joan Clark

1994: *The Lights Go on Again* by Kit Pearson

1993: *Ticket to Curfew* by Celia Barker Lottridge

1992: No award given

1991: *The Sign of the Scales* by Marianne Brandis

1990: *The Sky Is Falling* by Kit Pearson

1989: *Mystery in the Frozen Lands* by Martyn Godfrey

1988: *Lisa* by Carol Matas

Some Thematic Booklists

Historical fiction, with its depth and breadth, is a wonderful choice for booklists. These examples are thematic, pulling across time and geography. Use the keywords to develop other book lists, such as "Illness in History" or "Historical Disasters." Or why not have a booklist about girls who dress in boy's clothing? The options are limitless!

Alaska Through the Ages

Blessing's Bead by Debby Dahl Edwardson

Aleutian Sparrow by Karen Hesse

Jason's Adventures by Will Hobbs

Revolver by Marcus Sedgwick

The Great Death by John Smelcer

Brave Boys

Adventures of a Young Sailor by Paul Dowswell

The Jack Trilogy by Nancy Farmer

Spartan's Quest by John Ford

The Mark of Solomon by Elizabeth E. Wein

Gutsy Girls

Gemma Doyle Trilogy by Libba Bray

Cat Royal Quartet by Julia Golding

Boston Jane Adventures by Jennifer L. Holm

Bloody Jack Adventures by L.A. Meyer

Horse Stories

The de Granville Trilogy by K.M. Grant

The Horse from the Sea: An Epic Horse Story by Victoria Holmes

Rider in the Dark: An Epic Horse Story by Victoria Holmes

Black Horses for the King by Anne McCaffrey

Wind Rider by Susan Williams

I Rode a Horse of Milk White Jade by Diane Lee Wilson

Lives of Artists

I, Juan de Pareja by Elizabeth Borton de Treviño

I Am Rembrandt's Daughter by Lynn Cullen

Leonardo's Shadow: Or, My Astonishing Life as Leonardo da Vinci's Servant by Christopher Grey

Ivy by Julie Hearn

Marie, Dancing by Carolyn Meyer

The Smile by Donna Jo Napoli

Performers

The Black Canary by Jane Louise Curry

The Queen's Soprano by Carol Dines

In Mozart's Shadow by Carolyn Meyer

Penelope Bailey Takes the Stage by Susanna Reich

Royalty

Anna of Byzantium by Tracy Barrett

His Majesty, Queen Hatshepsut by Dorothy Sharp Carter

Warrior Princess by Frewin Jones

A Proud Taste for Scarlet and Miniver by E. L. Konigsberg

The King's Rose by Alisa Libby

Duchessina: A Novel of Catherine de' Medici by Carolyn Meyer

Young Royals series by Carolyn Meyer

Nine Days a Queen: The Short Life and Reign of Lady Jane Grey by Ann Rinaldi

Shakespeare

Shakespeare series by Gary Blackwood

Shakespeare's Daughter by Peter Hassinger

The Two Loves of Will Shakespeare by Laurie Lawlor

Wicked Will by Bailey MacDonald

The Fool's Girl by Celia Rees

The Triangle Shirtwaist Fire

Ashes of Roses by Mary Jane Auch

Lost by Jacqueline Davies

Uprising by Margaret Peterson Haddix

Witch Trials

The Sacrifice by Kathleen Benner Duble

The Minister's Daughter by Julie Hearn

Witch Child by Celia Rees

A Break with Charity: A Story About the Salem Witch Trials by Ann Rinaldi

The Witch of Blackbird Pond by Elizabeth George Speare

Author Index

Title Index

Keyword Index

About the Author

Photo by Amy Swackhamer

MELISSA RABEY, a teen librarian since 2001, has enjoyed historical fiction since she was a teenager herself and recommends it often to her teen patrons. Her undergraduate degree was in European history, focusing in particular on late seventeenth-century England. She has kept her interest in European history, as well as learning more about the Asian and Indian past. American Civil War novels are another favorite. After serving on YALSA's Popular Paperbacks for Young Adults Committee, Melissa was elected to the 2011 Michael L. Printz Award Committee.